KATAHDIN

An Historic Journey

KATAHDIN

AN HISTORIC JOURNEY

Legends, Explorations, and Preservation
of Maine's Highest Peak

JOHN W. NEFF
Illustrations by Michael McCurdy

Appalachian Mountain Club Books
Boston, Massachusetts

Editorial Direction: Sarah Jane Shangraw and Vanessa Torrado
Editorial Development: Saunders Robinson
Production and Manufacturing: Belinda Thresher
Cover and Interior Design: Eric Edstam
Cover and Interior Illustrations: Michael McCurdy
Cartography: Ken Dumas
Back Cover Photographs (l to r): *Members of a 1920 expedition to Katahdin crossing the East Branch of the Penobscot in a bateau; Myron H. Avery and friends gather at the summit in 1933; River drivers working a log jam along the West Branch of the Penobscot.* All courtesy, Maine State Library, Myron H. Avery Collection.

Distributed by the Globe Pequot Press, Inc., Guilford, CT.

Library of Congress Cataloging-in-Publication Data

Neff, John W.
Katahdin, an historic journey : legends, explorations, and preservation of Maine's highest peak / John W. Neff.
     p. cm.
    Includes bibliographical references and index.
    ISBN-13: 978-1-929173-62-4 (alk. paper)
    1. Katahdin, Mount (Me.)—History. 2. Katahdin, Mount (Me.)—Biography.
I. Title.
    F27.P5N44 2006
    974.1'25—dc22

                    2006009723

To Helen and to Jay, Lesley, and Eric.
We have together shared life's journey and a special
affection for this extraordinary mountain.

CONTENTS

FOREWORD

By Irvin "Buzz" Caverly

I FIRST CLIMBED KATAHDIN IN THE EARLY SPRING OF 1960, AND I continued exploring the mountain that summer: 23 times, 18 of which were after dark, assisting stranded or injured hikers. The next year, my friend and co-worker Ralph Heath and I made a beautiful climb after the first fall snow. We hiked 9 miles from Chimney Pond to Russell Pond via the Northwest Basin Trail, then an additional 8 miles to Old Warden Camp on Wassata-quoik Stream at the eastern boundary of Baxter State Park (4 miles each way). On that trip we discussed and planned a three-day, 26-mile journey from Russell Pond to Storywells for the fall of 1963. However, Ralph was killed in a rescue attempt during storm conditions, a tragic event that I think of often.

In June of 1963 Jan and I were married and lived at Russell Pond for the summer; the next four years we were assigned to Katahdin Stream. Overall, we had ten great seasons living in the park before I moved to a management position. Jan served 27 years in the park reservation office, many of those as reservation supervisor. As a team at Baxter State Park, our jobs defined our lifestyle. We shall always be grateful for our Baxter experience. Governor Percival P. Baxter was wonderful to us during his lifetime, and I feel lucky to have known him and to have trained and worked under his friend, former Park Supervisor Helon Taylor.

For more than 35 years, my good friend *Katahdin* author John W. Neff, has been an avid friend of Baxter State Park, spending considerable time and effort supporting park operations as a volunteer, trail maintainer, and participant in advisory meetings and workshops. He helped found and continues to serve on the board of Friends of Baxter State Park, an organization committed to supporting Governor Baxter's wilderness vision for the Katahdin area.

John's unwavering commitment to protect the wilderness values of the park have been successful due to his working knowledge of park terrain, operation, history, and his ability to interpret and communicate that knowledge to others. The detailed history that he has researched and articulated within this book is a tremendous contribution to this and future generations. His work assures that park history will live on.

During his lifetime, Governor Baxter assured that Katahdin and adjoining lands would forever belong to the people of Maine. John's contribution in the form of this book reminds us that the land belonged to the people at first, and that people were always the catalysts of history on the mountain. From the time when Native Americans lived and traded in the shadow of Katahdin, through the arrival of early explorers, the development of guide services and sporting activities, and the commencement of logging, Katahdin has stood strong while humankind revered it, explored it, and exploited it. Today, Katahdin is wilder within than it has been since Tracy and Love commenced logging operations on the Wassataquoik on October 16, 1883 (122 years ago today as I write this Foreword). The vision of Governor Baxter and the commitment of people like John will ensure it stays that way.

As one who has worked with John on numerous occasions, I am well aware of his love of Baxter State Park, his commitment to the natural resources, and his support of Governor Baxter's vision. I commend him for his work, congratulate him for his success, and recommend this book for all who enjoy nature at peace and our beloved park within the Maine Woods.

—Irvin "Buzz" Caverly
Ranger, Supervisor, and Director
of Baxter State Park, 1960–2005

NOTE

From Governor John E. Baldacci

AT THE HEART OF THE GREATEST EXPANSE OF FOREST IN NEW England rises Maine's highest mountain, Katahdin. Katahdin and the forests, rivers and lakes that surround it have been sources of inspiration for Native Americans, explorers, artists, sportsmen, hikers, and paddlers since time began. Katahdin is truly "the people's mountain."

Governor Percival P. Baxter, who called Katahdin "the greatest monument to nature that exists east of the Mississippi River," had the foresight to protect Katahdin beginning in 1931 through a gift of land to the people of Maine, laying the foundation for Baxter State Park and its more than 200,000 acres of protected forestland. When I visited Baxter State Park for the 100th anniversary Governor Baxter's first visit to Katahdin, I realized the high standards that Governor Baxter had set for me and all future governors.

Despite the protection afforded the Katahdin region today, many of the challenges present in Baxter's era continue to exist. These challenges, including changes in land ownership and loss of public access, are being acutely felt in the 100-Mile Wilderness region southwest of Katahdin along the Appalachian Trail. In 2003, I announced a vision for this region, based on shared values we hold as Mainers, called the Maine Woods Legacy. Its principles include strengthening the connection between economic health and conservation, sustaining a healthy forest products industry, supporting certified sustainable forestry by private landowners, and ensuring a Maine program of landscape-scale conservation of our woods, waters, and wildlife. This conservation includes strategic state ownership of those areas in Maine with the most critical recreational, scenic, watershed, and wildlife habitat resources, along with opportunities for the tradition of backcountry wilderness.

In publishing this significant book, the Appalachian Mountain Club (AMC) is carrying on its own fine tradition. The AMC published some of the first accounts of exploration in the Katahdin region in its journal *Appalachia*, and led the early development of many trails and shelters in the park. The AMC is involved in the region today, through its Maine Chapter and recently announced Maine Woods Initiative. The AMC, through its direct purchase and protection of 37,000 acres near the Katahdin Iron Works, creation of an ecological reserve, and support of sustainable forestry, and work with local communities, is among the leaders helping to make our Maine Woods Legacy vision a reality.

Katahdin, An Historic Journey: Legends, Explorations, and Preservation of Maine's Highest Peak captures the mystique of Katahdin along with the cultural and natural history of the mountain, and I commend John W. Neff for taking on this important project. I am also pleased that Irvin "Buzz" Caverly agreed to write a foreword to this book. In his 46 years at Baxter State Park, Buzz built his own legacy of stewardship and public service.

The protection of Katahdin is a symbol of what we can achieve together. Governor Baxter articulated this legacy best, when he said: "Man is born to die, his works are short-lived. Buildings crumble, monuments decay, wealth vanishes. But Katahdin in all its glory, forever shall remain the Mountain of the People of Maine."

—Governor John E. Baldacci
Augusta, Maine
December 2005

AUTHOR'S PREFACE

IT IS MY EARNEST WISH THAT YOU WILL JOIN ME ON A JOURNEY OF discovery and wonder. What follows is the account of a matchless personal pilgrimage for me, but I do not wish to take my journey into the heart and soul of Katahdin alone. I want to share the experience so others will find the same measure of reward I have known.

My love affair with the state of Maine began at its seacoast, my life enriched by the crashing of surf upon rocky headlands and the eternal rhythms of tide and wave. As a seasonal visitor in my younger days I was caught up, as were so many others, in the great natural beauty of this magnificent world at the edge of the sea. I was aware of only a hint of the treasures to be found inland, away from the sea. The sea was enough to capture my heart and so, except for a very brief and somewhat unrewarding time of suburban living, I stayed in Maine for the rest of my professional life.

My work brought me first to an island in Casco Bay. Later when my responsibilities led me to a lovely inland town, I began to discover the treasures of the great Appalachian Mountain chain, which, after its itinerancy up through the eastern United States, continues through Maine and into Atlantic Canada. What an eye and heart opener that discovery was for me. It was not long before I was led by friends to take the journey to Katahdin.

My Katahdin odyssey began in the early 1960s with a brief backpack trip to Chimney Pond and an exhilarating climb via the Cathedral Ledges to the summit. I was hooked. The experience was ennobling and filled my spirit in ways I found difficult to express. That first adventure led to many trips to the area across the years, as well as to many pleasant hours reading the enormous amount of Katahdin literature. It led to trail responsibilities in Baxter State Park and involvement in organizations committed to the preservation and conservation of the wilderness values found there. It has led to a deeply satisfying life, for Katahdin has made a priceless contribution to the quality of my inner spirit.

This is why I invite you to join me in considering the history, the stories, and the people who have made this a unique and special place. In her engaging biography of the schooner Bowdoin, Virginia Thorndike states, "In people's search beyond the horizons they can profit from looking at the past."[1] So let's journey back.

I approached the writing of this book—the vehicle of the journey—with several goals in mind. First, I wanted to create a comprehensive but accessible tale of the mountain. I've learned that although there is an abundance of literature about Katahdin—Myron Avery once stated that more had been written about Katahdin than any other mountain in the world—it tends to be scattered and not easily accessed. There are chapters in books as well as a few out-of-print books. There are articles in magazines, journals, and newspapers. There are innumerable small pamphlets and booklets. The list is long and rich in content, yet the public would find it difficult to access these materials without extensive library research.

There are, however, several notable exceptions, but they tend to deal with only one aspect of the area in and around Katahdin. The story of the Baxter family, the account of the extraordinary effort of Governor Percival P. Baxter to set aside the area for the people, and the history of Baxter State Park itself have been thoroughly and competently covered in recent years by Neil Rolde, John Hakola, and Trudy Scee. Several other works have sought to capture in more artistic ways the inner and more spiritual meanings of the Katahdin experience, Connie Baxter Marlowe's *Greatest Mountain* and Robert Villani's *Forever Wild* being two of the best. There have also been a few fine books dealing with one small piece of the overall picture; *Chimney Pond Tales* and several reflections on Henry David Thoreau's visit (one of which is covered in the AMC's *The Wildest Country*) are examples. Guidebooks, both old and new, always include excellent background material.

But no one, to my knowledge, has tried to bring together all the scattered elements of this magnificent story in order to help people more deeply appreciate the area, how humankind has affected it, and how it, in turn, has affected humankind. This I have tried to do: to touch on the Native American traditions and stories; to relate the accounts of the early explorers and climbers; to trace the histories of the trails and campsites; to convey the impact of the remarkable lumbering era; to tell of the bustling sporting camps that sprang up in the shadow of Katahdin; to tell again, though briefly, the extraordinary story of Governor Baxter's dream and how he fulfilled it; to follow the footsteps of the artists who have been touched by the mountain and to learn how they expressed themselves on canvas, in photographs, and in song and poetry; and finally, to hear some of the exciting and absorbing tales of twentieth-century events and adventures.

My principal purpose was to gather this material into one volume to fulfill a second purpose; that is, to share a deeper appreciation and reverence for this place to all those who journey to Katahdin, whether by foot, or in mind and spirit. It is my hope that by providing greater knowledge of trail histories and by retelling some of the Native American and early explorers' stories, I will enrich the memories of those who journey to or have journeyed to Katahdin.

A third purpose emerged as I engaged in the ever-fascinating research phase of this work. There has been and will increasingly be a need to preserve the personal memories of those who have intimate knowledge of various historical aspects of the Katahdin experience. We need to preserve them before those memories are lost.

A fourth purpose comes to mind in the light of the passage of years since I began this project. As each year unfolds we move inexorably toward that day when there will no longer be living memories of Governor Baxter, no intimate personal remembrances of his ideas and dreams for the Katahdin area. We will be left, therefore, to interpret his life's work without the benefit of that personal knowledge. We will, of course, still have the Deeds of Trust and Baxter's official and unofficial writings to guide us, but that may not be enough to ensure the full protection and preservation of his unprecedented gift to the people.

I will address this need by making available the history and the stories that will inform us as we make critical decisions about Katahdin and its future. In addition to that which has already been so well written, it is my hope that this work will raise awareness of the potential threats and make a contribution to the continuing effort to preserve the wilderness values of this very special and sacred place.

A brief word about the scope of this study: I have intentionally confined my attention to Katahdin itself and the area closely surrounding it. There is so much material available that I did not feel comfortable ranging far to the north; that is, to the South Branch, Trout Brook, and Matagamon areas, though many could make a case for doing so. Similarly, I did not explore material very far beyond the East and West Branches of the Penobscot nor to the Ripogenus area to the west, except when it seemed necessary to bring clarity to the text. Again, this was a matter of drawing some reasonable limits. Katahdin itself is the magnet and the center of this study.

A word also about the style of this work. Since we already have on hand two thoroughly competent and well-researched histories of Baxter State Park, both of which include many aspects of Katahdin itself, I have not attempted to write an academic work with all of the attendant exhaustive footnotes, references, and bibliography. I have, instead, tried to give more attention to the human stories that accompany the historical facts. I have worked diligently to be sure that all the facts given are accurate, but I have sought to tell the stories in vivid and interesting ways. People and their lively stories are generally center-stage throughout. A professor I once knew said that if one wishes to truly understand history, one must come to know the people who create and live that history. It is true! Thus, the center of my work is not Baxter State Park, nor even Governor Baxter and his remarkable gift to the people of Maine. The focus is always Katahdin itself and the spell the mountain has cast upon the wilderness around it and upon those who have been touched by its presence.

In the "Notes and Sources" section at the back of the book you'll find reference notes that can be explored by the reader if desired.

Regarding references to the aboriginal people who first lived in the shadow of Katahdin, it was important to me to use words that will be acceptable and appreciated by our state's native peoples. I have chosen, at the suggestion of some of their number, to use the term Native Americans. There are only a few exceptions when other terms are used for the sake of clarity or style. It is well for all of us to wean ourselves away from the term Indian, a largely pejorative term that carries much too much negative national history.

A brief word about spelling challenges I have encountered. Through the years many different spellings have been used for various family and place names. As a rule, in order not to confuse the reader, I have used the generally accepted modern spelling. When using quotations I have corrected the spelling to modern usage unless the author's spelling was important to the meaning of the text. Below are some of the variations encountered:

Ambajejus: There has been an enormous variety of spellings of this native name. This spelling, however, is not only the most common but is now used in all modern U.S. Geological Survey maps.

Daicey, Daisey, Dacey, Dacy, Dace and Deasey: We have sought to straighten out these variations in the text.

Eckstrom vs. Eckstorm: Fannie Hardy Eckstorm's original name was Eckstrom, but the spelling was turned around at some point and Eckstorm is now the commonly accepted usage.

Nesowadnehunk: Correct in both original and modern usage vs. Sourdnahunk or Sowdyhunk. The latter are spellings of how the word is pronounced in some popular modern usage.

Perimeter Road vs. Tote Road: For many years this road that circles Baxter State Park was referred to as the Perimeter Road, but it has recently been renamed the Tote Road, to honor its original purpose in the lumbering era and to recognize the efforts of the Civilian Conservation Corps (CCC) in the 1930s in building the road.

Tracy: Can be used interchangeably with Tracey. It is the same family.

Whidden Ponds vs. Whitten Ponds: Though both were used quite commonly in the past it would appear that Whidden has been accepted as the most accurate.

Windey and Windy: Both are used as we shall see but sometimes they are used interchangeably and thus incorrectly.

These are only a few. Others I will seek to clarify as we go along.

If there are mistakes or if I do not have a story quite right, I take full responsibility. I have sought to be as accurate as possible, but there will be unintentional lapses. I hope those errors will not in any way interfere with the experience of the reader.

And so, dear reader, I invite you on a singular journey to enrich and broaden your personal appreciation of:

Kette-Adene

Ktaadn

Katahdin

ACKNOWLEDGMENTS

THE ENDEAVOR TO MOVE THIS WORK FROM DREAM TO REALITY WAS aided by an enormously rewarding collaboration between the author and a host of willing partners who shared freely their personal experiences and knowledge of Katahdin history and story. Their interest in my venture and their willingness to help is keenly appreciated.

I want to express special thanks to the folks at the Maine State Library who were on every occasion willing to assist me, especially when I sought some rare resource or needed materials from the library's special collections. That institution houses the finest collection of Katahdin holdings anywhere and having them close at hand was a great gift. In addition to the library's general collections, the Myron H. Avery Collection and the Percival P. Baxter Collection were especially helpful.

Other libraries and collections were beneficial as well: the Special Collections of the Folger Library at the University of Maine in Orono, the Bangor Public Library, the Portland Public Library, the archive collection and library of the Appalachian Mountain Club, the Maine Appalachian Trail Club archives, the Portland Museum of Art, the Maine State Archives, the Northeast Archives of Folklore and Oral History at the University of Maine in Orono, and the archival collection at Baxter State Park.

I want to express profound thanks to those persons who shared so generously their personal experiences and knowledge of Katahdin area history and story. In the "Notes and Sources" section of the book, I have listed those who through an interview or correspondence aided in the writing of particular chapters. I salute especially the many people from the Millinocket area who were always willing to receive me for an interview, often serving coffee and goodies as we talked. That intimate personal sharing is one of the precious rewards of my Katahdin journey and will always be remembered with great fondness. I thank you one and all.

I do feel led to give special thanks to Baxter State Park Director (now retired) Irvin "Buzz" Caverly for his willingness to answer my many persistent questions about matters that only he could answer. In addition, his willingness to review the entire manuscript made a substantial contribution to its accuracy and reliability, and I appreciate the thoughts he has offered in the Foreword.

I offer a special thank you to other members of the Baxter State Park senior staff as well as a number of present, former, and retired rangers, all of whom were most generous in sharing information in addition to their own personal stories and memories. My special thanks go to Dean Bennett for much helpful advice along the way and for offering constructive ideas that I believe greatly strengthened my Epilogue.

My heartfelt thanks go to a dear friend, Janice Cox, who spent many hours reviewing the manuscript, correcting my bad writing habits and making valuable suggestions that improved the text out of her professional experience. If this work is deemed to have met a high standard it will be the direct result of her careful and thorough review. My friend, Phil Palmer, was also one of the readers and offered many helpful suggestions. If I have missed anyone I trust they will accept my apology, for I am grateful to each and everyone who has helped me in any way.

I am deeply grateful to the staff at AMC Books who shared my belief in this endeavor from the very beginning and went far beyond the call of duty to be sure the finished product would be one of which we could all be proud. Those with whom I worked most closely were Sarah Jane Shangraw, who, before leaving the organization, served as editor-in-chief and gave invaluable direction to the whole project as well as careful planning and editing; Vanessa Torrado, who took on the responsibilities of senior editor as the project was being completed and was very helpful during its final weeks;

Saunders Robinson, who helped develop the text; and Belinda Thresher, who coordinated production responsibilities, including photographs, maps, and design. I shall always be grateful for their patience with me and their strong commitment to consultation in all matters. I would also like to thank Eric Edstam for designing this book and Michael McCurdy for the dramatic illustrations he created for the book, including the one on the cover.

Finally, I extend profound gratitude to my wife, Helen, my soul mate and lifelong companion. She was the first to read the manuscript chapters, and I came to rely on her many valuable observations and suggested changes. Beyond that, she has been my greatest supporter and cheerleader in this effort, encouraging me when I was disheartened and believing in my attempt to bring alive the history and the stories of the Katahdin region. Her grace and patience during my personal journey to the heart and spirit of Katahdin will always be remembered.

Dramatic aerial view of the Katahdin massif, especially the Knife Edge from Pamola to South Peak. Courtesy, James W. Sewall Company, Old Town, Maine.

INTRODUCTION

The Katahdin Experience

Katahdin . . . is eminent and emphatic, a signal and solitary pyramid, grander than any below the realms of the unchangeable, more distinctively mountainous than any mountain of those that stop short of the venerable honors of eternal snow.

—Theodore Winthrop, 1856[1]

MOST OF THOSE WHO HAVE VISITED KATAHDIN HAVE BEEN PRO-foundly affected by the mountain. Of the thousands who visit the region each year, many return again and again, responding to an attraction they find irresistible. The mountain's allure is strong also for those who, though they have not visited the region, have come upon Katahdin through reading mountain history or admiring landscape art.

Katahdin's striking geology certainly contributes to its allure and mystique. Katahdin rises, solitary and majestic, from the great northern forest of Maine. The name given the mountain by Native Americans was "Kette-Adene," meaning greatest or preeminent mountain.* From a distance it seems to stand remote and singular. But the actual summit is one of a family of peaks that sit together upon a 4,200-foot tableland that emerges above treeline. Indeed, this seemingly singular mountain is a complex collection of summits, glacial cirques, basins, roiling streams, granite headwalls, lakes and ponds, moraines, a dramatic knife-edged arête, rare subarctic plants,

---

* The name later became "Ktaadn," which is closer to Penobscot usage. The name Katahdin was officially adopted in 1893 by the U.S. Geographic Board. Because the name Katahdin infers the word mountain, it is not necessary to call it Mount Katahdin; the proper name is Katahdin.

and rocky avalanches. Just to look at it is to know it has an enormously fascinating geological history. And while it stands resolute and unchanging for the moment in geologic time, the dramatic, sometime ferocious seasons and the constantly changing weather add liveliness.

Thousands reach the summit each year. Hundreds of them have walked the famed Appalachian Trail, nearly 2,200 miles from Georgia, to this, its northern end on Katahdin's summit. For these thru-hikers, reaching the peak and touching the summit cairn is one of the great goals of their months-long trail experience, and likely one of the highlights of their life. Of course, hundreds of others reach Katahdin's summit after one or two days of hiking from within Baxter State Park, and given the drama of the scenery, the effort, and the mountain's mysterious lure, this is often no less of a significant moment.

However, the summit is not at all the most prominent feature of the mountain or in the area. There is no definitive view of the summit as is true of, for instance, the Matterhorn. From the south, the summit is mostly hidden behind South Peak. From Katahdin Stream Campground, the summit is hidden by the Gateway at the edge of the lofty Tableland. From Russell Pond, the Whidden Ponds, and the Wassataquoik region north and east of Katahdin, the summit is hardly noticeable amid the lengthy massif that includes Pamola, Chimney Peak, South Peak, Hamlin Peak, and the string of North Peaks.

However, for nearly all who come, the Katahdin experience is about much more than just climbing another peak. Far more. In Katahdin many encounter the mystical. Some consider the mountain sacred because its presence and its overpowering grandness guide them toward inner contemplation of the vital center of all being. They are like pilgrims seeking the elemental heartbeat or pulse of the spirit. This is the most awesome aspect to the Katahdin experience. Native Americans call it the pulse of the Great Spirit.

How does one explain this compelling and enticing pull, this overwhelming lure that Katahdin has exerted on people across the many centuries since humans first looked upon it? The explanation starts with mountains as sacred places. Edwin Bernbaum* submits:

---

* Edwin Bernbaum is a mountaineer and scholar of comparative religion and mythology. His book *Sacred Mountains of the World* received a number of international awards and is already one of the great classics of mountain literature.

[The] highest and most dramatic features of the natural landscape . . . have an extraordinary power to evoke the sacred. The ethereal rise of a ridge in mist, the glint of moonlight on an icy face, a flare of gold on a distant peak—such glimpses of transcendent beauty can reveal our world as a place of unimaginable mystery and splendor. In the fierce play of natural elements that swirl about their summits—thunder, lightning, wind, and clouds—mountains also embody powerful forces beyond our control, physical expressions of an awesome reality that can overwhelm us with feelings of wonder and fear.[4]

Those who climb or spend time near mountains are usually seekers of an abiding experience of the inner spirit that will give deeper meaning to their lives. For them, the very reason for the journey is to have an encounter that is "wholly other," that transcends immediate human experience. Indeed, Bernbaum believes that people see mountains as representing their highest spiritual goals:

Floating above the clouds, materializing out of the mist, mountains appear to belong to a world utterly different from the one we know, inspiring in us the experience of the sacred. . . .

Mountains rise over the surrounding countryside in undisputed splendor, sovereigns of the valleys, plains, and lesser hills beneath them; they are commonly described as *majestic* and *mighty*. Unlike the reign of human kinds, theirs seem eternal and incorruptible, like that of the highest gods, who sit enthroned upon their lofty summits. . . .

Mountains have a special power to evoke the sacred as the unknown. Their deep valleys and high peaks conceal what lies hidden within and beyond them, luring us to venture ever deeper into a realm of enticing mystery. Mountains seem to beckon to us, holding out the promise of something on the ineffable edge of awareness. There, just out of sight, over the next ridge, behind the summit, lies the secret, half-forgotten essence of our childhood dreams.[5]

THE LURE OF KATAHDIN IS REFLECTED IN THE NATIVE AMERICAN stories of the mountain. Arnie Neptune of Maine's Penobscot tribe ascribes the draw of the mountain on people of all backgrounds to the call of the Great Spirit, the need for spiritual sustenance. The Native American attitude and stories are part of the rich tapestry of tradition surrounding Katahdin.

Katahdin continues to inspire storytelling. During my research of the mountain, most everyone I met had a story to tell—either a spectacular or intimate memory, or a story about a family member, neighbor, or friend. Justice William O. Douglas tells the story of standing one September day on the shore of a Katahdin-area pond with artist Maurice "Jake" Day. As they "stood on its smooth pebble beach, watching the play of sunlight on the richly colored hardwoods" [he] turned to Jake and asked:

> "How do you manage to wait for May to arrive?"
> "Got a secret," Jake said. "Come with me."
> We walked into the woods, where Jake found the stump of an ancient white pine. Whittling away the damp outer layer of wood, he came to a dry interior, where he cut many shavings. Holding these under his nose, he said with a grin, "The smell of these shavings carries me through the winter."[7]

People appreciate the stories because they humanize an inexplicably charismatic natural feature, and in their telling lay an active reverence for the mountain. Sometimes when one tells a particularly interesting story, a listener will quickly counter with his or her own story in a "can-you-top-this?" spirit. All want to show that they too share in the "Katahdin experience."

HOW DO WE EXPLAIN THE REMARKABLE HOLD OF THIS MOUNTAIN on the people of the state of Maine and others far beyond its borders? We've discussed its fantastic geology. What about the people who have played a role in its history? The mountain's history is peopled with explorers, lumberjacks, "sports," hikers, naturalists, and more.

The lumbering era brought dam building and great log drives employing hundreds of men each year. The camps and railroads built by the lumber barons would make the sporting camps possible, and for more than 50 years these camps provided a way for "sports" from far away to come and experience first hand the stunning wonders of the Great North Woods. That era also saw the emergence of professional guides who, for a fee, made all the arrangements for individuals and groups to travel to remote places to experience the great northern wilderness.

This book seeks to introduce all of the players in Katahdin's richly peopled history, from the early surveyors and explorers, to the scientists who came for discovery, to the sports and the hikers. Their ranks include Theodore Roosevelt, Edward Everett Hale, and William Francis Channing, Henry David Thoreau, and William O. Douglas.

And we must not forget those who have been moved and inspired by the mountain and who have sought to relay its majesty in turn to us. Artists ask us to consider beauty behind that seen by the eye, and are therefore powerful guides to the mountain and its mystique. Many artists have produced inspired works in the shadow of the mountain, most notably Frederic E. Church, one of the most significant painters of American history. But that was but the start of a procession of men and women who were richly inspired by the wilderness and especially Katahdin: George H. Hallowell, Charles Hubbard, Maurice "Jake" Day, Marsden Hartley, James Fitzgerald, and a host of present-day artists. There have been many photographers, including James Stodder, Amos L. Hinds, F. W. Hardy, Lore Rogers, and Albert Call. Filmmakers and poets too have contributed to the artistic legacy evoked by the mountain.

Perhaps in large part the lure of this sacred and historic place is built on the extraordinary circumstances under which the area was protected for all to enjoy. Incredibly, one man's lofty vision of setting aside Katahdin and the wilderness area encircling it for the people of the state of Maine became a reality. Governor Percival P. Baxter loved it so, he invested his personal fortune to share it with all of us.

IN KATAHDIN WE HAVE A WILDERNESS AREA BEING RETURNED TO and kept, as much as possible, as wild as it was before human encroachment made it more accessible. Someone has suggested the remote timberlands to the north and the presence of both the East and West Branches of the Penobscot River contributed to Katahdin's isolation over the years. The rivers kept rail and auto roads at bay for a long time and still exert a protective influence on the region.

The wildest places of the earth, those largely undisturbed by human presence, have always held for people a great fascination, and Katahdin, hidden in the depths of the Maine Woods, is one of the grandest.

Someone said it is not the destination, but the journey that counts. This is true of any time spent near Katahdin. There is so much to explore in the area that one can be nourished and filled in spirit and never reach the summit itself. Several of the great painters of Katahdin never climbed to the summit, finding their inner spirits nourished enough by simply being in the presence of the mountain and interpreting it. I have climbed to the summit many times and have, on some occasions, hurried on—across the Knife Edge to be thrilled by that exhilarating portion of the journey, across the Tableland to the south to experience again that vast expanse of glacial rock, or down to the Saddle in order to reach Hamlin Peak and the spectacular Hamlin Ridge. Indeed, the summit is but a small part of the whole adventure. And so, my fellow travelers, we will journey together to examine more closely the history of this mountain that holds such mystique for those who have come to know it.

Governor Baxter once said:

> Katahdin stands above the surrounding plain unique in grandeur and glory. The works of man are short-lived. Monuments decay, buildings crumble and wealth vanishes, but Katahdin in its massive grandeur will forever remain the mountain of the people of Maine. Throughout the ages it will stand as an inspiration to the men and women of this State.[9]

A summary of these words are now found on a bronze plaque at Katahdin Stream Campground within Baxter State Park, and they greet all hikers as they embark on their climb of the Hunt Spur, one of the more popular sections of the Appalachian Trail, to Katahdin's summit. Baxter's was a singular effort, not duplicated anywhere else in the history of this nation. That remarkable act, motivated by a sense of the sacred qualities of the wild areas, remains a part of what draws people to this mountain.

PART I

Early History

THE FIRST KINSHIP 1

The Native American Relationship with Katahdin

KATAHDIN STANDS AS AN EXTRAORDINARY LANDMARK, DOMINATING the landscape near the confluence of the two major tributaries of the great Penobscot River. The West Branch of the Penobscot begins its river journey as a series of small lakes and streams slightly northwest of Moosehead Lake, flowing from the height of land that marks the U.S.–Canadian border. The East Branch of the Penobscot flows out of the Matagamon/Webster Stream area north of Maine's Baxter State Park. After flowing through majestic forestlands, the two branches join forces at a place once called Nicatou, a Native American name that means "the place where the river splits," today known as Medway.

In 1857 John Sewall of Bangor, Maine, who later became a noted minister and professor, wrote:

> Here comes the East Branch on your left, mild, placid, maidenlike; here to the right the rushing West Branch, boisterous and masculine. At the foot of the hill they meet, flirt, foam a little, have their tantrums, but conclude to marry and settle down at once. . . .[1]

At this ancient crossroads, Katahdin rises in isolated grandeur, and in its shadow the Penobscot starts its journey to the sea, some 90 miles away.

Humans first came to the Katahdin region 11,000 years ago, following the slow retreat of the ice-age glaciers. The tribe of peoples living closest to the mountain in recent centuries is known as the Penobscot. The word Penobscot means "the place where the rocks and ledges descend and the river broadens out." This description is thought to refer specifically to Indian Island at Old Town, Maine, the Penobscots' principal and long-time residence, and indeed the name aptly describes the rocky ledges over which the river flows just below the island. The entire Penobscot River watershed, from Katahdin to the sea, was the territory of the Penobscots. Near the Atlantic Coast, their claim to the river and its tributaries was sharply defined—neighboring tribes respected the Penobscots' right to the lower watershed. Inland, however, territorial claims were not as obvious—primarily because there were no permanent settlements there, only riverine passages used for traveling and hunting. While the upper watershed was recognized as Penobscot territory, other tribes could freely pass along the canoe routes and portages for trade.*

EARLY ROUTES

Traditionally, Native American villages existed along the upper Penobscot River at Mattawamkeag and Passadumkeag, and in the Moosehead Lake region. Permanent settlements north of Mattawamkeag were unlikely, but seasonal campsites were located along the river and on the shores of the lakes and ponds. The West Branch served as the major route to the Moosehead Lake region, where travelers could also enter the Kennebec River. Unfortunately, it is difficult to locate and explore the old native campsites along the West Branch, as timber company roads, gravel quarries, and river

---

* The Penobscots are an Abenaki eastern woodland tribe, belonging to a much broader group of tribes east of the Great Lakes that share the family of Algonquin languages. The Passamaquoddies lived to the east of the Penobscots, and their tribal centers still exist at Pleasant Point Reservation near Perry, Maine, and the 24,000-acre Indian Township Reservation near Princeton. The Micmacs lived still further east, in New Brunswick and the other Maritime Provinces. The Maliseets (or Malecites) resided to the north, in what is now Maine's Aroostook County, and further eastward into New Brunswick along the St. John River Valley and the Bay of Fundy. The Abenakis lived to the west, along the Kennebec River watershed and western Maine. These tribes would have passed Katahdin during their inland travels.

dams have changed the landscape. Riverbanks were flooded to enable timber drives, and the long logs scarred the shore, erasing any evidence of prior human activity. However, as the Penobscots traveled up the river, they likely stopped at Nicatou before heading upriver on the West or East Branch.*

In his book *Above the Gravel Bar*, a study of Native American canoe routes in Maine, David S. Cook speculates that Native Americans often used an alternative West Branch route (which they called Kettetegwewick, "the main branch") to avoid the challenging falls and river terrain above Abol Deadwater. Traveling upriver they could leave the West Branch at Nesowadnehunk Falls and carry up Nesowadnehunk Stream to Chesuncook Lake, part of the West Branch flowage, via Harrington Lake. Cook notes that this was known as the "Oodoolwagenow-seezicook Ahwangen or 'the Entrails Route,' so known for its twisting course."[2]

From Nicatou, the East Branch (which Native Americans called Wasstegwewick, "the place where they spear fish")** led to the rich hunting and fishing grounds of Matagamon Lake. From there hunters easily portaged into the headwaters of either the Allagash or Aroostook River, which led to the mighty St. John River. Above Nicatou, the East Branch's swift water and falls made navigating either upstream or downstream difficult. At high water, an alternative route followed the Seboeis River across a number of lakes and streams to Matagamon Lake. Along the East and West Branches, and down to the river's mouth, Katahdin dominated the landscape. The Native Americans, traveling from place to place, oriented themselves by the mountain's prominent position.

Evidence suggests, however, that the Native Americans avoided exploring Katahdin itself out of spiritual reverence for the mountain. Their reverence grew out of the belief that all of creation—the natural elements, animals, people—are connected and infused with the same spirit. Katahdin, in their view, is where the earth meets the sky, where the secular and the divine converge; it is the origin of the Great Spirit.

---

* Later, the West Branch became a major thoroughfare between European settlements in Maine and Canada. The French, English, and Native Americans all traded along this riverine highway, within sight of Katahdin.

** Cook notes that Wasstegwewick is unmistakably close to Wassataquoik, the great stream tributary that drains the northern slopes of Katahdin.

FEAR OF THE MOUNTAIN

Native Americans avoided Katahdin's slopes also in part due to fear—lest they stir the wrath of the gods who dwelt there. The earliest written reference to this fear came from the pen of John Giles, who heard stories of Katahdin after he was captured by Native Americans in 1689. In his journals he tells of three young men who decided to climb to the summit. After three and a half days, they became "strangely disordered with delirium . . . and when their imagination was clear, and they could recollect where they were, they found themselves returned one day's journey. How they came to be thus transported they could not conjecture, unless the genii of the place had conveyed them."[3] Convinced that spirits were present, they and others did not approach the mountain again.

Rev. Marcus Keep's account of approaching the Great Basin's Chimney Pond in 1847 indicates his understanding of the Native Americans' perspective on the mountain's power:

> When we reached the lake on our way to Ktaadn, it was easy to see the origin of those fears which the Indians are said to have respecting the mountain as the residence of Pamolah, or Beg Debil. Clouds form in the basin, and are seen whirling out in all directions. Tradition tells a "long yarn" about a "handsome squaw" among the Penobscots, who once [dazzled] the young chiefs of her nation, but was finally taken by Pamolah to Ktaadn, where he now protects himself and his prize from approaching Indians with all his artillery and hail. . . . The basin is the birthplace of storms, and I have myself heard the roar of its winds for several miles.[4]

THE HERO WHO WOULD MEET KATAHDIN

Native American culture has a strong tradition of storytelling. Stories serve to define identity, reinforce heritage, explain the great mysteries of life, and educate the young.

A central legend in the region's tribal culture concerns the hero Gluskabe, whose name means "man from nothing." Gluskabe arose from the dust left after the Creator formed the world. This benevolent hero reportedly prepared the world for human habitation by reducing the size of monstrously proportioned animals.

It is said that Gluskabe undertook a long journey during which he went to Katahdin where the Great Spirit taught him all that he was later to share with his people. Gluskabe conveyed to his people knowledge of the Great Spirit's presence and power; he spent much of his time instructing the people how to live, survive, fish, hunt, and plant, and how to honor one another and the earth. He is attributed with the introduction of many innovations—including the birch bark canoe—and the institution of many of the ethical codes of conduct and models of behavior that have remained integral to the culture even to this day.

When Gluskabe's instruction was complete, he departed from the tribe. Some legends say that he did not tell the people of his departure, while others describe the people gathering at the water's edge as he packed his canoe (in some stories, described as made of stone) and bade them all farewell. Gluskabe remains a much revered and admired figure. Many still believe he will one day return to alleviate their suffering and restore the old traditions.

GODS AND MONSTERS

According to tradition, Katahdin is the dwelling place of *three* deities. The first is the much honored and benevolent Katahdin himself—kindly and friendly, human in shape yet a giant in stature. He is often described as having eyebrows and cheeks of stone, dwelling inside the mountain, and presiding over the great peaks and basins with his powerful influence and eminence. Fannie Hardy Eckstorm, a noted nineteenth-century authority on native culture and stories, published an interview with Clara Neptune, one of the oldest of the Penobscots, in her 1942 book *The Katahdin Legends*. Fannie recorded some of the stories Clara had heard from the tribal storytellers. Clara said that:

> Ev'ry mountain he got Injun in it. Katahdin, he man ... katahdin, he diff'rent, mountain once was man.[5]

According to one story about Katahdin—which, like most, has many variations—a young Indian maiden meets and marries Katahdin. Sometimes she is known as Red Rose, but the name may be a later addition to the legend. Eckstorm learned the story from Minnie Atkinson, who had heard it from a member of the Passamaquoddy tribe in the presence of an Indian agent. According to Eckstorm:

Once there was a girl who was called Red Rose. She was very beautiful. One day she wandered into the woods a long way from home. At length she came to a place from which she could see Mount Katahdin. As she looked at it she wished that she could have a husband as big and strong as the mountain. She had walked a very long way, and she was very tired. So while she thought of the husband she would like to have, she sat down by the foot of a tree, and presently she fell asleep. When she awoke there was an immense Indian standing before her.

"I am the Spirit of Katahdin," he said. "I know your wish. I have come to marry you."

He asked her to go to the mountain with him. It was a very long way.

"I cannot walk so far," she said.

"I did not ask you to walk," he answered. "I will carry you."

So he set her upon his shoulder, and went away with her to Katahdin. The entrance to the mountain was in its side between some rocks where it could not easily be found. The Spirit of Katahdin took her within the mountain, past the rocks, and there she dwelt with him most happily.

By and by a little boy and a little girl were born. As the years passed, however, Red Rose began to grow homesick.

"I wish I could go home," she said one day.

"You shall have your wish," answered the Spirit of Katahdin.

He gave her some medicine that made her once more young and beautiful. As a parting gift he said that whenever the girl passed her hand over her lips her words should come true, and that whatever the boy pointed a finger at should die.

So Red Rose went home to her tribe by the great waters of the Passama-quoddy Bay. She took with her the little girl and the little boy. When they reached home it was a time of famine. There was nothing to eat in the wig-wams; there was no game in the woods; there were no fish in the bay nor in the river and lakes. Everybody was sad. Red Rose felt sad also, but the little girl passed her hand over her mouth and said that there was game in the woods. At once the woods were full of game. The little boy pointed his finger at a deer, and it fell dead. Then he pointed at a moose, and that fell dead. He happened to point at an Indian, and he too fell dead. The little girl passed her hand over her mouth and said that all the lakes and rivers were full of eels. Then they were full of eels, and there was a great deal to eat. Everybody was happy, and there was no more famine.[6]

Red Rose returned to Katahdin, but journeys back to visit her tribe every 100 years. Many tribe elders claim to have seen her during her last visit and state, "she is very, very beautiful indeed."

Molly Spotted Elk, of the Penobscot Nation, learned stories about Katahdin from her mother, grandparents, and the tribal storytellers. In some of these stories Katahdin is a young boy who plays an important part in the dramatic creation of the mountain that would bear his name.

She relates a story in which Katahdin was a much-loved young brave who became very good friends with Gluskabe. They had many adventures together. Gluskabe taught Katahdin the languages of all living creatures and taught him that humans were the caretakers of the creation. At length, Gluskabe left the tribe to travel to far away places, but he promised to return one day. Katahdin, much saddened, missed his friend as the years passed. Later, after Gluskabe had been away for a long time, Katahdin fell in love with and planned to marry Zipsis, "Little Bird," a lovely young maiden.

However, misfortune befell them. Enemies attacked and defeated their tribe, and took Katahdin captive. After many years of hardship and suffering, Katahdin escaped and returned to his village, where he learned that Zipsis had journeyed to her home village. He set out to find her, but the way was difficult and he could not at first locate her.

When a messenger came with word of Zipsis' location, Katahdin set out immediately to find her. Along the way he encountered Medoulin, an old woman with evil powers who wanted to thwart him. Medoulin finally left Katahdin, and he continued his journey. He was warned about another evil spirit, Badugeal, "Thunder Cloud," but he still continued his journey.

Finally he found Zipsis, who was being held captive by a wandering tribe. He freed her, and they ran, with Badugeal in threatening pursuit. Katahdin and Badugeal fought hand-to-hand in a great struggle. In one last desperate effort, Katahdin threw Badugeal into the air, snatched Zipsis away from his grasp, and ran, this time with Medoulin now also pursuing them. Closer and closer Medoulin came, until she knocked Katahdin and Zipsis to the ground beside a lake. As Katahdin struggled to his feet, Medoulin shouted "Sahchuwee-mahchinen!" (You will die!).

Instantly a large copper kettle covered them, and before Medoulin could wish more evil a strange thing happened. Earth, rock, and pine trees descended upon the copper kettle and covered it, and it became a large mountain.

Before Medoulin could escape, the force of the earth rising skyward pushed her toward the edge of the lake.

While Medoulin was getting her breath to run around the lake and into the woods, Garmewun, the Rain Woman, appeared at her side. Clenched in each other's arms the two sisters struggled and when Garmewun, the good, had won over Medoulin, the evil, there was a great silence. Swiftly Medoulin vanished into the air, and Garmewun rose to the sky and became rain.

The story concludes:

Today when you see the dark clouds high in the sky world, it is a sign of battle between the earth and the sky gods. You will see the birds seeking safety among the trembling leaves of the trees. Then you will hear Badugeal thundering high above. Suddenly fire will fall to the ground with such force that it will hit a tree and burn it. My people call it "Skootbezal" (fire sticks) but the Pale-face people know it as lightning. Then Garmewun in her goodness comes from the sky land and gives to the thirsty land and the crops water to drink.

And for centuries, Katahdin has given my people a reddish, copper earth that they have used in their ceremonials. Some claim this earth is the copper kettle which has rusted, and others say that the earth has been stained by the bleeding feet of Katahdin, bruised and torn from his long journeys in search of Zipsis.[7]

Wuchoswen, the spirit of the Night Wind, sometimes referred to as the Wind Blower or Wind Bird, also inhabits the mountain. Endowed with great wings and huge claws, Wuchoswen creates the mountain's strong winds with his breath and his wings. Although he might flap his wings furiously at times, he is considered harmless.

In contrast, the renowned Pamola, the great Storm Bird who also lives on the mountain, is a malevolent and irascible creature. Pamola jealously guards the mountain and is angry when things do not go his way. When irritated, he creates violent winds and fierce storms. Pamola is of monstrous size, commonly described today as having the head of a moose, the arms and chest of a man, and the feet and wings of an eagle, celebrating, as U.S. Supreme Court Justice William Douglas, who visited the Katahdin region in the 1950s with artist Jake Day, once observed, "the three leading characters of the Maine woods to make himself supreme over each of them."[8] Artist Maurice "Jake" Day popularized this image of Pamola, though a much less threatening one, in his mid-twentieth century painting depicting Pamola in conversation with his friend Roy Dudley on Pamola Peak. While serving at Chimney Pond as the State Fish and Game Department warden in the 1930s and 1940s, Dudley created his own unique Pamola stories.

Pamola, watchful and unpredictable, usually expresses his anger along the Knife Edge or in the Chimney/Pamola Peak area. Marion Whitney Smith, in her book *Katahdin Fantasies: Stories Based on Old Indian Legends* published in 1953, wrote:

> Katahdin often frowns on those who violate its fastness, and demonstrates its inhospitality by sudden mists and icy blasts and clouds streaming across the mountain top, often called the "Plumes of Pamola."[9]

Edmund Ware Smith amusingly reflects that when the weather grows windy and cloudy it is because "Pamola's loose again. Someone's peeling bark off a birch tree at the New City clearing" or "Pamola's going to rock the valley [because] someone's exceeded the limit on trout at Six Ponds."[10]

From the summit of Katahdin the "plumes of Pamola" hover over the Knife Edge, Chimney Peak, and Pamola Peak. Courtesy, John W. Neff.

Whimsical painting by Maurice "Jake" Day of Pamola visiting with Chimney Pond Campground Game Warden Roy Dudley. Courtesy, Edward Werler.

THE FIRST KINSHIP / 13

One of the most popular stories about Pamola's fearsomeness concerns former Governor John Neptune of the Penobscot Nation. Roy Dudley reported to Eckstorm that, as a young boy, he heard the governor himself tell this story:

It is not to be wondered that the Indians peopled the mountains with Pamola, the fierce, avenging spirit who relished their destruction. Old John Neptune, famous Oldtown Indian of other days, called upon the Dudley family years ago when Mr. Dudley [Roy] was a mere lad, and related his experiences with the fury of the mountain.

"Folks say no Pamola, if they want to," he said, "but I know; I see him. Ol' Pamola there all right." He told how, though he had been warned against the deed, he went up into the mountain to hunt and stayed overnight in a shack with a strong door. In the night, when John was asleep, Pamola swooped down from his fastnesses in the crags and alighted in the yard by the shack, a great beast, with mighty wings that dragged on the ground, with a head as large as four horses, and with horrible beak and claws. He beat upon the door of the shack, and roared and howled and heaved again and again at the fastenings, but by good luck the door was frozen down and he could not budge it. So, with a last, long yell of rage and defiance, he flapped filthily and wickedly away.

Four others were less fortunate—they went into the mountain and never returned. Pamola got them somewhere. John had seen the entrance to Pamola's cave, and knew where, in the Northwest Basin, he hung out his lantern of nights, before his den, where he crawled with his prey.[11]

THE MOUNTAIN TAKES SHAPE

Katahdin literature is full of colorful stories that convey the sacredness of the mountain and that are inspired by Native American tales, but aren't actually so. Two such stories appear in a collection entitled *The Legends and Yarns of Katahdin*, published by Charles Watkins in 1942. In "The Coming of Pamola," the storm bird's wrath cuts and grinds the mountain into shape:

Many moons passed and the smoke of many a council fire was seen from the top of the mountain. The Indians did not dare approach the plateau for fear of the evil spirit. Peace and plenty were in the valley. However, Pamola, an evil spirit, was angry. He was not invited to the council of the "big rain," and so he continued to growl in his den in the Northwest basin. He was an ugly beast, head big as four horses, huge wings that dragged on the ground, had a horrible beak, and claws like big arrows. When he growled, the mountain shook with fear.

The Gods were celebrating the council of the "full moon" when Pamola swept down upon them. There was great confusion.

"Why do you disturb our council fire?" the Gods asked. "Who are you?"

Pamola growled and flapped his huge wings. The mountain shook. The lightning flashed and the thunders rolled. The terrific struggle lasted many days and the council ring was destroyed. Rocks rolled in all directions and made the big slides on the mountainsides.

The elves of the woods were so concerned that they met in the big ravine and wept for many moons. Their tears are still seen flowing down the big valley.

Pamola withdrew from the struggle and the Gods decreed "that he should be turned to stone on a peak of the mountain away from the plateau."

Pamola was very angry and as he sulked away from the peak, he flapped his huge wings and left only "the knife edge." Then when he passed "Chimney Peak" he raged so madly that he cut a big notch in the chimney between "Chimney Peak" and Pamola so that the other gods would never disturb him.[12]

In "Why Katahdin," the gods roll boulders into place to protect their new council ring:

Many, many moons ago, before the Big Chief ruled the day, the outdoor Gods held a big council fire out on the plains. The big smoke attracted many of the elves of the woods and the council was disturbed in their deliberations.

The Gods decided that they should find a new council ring where they could meet in secret and not be disturbed. They also wished that they could be covered by the clouds when in the council ring.

They searched for many a moon, but with no success. The big mountain in the West was too high (Mount Washington): other mountains in the northwest were not suited, so they implored the Gods of the mountains and hills to make possible for them a mountain in the wilderness, with a big council ring on top so that they could meet as they wished.

The earth groaned and trembled and a mountain, shaped like a huge man with outstretched arms, slowly rose in the vast woodlands. One of the Gods peered into the misty distance and saw the mountain way off on the horizon.

"That's our council ring," he said, and they quickly hurried in that direction. The huge form was more like a big wigwam and seemed to move farther and farther away.

Eventually they reached the top of the mountain and found a large plateau with plenty of big rocks for a council ring.

The Gods met for many a moon on the plateau. They were so contented that they made their plans in order that they would never be disturbed. They decreed that no Indian should ever climb to the big council ring, so they rolled huge bolders [sic] along the sides and piled big rocks across the trail in "the Garden of the Gods."

They also sent out the command that no trees or other bushes would be allowed to grow on the big plateau since the Gods wished a clear view of all their domain, except in cloudy weather.

The Indians at the foot of the mountain looked in awe upon the great mountain, for it was shaped like a big wigwam. When the clouds gathered on the top, the people of the forests felt that the Gods were in the council ring. And so the Indians named the mountain "THE PRE-EMINENT ONE," or Ktaadn or Kt-teddon.[13]

NATIVE AMERICAN LEGACY

Not long after the arrival of the Europeans in the seventeenth century, the Penobscots entered into a loose alliance called the Wabanaki Confederacy. Wabanaki means the "People of the Rising Sun" or "People of the Dawn." The alliance included the Penobscots, Passamaquoddies, Maliseets, Micmacs, and Abenaki. The alliance offered protection against the growing European presence, which was slowly wresting control of coastal and upland territories from Native Americans during the 1700s and 1800s, threatening the very foundations of their existence.* As seventeenth-century English hegemony moved northward, it conflicted with French territorial claims. The ensuing warfare and violence trapped the tribes in the middle of the

---

*While the alliance would soon be neglected, it was recognized and revived during the 1970s by Maine's Native Americans, who were interested in the sacred traditions and practices of their tribes.

conflict, which continued through the mid eighteenth century. Decimated by these conflicts and suffering from the rampant spread of new diseases, the Native American population never fully recovered.

However, their encounters and legends surrounding the mountain constitute the first human encounters with Katahdin, and their Earth-based spiritualism and reverence for the mountain form the basis of an enduring mystique.

Penobscot Elder Arnie Neptune describes the mountain as follows:

> The Spirit of Katahdin, great and kind leader of the Penobscots, lives within the massive mountain we call Katahdin in his honor. It is in this way that Katahdin is thought to embody the great teachings of the Creator. The sacred mountain is an inspiration to all who believe Katahdin to be the spirit who will lead mankind to his highest potential, by bringing wisdom to all who open their hearts and their minds to listening and learning.[14]

Dennis Kostyk, in his film *Wabanaki: A New Dawn*, tells us:

> It is on Katahdin that the Wabanaki people see the sun's first rays. The Wabanaki know the Spirit of the light and welcome each new dawn as it comes to the land.
>
> As their ancestors did, today's Wabanaki look to Katahdin as a sacred place where the Spirit roams freely and powerfully.
>
> To be with the mountain is to make a commitment to participate fully in life itself, to encounter the forces of life and to be in balance with them.
>
> For the Wabanaki, the mountain is central to all their beliefs and experiences.
>
> It is where Mother Earth reaches out to the sky. To go to Katahdin is to experience the spiritual aspects of Wabanaki life at its source, to feel the interconnectedness of oneself with that of ancestors and future generations.
>
> Going to the Mountain is but a single manifestation of the journey. For Wabanaki the journey is neverending. It is a continual search.[15]

EARLY EXPLORATION

2

From Colonial Surveys to First Ascents

IN AUGUST 1689, A BAND OF MALISEETS ATTACKED NINE-YEAR-OLD John Giles and his family near their Pemaquid settlement home along the central Maine coast. The raiding party killed his father and took Giles, his mother, and several of his brothers captive. Giles was later separated from his family and began a long canoe journey with his captors up the Penobscot River. Giles, though abused at first, survived and was eventually accepted into the everyday life of the tribe. However, after six years or more, the Maliseets sold Giles to a French seigneur, who finally gave him his freedom in 1698. Years later, after becoming the commander of a military garrison along the St. George River, Giles published an account of his captivity. The account includes several stories about Katahdin.

One tale describes a Native American maiden whose beauty made it difficult for her to find a suitable husband. One day, the maiden wandered off from her family's home in the Upper Penobscot valley, "under the White Hills, called Teddon [Katahdin]." Despite their efforts, her parents could not locate her. After much time and worry, her family finally found her with a handsome young man whose hair, like hers, flowed to his waist. The two were swimming in a lovely pool of water, but they vanished upon approach. The family imagined that the handsome young man was one of the kindly spirits who inhabited "the Teddon," and they began to look upon him as their son-in-law. According to the legend, when they were in need of game—deer, moose, and bear—they would go to the waterside, signify their wish, and the desired animal would emerge from the water.[1]

Giles relates one of the Native Americans' personal accounts of the mountain:

> I have heard an Indian say that he lived by the river, at the foot of the Teddon, the top of which he could see through the hole of his wigwam left for the smoke to pass out. He was tempted to travel to it, and accordingly set out on a summer morning, and labored hard in ascending the hill, all day, and the top seemed as distant from the place where he lodged at night as from his wigwam, where he began his journey. He now concluded the spirits were there, and never dared to make a second attempt.[2]

Giles' stories are the first published references to the mountain. Between the 1690s and 1760s, other non-Native Americans might have penetrated Maine's vast interior as explorers, traders, adventurers, missionaries, soldiers, surveyors, or sojourners. However, not until 1775 did Katahdin reappear in colonial accounts of exploration.

COLONIAL ENCOUNTERS

In 1760, the British military commissioned Colonel John Montresor, a young engineer officer, to explore the region between Quebec and the Kennebec River. Montresor was to study the feasibility of building a road from that city to Fort Halifax, a key frontier garrison along the Kennebec at Winslow. From Quebec, Montresor followed an old native path that connected Canada's Chaudière River with the Kennebec. The expedition itself reveals a strong and growing interest in opening up avenues of trade between the St. Lawrence River's thriving villages and the Atlantic coast, a region that is now Maine.

Although the natives were secretive about their canoe routes and portages, Montresor eventually reached Moosehead Lake, where he reported seeing Katahdin in the distance. He referred to the mountain as "Panavansot Hill," a possible corruption of "Penobscot," the name used by his native guides to identify the nearby river. The guides, who were from the St. Lawrence

Ascent routes of early explorers from the West Branch.

River area, spoke a language different from that of the Penobscot tribes. Montresor identified the mountain on the map he drew of his findings; it is the earliest known map showing Katahdin. The young colonel returned to Quebec and the St. Lawrence by the Chaudière River.

Katahdin next appears in John Chadwick's 1764 account of an expedition that may have included a partial ascent. Chadwick undertook the expedition with John Preble at the request of the governor of the Massachusetts Bay Colony. The two men were to map the Penobscot River from the Atlantic coast into Canada and to locate a possible land route for a highway between Fort Pownal (near present-day Stockton Springs on Penobscot Bay) and Quebec. Chadwick was a professional surveyor and well qualified for the task. In her brief history of the expedition, nineteenth-century historian Fannie Hardy Eckstorm speculated that several Penobscot native chiefs may have accompanied Chadwick to keep an eye on his activities while he was in their territory.[3]

Starting out in May, Chadwick journeyed up the Penobscot River to the island village of the Penobscot tribe at Old Town, where he hired his Native American guides. Following an ancient canoe route, the party traveled to the mouth of the Piscataquis River, which they then followed upstream, eventually going by way of Sebec and Onawa Lakes to reach Moosehead Lake.

Chadwick likely made his way from Moosehead Lake to the "Height of Land" (between Canada and the United States) and then down Canada's Chaudière River to Quebec City. He returned to Fort Pownal via the Northeast Carry to the waters of the Penobscot West Branch, passing very near Katahdin. Chadwick called Katahdin "Satinhungemoss Hill," a term Eckstorm suggests the surveyor may have invented from several native words describing what is now the Abol Deadwater. The location's dramatic view of the mountain may have made it a favorite campsite. At one point Chadwick describes Katahdin as "so lofty a pyramid."[4] Although Chadwick does not specifically mention making an ascent, he probably made a partial ascent along Abol Stream. He recounts the natives' reluctance to climb beyond the treeline and their belief that one native, in an earlier time, attempted to climb higher but never returned.

Because the natives would only allow his expedition to proceed if he promised not to make a formal map as he traveled, Chadwick later drew maps from memory. Katahdin appears on one of his maps as "Teddon"—the same name Giles had used earlier.

It is reasonable to assume there were other surveyors, as well as explorers, traders, adventurers, missionaries, soldiers, or sojourners, who came to the "lofty pyramid" to explore its treasures. Yet the gap of time between Chadwick's 1764 survey and the first recorded non-Native American ascent in 1804 is considerable. The account of that first ascent mentions Fort Mountain, west of Katahdin, suggesting the tantalizing possibility of an earlier ascent. The forays of Giles, Montresor, Chadwick and untold others had at last opened the West Branch to non-Native American travelers. For almost the next 80 years, the approach to Katahdin would be from the Penobscot up the south flank of the mountain.

THE FIRST RECORDED ASCENTS

In August 1804,* professional surveyor Charles Turner Jr. and a group of men ascended the West Branch from Mattawamkeag in bateaux and reached the summit from the south side of the mountain.** The expedition marked the first recorded ascent. Thus began a long history of ascents from the south side, which continued until the late 1830s when logging roads made the Wassataquoik Valley east of Katahdin more accessible. The commonwealth of Massachusetts commissioned Turner to survey the "Eastern Lands," an uncharted wilderness to the northeast of the commonwealth, which was called the District of Maine.

Turner's account vividly describes his approach, ascent, and the wonder felt at the summit:

> Having reached the top, we found ourselves on a plane [what we now call the Tableland] of rocks with coarse gravel in the interstices, and the whole covered with a dead bluish moss. This place, the westerly part of which was very smooth, and descending a little to the northward, contained about eight hundred acres. The elevation was so great a sensibility to effect respiration.

Turner writes that his party scratched their initials and the date on a

---

* To put this first ascent of remote Katahdin in perspective, note that the first ascent of Mount Washington was 162 years earlier (by Darby Field in 1642).

** Turner was born in 1760 in Duxbury, Mass., and became the first postmaster of the neighboring town of Scituate. He served in both houses of the Massachusetts legislature and as a U.S. congressman. In 1824, he became steward of the U.S. Marine Hospital in Chelsea, Mass.

sheet of lead, which they placed under a bottle of rum on the summit as proof of their accomplishment.

In his narrative, Turner also discusses Native American fear of the mountain:

> The two Indians whom we hired to pilot and assist us in ascending the mountain, cautioned us not to proceed if we should hear any uncommon noise; and when we came to the cold part of the mountain they refused to proceed ahead—however, when they found that we were determined to proceed, even without them, they again went forward courageously, and seemed ambitious to be first on the summit. On our return to Indian Old Town, it was with difficulty that we could convince the natives that we had been upon the top of Mount Catardin, nor should we have been able to satisfy them of the fact, so superstitious were they, had it not been for the Indians who had accompanied us.[5]

Turner's account certainly implies that he ascended the southwest ridge, now known as the Hunt Spur. Turner estimated that Katahdin was 13,000 feet in elevation, more than twice its actual measurement. Turner also noted that the surrounding lands, both the valleys and the steep wooded areas, had been badly burned. History does not record whether or not subsequent climbers discovered the rum or the lead sheet. Perhaps the next party to reach the summit did not wish to admit to consuming the rum that had been so generously left there. At the very least, no one has admitted to finding the sheet of lead. In 1816, a landslide, later known as the "Abol Slide" or the "Great Slide," devastated the mountain's south side. It was later reported that "an enormous declivity about mid-side of the mountain slid into a distant valley . . . an event, however, which has rendered the ascent in one of its difficult places altogether more tolerable and in other ways more easy."[6] In the years that followed, climbers were attracted to the foot of the slide and ascended the unstable rocks to the summit.

The second recorded ascent of Katahdin did not take place until fifteen years after Turner's. In 1819, Major Colin Campbell led a British expedition to the Katahdin region in what was the first known ascent of the Abol Slide. Campbell set out to determine the United States and British pre-war boundaries restored by the 1814 Treaty of Ghent. With the declaration of Maine as a separate state imminent, the British were anxious to take as much unclaimed land as they could. Later, some would suggest that their claims and boundaries were based on calculations favorable to the British.

The Campbell party, led by the region's most knowledgeable Native American guides, threaded its way from the Penobscot River along the West Branch's chain of lakes, deadwaters, and river courses. At the mouth of Katahdin Stream, the party spotted the fresh coloration of the recent avalanche on the mountain they called "Cathardin." Snow prevented the party from reaching the summit during two preliminary attempts, but they finally gained the summit on a brisk, clear October day. From the summit, the men observed the distant snow-covered peaks and took magnetic readings of key surrounding locations. In later years, other expeditions used the Campbell party's makeshift shelter located about a mile above the foot of the slide. Colonel Campbell must have enjoyed some fame from this feat, for he would be asked to guide another survey expedition the next year.

ESTABLISHING THE MONUMENT LINE (1820–1833)

On March 15, 1820, Maine became an independent state. The state's new status immediately prompted the formation of a Maine Boundary Commission that would formally survey the land and its boundaries. The commission, perhaps because of suspicions surrounding the 1819 British calculations, decided to authorize a joint expedition of British and American surveyors.

The 1820 expedition marked the first step toward setting a base Monument Line across Maine from its eastern to its western border with Canada. A Mr. Loring represented the United States, while a Mr. Odell represented Great Britain. Documents list Daniel Rose and Reuel Williams as Boundary Commissioners, positions for which they received $750 apiece. The Commission instructed Loring and Odell to lay out in a grid a series of measured "ranges" north and south of the base line, the resulting "townships" to be lettered and numbered. They were to report back by December 2, 1825.

An account of this trip, attributed by some to Daniel Rose, was first printed in the Appalachian Mountain Club's journal *Appalachia* nearly 150 years later. The account offers fascinating observations about the mountain.

> In ascending the Penobscot we had at different times, very indistinct and faint views of Katahdin Mountain. But as we entered the Lake Umbogegose [probably Ambajejus], its appearance was the most imposing and sublime

that can be imagined. . . . In that lonely desert, where we had hitherto seen nothing but an unvaried succession of forests and lakes—where we had found nothing to enliven or amuse, we were thus suddenly called upon to acknowledge the great Architect of Creation.[7]

In August, the party reached the mouth of "Abalajakomejus" Stream (today's Abol Stream). During the years before these early ascents the Native Americans had likely established a well-used campsite on the high ground across the West Branch from the mouth of this stream, just before Abol Falls. Early south-side explorers and climbers continued to use the site for its memorable view. The party climbed along the Great Slide and pitched their tents on the shelf formerly occupied by the crude shelter of the 1819 expedition. On August 10, they reached the summit after enjoying the rich waters of the spring on the vast Tableland.

Wherever our eyes reached there was a dead uniformity of forests, relieved only by a great variety of lakes. The mountains were very numerous and rose singly to great heights. The country appeared to be intersected by almost innumerable ramifications of the principal rivers, separating the mountains in every quarter.[8]

Like those who had come before, a member of the British contingent left at the summit the men's names under a small bottle in a pile of rocks. (There is no mention of finding Charles Turner's rum bottle.)

This expedition provided the most accurate measurement of the mountain's height at the time. While Turner had estimated Katahdin's height to be nearly 13,000 feet, the 1820 expedition set its height to be 5,385 feet. This estimation, formulated using only a British barometer, was a mere 118 feet more than the actual height—not bad for the instruments being used at the time. The challenge of carrying out the survey across northern Maine's untamed forests and mountains required at least five additional trips before the Monument Line was complete.

The earliest known account of the spelling "Katahdin" was put to print by Moses Greenleaf, a wilderness geographer and mapmaker. He used this spelling on his 1815 map of the area. The name took hold. Greenleaf performed a great deal of survey work in the years before and after statehood in 1820 and, at one time, even proposed extensive canal building to link the waterways of the Penobscot with the St. John/Allagash watersheds.

Joseph C. Norris Sr. and his son continued the effort to establish the Monument Line begun by Loring and Odell. In 1825, the pair started out at the Maine-New Brunswick border from a certain yellow birch tree that had been marked in 1797 and encircled by an iron hoop. They headed west across the newly established state.

The survey went well the first year, and the surveyors closed in on the Katahdin region. By late September they had almost reached the Penobscot's East Branch, when Norris left to complete other survey obligations. He was unable to resume the task until early November. Notwithstanding the approach of winter, Norris doggedly forged on after he returned. Soon, after being one of the first non-natives ever to visit the Wassataquoik Valley, he had run the line over and beyond the Turner Mountain massif. Norris endured and overcame numerous difficulties. Because he was attempting to run an accurate straight line, he and his party could not circumvent steep terrain and nearly impenetrable forest growth.

Norris likely ran the line as far as Hamlin Peak that year and thus became the first to climb that summit. However, when he finally peered over the edge of the plateau west of Hamlin Peak, he realized that it was impossible to continue the line down the cliff face into the Northwest Basin. Thus he wisely abandoned his effort for the year.

The time of the year and the purpose of this adventure make it a singular achievement. Norris observed the same large tracts of burned land that Turner had noted 21 years earlier. However, Norris went a step further and declared the timber in the area utterly useless. He was also the first to view the Northwest Basin and the Klondike, neither of which had been thoroughly explored.

Other Monument Line expeditions took place in 1826, 1827, possibly in 1828, and in 1832, but those efforts concentrated on the area west of Katahdin from Quebec and did not include a return to the Northwest Basin. Approximately 8 miles remained incomplete. Finally in 1833, Edwin Rose mounted an expedition to run the Monument Line from the Katahdin plateau toward Chesuncook Lake. He and his party forced their way into the Northwest Basin, across the northern portion of the Klondike, over South Brother Mountain, down into the Nesowadnehunk Valley and over the ridge north of Doubletop Mountain. From his travels Rose produced the first detailed map of the region.

The portion of the Monument Line that crossed the Katahdin range from New Brunswick westward did not align with the portion coming eastward from Quebec. The two lines missed each other by approximately 0.5 mile just northwest of Doubletop Mountain. This unexplained miscalculation was never corrected and still appears on modern maps.

The success of the 1833 expedition concluded the effort to establish a Monument Line across Maine. Only a few years later, a new era of scientific exploration would begin, a time of discovery and formal recording of the features of Katahdin's wilderness. After these surveys, homesteaders would begin to move into the region for farming and logging.

EARLY SCIENTIFIC EXPLORATION

In 1832, a year before the Monument Line's completion, John James Audubon, distinguished ornithologist, wildlife artist, and astute observer of nature, visited Maine with his family. From Canada, he traveled down the "Military Road" to Bangor. Although the road was rough and rainfall came in torrents at times, there were glorious autumnal days when Katahdin would have been visible in all its grandeur. At one point, Audubon observed in his journal: "Mountains which you well know are indispensable in a beautiful landscape, reared their majestic crests in the distance." He may have harbored the wish to travel toward this monarch of the wilderness. It is a pity that he could not have ascended Wassataquoik Stream, still pristine prior to the start of the great logging era along its banks.

In late July 1836, Rev. Joseph Blake, a recent Bowdoin College graduate who later became an accomplished botanist, traveled the carriage road from Bangor toward Katahdin with two companions. They were among the first to travel through virgin forest by carriage to Nicatou. There they hired a bateau and guide to take them up the West Branch toward the mountain.

Their guide took them only as far as the Debsconeag Lakes. From there, they were on their own. They spent a lovely evening camped along the Abol Slide but awoke the next morning to lowering clouds. The party continued climbing but soon encountered sleet, freezing rain, and numbing cold. After reaching the Tableland, they wisely retreated to the river and continued their trip up the West Branch to Moosehead.

The weather had not improved two weeks later when Jacob Whitman Bailey, a chemistry professor at West Point, led the first scientific expedition to Katahdin to make geological and botanical observations. Bailey's father-in-law, Professor George Washington Keeley, and Professor Phineas Barnes, both of Waterville College (now Colby College) accompanied him. They crossed the new bridge at Mattawamkeag and began the rough journey by foot to Nicatou. From there, they traveled along the usual West Branch route and climbed the Abol Slide to the summit. Somewhat frail, Bailey turned back before reaching the summit, while the others made it to the top despite the rainy, windy conditions.

The published account of Bailey's expedition contains the first scientific observations of the region and the first published sketch of the mountain and its terrain. In the sketch, Bailey identifies Doubletop Mountain as "Sugarloaf." From his river vantage point, the mountain resembled a large loaf of unrefined, dark sugar, purchased in those days in solid cone-shaped molds.[9]

In September 1837, Charles Thomas Jackson, a Harvard College graduate and Maine's first state geologist, organized a second major scientific expedition. Jackson intended to carry out a geological reconnaissance of Maine's public lands. Although not a native Mainer, he had heard of Katahdin from his brother-in-law Ralph Waldo Emerson, a fellow citizen of Concord, Massachusetts. Emerson had visited Bangor as an interim pastor and likely brought back stories of Katahdin ascents and the Monument Line efforts. A few years later, Emerson's friend Henry David Thoreau would also undertake a foray to the northern forest and Katahdin.

Jackson's group included Rev. William Clark Larrabee, then principal of the Maine Wesleyan Seminary at Kents Hill, who later provided a detailed account of the journey. The group of ten headed up the Penobscot in bateaux and canoes from Old Town. They ascended the West Branch by way of Millinocket and Ambajejus Lake to the ancient native campsite above Abol Falls, later known as Abol Meadows to some early explorers. Today, the Jackson and Larrabee accounts are regarded as classics. In his account, Larrabee recounts their moment on the summit:

> At last, with many a weary step, and many a hair-breadth escape, we reached the cloud-capped summit. . . . The cloud, which, from below, appeared resting so quiet on its mountain perch, was all in a whirl. The wind blew so violently, that one of the company, with comic gravity, inquired how many men it might take to hold one's hair on. Nor were wind and cloud all. The snow came thick and fast, and the cold was so intense that out of ten men, protected by overcoats and mittens, not one could unscrew the tube of the barometer, so benumbed were our fingers. . . .

An Indian of the Penobscots [Louis Neptune], who was one of the party, averred that Pimola, the mythological demon of the mountain, had sent this terrible storm upon us, in punishment of our impiety in visiting his dominions. . . .

After much difficulty, we succeeded in taking barometrical observations, and obtaining such geological information as the circumstances allowed; and then, finding that longer delay might be dangerous, on account of the intensity of the cold, and the violence of the storm, we started on our return.[10]

After the party reprovisioned in Bangor, they traveled up the East Branch and stayed at the Hunt Farm. From there they explored the Seboeis and Aroostook Rivers. They managed this incredibly vast exploration during the fall season. Arthur H. Norton, writing in *The Maine Naturalist*, reports that Jackson had to:

Force his fleet up streams with low water, across freezing lakes, and to endure storms of rain and snow. Jackson, on the other hand, recounts these obstacles as calmly as other mere incidents, which he was duty bound to report. Nor did he neglect to make a considerable collection of minerals and rocks along the route, bringing out five boxes of specimens.[11]

Jackson was known for this steadfastness in the face of nature's forces—and his stubbornness. Herbert Adams called Jackson "one of the crankiest and most colorful men in all American science."[12] Jackson was at the same time a physician, educator, chemist, and geologist—a true son of the sort of American Renaissance taking place in Concord, Massachusetts. He later did geologic work in the White Mountains, and it is this man, rather than President Andrew Jackson, for whom Mount Jackson in the Presidential Range is named. He was later beset by great mental stress and died at a mental health facility in 1880—a sad end for a brilliant man whose expeditions and studies demonstrated how valuable Maine was to the United States.

THE HUNT FARM

After the Military Road, linking Mattawamkeag and Houlton, was built in the early 1830s, loggers and timber owners began to cast a longing eye toward the vast areas of timber in the direction of Katahdin. Moving westward from the Military Road, they could harvest timber and drive the logs down the Penobscot to the sawmills at Old Town and Orono.

William Harmon Hunt of Carthage, Maine, saw the potential of this emerging "industry" and decided to provide accommodations for loggers and "entertainment" for recreational travelers along the river. He moved his family to a tract of land he bought on the east side of the East Branch around 1832. By 1835 he had erected a timber farmhouse using the region's first rip saw and cleared land for cultivation. He cut a rough road from Stacyville westward to his farm site, located across from an intervale just above Whetstone Falls.

About the same time Hiram Dacey of Skowhegan, Maine, established a smaller farm at what is now Lunksoos Camp, only two miles north of Hunt's farm. The Wassataquoik flowed into the East Branch at a point halfway between the two farms.

Hunt's farm would become very important to the growing number of people ready to venture into the wilderness to climb Katahdin's lofty summit. Until then, an expedition to Katahdin involved either a long canoe trip from Bangor up the West Branch to the Abol Deadwater or an even lon-

The Hunt Farm along the East Branch of the Penobscot. Hunt Mountain is in the distance. Courtesy, Special Collections, Bangor Public Library.

ger trip from Moosehead down the West Branch to Abol. Such expeditions were physically demanding and expensive. They required canoes, bateaux, provisions, guides, and boatmen for an extended period of time. The trips appealed only to those most ready for the rigors of wilderness travel. Previous trips to the mountain—the surveys, the Boundary Commission work, and the scientific explorations—were major expeditions, financed either by the state of Maine or its parent, the commonwealth of Massachusetts. Almost all of these early expeditions approached Katahdin from the south. From the West Branch, expedition leaders could ascend the Tableland and summit by the Southwest Spur or the Abol Slide.

The farm provided easier access to Katahdin from the east side. By using the recently constructed Military Road, the new road to the Hunt Farm, and traveling up the valley of the Wassataquoik, reaching Katahdin was a great deal faster, less expensive, and less complicated than a full-scale expedition. Furthermore, people could now travel in small private parties.

In this new era, the popularity of the mountain's east side grew in conjunction with the steady development of logging roads along Wassataquoik Stream toward Katahdin beginning in the mid-1830s. The approaches changed completely, as travelers almost totally abandoned the south side in favor of the east.

On a fall evening in 1837, Charles T. Jackson made his way up the East Branch and became one of the first travelers to stay at Hunt's farmhouse. Hunt had carefully positioned his farm site where the East Branch broadens briefly to allow easy fording. The farmhouse was on a high bluff, situated so Hunt and his guests could see both upriver and down. Across the river one could see to the west and northwest what are now named Hunt Mountain and Deasey Mountain.

When Jackson and his party stayed there in October 1837, he reported that the Hunt Farm was well-established and that Hunt had brought the soil to an excellent state of cultivation. Hunt had built his one and a half-story farmhouse out of hand-hewn squared logs, boarded over. A large kitchen, several fireplaces, outbuildings and a large barn offered ample space. Jackson added that Hunt had raised 100 bushels of wheat and an abundance of potatoes and hay—some of which was sold to the loggers for the animals they kept at the logging camps deeper in the wilderness.

Hunt himself may have only operated the farm for some fifteen years; his sons and subsequent owners continued to provide accommodation for many years. In 1857 Henry David Thoreau, during his voyage down the East Branch, stopped briefly at the farm. While the family was absent, some men cutting hay occupied the house. Thoreau had wanted to climb Katahdin from the east on this occasion, but abandoned the plan because his companion had foot problems. Jackson and Thoreau were not the only distinguished visitors in those early years; the farm guestbook must have included many others.

Indeed, the farm became known as the last place of comfort and civilization before adventurers endured primitive camping on the last push to Katahdin.

At first, travelers came by carriage from Mattawamkeag or by canoe along the river. When the European and North American Railroad opened in 1869 north of Bangor to Mattawamkeag, reaching Hunt's by carriage along the Military Road became even easier. However, a great fire later devastated lumbering operations along the Wassataquoik, and use of the east side decreased. The coming of the Bangor and Aroostook Railroad in the mid 1890s made Medway, Millinocket, and the lakes along the West Branch more accessible. Thus the scene would once again shift to the south and southwest side of Katahdin.

THE HALE-CHANNING CLIMB (1845)

Various adventurers and even some loggers may have climbed to the summit from the east side in the eight years after Charles Jackson stopped at the Hunt Farm. Even so, Edward Everett Hale and William Francis Channing, two young Bostonians, made the first recorded eastern ascent (other than the Monument Line surveyors). Both gentlemen were from well-known families and were classmates at Harvard College.

Hale, the grandson of Revolutionary War hero Nathan Hale, began preaching after graduating from Harvard and served two pastorates, in Worcester and in Roxbury. He later became Chaplain of the United States Senate. Hale edited histories and wrote the classic *The Man Without A Country*. Channing, the son of William Ellery Channing, came from a family of clergymen, authors, historians, and social justice reformers. He transferred from Harvard to the University of Pennsylvania where he received his medical degree. He later abandoned medicine for research in the field of physics.

Hale and Channing had become interested in mountain climbing while exploring Mount Washington's trails and summits. In 1845, they decided to climb Katahdin. One of their Harvard mentors, Dr. Asa Gray, a noted American botanist, asked them to bring back plant specimens he could compare to Mount Washington's flora. The young men took a steamboat from Boston to Bangor and then a stage to Mattawamkeag. During their travels, they noted that Mattawamkeag was a real frontier town, as a deer had wandered into the village the day they were there. In town, they engaged a lumberman as their guide, a man who probably worked along the Wassataquoik in the winter and knew the country well. He told them that he, as well as other loggers, had ascended Katahdin on two or three occasions.

The two adventurers had originally hoped to ascend the West Branch, climb the mountain from the traditional south side, and return via Moosehead Lake. However, because of high water, they instead traveled by wagon or stage to Benedicta, then by foot to the Hunt Farm on the East Branch. Hale described the farm in the following manner:

> The position of Hunt's Farm . . . is for picturesque beauty utterly unsurpassable. From a thick forest you came out upon a hillside to his clearing, grass and grain covered, sweeping down the hill to the river. The river here takes a long circuit, enclosing on the opposite side a noble piece of intervale covered with the richest growth of hardwood timber, whose varying and brilliant shades contrast with the more sombre evergreen growth of two or three fine mountains which rise immediately beyond. Hunt's house is just on the river opposite this forest peninsula. It is a large, rambling place, partly built of logs and partly of frame . . . and is the last inhabited station of the loggers in this quarter.[13]

Leaving the farmstead, one of Hunt's boatmen took them 0.5 up the East Branch and crossed the river to the north bank of the Wassataquoik, where they began their adventure of hiking and camping in the wild. Hale's account provides interesting details about the rough terrain, staying in logging camp shelters, visiting Grand Falls, and lamenting the loss of some of their supplies to marauding bears. As expected, they could not reach the summit that first day, so at sunset they prepared themselves for a night at or near treeline.

The morning brought a beautiful sunrise, and the two men expected to easily reach the summit. However, a spell of strong winds, mist, and rain prevented them from reaching the highest peak. They surmised that Pamola's anger may have caused the weather, for they had heard of the Native American stories about Katahdin's guardian spirit. Although the account does not explain what path they took to the summit, they probably trekked along the upper waters of the Wassataquoik Main Branch, up Russell Mountain, across the North Peaks (perhaps the first to do so), to Hamlin Peak. It was likely in that area that weather drove them back.

Both Hale and Channing looked back on their trip with great appreciation. They had fulfilled their desire for high youthful adventure and were able to bring home hundreds of specimens, the first Maine plants for Dr. Gray's collection.

YOUNG'S BOTANICAL EXPEDITION

In August of 1847, Dr. Aaron Young Jr., Maine's state botanist, led the Botanical Expedition to Mount Katahdin. The expedition received $600 from the Maine legislature to undertake the region's first survey by a trained botanist. Dr. George Thurber of Providence, Rhode Island; John Emerson of Glenburn, Maine; James Cowan of Bangor; Rev. Ariel P. Chute of Harrison, Maine; and John K. DeLaski accompanied Young. Both Thurber and DeLaski provided lively and detailed newspaper and journal accounts of the trip. Cowan, who had cut timber along the Wassataquoik, served as guide.

From Bangor, the expedition journeyed up along the Penobscot in a large two-horse wagon and reached the Hunt Farm via Mattawamkeag and the Aroostook Road on a Saturday night. The road into Hunt's was in wretched condition, but they found a large, productive, and comfortable farm awaiting them. The next morning, following the Sabbath service led by Chute, the party shouldered their packs, crossed the Penoboscot's East Branch by bateaux, and began their trek by foot up the Wassataquoik Tote Road. Young reports that he brought a large tinbox for specimens, a barometer, telescope, and compass. Chute carried a teakettle and a tin molasses flask, and another in the party packed in a large frying pan.

After leaving the Hunt Farm, the party ate a breakfast of "stew fungay," a concoction of hard bread softened with hot water, leftover fried pork fat and a "wee taste of molasses." While some of the group fussed about starting the day in this manner, others pronounced it a delight, as long as it was accompanied by plenty of strong black coffee.

The group ascended Katahdin from the Russell Mountain area via the North Peaks. On their way they passed several of the Monument Line cairns, placed more than two decades earlier. They followed Hale and Channing's 1845 route, which was growing in appeal because of its more gradual, though roundabout, ascent. After observing "the solemn grandeur" from the summit, the expedition added stones to the cairn and sang *Old One Hundredth* (the Doxology). On the descent, some of the party were lost for a time and had to make their way through the wild tangled forest, finally uniting with others along the Wassataquoik. Dr. Young's expedition was quite successful, collecting many specimens, and providing important information about the region.

DeLaski wrote that from the summit the many lakes scattered across the forest below resembled "a splendid mirror broken into a thousand fragments."[14] Thoreau in a later published account of his own 1846 Katahdin trip under the title *The Maine Woods* borrowed the simile when he likened the scene he viewed to "a mirror broken into a thousand fragments, and wildly scattered over the grass, reflecting the full blaze of the sun."[15]

THE MARCUS KEEP ERA (1846–1861)

Very few who have climbed Katahdin's Knife Edge or Pamola Peak from Keep Ridge know the remarkable story of the man for whom the ridge is named. Rev. Marcus Rodman Keep was born in Swanton, Vermont, in 1816, graduated from Middlebury College, briefly attended Andover Seminary in Massachusetts, and graduated from Bangor Theological Seminary in 1846. During his time in Bangor, Keep heard of expeditions to Katahdin in the northern wilderness. Perhaps lured by the possibility of taking part in such adventures, Keep traveled north in 1846 on the still very rough Military Road to begin his pastoral duties in Ashland. He may well have heard more stories about Katahdin as he passed through Benedicta and Sherman, and he certainly caught a glimpse of the mountain from those outpost villages. Fascinated, he quickly discovered how to reach Katahdin easily by traveling west to the Penobscot East Branch from Sherman and ascending Wassataquoik Stream.

That summer, Keep, along with his friend James H. Haines, journeyed to the Hunt Farm to begin the first of his many trips along the Wassataquoik route. The men followed the logging road along the stream but then veered south to Katahdin Lake. From the lake they navigated through unexplored forest by compass. After crossing Sandy Stream and Avalanche Brook, they reached the foot of a great avalanche on the side of the East Spur (Keep Ridge). The formidable slide, which probably occurred in the early nineteenth century, allowed spectacular access to the East Spur. After ascending the slide and the ridge, Keep and his party reached Pamola Peak, from which they would see the great Knife Edge, the summit, and the Great Basin far below. Keep found the spectacular views deeply moving and built a small cairn on Pamola as evidence that he had been there.*

Keep's account of his trip the following year indicates that he did not go farther than Pamola on this 1846 excursion. Keep, touched by his experience on the mountain, planned to more thoroughly explore the region the next year and to build a trail for others to use.

In September of 1847, he returned with a flock of other friends including Lawrence R. Chamberlain; Rev. J.R. Mansell of Brewer; Rev. A.J. Bates of Lincoln; H. Pratt of Bangor Theological Seminary; D.N. Rogers; Rev. R.N. Mesurva of Patten; and B.A. Gray. The group dubbed Keep the Captain, Gray the Gunner and Fisherman, and Mansell the President in Council. Because Keep knew the way, he also served as the guide.

From the Hunt Farm, the party proceeded up the Wassataquoik Tote Road, which they called "the supply road." In a single file, Gray led, followed closely by Keep, and Mansell took his place at the end of the line. What a sight it must have been to see this hearty group filing by! When they turned south from the logging road they discovered rough new logging roads leading toward Katahdin Lake. In Keep's account of this trip, he reflected on the value of building a "Katahdin Mountain House" at the lake's outlet, which offered a magnificent view of Katahdin.

Beyond the lake lay virgin forest. The party crossed Sandy Stream and followed Keep's previous route up Avalanche Brook. They camped on a Saturday at the foot of the avalanche where there were wonderful views and continued their ascent of the slide the next day. Keep recalled:

> Although it was hard climbing, we ascended pretty fast, and the clear morning air gave an indescribable beauty to the prospect below. . . . The most

---

* The two did not likely know that during that same summer Henry David Thoreau traveled up the Penobscot West Branch and made his climb almost to the summit from the south side.

zealous went ahead, and were soon out of sight, until, near the head of the slide, we heard them from the distant topmost peaks calling out, "Come on, ye brave!"[16]

When Keep finally stood atop Pamola, some of his comrades had already started across the Knife Edge. Keep reported finding a moss-covered cairn on one of the ridge's peaks. As no record of anyone traversing the Knife Edge before Keep's party exists, the architect of the cairn remains a tantalizing mystery.* After a satisfying pause at the summit, the party retraced its steps across the precarious ridge.

When the men reached the slide's head, they halted their descent in order to pick cranberries. The cranberries were so abundant that Keep speculated that the fruit could well be turned into a successful business enterprise with the proper investment. While most of the party descended the slide to their earlier campsite, Keep and Gray spent the night there, keeping themselves warm by burning dead roots.

The party continued its descent Monday morning and, after spending an uncomfortable rainy and windy night at the outlet of Katahdin Pond, pushed on. Their march from the lake to the Hunt Farm was a wet and soggy affair. They finally arrived in the late afternoon at the farm, where they reveled in the warmth, comfort, and home cooking of the welcoming wilderness inn.

One of the most significant results of this trip was Keep's decision to cut a footpath to the East Spur avalanche by way of Katahdin Lake. Keep asserted: "When this is done, any one may 'go to Katahdin' who wishes."[17] He wanted to open access to both Katahdin and the mountainside's abundant cranberries. In order to facilitate the trail's construction, Lawrence Chamberlain drew a map on linen cloth, which can be seen today at the Maine State Library in the Baxter Map Collection.

Especially impressed with the view of the Great Basin and its beautiful pond from Pamola Peak, Keep and several others made a special trip back to the area in October that year. Keep wrote that he believed he was "the first human visitor to this fabled residence of the Indians' Pamola."[18]

Keep described in detail the basin, its lovely tarn and outlet flowage, and

---

* Keep had the impression that the promontory we know as South Peak today was higher than the true peak, and he held to that opinion for a decade or more until he finally admitted his error.

A view of Katahdin from Katahdin Lake. Courtesy, Maine State Library, Myron H. Avery Collection.

the ponds below the glacial moraine. He ends his brief description of the visit with these words:

> On the 15th of October, when I entered [the Great Basin], and went to the upper lake, all was still as the house of Nymphs except when we ourselves spoke, and then the thousand echos were like the response of fairies bidding us welcome. In this way our voice singing alone would find itself in the midst of a numerous choir singing a "round."[19]

TRUE TO HIS PROMISE AND HIS CAREFULLY LAID OUT PLANS, KEEP returned in 1848 with John Stacy, a noted woodsman in the area, to mark and cut a path from Wassataquoik Stream to Katahdin Lake and on toward the Keep Ridge. His trail, "The Keep Path," remained in use until heavy lumbering finally obscured it in the late 1870s. The path was the first formal trail to the mountain, since the trails on the south side had never been as carefully marked and cut.* The Keep Path ended at the foot of the east slide, from which one could easily ascend the rest of the way.

In 1849, Keep married Hannah Taylor. The couple spent their honeymoon climbing Katahdin, though the record does not indicate Hannah's opinion of that arrangement. With the honeymoon party that summer was a group of four other women. Keep had recruited Martha Mason of Bangor and Caroline Eastman of Bradford the previous winter, and Almira Lowder of Bangor and Esther Jones of Enfield nearer to the departure date. John and Thomas Lawton of Passadumkeag were also in the party. Some of Keep's acquaintances ridiculed the idea of women climbing Katahdin, but Keep remained convinced that women were entirely capable of sharing in the hardships and challenges. From the Hunt Farm, the party followed the supply road along the Wassataquoik by foot, turning south toward Katahdin Lake where they picked up the marked trail Keep had cut the year before.

They reached the base of the east slide on a Saturday evening and the following morning held "Camp Meeting" while looking out across the vast wilderness. Keep wrote that it was a "fit time and place to contemplate the history of the creation."[20]

The party arose Monday morning to a beautiful and promising day. Their goal was to name the peaks along the Knife Edge on their way to the summit. They named the first peak (Pamola) Mount Alma, for one of the ladies in the party. Next came Mount Etna (Chimney Peak), Mount Lawrence, Mount Cario (South Peak) and finally the summit, which they named Mount Moriah. Although Keep may have used these names in subsequent years, they were never officially recognized by others and were not used again.

KEEP RECORDED FINDING A BOTTLED NOTE NEAR PAMOLA CLAIMING that Elizabeth Oakes Smith had ascended Katahdin's summit only a few days earlier. Mrs. Smith, a native of Maine, was the wife of Sheba Smith, who founded the *Portland Daily Courier*, the first daily newspaper east of Boston. The couple had moved, however, in 1837 to New York State where

---

* By comparison, the first path on Mount Washington, the highest peak in New England, was cut in 1809, 29 years before the Keep Path was cut on the east side of Katahdin.

EARLY EXPLORATION / 39

their home became a lively social center for men and women of broad cultural acclaim. She wrote novels and poetry and was a pioneer women's orator, ardently advocating for women's rights and the abolition of slavery. She was a friend of Ralph Waldo Emerson.

The record shows that James Haines, Keep's travel companion two years earlier, guided Mrs. Smith and several friends to Katahdin. In his account, Keep quoted the letter in the bottle, which taunted him for boasting that his wife would be the first woman to reach Katahdin's summit. Keep strongly suggested that the Smith party got no farther than Pamola Peak. He therefore always claimed that his wife and her female companions were the first ladies to reach the summit.

KEEP RETURNED TO KATAHDIN ONE OR MORE TIMES A YEAR, EVEN into the 1860s, to maintain the Keep Path, guide other parties, and further explore the Wassataquoik Stream region. He guided Rev. Joseph Blake's second trip in 1856 as well as the Holmes-Hitchcock Geological Survey in 1861, which may have been the last of his regular visits. After Charles Hamlin visited Katahdin in 1881, Hamlin recounted that he had prevailed upon Keep to join him and others to tent together in the Great Basin. Keep, then 65 years old, did join them, his first visit since 1861.

In 1859, "in consideration of services and money expended by Marcus R. Keep in opening a pathway from the East Branch of the Penobscot River to the summit of Katahdin Mountain,"[21] the Maine legislature gave Keep a 200-acre grant of wilderness land in the western half of Township 3, Range 8. Given the privilege of choosing the location, Keep selected an area at the outlet of Katahdin Lake. According to Katahdin historian Myron Avery, Keep had, prior to the legislative petition, received permission in either 1857 or 1858 to erect a crude log cabin at this site on the north side of "Katahdin Brook," just below the outlet dam.

Keep was considered by many to be a bit of a character. Rev. Blake once said of him:

He had been over the ground to the mountain I know not how many times. He had himself made a path through the woods, so far as it was made, had blazed the trees, brushed out the path, and in miry or swampy places laid logs or brush.[22]

Keep also had no small interest in botanical and geological matters. At one time he published papers on geological studies (that he had carried out on "horsebacks") and other natural features of the Maine countryside. In Keep's honor, the late Prof. C.S. Sargent named a northern Maine thornbush *Crataegus keepli*. According to the *Portland Sunday Telegram*, Sargent noted:

> This species is named for Marcus Rodman Keep. "Parson Keep," for forty-eight years a resident in Aroostook County, a clergyman and missionary at large, widely identified with the educational and agricultural development of his adopted state, a friend of the poor, and a helpful advisor of all who sought information on the flora of northern Maine.[23]

Myron Avery reported in his *Annotated Bibliography*: "Marcus Keep was considered to be a little odd. He would start off and be gone a week without letting anyone know where he was going. One leg was a little shorter than the other, his feet were large, his stride long—born of the impatience of his enthusiasm." Keep died in Ashland in 1894, at the age of 78.

PART II

Opening the Wilderness

THE "GOLDEN AGE"   3

Wilderness Adventures and Dreams of Development

Mt. Ktaadn is so inaccessible that practically it is remote even to New Eng-
landers. It is probably true that a greater number of eastern men now annually visit Pike's Peak than penetrate to the Maine mountain and a hundred
Bostonians have been among the Alps for one who has climbed Ktaadn.
—Charles E. Hamlin, "Routes to Ktaadn," *Appalachia*, December, 1881[1]

BY THE 1850S, ACCESS TO KATAHDIN THROUGH THE WASSATAQUOIK
Valley had become the generally accepted route and would remain so for
the rest of the century. Improved roads that reached the East Branch from
Stacyville, the extension of logging roads toward valuable timber, the attraction of the Keep Path and other hiking trails, and increased interest in
the dramatically beautiful Great Basin made the mountain more accessible
from the east. Although parties continued to climb to the summit from the
West Branch side, the Wassataquoik Valley remained the route of choice.

Lumbering routes, which served as hiking trails to Katahdin, were in
constant flux. As loggers carved out new roads and built new depot camps
in the once virgin valley, they abandoned the decimated areas. By the mid-
1860s, there were reports that the Keep Path itself had deteriorated greatly.
The lumbermen, whose work opened access for explorers, had not yet tamed
the Nesowadnehunk Stream and the Sandy Stream/Millinocket Lake drain-
ages on the south side for driving timber. Exploration therefore took hold
on the east side.

Around 1874, the construction of the Lang and Jones Trail from Katahdin
Lake, across Sandy Stream and Roaring Brook, toward the Great Basin shifted
attention from the Keep Ridge to the Great Basin as a major destination.

Later, as the Wassataquoik Tote Road neared Katahdin's northern slopes, interest in approaching the mountain from the Russell Pond area via the North Peaks grew.

In addition, with the 1869 completion of the European and North American Railroad from Bangor to Mattawamkeag, access to Stacyville became easier by horse-drawn stage and interest in approaching Katahdin from the east increased. Popularity of this approach increased further with the 1894 extension of the Bangor and Aroostook Railroad to the Stacyville area and Aroostook County. However, because the B&A also stopped at Norcross on South Twin Lake, interest began slowly to shift back to the south (West Branch) side. The shift continued with the lumbering industry's eventual collapse in the Wassataquoik Valley due to several devastating fires and the dwindling supply of commercially viable timber.

It was against this backdrop that adventurers, in the spirit of scientific exploration, personal enrichment, and ambition, were drawn to the mountain.

BOTANY AND GEOLOGY ON KATAHDIN

A recent Bowdoin graduate, Rev. Joseph Blake, attempted to reach Katahdin's summit from the south side in 1836. However, he and his companions turned back upon reaching the Tableland, a memory that he might well have wanted to erase. Twenty years later, Blake had become a first-rate botanist whose second Katahdin adventure in 1856 focused on observing flora and collecting rare specimens.

One of the five who accompanied Blake was Colonel Eliphalet Whittlesey, a Bowdoin professor who later served as a Union officer during the Civil War. Rev. Marcus Keep, whom Blake identified as "a minister in the wilds of Maine," served as their guide. The party traveled from Bangor to the Hunt Farm. From there, they followed the Wassataquoik Tote Road, eventually swinging south to Katahdin Lake and onward to a rock slide, which they ascended to the Keep Ridge. Upon reaching the summit of Pamola and looking down some 2,000 feet to Chimney Pond, Blake reported:

> A most interesting feature of the mountain is this basin, an area of I know not how many hundreds of acres shut up within the mountain which comes around as nearly to enclose it, and whose walls tower above it some 3,000

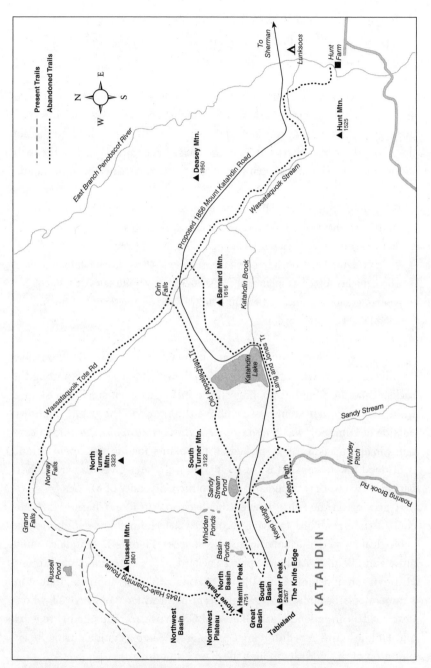

Nineteenth-century routes to Katahdin from the East Branch.

feet. It is said to contain five or six ponds, one of which is visible and seemingly within a stone's throw as you stand on the dizzy heights above; a place in which clouds gather, the winds run, and echo dwells.[2]

Upon reaching Katahdin's summit, party members wrote letters to wives and loved ones on birch bark sheets, which they had brought from their birch grove campsite at the foot of the slide. On their way back to Bangor they mailed the birch bark letters home. Blake's account, written in the early 1860s when the shadow of civil war began to overtake the land, continued:

> We passed a fine beautiful day on the mountain, our country's birthday. Our prayer was that God would bless our land, healing all dissentions and bringing good out of evil, that our Union might last and our country prosper. . . .
>
> But Katahdin, though in days long past, floods have dashed upon it and some mighty force has splintered and shattered its granite sides, still stands, young, grand, sublime, and so our country survives the deluge of fire and blood that has swept over it.[3]

On his way down from the precipitous Chimney Peak, Blake made a notable discovery when his hands touched a small grassy ledge among the rocks. There he found at his fingertips a little cluster of small star-shaped white flowers, their stems barely above the ground. The plant, unknown outside of Labrador, was the *saxifraga stellaris var. comosa*. Unable to contain his enthusiasm, Blake picked all the plants for his specimen tin and continued his descent. Most of the plants were later given to various herbariums; two were retained and given to the University of Maine.

Carrying on the spirit of scientific discovery, in 1861, Charles H. Hitchcock, a state geologist for Maine, and Ezekial Holmes undertook a major geological survey of Maine's natural resources. George L. Goodale, a botanist and chemist; Alpheus Spring Packard Jr., an entomologist; Edmund H. Davis, an assistant; C.B. Fuller, a marine zoologist; John C. Houghton, a mineralogist; Manly Hardy, an assistant naturalist; a Mr. Maxwell, who is described as an independent hiker; and G.L. Vose accompanied Hitchcock and Holmes. The expedition engaged Marcus Keep as guide during its exploration of the Wassataquoik Valley and Katahdin.

Keep rendezvoused with part of the group at the Hunt Farm and led them to the Keep Ridge by way of the slide. Crossing the Knife Edge, they ascended to the summit and descended to the Great Basin for the night. The following day the party followed Roaring Brook down to Sandy Stream and back to Katahdin Lake and the Hunt Farm. In his own embellished account of the trip, perhaps his last regular annual visit to Katahdin, Keep described Wassataquoik Stream at the outbreak of the Civil War:

> In this stream the perpetual roar of waterfalls in the deep silence of the wilderness is the true song of nature, unmoved by any of the passing sounds of mechanical life. The song of the falling waters and warbling birds, and ever the moaning of continual winds, are all without the jarring sounds of violence and wrong, for the children of nature shout on the wings of freedom and joy, they all join in the smiles of spring, and the sweet weather bird can sing her treble note with the deepest bass of the woodland; till the low moan of the wind sings the funeral dirge of the common sisterhood, and altogether lie down for their winter's sleep in the arm of their common mother. To such sounds of harmony, and to such children of innocence, we turned away from the news of raging battles, to hear no more of them till our return.[4]

The Hitchcock-Holmes expedition attracted extensive coverage and may well have stimulated the strong interest in recreational climbing that seemed to grow from that point on.

In 1869, Harvard professor Charles E. Hamlin embarked on a series of remarkable explorations in the Katahdin region. Hamlin, a member of the geology department, began a thorough geological study of Katahdin and its surrounding area and continued to explore the area during trips in 1871, 1879, 1880, and 1881.

In 1881 Hamlin published an important article in *Appalachia* in which he described the salient physical and geological characteristics of the Katahdin area. In a second article the same year, "Routes to Ktaadn," Hamlin gave a thorough description of the various routes to the mountain. The oldest ascended the West Branch and the Abol Slide to the Tableland. In that same article, Hamlin suggested cutting a trail along the Southwest Spur (the present day Hunt Spur) to the summit, likely the first to voice the idea. Two decades later, Irving O. Hunt completed such a trail, which later bore his name and became part of the celebrated Appalachian Trail. The second route led from Brownville to the "Joe Merry" lakes and on to the West Branch and up the Abol Slide. The third route involved canoeing from Moosehead Lake to

Northeast Carry and down the West Branch to Abol Slide. The final route was from Sherman to "Hunt's House" on the East Branch and on to the Keep Ridge or, alternatively, to the Great Basin. Today his article serves as an important source of information about those historic trails.

In the same article, Hamlin describes the mountain's towering stature:

> Ktaadn, seen from the level of the country and standing apart, towers in most majestic style above the whole region round. Not a few summits, in themselves picturesque and striking, dwindle in the presence of their superior. None, near or remote, presents itself in any degree as a rival; but all, like dwarfs around a giant, serve, by the strong contrast they afford, to proclaim Ktaadn undisputed monarch of the great wilderness he overlooks.[5]

Several smaller scientific efforts followed Hamlin's explorations. John De-Laski, a member of the earlier 1847 Aaron Young Survey, returned in 1871 to study the effects of glacial action at the summit and across the Tableland.

In 1873 and again in 1874, Merritt C. Fernald, the president of what is now the University of Maine, and botanist F. Lamson Scribner took the Keep Path to the summit. They wanted a more accurate measurement of Katahdin's height, which they declared to be 5,215 feet, still off the modern measurement of 5,267 feet. John Stacy guided the party, which also returned with a large body of important botanical observations and specimens.

The final series of major explorations of the nineteenth century was that of George H. Witherle. Witherle was a prominent maritime merchant and ship owner in the Penobscot Bay town of Castine. Unable to matriculate at Harvard College because of poor eyesight, he dedicated himself to town and state affairs. An early conservationist, he bought old Fort George and a substantial tract of woods to protect them for public benefit.

With a "record of exploration . . . unsurpassed in the 19th Century,"[6] Witherle made eleven trips between 1880 and 1901, during which he covered most of the Katahdin region. He reportedly climbed Katahdin nine times, the last at age 70. Often his wife Sarah, and sometimes his daughter Amy, accompanied him. Paul Peavey and his son Clarence, both from Patten, Maine, frequently guided them.

On his second trip in 1881, Witherle traveled to the Great Basin from the East Branch where he met Charles Hamlin, whose guide was none other than Rev. Marcus Keep. Hamlin had convinced Keep, who no longer visited

George H. Witherle's 1899 campsite part way up the Abol Slide. Witherle is to the right. His guide George McKenney is to the left. Courtesy, Maine Appalachian Trail Club.

the mountain as frequently as he had in his youth, to journey "one last time" into the Great Basin. Hamlin and Witherle teamed up for several days exploring the area around the basin and making detailed observations.

Deliberately visiting unexplored areas, Witherle's subsequent trips encompassed the Traveler Mountain area, both the West and East Branches, the Northwest Basin, the Klondike, Doubletop Mountain, the Nesowadnehunk Valley, and more. The Appalachian Mountain Club later published Witherle's articles and personal journals of his findings.

CLIMBING FOR THE FUN OF IT

During the first half of the nineteenth century, few had seriously considered Katahdin's recreational climbing potential. However, in the 1850s the Wassataquoik Valley became more accessible and news spread of this remote and wild region's undiscovered treasures. The Keep Path grew more and more popular as a way to reach the summit. Keep himself no doubt escorted an increasing number of climbers along his path.

The Reverend Dr. John Todd traveled along this route in 1851. He related in his stirring account the awesome experience of camping along the "Quasatiquoik" and finally reaching and traversing the Knife Edge:

> Onward we plodded, now swallowed up in the great forest, and now out on the banks of the wild, roaring but beautiful Quasatiquoik. On its banks our tent would sometimes be pitched, our teakettle hung on the pole, over the camp-fire, while the hard sailor's bread was roasting, and the small piece of pork was frying. This was our food three times a day, and it became very wearisome. . . . In the course of our tour we had occasion more than once to feel grateful towards the Rev. Keep, whose hatchet for the last five or seven miles had done a great and good work in cutting out a kind of path, and marking the trees.

After several days and nights of climbing Katahdin, Todd described his feelings as he attained the summit:

> Your first feeling is, you want to be and must be alone. When I reached the summit, my companion and guide were more than half a mile off, and right glad I was. I did not want to see or hear any thing human. I did not want any one to ask, What means the tear in your eye? You are communing with nature and nature's God, and you feel as if you had no right to be there.
>
> . . . Nature is here unfashioned by man, stern, savage, awful, but beautiful. The eye rests on no garden, cultivated field, lawn, pasture for flock, nor even a place to bury the dead. . . . Here the winds, untamed, hurry and dash against old Katahdin. . . . Before I was born you were here! When I and my generation are all in the grave, here you will stand unaltered and the same, lifting up your granite head, listening to the whispers of the clouds, the roar of the storm, the dash of thunders, and still proclaiming the power of God![7]

Just two years later, in April of 1853, an adventurous Rev. William L. Jones of Minot Center and his companion "J.F." traveled north by horse along the Penobscot. They trekked up the Wassataquoik to Katahdin Lake and reached the Knife Edge via the Keep Path, where they must have encountered snow. This excursion was the first in which a party of only two had traveled into the Katahdin wilderness. At the summit the men found a considerable rock cairn supporting a bottle containing birch bark pieces inscribed with the names and dates of other climbers. No doubt they added their own names to the record.

In 1855, Rev. Thomas Wentworth Higginson led a party that included five ladies from his Unitarian church in Worcester, Massachusetts. They traveled to the Hunt Farm and from there followed the Keep Path to the Knife Edge and the summit. Higginson was a close friend to Henry David Thoreau and Edward Everett Hale; the three were members of The Worcester Circle, a regular gathering of literary friends. In the winter of 1851–52, Thoreau attended a lecture by Higginson on the subject of Mohammed. Higginson was an abolitionist and a secret supporter of John Brown at a time when such a stand was unpopular. He later served as a colonel in the Union Army during the Civil War and headed the first regiment of "negroes" in the war. After being wounded, he devoted himself to writing and became a well-published author. Higginson also served as president of the Appalachian Mountain Club in the 1880s.

Higginson's party hired as their guide the venerable John Stacy, who had helped cut the Keep Path to Pamola back in 1848. According to Higginson, one of the group's campsites was at the foot of a major rock slide in the midst of a magnificent birch grove. There had been a few references to this grove in the past, but over the following years there would be more frequent mention of the special beauty of that very handsome grove of birch trees. Sadly the grove fell victim to logging in the late 1930s.

Higginson's thorough account describes his summit day as "fantastic" and exuberantly recounts finding an abundance of cranberries on his descent.

One of the most remarkable things about this trip chronicle was that it was penned as if one of the ladies had actually written it. Pastor Higginson must have taken a great deal of delight across the ensuing years as people tried to determine which of the five ladies had authored the account. Higginson finally revealed before his death that he, indeed, had been the author.

In 1856 one of the most significant trips in Katahdin and perhaps American history took place. The noted American landscape artist Frederic E. Church of the Hudson River School traveled to the region to experience the Katahdin wilderness. One of Church's companions, Theodore Winthrop, later published an account these travels in his minor classic *Life in the Open Air.*

The party started in New York City and traveled through the Adirondacks to Lake Champlain and into Vermont. They crossed New Hampshire and Maine to the Rangeley Lakes. After reaching Moosehead Lake, they portaged the Northeast Carry and canoed down the West Branch. They stayed at the ancient Abol Deadwater campsite the night before they ascended Katahdin. Winthrop described Katahdin as "the best mountain and in the wildest wild to be had on this side of the continent."[8]

This was only one of many pilgrimages Church made to Katahdin. The mountain and its surroundings touched him deeply and greatly influenced both his life and artistic work. Church had actually visited the region earlier, but it was the combination of Winthrop's stirring account and the sketches that Church drew along the way that made this journey such a landmark.

Winthrop, in a comical mood, wrote as he gazed upon the mountain from the river as he waited for Church to finish sketching:

[I] discovered a droll image in the track of a land-avalanche down the front [of the mountain]. It was a comical fellow, a little giant, a colossal dwarf, six-hundred feet high, and should have been thrice as tall, had it had any proper development,—for out of his head grew two misdirected skeleton legs, "hanging down and dangling." The countenance was long, elfin, sneering, solemn, as of a truculent demon, saddish for his trade, an ashamed, but unrepentant rascal. He had two immense ears, and in his boisterous position had suffered a loss of hair, wearing nothing save an impudent scalp-lock. A very grotesque personage. Was he the guardian imp, the legendary Eft of Katahdin, scoffing already at us as verdant, and warning that he would make us unhappy, if we essayed to appear in demon realms and on Brocken heights without initiation?[9]

In 1857, a group of twelve students from the Bangor Theological Seminary mounted a major recreational expedition, which included three bateaux, six boatmen, and enormous supplies of food and gear. Party member John Sewall wrote an account not long after the trip, but it was not published until 1904. Its author had by then become Rev. John S. Sewall, DD. The group left Bangor in June by rail to reach Mattawamkeag and traveled up the West Branch by foot and bateaux. Because of the time of year black flies and mosquitoes pestered them mercilessly almost every step of the way. The trip was not without moments of humor and sadness:

> He [Katahdin] is a rigorous hermit, with a heart of stone and with a face of stone as well, and yet he always has a cordial welcome for all who venture to brave the solitude in the midst of which he reigns. . . .
>
> As we were poling and paddling along [on the Pockwockamus Deadwater] we came suddenly upon the floating body of a poor fellow who had been swept off and drowned while driving logs some four or five weeks before.[10]

The boatmen knew of the drowning and the unsuccessful search by the river drivers to find the body. The Sewall party found a quiet cove, walked back along the shore of the river and pulled the body onto the bank. They dug a shallow grave, and all hands gathered for a solemn service of Christian burial. Later, one of the men found a piece of slate rock near the mountain and on it scratched the name of the unfortunate fellow and the date of his death. On the group's return trip down the river they stopped to nail the marker to a tree near the grave.

Historian Fannie Hardy Eckstorm immortalized this tragic story of death on the river in her riveting collection of log driving stories, *Penobscot Man*. She movingly describes the circumstances that led to George Goodwin's death as he stood at his post on a huge gray rock along Abol Falls during the river drive. The story includes more about the Sewall trip and the reaction of the Native Americans and river drivers to the burial service.

> There, two rods from the water, three at most, close by the place where they found him, still rest the bones of the man who was drowned on the Gray Rock of Abol and, by a miracle of God, after death found mercy.[11]

Finally arriving at the trail up the Abol Slide, the Sewall party followed its guide single-file, "every inch of the way hotly contested by vandal hordes of insects." It was a beautiful day at the summit, and the group found it difficult to leave until late afternoon. Their late departure forced them to spend the night in a makeshift shelter at the foot of the slide.

Although by the late 1850s, several expeditions had already entered and explored the Great Basin, an 1859 trip there provided an important milestone: the first female visitors. Colonel Luther B. Rogers of Patten led a 22-person group along a path that Keep may have marked earlier in the decade. This expedition began Rogers' long association with the mountain. John Stacy acted as their guide.

Rogers identified Harriet Scribner as the first lady to actually enter the Great Basin. Keep found proof of this feat in documents he discovered in the basin when he accompanied the 1861 Hitchcock-Holmes expedition.

In recognition of Ms. Scribner's achievement, the group decided, as they gathered on Chimney Pond's shores, to nominate her for president of the United States in the next election. Further, so grateful were they for his leadership, they nominated Luther Rogers for vice president. Whether or not this act represented a political commentary upon the then-presidency of James Buchanan, a Democrat, we do not know. It was only a year later that Abraham Lincoln was nominated for president by the Republican Party. There is no record of Ms. Scribner receiving votes at the party's national convention.

Sometime in the fall of 1862, George Pickering embarked on a trip from Moosehead Lake down the West Branch:

> Into regions seldom visited except by lumbermen, and a few sensible people who prefer roughing it at Katahdin during dog-days, to dissipating at Saratoga. The gratification derived from this excursion in the midst of the noble scenery strown [sic] with lavish hand along the route, induces me to attempt a description of the prominent points of interest, in the hope that others may be induced to visit the wilds of our State, for their own pleasure, and to do justice with pen or easel to sight and scenes worthy of the most gifted artists.[12]

Pickering's account offers another stunning addition to Katahdin literature. After running the dramatic Horse Race section of the river, the group dropped down to:

> Soudnehunk dead-water, as smooth as polished steel, and as clear as crystal. A mile further, and we are at the falls bearing the same elegant and classic name.
>
> "Now," said Tom [Pickering's guide], "I will show you the finest sight in America!" With a sweep of his paddle he brought the canoe into a little nook, and bade me look up! Well, friend Thomas, although you have seen but precious little of America, your opinion cannot be far from correct.
>
> Three miles off, like a huge uncut emerald, towered Mt. Katahdin, its base swept by the water at our feet, with a front of two miles. Its grandeur was oppressive. There it stood, stern, solemn, silent.

The next day the party continued down the West Branch, finally pausing to take one last look at the mountain:

> Stopping a moment at the mouth of a small brook, Tom remarked, "It rises somewhere on Katahdin, but no man knows the spot. Taste the water; did you ever drink better? It never freezes and is of even temperature winter and summer. We shall not see Katahdin again for sometime; let us drink good bye to it!" Agreed! So over and over we drank the monarch's health, and poured libations copious enough to satisfy the utmost demands of the mountain gods, and the piety of the most devout priest.[13]

In the 1860s and 1870s Frederick S. Davenport of Bangor wrote of a number of trips made to Katahdin. One of them relates an unusual way of celebrating climbing Katahdin. Upon reaching the summit on a beautiful Sunday, he and his companions sang the "Te Deum" in English and followed with a plaintive rendition of "The Magnificat" in Latin. The record does not mention how many other parties were on the summit that day to hear this "heavenly choir" but, given the year, they were likely quite alone and felt few musical inhibitions. In 1864 he noted the summit was crowned by a pile of ten to twelve stones which protected a bottle and a tin box containing the names of climbers and the dates they reached the summit. In 1876, Davenport accompanied the artist Frederic E. Church on a canoe excursion to the region. Finally, in an 1877 account, Davenport lamented that the bottle and the tin box had disappeared from the summit, he hoped not stolen.

Three brothers, George T., James W., and Joseph Sewall, along with their friend and relative Edwin "Ned" Hunt, traveled to Katahdin in 1876. Their journey proved to be a memorable experience for the four Old Town boys. George wrote a fine account of the trip that included many of his own excellent sketches. The account was discovered only recently and first published in 2000 under the title *To Katahdin*.

The boys approached Katahdin by canoeing down the West Branch. That year the low water left the river relatively free of logs that would normally clog it during the spring drive. After arriving at the mouth of Abol Stream, they, like so many others before them, camped on the south side of the river where there was a commanding view of the mountain.

After spending an extra day in quiet exploration of the area they experienced a pleasant evening before their hike to the summit.

The night dropped down, cool and fragrant, in the train of departing day. The singing sun ringed with a lingering flush of pink the western slope and the eastern tip of the silent and shadowy mountain. . . . Only a light stir faintly ruffled the surface of the river, in which the inverted mountain hung trembling, its color intensified by the reflection. . . .

We resolved to make the morrow the day for climbing Katahdin, and so prepared for a tolerably early start. We cooked enough bread for both breakfast and dinner; Ned made ready a "bean hole" in which to leave his beans baking while we were gone; we picked over and parboiled the beans themselves; and then turned in to await the morning.[14]

Ascending the Abol Slide route, they arrived at the spring on the Tableland and named it "Spring Edwin," to honor the first of the four to reach it. They had a wonderful summit experience that day, and carefully described the views and expressed their awe. Shortly, they began a reluctant descent and retraced their steps to the river. After spending an additional day at their campsite the boys continued down the West Branch. It was, indeed, a rousing trip, resulting in an equally spirited account.

THEODORE ROOSEVELT ON KATAHDIN

In the summer of 1878, guide William "Bill" Sewall (a distant relative of the Sewalls in the previous story) awaited the arrival of a client at his Island Falls home, 35 miles east of Katahdin. Sewall operated a guide service and ran animal trap lines for a modest living. Sewall was the first child born in this frontier village and his family home the first house built there. As he waited, he could not have imagined that he was about to take part in one of the most significant moments in American history.

Sewall had been engaged to take a sickly young Harvard College junior under his wing for three weeks to determine if an adventure in Maine's wilderness might improve his stamina and health. Sewall must have wondered what he was getting into with this unknown "kid." But when the buckboard arrived, Sewall extended his hand to welcome Theodore "Teddy" Roosevelt.

That day four others arrived with Roosevelt: his cousins Emlen and James West Roosevelt, friend Will Thomson, and his friend and tutor Arthur Weeks. They came by train from New York City to Boston, and then on the European and North American Railroad to Mattawamkeag. There they hired a buckboard to take them to Island Falls. As he greeted the party, Sewall observed that Roosevelt appeared to be a "thin, pale youngster with bad eyes and weak heart."[15]

Roosevelt needed a strong physical endeavor to help him overcome a severe asthmatic condition that had plagued him since he was three years old. The uncertainties of his sickness had profoundly affected the Roosevelt family—delayed vacations, constant nearly life-threatening attacks, and a grave concern about his future. In addition, he suffered from headaches, stomach problems, colds, and frequent fevers. On top of all that, his father's death the previous summer had greatly affected Roosevelt.

Despite these obstacles, Roosevelt resolutely chose a number of challenging conditioning programs, including the summer trip to Maine. Rather than take the young man on a few easy trips into the wilderness and send him packing back to Harvard, Sewall challenged him. As a result, something quite extraordinary occurred. Within days of Roosevelt's arrival, Sewall began to admire the young man's grit, high spirit, and eagerness. They became friends quickly.

Sewall touched Roosevelt in a number of important ways. Though not formally educated, Sewall not only read his Bible regularly but was widely read in the classics and refused to drink or smoke. He had an innate capacity to reflect profoundly on history and politics. Roosevelt found in Sewall some of the fatherly qualities that his life now lacked. He admired Sewall's shrewd and dauntless nature, and viewed him as a true son of the wilderness, self-made, keenly loyal and honest. Roosevelt found Maine's wilderness and the strong and good people who had settled the frontier equally captivating.

After three weeks of camping, canoeing, fishing, hunting, and tramping with Sewall and Sewall's nephew Wilmot "Will" Dow, Roosevelt returned to Harvard with renewed vigor and energy. He made plans to visit Sewall in Maine on two occasions in 1879. In March Sewall met Roosevelt at Mattawamkeag and drove him to Island Falls in a sleigh. Roosevelt experienced the wilderness while it was still locked in the grip of snow and ice, and he loved every minute of that visit.

In the summer of 1879, Sewall decided it was time for Roosevelt to climb Katahdin, a goal the young man had expressed after seeing the mountain the summer before from his room at the Sewall home. Both Sewall and Dow had climbed Katahdin on several occasions and knew the way. In addition to Roosevelt, the climbing party included his cousin Emlen Roosevelt and a tutor-friend Arthur Cutler, who had made the arrangements for Roosevelt's first visit the year before.

The group likely traveled to the Hunt Farm before heading by way of the Wassataquoik Tote Road to the north end of Katahdin Lake, where they camped and hunted for several days. Because logging operations had obliterated the Keep Path and some of the other early spotted trails, the group sought an alternate route. They probably followed the Lang and Jones trail, which people had just begun to use to reach the Great Basin. Roosevelt eagerly shouldered a 45-pound pack over the trail's difficult and demanding terrain.

Although there are few details about Roosevelt's climb to Katahdin's summit, we know that Emlen and Cutler turned back short of the summit, and Sewall and Dow accompanied Roosevelt to the top. Roosevelt later recalled the trip with great joy and a strong sense of accomplishment. He remembered losing one of his heavy walking shoes crossing a stream "at a riffle" and completing his climb in moccasins. Heavy rains completely soaked their tents and bedding the night after they reached the summit. Roosevelt remembered with considerable satisfaction, that, "I find I can endure fatigue and hardship pretty nearly as well as these lumbermen."[16]

After resting briefly at Island Falls, Roosevelt, encouraged by the rigors of the trip, arranged to have Sewall take him on a vigorous ten-day trip into the remote Munsungan Lake area, followed by a three-day, 110-mile adventure by wagon and foot. By the time Roosevelt left for Harvard, their friendship had taken on a permanence that would never be shaken. Though Roosevelt never visited the Maine wilderness again, a steady correspondence between the two continued through the years.

Roosevelt invited Sewall and Dow, whom he called "mighty men of the axe and paddle," to help build and manage the Elkhorn Cattle Ranch in the Dakotas territory that Roosevelt bought in 1883. The two moved there in 1884, their families joining them in 1885. Sewall played a major role in Roosevelt's pivotal decision to return to New York City to run for political office. Roosevelt agonized over such a life-shaping decision. One day he and Sewall, while inspecting their beloved prairie, had a long talk. Roosevelt told him of his struggle and asked him his opinion. Sewall counseled him to pursue a political career. He believed that Roosevelt's elemental integrity would some day carry him as far as the presidency. Although Roosevelt laughed at that remark, he apparently took Sewall's counsel to heart, and the very next day departed to pursue the nomination of the Republican Party for mayor of New York.

As Roosevelt pursued the Republican presidential nomination in the spring of 1912, he responded to a letter from Sewall:

> Your letter contains really the philosophy of my canvass. After all, I am merely standing for the principles which you and I used to discuss so often in the old days both in the Maine woods and along the Little Missouri. They are the principles of real Americans, and I believe that more and more the plain people of the country are waking up to the fact that they are the right principles.[17]

After Roosevelt returned to New York, the Sewalls and the Dows returned to Maine, but their friendship and correspondence with him continued.* Roosevelt biographer Hermann Hagedorn wrote of the friendship:

> "Bill" Sewall was guide, philosopher and friend to Theodore Roosevelt in that period in his life when a man's character, emerging from the shelter of home traditions and inherited beliefs, is most like wax under the contact of men and events. . . .
>
> . . . To the city boy the backwoodsman was the living symbol of all that he had admired most in the heroes of the past—sea-rover and warrior, colonist and pioneer—strength of arm and strength of heart, fearlessness and resource, self-respect and self-reliance, tenderness, patriotism, service, and the consciousness of equality with all men. . . .
>
> The friendship, established in Maine and sealed and strengthened by joys and hardships shared in Dakota, endured unwaveringly through the changing political fortunes of Theodore Roosevelt, to the day of his death.[18]

---

* After he became president upon the assassination of William McKinley in 1901, Roosevelt invited the Sewalls to meet him when he spoke at the 1902 Bangor Fair. They were his special guests in Washington, D.C., at the time of his own inauguration in 1905 and again in 1909 as he prepared to leave office. They attended the inauguration of Roosevelt's successor, William Howard Taft, and were among those attending Roosevelt's Farewell Luncheon that same day. Later Sewall served on the Committee for a National Theodore Roosevelt Memorial and attended its meeting in March of 1919, only a few months after Roosevelt's death in January of that year.

Roosevelt himself spoke of his admiration for Sewall and his appreciation for his experiences in the Maine wilderness:

> It is more than forty years ago that I first went to Island Falls and stayed with
> the Sewall family. . . . I was not a boy of any natural prowess and for that very
> reason the vigorous out-door life was just what I needed. . . .
>
> But the bodily benefit was not the largest part of the good done me. I was
> accepted as part of the household; and the family and friends represented
> in their lives the kind of Americanism—self-respecting, duty-performing,
> life-enjoying—which is the most valuable possession that any generation can
> hand on to the next.[19]

Roosevelt's experiences in Maine, including his climb of Katahdin, were
formative influences that contributed to his commitment to the preservation and conservation of the country's land. Roosevelt set aside vast tracts
of land in the western states for the National Park System. His effort was
one of the great hallmarks of his presidency and a lasting legacy to future
generations of Americans.

AVALANCHE AT THE GREAT BASIN

In the 1880s, Colonel Charles A.J. Farrar produced an important guidebook
on the northern wilderness for travelers wishing to explore the Moosehead
and Katahdin regions. He relates the astounding tale of an 1885 excursion
of a group of young men. While camping in the Great Basin, a raging storm
followed by a thunderous avalanche of rocks awoke them during the night.
In the darkness, they felt terror at possibly being in the path of the devasta-
tion. Fortunately, they were not. The next morning they discovered that a
great slide of rocks and debris fell from the cliffs above the basin and had left
a huge white gash in the side of the mountain.

However, that is only half of the story. Late the next night one of the men
observed an unusual display of shooting stars. He woke the others and, as
they gazed at the wondrous show of light, a great fiery ball hurdled from
the sky toward the basin. Frightened for their lives, they fled, glancing back
from time to time to be sure they were out of its path. According to Farrar's
story, the men felt great heat and saw a brilliant light just before the object
struck the ground. At its impact, the mountain itself shook, and they were

thrown to the ground. It was an immense boulder that crackled from time to time as it cooled in the night air. When the men examined the gigantic meteor the next morning, it was still warm. It is said that each of them brought a fragment home.

Other sources give credence to avalanches descending from the cliffs above the Great Basin in the early 1880s. Walter Leavitt has pointed to evidence of such activity in the basin between 1875 and 1886 found in several of Frederic E. Church's paintings. The group could have been camping there during one of those glacial slides. However, no other references in Katahdin literature support the claim of a meteor hitting the Great Basin. Whatever is true, the accounts make for two very special stories in the shadow of Katahdin.[20]

YOUNG ADVENTURERS

In 1887, Lore A. Rogers made his first trip to Katahdin at age twelve.* He and his older brother and two friends trekked down along the banks of the East Branch from Happy Corner, near Patten, and crossed the river at the old Dacey Farm, now the site of the Lunksoos Sporting Camp.

As the boys journeyed up the Wassataquoik, they came upon a group of loggers carefully probing the stream with their peaveys in the hope of finding the body of a fellow lumberman lost in the spring river drive. At Katahdin Lake, the boys discovered and followed a trail marked by a small Appalachian Mountain Club (AMC) group the year before. They were actually closely following a larger AMC group moving toward the Great Basin (see next section for details about the AMC trip). They reveled in the extraordinary view of Katahdin from the lake and the next day made their way into the Great Basin.

At the Great Basin they found the lean-to built the year before to accommodate the AMC excursion that was then exploring the basin area. They set up a campsite under a granite outcropping that would shelter them in case of rain. In a thrilling surprise, they found a tin box containing pieces of paper with the names of their father Luther B. Rogers and uncle Edwin S. Rogers. Both men had camped at that site in 1859 with a group that included

---

* Rogers graduated from the University of Maine and become a dairy researcher with the U.S. Department of Agriculture. He helped found the famous Lumberman's Museum.

the first women to reach Chimney Pond.

The next day, the boys, after climbing up the yet unnamed avalanche/ slide onto the Tableland, chose to ascend Hamlin Peak first because of the larger AMC group occupying the summit. This may be the first record of congestion on the summit forcing a change of plans. The boys climbed to the summit later in the afternoon and added their names to the summit cairn register. The adventure was one Lore Rogers would never forget across his many years of visiting Katahdin.

In his 1960 account of this trip Rogers wrote:

> Since then I have been on Katahdin more times than I can count and under the most diverse conditions. I think I have been there in every month of the year: in the early autumn when, from our camp at the timber line, we looked out through trees covered with a cold, dry snow to the distant farms warm in the October sunshine; in the arctic cold of midwinter when caribou would dispute our right to the use of the paths through the scrub; in the late spring and early summer when the great snow banks fill the ravines and the beds of the brooks that make a dry trail in the summer are filled to overflowing with icy water.
>
> In all these trips the mountain has been kind to me . . . but the one that stays clearest in my memory is that first one now 73 years in the background.[21]

THE APPALACHIAN MOUNTAIN CLUB ARRIVES

In 1876, a group of scientists in Boston founded the Appalachian Mountain Club (AMC). The members were interested in furthering geological and other research in the White Mountain area. Soon the AMC became interested in the even more remote Katahdin wilderness. Katahdin explorers Charles Hamlin and George Witherle became AMC members in 1877 and 1883, respectively, and publication of both men's accounts of their explorations in the AMC journal *Appalachia* stimulated interest among AMC adventurers.

In 1886 the club sent an advance five-person party to Katahdin to prepare for the anticipated arrival of a larger AMC party in 1887. The advance party trekked to the Great Basin by way of the North Peaks on the newly constructed Tracey-Love Trail (now the North Peaks Trail). On their return, they explored possible routes from the Great Basin back to Katahdin Lake. As a result of the effort, the club hired Clarence Peavey, the guide for the 1886 group, to cut a trail from the Wassataquoik Valley to Katahdin Lake and the Great Basin. The trail was known as the Appalachian Trail for close to 50 years, until the 1930s, when the name began to identify the great trail that followed the more than 2,000-mile ridgeline of the Appalachian mountain chain from Maine to Georgia.

Peavey completed the preparation of the trail and shelters just in time for the arrival of nineteen club members, five guides, and 26 others in August. The group brought trail signs to erect at key locations and hand tools for trail improvement work. After this successful 1887 trip and one the next year, an organized AMC group did not return to Chimney Pond until 1916.

Early in its history, the AMC established August Camp, where members convened to participate in challenging mountain projects as well as camaraderie. The 1887 excursion was a part of that tradition. Over the years, the AMC held a number of August Camps in the Katahdin area, especially during the 1920s and 1930s. During these trips, club members maintained old trails, provided important signage, and explored possible locations for new trails—all valuable contributions to the health of the Katahdin area.

The AMC published the first guide to the Katahdin area in 1917 and the first contour trail map of the region in 1925. The club continued to publish valuable historical material in *Appalachia* well into the 1950s. The AMC's work in the area so impressed Governor Percival Baxter that in 1934 he gave the club permission to build a cabin of its own at Chimney Pond. Although the cabin was never built, the club continued to be a major force accommodating the new wave of interest in Katahdin that began in the 1930s.

In 1941, the AMC and Baxter State Park signed a formal agreement allowing the club to maintain certain designated park trails. However, in response to the park's administrative evolution in the 1940s, the AMC's contributions waned. AMC signage was present in the park well beyond the 1960s—the green-lettered white signs were small but powerful symbols of more than 50 years of service to the region and its visitors.

DREAMS AND SCHEMES

As Americans migrated west in the nineteenth century, they believed that it was the nation's destiny to tame the great western wilderness and make use of its remarkable resources. The remote Katahdin area was subject to the same romantic notions.

During his 1847 expedition, Marcus Keep envisioned a "Katahdin Mountain House" at the Katahdin Lake outlet and a thriving cranberry industry on the slopes of Pamola. In the ensuing years, the eastern approach to the mountain opened and the resort dreams persisted. Entrepreneurs noted that bridle paths to high peaks and resort inns had by then brought new commercial income to the White Mountain area in New Hampshire. By 1853, the Tip Top House, had been built on Mount Washington, and in 1861 Abel Crawford rode on horseback from Crawford Notch to the summit on his newly completed bridle path. By 1869 a cog railroad was transporting visitors to Mount Washington's summit.

In April 1856, Maine's legislature approved a petition allowing Shephard Boody, an enterprising Bangor lumberman, "to locate, construct and maintain a road from some point on the Aroostook Road . . . by the most convenient route to Mount Katahdin . . . and to construct and maintain a way from the west end of said route to some point on or near the summit of said mountain."[22] The petition suggested building the road as far as possible toward the mountain and an additional bridle path to the summit. The Mount Katahdin Road Company was thus born with the right to purchase land and collect tolls.*

In 1858, Boody employed the J.W. Sewall Company of Old Town to survey a location for the road. The party left Patten on November 1 under the leadership of David Haynes, Chief Surveyor. Recognizing the value of his knowledge of the area to be traversed, Haynes engaged venerable Katahdin trailblazer Marcus Keep as guide and chainman. Charles Lyon acted as the second chainman and Thomas Haynes as the ax man.**

According to the field notes and map, the group followed established trails to the summit, where they began the survey through undeveloped lands. The

---

* Boody engineered the famous Telos Cut (Canal) between 1841 and 1842 that diverted logs from Allagash waters heading toward the St. John River and Canada to American Penobscot waters. The project was also known as Shephard Boody's Cut.

** In that era the standard forest measurement (taken from English usage) was a chain of 100 separate links each 7.92 inches in length, for a total of 66 feet. One chainman served as the "tail chain," remaining at a fixed location. The other served as the "head chain," moving forward to the next fixed position. The Chief Surveyor kept the measurement and angle records, and the ax man made the appropriate markings on trees and other landmarks.[23]

surveyed road traveled from Katahdin's summit to the saddle it shared with Hamlin Peak. From there it descended to Chimney Pond, skirted the lower slopes of Pamola, and crossed Roaring Brook not far south of the present day Roaring Brook Campground. The road, after passing Katahdin Lake, followed the Tote Road along the Wassataquoik to the Dacey Farm on the East Branch. The surveyors proposed that the road then follow a nearly direct line to Sherman at the Aroostook Road. For whatever reason, they did not suggest utilizing the already well-used logging road from Stacyville to the Hunt Farm, perhaps because the new road was to be a private enterprise.

Because the survey did not begin until the first week of November, the party likely ran into intense cold and the onset of snow. Though little of that is recorded in the field notes, it was because of the bitter weather that they were forced to stay for two nights at Marcus Keep's newly built log cabin near the Katahdin Lake outlet. The party filed their results on March 28, 1859. Two days later the legislature approved the Mount Katahdin Road Company's "right to select ten acres of land . . . [for] twenty years, for the accommodation of travelers and visitors to Katahdin Mountain, and to take timber . . . for building purposes . . . and that suitable buildings thereon shall be completed within five years."[24]

Within a few months of the ruling, Boody sold the Mount Katahdin Road Company to William Dawson for $100. Whether for lack of capital support or due to the impending Civil War's disruptions and uncertainties, the bold dream quickly disappeared.

In 1861, Charles H. Hitchcock and Ezekial Holmes proposed building a hotel on the remote and pristine shore of Chimney Pond. In the account of their geological expedition they mused:

> If a good carriage road could be built from the Hunt farm to Chimney Pond in the Basin, and a good foot or bridle path from there to the summit, an immense number of visitors would be attracted to Mt. Katahdin, especially if a hotel should be built at Chimney Pond, the most romantic spot for a dwelling-house in the whole State. As the roads are now constructed, it is easier for travellers to ascend from the west branch of the Penobscot, because less time is required away from the water. With the road thus constructed, travellers would hardly know that they were climbing a high mountain. With the present conveniences, lovers of adventure and recreation will find a trip to Mount Katahdin invigorating, and fraught with pleasure.[25]

Still later, in his account of an 1881 trip into the Great Basin with Charles Hamlin, Keep expounds on his dream of establishing a bridle path into the Great Basin and possibly to the summit itself. In his report of that same trip, Hamlin, speculating that the Bangor and Aroostook Railroad might soon near the East Branch approaches to Katahdin, suggested that:

> The first step toward "opening Ktaadn to the public" will be to construct a stage-road from Sherman to Ktaadn Lake, to build a hotel upon a beautiful site a mile beyond the outlet, and thence to establish a bridle-path into the Basin, a cabin being provided there as a shelter for visitors. Later will come a hotel in the Basin with foot and bridle paths to the summits.[26]

In 1885, Madison Tracy and others in the Tracy and Love logging operation began to build the North Peaks Trail from the Wassataquoik's Middle Branch to Hamlin Peak and Katahdin. Late that season, Tracy rode his saddle horse to treeline and stated publicly that a resort and bridle path should be developed on the northern slopes with a buckboard connection to the Wassataquoik Tote Road.

In a 1916 *Appalachia* article, William Dawson urged developing public facilities at Sandy Stream Pond. He described the lovely tarn, nestled between South Turner and the Katahdin massif, as a place of special beauty and ideal for a "commodius hotel" and log cabins after the Swiss chalet design. To accommodate this development he suggested a good road for wagons and later automobiles be built from the Millinocket–Greenville Tote Road. He further suggested building a packhorse trail to Chimney Pond where a comfortable cabin would be erected and a hotel at Cushman's [Sporting] Camp at Katahdin Lake. Nothing further is heard about these schemes.

In 1931, a *Portland Press Herald* editorial boldly and eloquently proposed building a toll road into the Great Basin using private capital so that the public could experience Katahdin's beauty. This would give Maine an incomparable tourist attraction. After a number of irate letters were written to the editor in opposition, the matter was dropped and never pursued further.

In 1935, Governor Louis Brann requested the National Park Service assess the feasibility of establishing a national park in the Katahdin region. The NPS report suggested building a buckboard road from the old lumber camp along Roaring Brook to the promontory between the two Basin Ponds where a substantial lodge and cabins would be erected. The road would then carry travelers up to Chimney Pond, where they could stay in another spacious lodge and buy supplies. From there, a horse trail would extend to the summit. There were proposals for an emergency shelter just below treeline and at least one refuge shelter on the Tableland. The park never implemented the plans but did improve the road from Windey Pitch to Roaring Brook.

In 1945, even Governor Baxter suggested erecting a shelter at or near the summit "to give protection to those who may climb the mountain and may be caught in a storm or compelled to remain overnight."[27] However, Baxter had a change of heart and never pursued his suggestion. In fact, he became a firm advocate against building any new structures in the park.

In 1950, State Senator John F. Ward of Millinocket suggested in an address to the Bangor Kiwanis Club:

> In World War Two during the winters and springs Army Arctic Rescue Teams from the Presque Isle Air Base were sent to Millinocket and on into the Katahdin Region, for practice maneuvers. These teams were made up of some of the most expert and outstanding skiers in the country. When they saw and used the slopes going down into the basins at Katahdin, they stated the region could be developed into one of the finest skiing areas in the country.[28]

A variety of other development schemes rose and fell, countered inevitably by the incomparable Baxter dream of preserving the very wilderness values that continue to lure people to this sacred place.

As the nineteenth century came to a close, the massive lumbering efforts along the Wassataquoik Valley slowed and, with the approach of the railroad, Katahdin became more accessible from the south and the east than ever before. Some sporting camps had already been built and more would follow. More permanent trails would be built and maintained. Artists would come and be touched by Katahdin and its beauty and majesty. Governor Percival P. Baxter would soon see Katahdin for the first time and vow to himself that this magical place must someday belong to the people of the state of Maine.

LOGGING

4

Daring Drives and Lumberjack Tales

EARLY LUMBERING

When European seafaring explorers reached the shores of New England in the early 1600s, they discovered, much to the delight of the trading companies that sponsored their voyages, abundant forestland. Wood was easily available for constructing homes, protective forts, and great wooden ships with their towering masts. By this time, the English had largely cut their forests at home, turning the land to farming, and timber was valuable.

In 1605, Captain George Weymouth sent back glowing reports of southern Maine's seemingly limitless virgin forest. The sight of such massive groves of towering white pines from Maine's coast stirred explorers' imagination:

> Early explorers were awed and immensely disturbed by the ghostly silence through which they would travel for mile upon mile, hearing nothing to relieve the stillness except the rapping of the woodpecker or the scolding of an occasional squirrel. Yet there were others who responded to the very loneliness and vastness, much as the sailor is drawn to the sea. In the integrity and simplicity of the indomitable spruce they found its majesty. . . .
>
> . . . The first explorers had eyes for only the pine [which] towered above the sea of spruce forming a second story canopy of greenery. They stood in

groves, conclaves of giants, to be descried from any high advantage. Like the whales they were much too large to hide from searching eyes.[1]

By the late 1600s, Europe was experiencing a shortage of pines for use as ship masts. At that time, England established its "Broad Arrow" marking of the giant pines to reserve them for the Royal Navy. According to G.T. Ridlon, an early Maine writer, these giant white "King's Pines" were like monarchs in the northern forests:

> He who sits far below the foliage of the old forest monarchs when they are touched by the passing winds will hear voices that sound like the distant ocean's roar; their music ranges through infinite variations in sweetness, compass, and power. There are swelling strains like the chorus of a mighty orchestra; sounds as solemn and awe-inspiring as the piteous music of the *Miserere*, or the wail of a lost soul. Again it floats in gentle undulations like the dying echoes of a vesper chime, or the symphonies of an angel's song.[2]

English interest in New World timber was so pervasive that settlers set up the first American sawmill in York, Maine only a few years after the Massachusetts Colony's birth. In many ways, Maine was the mother of the American lumbering industry. Sawmills slowly spread along the coast of Maine, feeding on the timber so readily available near to the bays and the inlets of the North Atlantic shore.

In its early days, the timber industry was primarily a coastal enterprise. Because there were large tracts of trees near the coast, cutting further inland was unnecessary. Individuals and families harvested the trees at small sawmills beside modest-sized falls at the head of tidewater or only slightly further upstream.

As England's population and appetite for lumber increased, the industry outgrew Maine's coastal timber supply. Sawmills spread inland where supplies were more plentiful. However, limited equipment made it difficult for individuals and families to tap into the vast timber reserves of the upland forest.

To bring timber to the coastal markets, the lumber industry developed advanced systems and techniques, contributing to extraordinary growth in commerce in post-revolutionary America. The lumber industry built infrastructure and larger mills. It laid out rough roads to inland settlements, bringing opportunity for increased trade and growth further afield. It brought together the capital and labor required and advanced commerce, development, and progress.

One of the most significant developments during this era was the innovative use of New England's streams and rivers for floating or "driving" logs downstream to the sawmills nearer to the coast. Fannie Hardy Eckstorm, who observed this era first-hand in the late years of the nineteenth century, called the innovation an unappreciated "native art brought to the highest perfection through overwhelming discouragement."[3] Eckstorm wisely identified two technological advances as responsible for the success of the river drives.

The first was the development of the bateau, which increased the drivers' mobility on the water. The boat was sturdy enough to withstand a river full of floating logs and stable enough for men to stand in while they were working the river. On the other hand, they were light enough for a few men to shoulder across the river carries. Additionally, their shallow drafts enabled them to clear river rapids when necessary.

There is some mystery about the evolution of the bateau, but clearly it was an adaptation of the dory, which had served the coastal fishermen for so many years. Because the bateaux were often referred to as "Maynards," after one of their prominent builders, Hosea B. Maynard of Bangor, it is often assumed that he was the first to make the design adjustments that were to serve the river men for many decades. Whatever their origin, bateaux were to prove indispensable to logging operations well into the twentieth century.

The second advance was forwarded by a resident of Stillwater, Maine. Joseph Peavey stood on the town's bridge over the Stillwater River (a branch of the Penobscot River), watching the river men guide logs under the bridge and over the falls below, and felt he could improve on the tools they were using. Legend has it that he strolled over to his son's nearby blacksmith shop and, after some minor experimenting, turned his idea into the Peavey Cant Dog, a metal-tipped pole with a hook attached near the tip. It could act as a lever to turn or pry logs—and it was to be a revolutionary and versatile tool that would become indispensable to river drivers. According to Eckstorm, "The noted lumberman John Ross once declared in a meeting of lumbermen that with a Maynard boat and six men with peaveys he could do more than with twenty men and the old tools."[4]

As the lumber industry spread inland, it utilized the railroads and steamboats that accompanied expansion. Dams impounded large amounts of water for the spring drives; canals were dug around falls; sluiceways allowed logs to pass through the dams; booms held logs at key lake and river locations; lumber camps housed the personnel as well as the livestock; and the great Telos Cut diverted water from the St. John to the Penobscot to avoid driving logs through Canada. It was an exciting and stirring era in American and Maine history.

In his compelling book *Tall Trees, Tough Men*, Robert E. Pike paints an entertaining picture of this piece of New England history. He relates with obvious appreciation the stories of the terrain and the trees, the tools, lumberjacks, logging camps and their personnel, river men, sawmills, and much more. Pike finishes his study with these words:

> In some parts of the United States the epic of history has been the filling up of vast spaces, but in New England it has been the long struggle with the wilderness. For generations the forest was the settler's friend and foe—it furnished him with his home and his fuel, but it was an obstacle to his plow and frequently the cause of his death, as is attested on numerous gravestones.
>
> . . . Many of the distinctive qualities of the Yankee temperament can be accounted for only by the proximity of the forest—of a feeling, unconscious but deep, of the presence of nature.[5]

LUMBERING IN KATAHDIN'S DOMAIN

Lumbering unfolded in the shadow of Katahdin's great granite peaks in the summer of 1828. Ten men looking for marketable timber found a grove of towering pines near the present site of East Millinocket. The group cut the logs, dumped them into the river, and retrieved them later downstream in what may have been the first Penobscot River drive. The men quickly realized the market potential of the vast untouched forest, and within a few years the first settler along the West Branch arrived. Thomas Fowler Sr. and his family moved from Pittsfield, Maine, to carve a farmstead out of the wilderness just below Grand Falls, at the foot of its ancient carry.

Lumbermen utilized five rivers and streams to bring logs from Katahdin's interior region to the hungry sawmills near Old Town: the West Branch of

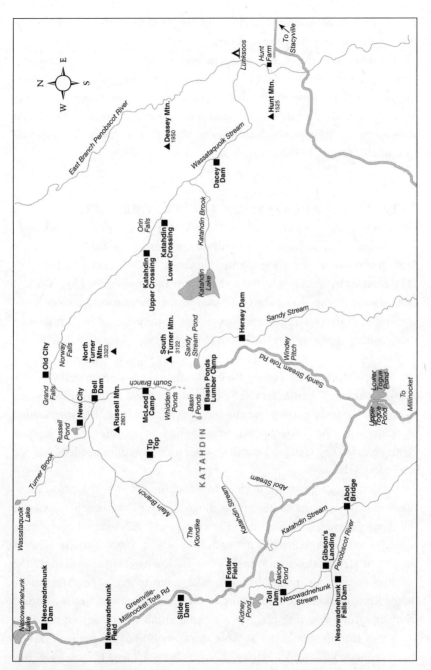

Major logging era sites.

the Penobscot, Nesowadnehunk Stream, Sandy Stream, the East Branch of the Penobscot, and Wassataquoik Stream.

The logs cut in the regions adjacent to these rivers were sent downriver to the Penobscot Boom at Old Town, where they were sorted and owner-identified before being diverted to various sawmills that dotted the river banks from Old Town down to Orono and Veazie and finally to Bangor. At Bangor the cut lumber was hoisted onto ships that took it to ports-of-call throughout the Western Hemisphere.

BATEAUX AND PEAVEYS ON THE WEST BRANCH

Constituting the central artery of Maine's largest watershed, which covers two and a half million acres of forest timberland, the Penobscot's West Branch was one of the great log-driving rivers of America's Northeast. In 1825, Maine's legislature granted a charter for the creation of a log boom at Old Town. Prior to use of the Old Town boom, crews had to be employed day and night to catch their employer's logs as they floated by. But now an independent company used its boom to catch all logs—for a fee.

Just a year after loggers felled the first pines in 1828, a Colonel Stanley settled at Mattawamkeag to aid the lumbermen who were operating in the area. A year later, Thomas Fowler Sr. cleared his Grand Falls farm and began many years of service to loggers and travelers alike in a vast area surrounded by wilderness. The Fowlers provided accommodation, took care of logging camp animals, engaged guides and stocked up on supplies needed by those who passed through.

By 1835, logging had come close to Katahdin. Charles T. Jackson mentioned in the account of his 1837 geological survey that his party visited "Gibson's Clearing." He described the area as uninhabited and comprising some 80 acres on the Penobscot's eastern side, just south of where Nesow-adnehunk Stream flows into the West Branch. The clearing was likely the result of an attempt to establish a farm or camp to aid logging operations below Ripogenus Gorge somewhere near the mouth of the "Sourdnahunk." Thoreau wrote that after his 1846 Katahdin climb he considered paddling upstream from his campsite at Abol to repair one of his bateau poles at an abandonded Gibson's Clearing. Because his party was low on food they elected instead to head downriver, making do with what they had on hand. Rev. Joseph Blake's account of his 1836 excursion to Katahdin relates that after descending the mountain, his party slept in a cabin at a large riverside clearing where two men were cutting hay. This was likely the same Gibson's Clearing. Why the name "Gibson" was given to this clearing is not known. We do know that a Robert Gibson was one of the petitioners to the legislature in 1835 who requested the right to establish a log boom at the head of Ambajejus Lake. Along the forest floor there may still be evidence of this unique though brief attempt to carve out of the wilderness a working farm along the West Branch.

The first dam on the West Branch was built at the outlet of Chesuncook Lake somewhere around 1840, and other dams followed at key locations. In 1846, the Penobscot Log Driving Company formed in order to deliver all logs cut along the West Branch to the great Penobscot Boom at Old Town. Each logging company marked its logs on the butt end with a distinctive symbol so they could be separated and accounted for at the boom.

The company continued for 57 years until it relinquished its rights in 1903 to the West Branch Driving and Reservoir Dam Company, a subsidiary of the then recently formed Great Northern Paper Company in Millinocket. However, downriver of the Millinocket mill, the Penobscot Log Driving Company continued to deliver logs from the lower sections of the river to the boom until well into the 1930s.

The great log drives along the West Branch are stirring stories of hardship and determination. During winter's deep inland snow, the loggers felled trees and yarded them to the streams' edge and onto the frozen lakes and ponds. After the spring melt filled the impoundments behind the dams, the logs were pushed into the streams and the water released through the sluices. The water carried the logs downstream to Old Town. Often at great danger to themselves, the drivers followed and dislodged logs that frequently jammed along the river. An account called "A Tramp in the Shadow of Katahdin," describing the effort to free a jam at Ripogenus Gorge, appeared in an 1863 issue of the *Northern Monthly*, a magazine of life in Maine:

But how are all the logs driven through such a place? Listen, and I will tell you. In the first place, imagine the lake filled with logs, moving slowly toward the foot. At the throat of the outlet, on each side, stand men with pickpoles and handspikes, to prevent the logs from jamming. There goes a log over the falls, throwing up the water as it plunges like a whale fluking: flip, flip, flip, there they go, a dozen at a time, and thus they pitch over, thirty thousand a day.

Suddenly the man stops; there is trouble below, and a hundred men start to break the jam. The place reached, out swarm the red shirts, handspike in hand. They start a log here, lift up a log there, cut this, pull out that, and with a crash, ten thousand logs start at once. A rush is made for the shore; every man looks out for himself first, and his neighbor afterward. Feats of jumping are performed that would put the Ravels to blush, and an agility shown that Blondin might envy.

Should one false step be taken, a nerve falter, an eye miss its calculation, to powder would be ground the being who fell among the tumbling mass. But see the bravado of yonder Frenchman. He dances about on the logs like a cat on hot coals. There is twenty feet of water between him and the shore, and the logs are moving ten miles an hour. If he goes another hundred feet, over the next pitch he shoots and is lost. How can he escape? Look! There comes a log just outside the mass. He jumps upon it, swings his pole quicker than lightning, sheers the log toward the shore, catches a hanging branch, and is jerked up the bank by his shirt-collar, by the hands of his admiring comrades.[6]

The West Branch river drives were notorious throughout New England. Eckstorm described John Ross, the most famous drive boss of the mid-1800s, as follows:

The West Branch Drive was a little army, drilled and commanded by a military genius, and its virtues were preeminently the virtues of fighting men. For fifty years John Ross worked on the river, for about thirty he was one of the heads, when he was not sole head, of the West Branch Drive, and he trained his men to a degree of efficiency never known before. They came to believe that there was not a place on earth or under it that the West Branch Drive could not take logs out of, if John Ross gave the word.[7]

Because of the West Branch river drive's significance to the timber industry, a number of memorable stories describe those extraordinary days. Eckstorm told one of the most unforgettable titled "Lugging Boat on Sowadnehunk":

One May day long ago, two boats' crews came down to the carry and lugged across. They had lugged three miles on Ripogenus, and a half mile on Am-

River drivers working a log jam along the West Branch of the Penobscot. Courtesy, Maine State Library, Myron H. Avery Collection.

bajemackomas, besides the shorter carry past Chesuncook Dam; they had begun to know what lugging a boat meant. The day was hot,—no breeze, no shade; it was getting along toward noon, and they had turned out, as usual, at three in the morning. They were tired,—tired, faint, hot, weary with the fatigue that stiffens the back and makes the feet hang heavy; weary, too, with the monotony of weeks of dangerous toil without a single day of rest, the weariness that gets upon the brain and makes the eyes go blurry; weary because they were just where they were, and that old river would keep flowing on to Doomsday, always drowning men and making them chafe their shoulders lugging heavy boats. . . .

So it was in silence that they took out the oars and seats, the paddle and peavies and pickaroons, drew the boats up and drained them of all water, then, resting a moment, straightened their backs, rubbed the sore shoulders that so soon must take up the burden again, and ran their fingers through their damp hair. One or two swore a little as relieving their minds and when they bent to lift the boat, one spoke for all the others.

"By jinkey-boy!" said he, creating a new and fantastic oath, "but I do believe I'd rather be in hell to-day, with ninety devils around, than sole-carting on this carry."

That was the way they all felt. It is mighty weary business to lug on carries. For a driving boat is a heavy lady to carry. . . .

They were lugging that May morning only because no boat could run those falls with any reasonable expectation of coming out right side up.

But there was a third boat in the group that day. Big Sebattis Mitchell was in the stern. He and his bowman approached the carrying place. Suddenly "Big Sebat," with his paddle still across his knees, suggested they forget the carry and run the falls.

Thus at the upper end of the carry Sebattis and his bowman talked over at their leisure the chances of dying within five minutes. At the other end the two boats' crews lay among the blueberry bushes in the shade of shivering birch saplings and waited for Sebattis. . . . They pictured him draining his boat and sopping out with a swab of bracken the last dispensable ounce of water, then tilting her to the sun for a few minutes to steam out a trifle more. . . .

So, looking at the logs ricked up along the shores and cross-piled on the ledges, looking at the others drifting past, wallowing and thrashing in the wicked boil below the falls, they lounged and chaffed one another. . . .

"Holy Hell!—Look a-coming!" gasped [one of them]. "Man! but that was a sight to see!" They got up and devoured it with their eyes.

On the verge of the fall hovered the bateau about to leap. Big Sebat and his bowman crouched to help her, like a rider lifting his horse to the leap. And their eyes were set with fierce excitement, their hands cleaved to their paddle handles, they felt the thrill that ran through the boat as they shot her clear, and, flying out beyond the curtain of the fall, they landed her in the yeasty rapids below.

Both on their feet then! And how they bent their paddles and whipped them from side to side, as it was "In!"—"Out!"—"Right!"—"Left!" to avoid the logs caught on the ledges and the great rocks that lay beneath the boils and snapped at them with their ugly fangs as they went flying past. The spray was on them; the surges crested over their gunwhales; they sheered from the rock, but cut the wave that covered it and carried it inboard. And always it was "Right!"—"Left!"—"In!"—"Out!" as the greater danger drove them to seek the less.

But finally they ran her out through the tail of the boil, and fetched her ashore in a cove below the carry-end, out of sight of the men. She was full of water, barely afloat.[8]

The story would still be memorable if it ended here, but the pride of Penobscot men forced a more tragic conclusion. Unwilling to be outdone, the other two crews returned without a word to their bateaux, lugged them back up the carry, and launched them into the seething waters. Six men rode in each boat; one of the sternmen was Joe Attien, Thoreau's guide on several of his trips to Maine. The strange luck that attended Big Sebat and his bowman did not hold. The river threw all twelve into the dangerous waters, shattering the boats and drowning one.

Below the foaming water of Nesowadnehunk Falls, the river flows calmly past Katahdin along the Abol Deadwater. As the river turns south at Abol Stream's mouth, it drops along Abol Falls to more broiling falls at Pockwockamus, Debsconeag, Passagamet, and finally Ambajejus. Eckstorm gave a stirring description of the gray rock of Abol:

There are many gray rocks on Abol: Mount Katahdin put them there. Katahdin rules all that West Branch country, a calm despot. Mute, massive, immense, hard-featured, broad shouldered, nowhere can you get in the country where the broad forehead of Katahdin is not turned upon you. Snow and rain it sends to that region; it floods the river from its flanks; its back cuts off the north wind, making the valley hot; the road of the farmer it has closed, and the way of the lumberman it makes unduly difficult, by sowing the whole country with millions of tons of granite chipped from its sides. From Abol all the way down those many falls ... the river in a half dozen places is choked with these great granite boulders, quarried by the frost from the sides of Katahdin, and by the ice transported all over the country. Katahdin makes all that region what it is; it made the falls, and, indirectly, the backbreaking carries around them; it made the sand on Abol, the first place on the way downstream where you notice clear sand above the freshet level; it turned the course of the glaciers and so directed the horsebacks of the glacial drift; ... and it made all the gray rocks. In this region a "gray rock," or a "great gray," is the accepted synonym for a boulder of Katahdin granite."[9]

Thoreau's account of his 1853 return to the West Branch waters increased the West Branch country's mystique. He published stories of the wilderness, the logging activities, the native peoples and woodsmen he met. That year, guided by Joe Attien, he traveled by canoe across Moosehead Lake into the upper waters of the West Branch. His party paddled downstream as far as Chesuncook Lake. Later, on another excursion, Attien suffered a tragic death at Grand Falls.

A GREAT LOG BOOM AT THE FOOT OF AMBAJEJUS FALLS CORRALLED logs moving down the river. Ambajejus Lake was the first major body of water after Chesuncook Lake and it was necessary early in the drive to keep the logs from spreading across that huge lake system.

The logs were contained in the boom area by large floating logs joined by cables. When enough logs were impounded the cable ends were drawn together and the huge log boom towed across the lakes and sluiced through the North Twin Dam back into the main flow of the river.*

The Penobscot Log Driving Company and later the Great Northern Paper Company ingeniously controlled the water levels of the Penoboscot's vast lake system, which included Ambajejus, Pemadumcook, North Twin, South Twin, Quakish, Shad, Elbow, and Millinocket. A series of dams raised and lowered water levels, allowing logs to travel smoothly to the mills, first at Old Town and Orono and later at Millinocket and East Millinocket. Ambajejus Lake's water level may have been as much as twenty feet lower before the dams existed. Most of the dams are still in use today for power generation and recreation.

---

* In 1835, a rough boom house on a small island near the foot of the falls gave shelter to those working the boom. A later boom house, built in 1907 by the Great Northern Paper Company, is still there, now listed on the National Register of Historic Places and steadily being restored by the dedicated efforts of a remarkable man, Chuck Harris. Inside the Boom House Harris has collected and preserved an exceptional record of the old boom operation and the West Branch Drive. It is important to preserve this remarkable collection for it tells the story of one of the exceptional moments in American history.

The Great Northern Paper Company and its successors altered the river's original course in order to avoid a huge bend below Quakish Lake and the very rough and dangerous Grand Falls (also called Grand Pitch). A canal allowed the river to flow from Quakish into Millinocket Stream and back to the original river course. The Great Northern mill stands where that canal joined Millinocket Stream.

The earliest explorers ascending the Penobscot, including Thoreau, quickly discovered that it was easier to paddle up Millinocket Stream and carry the short distance over to Quakish Lake than to carry around a much longer and more difficult route that included Grand Falls, Island Falls and Rhines Pitch. Tom Fowler Sr. of Pittsfield, cleared his first tract of land at the mouth of Millinocket Stream in 1829 or 1830. Realizing later the importance of the 2-mile carry to Quakish Lake, he moved the farm upstream to the carry site, and left the old farmstead to his son. Native travelers had no doubt used the carry site for hundreds of years. The senior Fowler's second homestead remained in the family until the early 1880s when Charley Powers bought it. In 1899, the homestead became the site of the new Great Northern Paper Company mill, which gave rise to the establishment of the town of Millinocket.

Mythical stories and songs have grown up around the fabled West Branch log drives. One of the stories links the legendary Paul Bunyan to Maine and claims that Bunyan died while still lumbering in the western forest at the ripe old age of 91. At his request, his body was brought back to Maine and buried along the banks of his beloved West Branch where he had gotten his start. Some of his old logger friends fashioned his casket from molasses hogsheads.[10]

The rousing verses of "How We Logged Katahdin Stream," attributed to a Dan G. Hoffman, gives tribute to the Katahdin Stream loggers:[11]

Come all ye river-drivers, if a tale you wish to hear,
The likes for strength and daring all the north Woods has no peer;
'Twas the summer of 1860 when we took a brave ox team
And a grand bully band of braggerts up to log Katahdin Stream.

Chorus:
So, it's Hi derry, Ho derry, Hi derry, Down!
When our driving is over we'll come into town!

Make ready, ye maidens, for frolic and song!
When the woodsman has whiskey, then naught can go wrong!

Bold Gattigan was foremen, he's the pride of Bangor's Town,
And there was no other like Chauncey for to mow the great pines down;
Joe Murphraw was the swamper, with Canada Jacques Dupree,
We'd the best camp cook in the wilderness I know, for it was me.
[Chorus]
We left from Millinocket on such a misty day
We dulled our axes chipping the fog to clear ourselves a way,
Till at last we reached the bottom of Mount Katahdin's peaks supreme
And vowed that we within the week would clear Katahdin Stream.
[Chorus]
O, Chauncey chopped and Murph he swamped and Canada Jacques did
     swear,
Bold Gattigan goaded the oxen on and shouted and tore his hair,
Til the wildwood rang with "Timber!" as the forest monarchs fell,
And the air was split with echoes of our ax-blows and our yell.
[Chorus]
For six whole days and twenty-three hours we threshed the forest clean—
The logs we skidded by hundreds,—O, such a drive was never seen!
We worked clear round the mountain, and rejoiced to a jovial strain,
When what did we see but that forest of trees was a-growing in again!
[Chorus]
Then all of a sudden the mountain heaved, and thunder spoke out of the
     earth!
"Who's walking around in my beard?" it cried, and it rumbled as though in
     mirth.
The next day we knew, a hand appeared—no larger than Moosehead lake-
And it plucked us daintily one by one, while we with fear did quake!
[Chorus]
Paul Bunyan held us in one hand! With the other he rubbed his chin.
"Well I'll be swamped! You fellers have logged my beard right down to the
     skin!"
"We thought you was Mount Katahdin," Gattigan shouted into his ear,
"We're sorry, but 'twouldn't have happened if the weather had been clear."
[Chorus]

Well, good old Paul didn't mind it at all. He paid us for the shave—
A hundred dollars apiece to the men, to the oxen fodder he gave.
And now, ye young river-drivers, fill your glasses—fill mine too—
And we'll drink to the health of Bold Gattigan, and his gallant lumbering
crew!

"YOU CAN ALWAYS TELL A SOURDNAHUNK LOG"

In his 1851 classic, *Forest Life and Forest Trees*, John S. Springer describes
the log drive along Nesowadnehunk Stream and its final plunge into the
Penobscot's West Branch just below Nesowadnehunk Falls:

> Logs are now driven down streams whose navigation for such purposes was
> formerly regarded as impracticable—some from their diminutive size, and
> others from their wild, craggy channel. There is a stream of the latter de-
> scription, called Nesourdnehunk, which disembogues into the Penobscot on
> the southwest side of Mount Ktaadn, whose foaming waters leap from crag
> to crag to crag, or roll in one plunging sheet down perpendicular ledges be-
> tween two mountains. On one section of this stream, said to be about half
> a mile in length, there is a fall of three hundred feet. In some places it falls
> twenty-five feet perpendicularly. Down this wild pass logs are run, rolling,
> dashing, and plunging, end over end, making the astonished forest echo with
> their rebounding concussion.[12]

The waters of Nesowadnehunk, known affectionately as the "Sourdnahunk," flow from the western flanks of the Katahdinauguoh, the mountains
on Katahdin's western side—Barren, OJI, Coe, North and South Brother,
Fort, Mullen, and Bald. The stream flows out of Nesowadnehunk Lake,
northwest of Katahdin. At times of high water, especially in the spring, its
current can be quite strong. At other times, it is much more placid as it
flows through areas of incomparable beauty. In order to cut timber along
the Nesowadnehunk, loggers had to solve the problem of the raging cascades located in the stream's last two miles to the river.

It was not until 1878 that the legislature granted a formal charter creating
the Sourdnahunk Dam and Improvement Company. The charter allowed
the company to construct dams and make any improvements necessary to
facilitate driving logs down to the Penoboscot's West Branch. The company

charged 63¢ for every 1,000 feet of timber, to be paid within ten days of the log's arrival at the Penobscot Boom in Old Town.

The company's first action was the erection of a toll dam at the head of the cascades, a mile below Daicey Pond. In the spring of 1879, bateaux ferried men and supplies up the West Branch to the site chosen for the dam. Alfred Hempstead, in *The Penobscot Boom*, tells the story of the toll dam's construction:

> A head wind had held up the batteaux men for a day and the carries were hard to make. The eight men had to take their supplies on their backs across all the carries and then take the four batteaux. It required all eight men using poles to carry each batteau. Everything was carried on their backs from the West Branch to the camp, but this was done with the aid of the big crew. . . .
>
> . . . This was the first time, so far as it has been possible to discover, that dynamite was used in the woods of Maine. The two batteau loads of dynamite . . . came from Old Town. The railroad would not accept it and no one would take it with a team, so it had to be poled up the river all the way. The men had a hard time, especially taking it across the carries.[13]

The company collected its first toll on September 9, 1880, from timber harvesters driving logs through the dam into the roiling Little and Big Niagara Falls below; boulders had been blasted out of the way to allow for a smoother flow of logs. High water blew out the dam on at least three occasions across the years, requiring many repairs. The last blowout occurred in September of 1932 when a devastating storm hit the valley and washed away most of the dam. The remains are still visible just off the Appalachian Trail below the Daicey Pond Campground. Hempstead reports:

> Even after the dams were built, which made log driving possible, Sourdnahunk logs were recognizable as far as they could be seen. They were distinguished by battered ends, large numbers of scars and the absence of bark, for the logs that came out of Sourdnahunk Stream were scoured with gravel and rossed* by granite rocks.[14]

Two additional dams were built farther upstream. Construction of the dam at Nesowadnehunk Lake's outlet likely began the same year as that of

---

* Meaning, to remove the rough exterior of bark from a log.

the toll dam (1879), and the Slide Dam was built the next year. The Slide Dam received its name from an avalanche falling into the valley. According to Katahdin explorer George Witherle, shortly after the end of the Civil War, a great avalanche off the slopes of North and South Brother partially filled Nesowadnehunk Stream. That makes the path of the slide as much as 3 miles in length, an astonishing natural occurrence. Overwhelming evidence indicates that the great slide briefly dammed the stream from the eastern side of the valley. There were further slides into the valley as a result of a devastating 1932 storm in the region.

The Great Northern Paper Company acquired the entire Sourdnahunk operation sometime after 1899 and began constructing a rough access road to allow crews to reach and re-supply their camps easily. The road crossed Abol Stream and traveled along the Abol Deadwater on the north side of the Penobscot River, to Nesowadnehunk Stream. A crib-work bridge, built around 1933 near the mouth of Nesowadnehunk Stream, provided access to valuable timber on the west side of the stream where a small logging camp was built. Before this bridge was built, however, the main stem of the tote road turned and continued up along the east side of Nesowadnehunk Stream and on toward Nesowadnehunk Lake. This old road later merged with the Great Northern Millinocket Tote Road that had been built by 1913 across Togue Pond, skirting the lower flanks of Katahdin and moving also toward Nesowadnehunk Lake.

A "winter" road traveled from the lumber camps up the west side of the stream to further timber areas. That road, which for a short time became part of the Appalachian Trail, allowed the trail to cross the West Branch on the massive crib-work dam over Nesowadnehunk Falls.

TWO MOMENTOUS AUTO TRIPS INTO THE "SOURDNAHUNK" COUNTRY took place on September 28, 1922. George O'Connell, the superintendent of the Duck Pond and Sourdnahunk Road Construction Company, drove the first automobile to enter the area. He followed the tote road along the West Branch to Nesowadnehunk Stream and crossed the lumberman's bridge to the other side. That same day Ralph Drinkwater and three companions drove a Ford to Nesowadnehunk Stream, but continued up the tote road on the stream's east side all the way to within sight of Nesowadnehunk Lake. The difficult trip represented a considerable feat for the time.[15]

The road from Togue Pond and the road from the West Branch eventually joined south of Foster's Field, where a lumber camp grew up in later years. A white building, which served as a landmark there, became the house of the scaler, who recorded and measured the logs passing through the camp. The house later was given to York's Twin Pine Camps and is today the Daicey Pond Campground ranger's cabin.

The converged road was originally known as the Sourdnahunk-Millinocket Tote Road, but, after linking up with the tote road from the Greenville region in 1929, it was known as the Greenville-Millinocket Tote Road. The tote roads joined at Nesowadnehunk Field and gave rise to another major lumber depot camp in the shadow of Katahdin.

There are two intriguing stories from the Nesowadnehunk region. The first concerns a haunted depot camp on the road leading to Strickland's Mountain just east of Nesowadnehunk Lake. According to one account, several gigantic boulders in the river gave way and crushed a river driver to death as he tried to free up a jam. His fellow drivers brought the body back to Jack Reed's depot camp where they buried him. In the years to follow the dead river driver's spirit was said to have haunted the depot:

> On every moonlight night in the winter a listener standing outside the camp can hear the sound of rolling stones that apparently are grating, grinding, hurtling, plunking over each other, as though sliding down a steep bank. Diligent search has been made for the source of this strange noise, but so far no one has solved the mystery. Old lumbermen remember that the camp was considered to be haunted for many years, and the sound of the rolling stones has been heard on many a moonlight night in the past. Many lumbermen who are on their way into the Sourdnahunk Region prefer to push by the depot camp and make a night tramp rather than sleep over that grave and hear those grinding stones.[16]

Another unknown river driver drowned in the 1920s along the Nesowadnehunk between Foster's Field and Slide Dam. A memorial still exists in the form of a cross, erected at the side of the Baxter State Park Tote Road. The victim's identity was unknown even to his fellow river drivers, who knew only that he had come from French Canada and spoke no English. With no roads into the Nesowadnehunk region, fellow drivers made a makeshift coffin out of two pork barrels and buried him at the edge of the riverbank.

In the 1930s, when the Civilian Conservation Corps (CCC) crews were constructing the Sourdnahunk-Millinocket Tote Road, they came across the pile of stones that marked the remains of the grave. They had heard the story from some of the old lumbermen and decided to clear the area of underbrush.

Later still, Governor Baxter, while traveling in the area, noticed the pile of stones alongside the road and questioned John O'Connell, a ranger at Katahdin Stream Campground. Taken with the historical aspect of this story, in the shadow of his beloved Katahdin, Baxter arranged for the grave to be suitably identified as that of the Unknown River Driver.[17] Thereafter, when Baxter visited the park he always checked to be sure the memorial was receiving proper care.

The wooden cross and sign still stand along the old Tote Road north of Foster's Field where the road passes near the stream. They commemorate a piece of "Sourdnahunk" history and warn of the dangers that stalked every log driver as he worked along the streams and rivers of Maine.

SANDY STREAM

Sandy Stream has never achieved the notoriety of its two neighboring watersheds, the Wassataquoik and the Nesowadnehunk. But in reality Sandy Stream drains a huge area to the southeast of Katahdin, and its importance for driving logs was noted early by the lumber barons. It rises from the waters of Katahdin's Great Basin itself, flows through Basin Ponds and down Roaring Brook, finally joining another tributary below Sandy Stream Pond. From there the stream flows south into Millinocket Lake and down Millinocket Stream to the West Branch.

The preparation of Sandy Stream for log driving began in 1874 when the Sandy Stream Dam Company was incorporated by Isaiah Stetson, Francis A. Reed, William R. Hersey, and Edwin A. Reed. They were authorized to construct dams, make improvements and charge tolls at the rate of 40¢ per 1,000 feet of logs. As with similar charters of that era the toll was to be paid within ten days of when the logs reached the Penobscot Boom in Old Town. After the initial cost of building the dams had been recovered, tolls were to be reduced and thereafter charged only at a rate sufficient to maintain them.

The lumbering operation itself likely began upon the completion of the dam during the summer of 1874 or the following winter. Francis Reed and his

A 1909 photograph by Samuel Merrill of Hersey Dam along Sandy Stream. The trail from Avalanche Field to Katahdin Lake passes near this site. Courtesy, Maine State Library, Myron H. Avery Collection.

son Edwin had joined the operation to help Francis' father-in-law, William Hersey. The Reeds manufactured shingles and lumber in Springfield, Maine, so they knew the business fairly well. Hersey died shortly after they formed the partnership, leaving the Sandy Stream operation to the Reeds. With his father spending most of his time with the family business in Springfield, young Edwin Reed assumed the responsibility for Sandy Stream.

A 1915 article from Maine's *Lewiston Journal Illustrated Magazine* tells more of the story:

> Those were the days of crude, hard labor in lumbering. Sandy Stream had never been driven. For six miles at the upper end the stream was very rapid

and it was a ten-mile stream into Millinocket Lake. The telephone and dynamite were not then in use. With four oxen, some gunpowder and the old-fashioned fuse, the operators did what they could to clear the stream and build their dams.

This lumbering operation took three years and was a financial loss in the end. The first year, a crew of seventy-five men drove seventeen days without getting out a log. Yet, for a mile and a half along the wood road, the logs stood forty tier deep. The prospects of the season were shattered when the new dam above the falls (Hersey Dam) went out. This hung the drive and was a great setback. The dam had to be rebuilt the second year and this so delayed operations that it was necessary to return a third year to get the logs out. In the meantime the price of lumber went down so that the Reeds were heavy losers. They were many times advised to save themselves by going into bankruptcy, but [they] were made of different mettle.[18]

One harrowing experience of the brief Hersey-Reed operation was remembered in song by one of the members of the crew. In April 1875 Edwin Reed set out with 25 men he had recruited back in Springfield to work on Sandy Stream. After getting into trouble at an inn in Medway the crew continued its trip up an old tote road to a supply camp on the western shore of Millinocket Lake. They set a roaring fire going and settled in to sleep. Sometime in the dead of night sparks from the fire set the roof ablaze and the crew made a hasty retreat before the camp burned to the ground.

As they took stock of their situation matters looked rather grim. They were 15 miles from their driving camp, without food, surrounded by 5 feet of April snow. They crawled on the snow, waded up slippery streams, and finally got within 3 miles of the camp and collapsed from exhaustion. Edwin Reed, the only one at that point who knew the way, bravely continued to the driving camp where he recruited one of the hearty workers to go back with food and help the others reach the camp.

The "Sandy Stream Song," written and originally sung by one of the members of that crew of 25, became one of the classic lumberjack songs of the nineteenth century. It was sung frequently in the lumber camps of eastern and northern Maine.

After the demise of the short-lived Hersey-Reed operation the Sandy Stream watershed was quiet for a time, though it was this early lumber operation that played havoc with the Keep Path and other trails to the Keep

Ridge and the Great Basin. Then in 1901 another charter was granted to the Sandy Stream Dam and Improvement Company led by Edward Blake, Harry F. Ross, and John Ross. This was the same John Ross who, in his younger days, had managed many of the renowned West Branch log drives. They cleared the river by dynamite, built seven or eight dams, and began to operate under much more favorable conditions than in the past. This operation later became a part of the Great Northern Paper Company. After rebuilding the operation's infrastructure, they logged the area for many years, slowly moving upstream along Roaring Brook as far as Basin Pond, where in the 1920s there was a huge depot camp.

The lumbering trails and roads of this operation were used extensively by hikers seeking to reach the Great Basin in the early days of the nineteenth century. Later the trails passed from being tote roads used by hikers to hiking trails that once were old tote roads. There is a big difference.

In the early 1920s the Great Northern Paper Company began construction of a tote road north from its Greenville-Millinocket Tote Road near Togue Pond. That road, now called Roaring Brook Road, was gradually extended to facilitate the supplying of the lumber operation along Sandy Stream. For a long time it ended at Windey Pitch, a steep pitch in the terrain that seemed insurmountable. By 1923 the road was built up enough to allow automobiles beyond that obstacle, ending at what is now Baxter State Park's Roaring Brook Campground. The rougher road from there all the way to Basin Ponds was maintained until the early 1930s.

The first automobile beyond Windey Pitch was an Overland driven by William Flowers of Millinocket, who in 1923 drove in as far as the old Great Northern Paper Company Depot Camp at what is now Avalanche Field. For some years, automobiles could largely negotiate Windey Pitch but only if the conditions were right. It was not until 1935 that the road was made permanently passable by the CCC.

An unusual story about the Sandy Stream watershed lumber operation involves Togue Pond. In all of the early maps before the Great Northern Paper Company built its road into the Sandy Stream area, Togue Pond is shown as only one pond with a distinct narrowing in the middle between the north and south shores. In fact, in several old maps, the pond is identified as Katahdin Pond (not to be confused with the larger Katahdin Lake to the northeast). This difference can be attributed to the variety of names given to landmarks by early explorers and mapmakers in the region. Obviously, the name Togue Pond prevailed.

When the Great Northern Paper Company finally began to build its access road toward Windey Pitch and Roaring Brook in the 1920s it decided to build directly across Togue Pond, utilizing the very narrow area between the north and south shores. Some have speculated that the terrain beyond either the east or west shores was so marshy that it did not offer a good road foundation. The company, of course, installed a culvert so the waters of one side could mingle freely with the waters of the other. From that point on, maps identify both an Upper Togue Pond and a Lower Togue Pond. One cannot be entirely sure of the above scenario, but it is one likely explanation for the identification of only one pond in the earlier maps.

THE INCOMPARABLE WASSATAQUOIK

It is well accepted that Wassataquoik Stream was one of the most significant and notable watersheds in the Katahdin region. Joseph C. Norris, when he ascended the Wassataquoik in 1825 on his first Monument Survey Expedition, surmised that the massive water flow he discovered there could sustain a great many mills built to harness the power in that big stream. Myron Avery, who wrote extensively about the whole Katahdin area in the 1920s and 1930s, had a special love of the Wassataquoik region and has written eloquently of its uniqueness:

The story of the Wassataquoik is an epic—an epic such as could develop only in Maine. Its history is the forward march of the lumber industry. It is the story of pioneering and of untold labor and hardship. The stream itself, in brief, is a brawling mountain torrent of the clearest water, tumbling along a bed choked with enormous pink boulders. It flows generally southeast, breaking through the mountain range composed of Lunksoos, Hathorn, Dacey and Hunt Mountains, to enter the Penobscot East Branch near the Hunt Farm, west of Stacyville. The stream rises in that little known wilderness north of Katahdin. Its upper course consists of three branches which unite within the space of a mile. The first and lowest is the South Branch which flows north through the narrow valley between Turner Mountain and Katahdin. The second, flowing from the north, is curiously named Turner Brook and drains several small lakes to rise in that beautiful mountain tarn, Wassataquoik Lake, located in a gorge between South Pogy and Wassataquoik mountains, and occupying one of the most spectacular settings of any body of water in the state. The third branch, properly called the Middle Branch, although sometimes known as the North Branch, rises in that great elevated spruce flat, called the Klondike, lying between Katahdin and The Brothers.

The Wassataquoik has known all phases of lumbering; it has floated the drives of the old pine days, now obscured in a dim tradition; it has battled the long spruce logs and finally yielded, subdued, when in the march of industry the long logs gave way to the pulpwood drives.[19]

Another has described the Wassataquoik as a "troubled stream, impossible of navigation, filled with granite boulders, some of which are of enormous size."[20] In 1958 Edmund Ware Smith reflected on this remarkable valley:

> Deep within the fastness of Maine's Baxter State Park, flanked by mountains seldom seen and rarely climbed, lies an enchanted valley which, to those who have traversed it, represents the cone of silence and the core of solitude. Isolated, nearly trackless except for game trails, haunting in its loneliness and litany of falling water, the valley of the Wassataquoik is New England's last wilderness. . . .
>
> This bold, bright watercourse, always beautiful, sometimes ruffian, thunderous with cascades and walled with scoured ledges, seems somehow to resent the inroads of man. . . . It is true that the Wassataquoik log drives were the most difficult and dramatic of Maine's lumbering history.[21]

We journeyed along the Wassataquoik when we followed the paths of the early Katahdin explorers and climbers of the nineteenth century. Their interest in utilizing this significant waterway to reach Katahdin's summit coincided with the building of a logging road from Stacyville to the shores of the Penobscot East Branch in the 1830s. Timber was beginning to be cut along this road and dragged to the East Branch for the river trip down to the Old Town and Orono mills. Sensing the potential for serving this new lumber industry, William Hunt built his farm on the East Branch where that road ended at a place in the river that could easily be forded.

It is obvious that those who cruised the forest to find suitable and marketable timber were impressed by the rich forest resources of the Wassataquoik watershed and made plans to open it up for cutting no matter what difficulties might be encountered. Construction of the road that would eventually ascend along the stream almost to its headwaters was begun about 1841 and the cutting began. With the Hunt Farm serving as a supply center and jumping off place the loggers began their slow and inexorable march up this great stream to the very edge of Katahdin's ramparts.

The name of the stream—Wassataquoik—is Native American, of course, and is thought by some to identify a stream where fish were speared by torchlight. The East Branch was noted for its salmon, which were often speared at night by torchlight even in later years. It is likely that this practice may have taken place where the stream empties into the East Branch. The name has also been said to mean a bright and sparkling mountain stream.

There is no hard evidence that the search for the great "mast pines" that could be used for the British and American navies lured early pine loggers to the Wassataquoik region but it is a possibility. It is, however, fairly certain that no large-scale cutting took place along the stream until the road building began in 1841. That road followed near the east bank of the stream except where it circled around Dacey Mountain to avoid a difficult gorge. When Edward Everett Hale and William Francis Channing ventured into the Katahdin wilderness along this road in 1846 there were already a number of lumber camps, and they stayed overnight at several of them.

These initial operations were to cut long pine logs, and it proved to be a very tough job. The logs often jammed in the river and were sometimes impossible to push back into the river before the high waters of the spring subsided. We must remember that the "Old Pine Days" came before the dams were built and before the stream could be cleared of major boulder obstacles. It was a Herculean task. Dealing with log jams in this uncontrollable and unpredictable flow of water must have been an awesome and terribly dangerous task.

During those early pine logging days the recreational hikers and climbers began to follow the logging roads toward Katahdin. When the rough and coarse roads moved closer and closer to Katahdin Lake, it made Pamola and the Great Basin more accessible than ever before. As the road system began to move even further up the stream itself the whole area north of Katahdin became easily accessible as well. Because of the accounts of hikers and explorers in the 1860s and 1870s we know that logging was taking place, but few details about those operations have been found. We have already noted the constantly changing trail locations because of lumbering activity. It is likely that the logging was confined at first to the lower Wassataquoik as far as Orin Falls and involved the cutting of some spruce along with the pines.

All this changed in 1883 when Foster J. Tracey from New Brunswick and his son-in-law Hugh Love began the first large-scale spruce operation along the stream on property owned by T.H. Todd, also of New Brunswick. The same year the land was bought in 1881, men were sent in to begin the task of clearing rocks from the stream bed and to commence the building of the necessary dams and camps. All this was in preparation for the company's first drive in 1883.

The Tracey-Love operation had an impressive history in the region. They were the first to use dynamite extensively to clear the stream of the large obstructive boulders that interfered with the spring drive; also they did extensive dam building to ensure that an abundance of water could be impounded and later released for the drive. One report suggests that 23 dams were built eventually from Dacey Dam (not far from the East Branch) to Russell Camps (not far from present-day Russell Pond). Perhaps it was all this expensive activity that gave rise to the old lumbermen's legend that Wassataquoik Stream was laid out by the native god Pamola for the purpose of sending timber operators to the poorhouse.

We can at least be sure of the date when this operation was initiated because on the side of a massive boulder by the shore of the stream near the site of Mammoth Dam this inscription was chiseled:

> Tracey and Love
> Commenced operations
> on Wissattaquoik
> Oct. 16th 1883

Tracey had found the road that was built in 1841 in fairly good shape and began that summer to extend it on up the stream.

Unfortunately the Tracey-Love operation ran into two major obstacles that challenged the fortitude and resolve of all those involved. The first came in the summer of 1883 in the form of a great cyclone, which blew down vast areas of timberland and forced the owners to cut only felled timber that first year. Then the very next year, the first of two great fires to break out in the region caused 22,000 acres to burn, forcing the crews to cut only the burned timber for several years. The fire, it is said, was started by a campfire spark, while two men were fishing for salmon at Norway Falls below Old

Loggers at Old City Depot Camps. Courtesy, Maine Appalachian Trail Club.

City Camps. The two had made the fire to drive away the mosquitoes, a spark flew out, and the fire got out of control.

Even with all the obstacles the Tracey-Love operation lasted until 1891. The operators built most of the dams from the Russell Pond area downstream and some of the names of those dams are still preserved in the Katahdin literature: Dacey, Bell, Mammoth, Robar, and others. Many of the falls and cascades along the Wassataquoik had to be made passable for logs: Orin, Norway, Grand, Ledge, and many more. In addition, lumber camps and depots were erected in various locations: Lower and Upper Katahdin Crossings, Nine-Mile, Halfway House (also known as the Parker House), Butterfields, Old City, New City (also known as Russell Camp at first), and many other camps on the tributaries. The Old City Camp was an extensive clearing with level hay fields and numerous buildings. The New City Camp had ten or twelve buildings and barns, hay cutting and cultivation equipment, a blacksmith shop, and even a schoolhouse for a time. These sites and the buildings constructed are, of course, becoming more and more obscured from view, to be found only by the most alert. Of course, there are no trails along most of the Wassataquoik today, further enhancing its isolation.

Of special interest was the major work done at Grand Falls to rid the stream of large boulder obstructions and to divert some of its waters around the treacherous falls. Those who are alert when visiting spectacular Grand Falls today may be able to find evidence of this activity amid the sheer beauty of the place.

The firm of Ayer and Rogers took over from Tracey and Love in 1891. One of the partners in this operation was Colonel Luther B. Rogers, whom we met in a previous chapter when we recalled his visit to the Great Basin in 1859. The other partner was Fred W. Ayer, owner of the Eastern Manufacturing Company and the head of the West Branch log drive in 1899. He and Herbert W. Marsh were the builders and operators of the tramway that allowed log hauling between Eagle and Chamberlain Lakes in the Allagash country from 1903 to 1908.

The firm opened up the old road system, rebuilt some of the camps, and pushed the cutting further up the Wassataquoik branches toward its headwaters. The firm established its headquarters at the old Dacey Farm site, a few miles above the renowned Hunt Farm. It was then known as the Patterson Place, and Rogers later built at the site an elaborate log sporting camp he named Lunksoos, which was managed along with the lumber operation for many years. A very good road was built along the South Branch of the Wassataquoik from the site of Bell Dam toward Katahdin. This old path is utilized today as the Tracy Trail (known also as the Wassataquoik Stream Trail and in the past as the Tracey Horse Trail).

In 1901 lumber operations along the Wassataquoik passed to the Katahdin Pulp and Paper Company. Again, the roads were improved and extended. Sadly, another much more destructive fire broke out in 1903, burning a huge acreage along with most trails, camp buildings, and other infrastructure caught in its path. The Old City site was never rebuilt after this fire and only a grown-up field marks the location today. Some 132 square miles of timber were destroyed by this fire, which apparently began in the Matagamon area by a group of men putting in a telephone line. It then spread to the slopes of Traveler Mountain and swept through Pogy Notch into the valley where the three Wassataquoik branches converge. It is thought to have been one of the most destructive fires in Maine history and is often referred in the literature as the "Great Burn."

Myron Avery described the transition that took place about this time:

So far the Wassataquoik had battled on fairly even terms with the invading lumbermen. The extreme difficulty and cost of driving this most uncertain of streams had baffled and eventually checked the enterprise of the successive spruce loggers. But the lumber industry was moving on. The cutting of long logs was giving way to the pulpwood industry and with this change was ushered in the third era of Wassataquoik history.

In 1910 Edward B. Draper . . . became manager and treasurer of the Katahdin Pulp and Paper Company. To salvage some of the burnt timber and to cut additional timber [the Company] recommenced cutting in the Wassataquoik. Profiting from the experience of the previous spruce loggers, Mr. Draper had the logs cut into pulpwood of four-foot lengths before they were dumped into the stream for driving. The Wassataquoik raged as in the days of old but it had little effect on the short logs. A sudden drop of water—the stream's final strategy—or a jam were not the catastrophic events as in former times. The stream was at last checked and subdued. Its reign of terror was over.[22]

The so-called Draper Operation soldiered on until 1914. Along the headwaters of the stream's branches old dams were rebuilt and new ones were constructed along the Middle Branch, especially toward the northwest sides of Katahdin's Tableland. As one hikes the trails to the North Peaks and the Northwest Basin there are still obscure reminders of those cutting activities. The slowly decaying evidence of dam structures, old camps and sluiceways are evident just off-trail.

The Draper Operation also reopened and extended timber cutting in the Wassataquoik Lake region, especially up and over the slopes of North Pogy and South Pogy mountains. Tote roads as well as sluices and snub hills to open up steep places were built and utilized all through the region. A huge, sturdy and partly enclosed 1,600-foot sluice brought logs thundering down the slopes of South Pogy into Wassataquoik Lake where they were cut into four-foot lengths and, after being piled up on the lake ice during winter, began their long journey down the Wassataquoik system in spring to the mills far to the south. The tragic story of the death of a Russian lumberman who was caught in the sluice and unable to avoid the oncoming logs is still told throughout the Katahdin region. The Draper Operation was an extremely extensive one, reaching from the Northwest Basin to the Pogys, to Katahdin Lake, north toward the Trout Brook and Webster Brook area, and all the way to Chamberlain Lake.

In 1915 another disastrous fire struck the region. It is said that it was started somewhere above Little Wassataquoik Lake from a match used by an old fisherman lighting his pipe. The fire most certainly was fueled by the dry slash left from extensive lumber cuttings. Though the Draper Operation had been phased out the year before, the fire caused the final abandonment of timber cutting in the Wassataquoik watershed.

Across the years there have been other major fires in the shadow of Katahdin. Although the destructive fires that affected the Wassataquoik certainly made a lasting mark on the region north and east of Katahdin, other fires left their mark on its slopes in other directions. There is, for instance, considerable evidence that there may have been a major fire in the forestlands south of Katahdin's treeline somewhere around 1795. Some of the early-nineteenth-century explorers and adventurers noted the presence of burnt lands and later foresters noted the scars that remained in the woodlands.

There is some evidence of an extensive fire in 1837 in the lower Wassataquoik Valley as far east as Dacey Dam. In addition, fires in 1884, 1903, and again in 1915 greatly affected logging operations along the stream. Then in August 1923, a fire broke out in the Basin Ponds area, most likely fueled by the slash left from the Great Northern Paper Company operation there. Fortunately, that fire was quickly contained and extinguished by the loggers themselves, aided by members of an Appalachian Mountain Club group camping at the Great Basin.

In the early and mid-1930s a number of fires threatened areas along the West Branch within sight of Katahdin. Smoke from these fires on one occasion reached Millinocket and caused some worry. It was during one of the fires that Fred Pittman's Katahdin View Sporting Camp on the south bank of the West Branch was destroyed. It was never rebuilt.

An extensive fire of more recent memory broke out in July 1977 and eventually burned more than 3,500 acres along the West Branch south of Baxter State Park and up toward Abol Hill, coming perilously close to the steeper slopes of Katahdin. The fire was fueled by debris caused by an enormous windstorm that occurred three years earlier. Firefighters finally brought the fire under control fourteen days later. Evidence of the blowdown, the fire, and the encouraging signs of recovery can still be seen along the Baxter State Park Tote Road and along the Appalachian Trail between Daicey Pond and Abol Bridge.

Myron Avery thus concluded his 1929 article on the Wassatquoik:

The Wassataquoik of to-day presents a curious contrast. It is entirely deserted and abandoned. The growth of Millinocket to an imposing outpost of civilization, and the development of the Great Northern Paper Company's tote-road from Millinocket to the Basin Ponds has heightened its isolation by diverting from the east the usual travel to Katahdin. The spruce and pine of its glorious lumbering past are gone.

Bared rock, a burned soil, a scraggly growth of "pople" and—the aftermath of the two terrific fires—an old field or two, ruined dams and tumbling down camps and an overgrown road are the mute and unconvincing records of its story. From the wilderness to a wilderness again, another life cycle of the Wassataquoik is complete.[23]

In a later article, Avery expresses his regret that:

These remains, which are more a memorial than a disfiguration, have become obliterated to a degree that it is difficult to appreciate and understand their precise mechanism. It is a token of a hardy and proud race of men. Rather than seeming to be an intrusion of the artificial into the wilderness, the lumbering history of this region seems insolubly bound to it. It is all very much a part of the whole. Rather than being a detraction from the area, what is left from these activities is a tribute to a glorious past, and there is good reason, apart from any other consideration, to preserve this memorial of a race, who—with all their faults and shortcomings—were indeed men.[24]

LOCAL STORIES AND HISTORIES FROM THE LUMBER ERA ABOUND; here are but a few snippets.

Sometime in the 1880s Israel Robar was allowed by the timber operators to erect a crude camp along the Wassataquoik where the waters of what later became known as Robar Pond and Stream entered. Robar may have been a logger himself at one time, but he soon became well known as an outstanding hunter. During the 1880s and into the 1890s Robar welcomed hikers on their way to or from Katahdin, and many set up their overnight camp there, even if Robar himself was not present. The site would later become known as Roger's Halfway House, likely because it was approximately halfway between the sporting camp Edwin Rogers operated on the East Branch and the New City logging depot camp.

Having read and remembered many of the stirring Leatherstocking Tales written by James Fenimore Cooper, and having accumulated a wealth of tales of his own and others' adventures in the area, Robar was a great favorite around the evening campfire. A dam was built near the Robar camp by the Tracy and Love Operation, and hikers could easily cross the Wassataquoik there and continue their journey to Katahdin Lake. This semi-hermit lived in the midst of the Wassataquoik wilderness, making a meager living as best he could, and was always willing to tell, and most likely embellish, his stories.

At the Poplar Burying Ground, downstream and not far from where the Wassataquoik flows into the East Branch, the bark of the poplar trees has been carved with the names of log drivers drowned in various lumber operations across the years. At other places along the stream it is said that the names of loggers are carved on rock boulders where they lost their lives. As a further memorial to the many who died along the stream there was also the tradition of nailing the boots of the deceased to a tree near where the driver was buried. At times crosses were planted atop burial mounds along the side of the old tote road. These nearly forgotten memorials were important reminders of a remarkable way of life, often requiring the facing of the narrow line between life and death in the wilderness of Katahdin.

There is a recurring mystery associated with the first large dam going upstream from the East Branch. There are those who know it as Daisey Dam, derived from the name of a log driver who lost his life in the river at the site where the dam was later built. A jam had formed and Daisey and others went to open it up. The jam broke and all got to shore except Daisey, who was crushed in the breaking mass of logs. They never recovered his body and later named the dam in his memory. This story was told to a hiking party in 1920 that included Governor Percival P. Baxter. But a strong case can be made that the dam carries the name of Hiram Dacey, who came in the 1830s and built his farm along the East Branch about a mile above where the Wassataquoik flows into the East Branch. It is certainly logical to assume that Dacey gave his name to the mountain he saw across the river from his farm and that later the name would be used for the dam. Complicating the mystery, the spelling of the name has also varied across the years: Daisey, Dace, Dacy, Dacey, and even Deasy and Deasey. Perhaps some day the mystery will be solved when an as yet unknown source is discovered.

SPORTING CAMPS

5

Camp Histories and the Advent of Tourism

UNTIL THE EARLY 1830S, KATAHDIN WAS REACHABLE ONLY BY mounting a major expedition requiring river travel by canoe or bateau along the Penobscot West Branch. However, the opening of the Military Road from Bangor to Aroostook County in 1832 allowed small private hiking parties to reach the east and north side of Katahdin. Using the Hunt Farm on the Penobscot East Branch and the logging camp clearings along Wassataquoik Stream as nighttime shelters, people came from Sherman and Stacyville in increasing numbers to climb the mountain. Later in the century, when logging in the Wassataquoik watershed diminished, recreational access from that side began to wane. This decline occurred as significant developments allowed greater access on the West Branch side of Katahdin once again. A new era of recreational tourism, featuring the sporting camp, rode the newly laid rails of the Bangor and Aroostook Railroad as it approached Nicatou where the East and West Branches join.

WEST BRANCH SPORTING CAMPS
In the early 1890s, the completion of the Bangor and Aroostook Railroad (the B&A, as it became known) from Brownville Junction through Norcross

and Medway to Aroostook County opened up new access to northern forest wood. This also resulted in an explosion of new sporting camps on the lakes and rivers throughout the region.

Access to Katahdin was greater than ever before, and many who lived in nearby towns and villages realized the commercial value of providing those living in the ever-expanding cities with accommodation in remote areas. Most sporting camps opened for business following the arrival of the railroad.

The operation of steamboats on the lake system south of Millinocket also played a large role in the rise of the sporting camps' popularity. The Bangor and Aroostook Railroad established a flag stop at Perkins Cove on South Twin Lake and a full station at Norcross at North Twin Lake. These two stations opened up access to an entire system of lakes and streams—South Twin, North Twin, Pemadumcook, the Jo-Marys, Ambajejus, and others.*

From 1893 to 1894, two hotels were established along the shores of South Twin and North Twin lakes. At the South Twin Lake flag stop, Pearl S. Willey built the South Twin House, a small hotel at Perkins Cove, shortly after the tracks were laid. A sporting camp complex on Nahmakanta Lake was run in connection with this hotel. The business was successful but never quite rivaled the one on North Twin Lake.

In 1894, near the Norcross station, W.R. Stratton built the first Norcross House on a hill overlooking the foot of North Twin Lake. The hotel did well, but ill health forced Stratton to sell it to Fred A. Fowler around 1897. Although the hotel burned later that season, Fred courageously decided to build a much larger hotel closer to the lake and railroad. Shortly thereafter, Fred's brother Albert F. Fowler joined the business.**

A 1901 promotional ad claimed that the Norcross House was "visited by more fishermen, canoeists, and hunters than any other hotel on the main line of the B&A."[1] At that time the roundtrip fare from Boston to Norcross was $14.50. The hotel offered hot water, steam heat, and full guide service.

---

* These lakes were extensively utilized to bring logs from the forest drainage beyond. The water flow was controlled by a series of dams built by the newly formed Great Northern Paper Company. The West Branch flowed through Ambajejus, North Twin, and several smaller lakes on its way past Millinocket and Medway to its rendezvous with the East Branch, making the upriver stretches toward Katahdin more accessible than ever before.

** Fred and Albert were grandsons of a pioneer in the area, Thomas Fowler Sr., who came into the region around 1829 and built farms at Grand Falls on the West Branch and on Millinocket Stream. On his way to Katahdin in 1846, Thoreau stayed with Tom Sr.

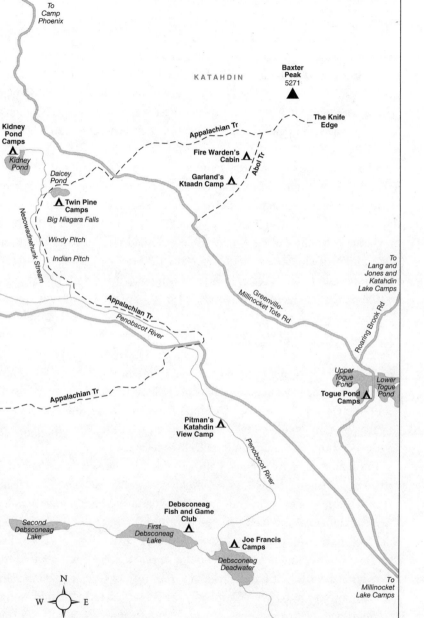

Sporting camps in the shadow of Katahdin (West Branch side).

A popular emporium, the Norcross Supply Store, provided camp supplies, guns, fishing gear, cooking outfits, bedding, moccasins, and a host of other items for a wilderness excursion. A jumping off place for timber cutting activity in the region, loggers often stayed at Norcross House on their way to and from the depot camps. The hotel offered two types of accommodation—an austere facility for those of meager means or who wished to rough it, and a refined facility for the tourist desiring more elaborate lodging. For many years the Fowlers were known for their generous hospitality and knowledge of the lake region.

Soon after establishing the hotel the Fowlers founded the Norcross Transportation Company, a steamboat business that transported sportsmen throughout the lake system to sporting camps. Eventually they had an entire fleet of steamboats, including the Gypsie, the Anna Bell, the Ora, the Rainbow, and the Minnie Ha Ha. Willey also established a leaner steamboat business at South Twin, operating the Irma and the Frances across the lake system for his guests. In the early days the steamboats made daily rounds after boarding the passengers at the Norcross House or South Twin House piers.

One of the notable results of this steamboat activity was the establishment of additional sporting camps on the Penobscot West Branch and its tributaries, all of them upriver from Ambajejus Lake. The camps in that region were all established around the same time in the late 1800s—Camp Wellington at the head of Ambajejus Lake, Kidney Pond Camps, Twin Pine Camps on Daisey (Daicey) Pond, Camp Phoenix on Nesowadnehunk Lake, Joe Francis Camps and Katahdin View Camps on the West Branch, and Debsconeag Outing Camps on First Debsconeag Lake.

The Bangor and Aroostook Railroad aided in the success of sporting camps by publishing its own annual booklet, *In the Maine Woods*, which advertised the ease of going by train into the wilderness. The company extolled the exceptional hunting and fishing opportunities that rail travel afforded. Such use, of course, helped pay for new railroad extensions northward so everyone was a winner. An 1898 issue of *In the Maine Woods* advised the adventurer in search of Katahdin to take the steamer Gypsie to Ambajejus Lake and travel up the West Branch by canoe, stay at Irving Hunt's camps on "Sourdnahunk Stream," where the fish rose to almost any fly, and camp at the foot of Abol Slide the night before climbing to the summit. The article suggested that the adventurer engage a guide to carry a gun for shooting caribou on the Tableland.[2]

Life at the Camps

The sporting camp proprietors leased land from timberland owners with the understanding that the proprietors would not interfere with timber operations.* With the lease secured, the proprietors built a number of basic buildings: guest cabins, a kitchen and dining room, a central gathering lodge, and a variety of outbuildings. The proprietor, almost always a male, was responsible for construction, ongoing maintenance and guiding, while his wife ran the dining room, cleaned, and cooked. Guests enjoyed food from a nearby garden, kept fresh by a hand-dug root cellar, fish caught in nearby ponds and streams, and baked breads and pastries. Food was prepared on a giant wood stove; light was provided by kerosene lamps, heat by wood, drinking water from a nearby pond or brook, and other water by gravity feed from a rain barrel. Some camps even offered linen tablecloths and napkins, all of which had to be washed and ironed (non-electric, of course). There was much camaraderie around the tables during the evening meal—somewhat civilized after all.

Reaching the camps was part of the camp experience itself. Access to the camps was varied and continued to change as the timber roads opened up more tracts of land to the automobile during the early twentieth century. Camps on the east side of Katahdin were reachable by buckboard from Stacyville. On the south side one might be brought in by a combination of the steamboat from Norcross, a canoe trip up the West Branch, and finally by foot or buckboard up the Nesowadnehunk Valley.

Just after dawn at a typical camp, a pitcher of hot water was delivered to each cabin for a morning "bath." After a hearty breakfast, guests selected their activities, which ranged from canoeing and taking guided fishing trips to hiking nearby trails and preparing for the two- or three-day trek to Katahdin's summit. Most sporting camps had simple outlying cabins or shelters on nearby ponds and rivers where one or more guests, often with a guide, stayed for a few nights of even more remote fishing and exploring. Here they would sleep and enjoy the food prepared by the guide.

As darkness fell at camp proper, proprietors, guests, and guides planned the next day's excursions, shared tales, or retreated to the library and even-

---

* These lease arrangements are a time-honored tradition in Maine. Over time, leases usually passed from one proprietor to another, with compensation being paid for the value of the buildings and the business.

tually to their cabins to sleep. There was usually a great mix of guests—politicians, businessmen, artists, the rich and the not-so-rich, the ordinary and the extraordinary—all sharing equally, socializing together as one, drawn together by their love of the Katahdin area and its great riches.

In the off-season most proprietors lived in town, though a few stayed at the camps through the winter and some even stayed open for winter guests. Necessary repairs and maintenance were addressed before the snows came. Usually the proprietor returned to the camp during the winter to cut pond ice, which was stored in an outbuilding under sawdust and used during the summer and fall seasons. In the spring, the proprietors cleaned, cut wood, made repairs, and readied the camps for the first guests' arrival around Memorial Day.

Colt Camp

Samuel Pomeroy Colt, named after his uncle who founded the Colt Firearms Company, grew up in Rhode Island. The youngest son of Christopher and Theodora Colt, Samuel was a lawyer with a reputation for extravagant spending. Colt, who preferred the sobriquet "The Colonel," built a private camp on Nahmakanta Lake but later abandoned it in order to build on Kidney Pond around 1890. Part of Kidney Pond's appeal was its easy accessibility from the Penobscot's West Branch via a logging road and a toll dam near Daicey. With the timber owners' permission, and with the help of Lewis "Lewey" Ketcham, Colt built on a point of land now known as Colt's Point. Ketcham, a member of a New Brunswick tribe, had built Colt's first camp at Nahmakanta Lake. He had also worked with John Ross on the great West Branch river drives and was considered one of Maine's best guides.

Colt Camp offered its visitors lavish amenities—a pool table, two bowling alleys, an upright Steinway piano, and all the comforts of home in the middle of the wilderness. A great stone fireplace graced the main living room, and the porch offered a stunning view of Katahdin and the surrounding mountains. Ethel Barrymore, a famed Broadway actress, married Colt's son Russell around 1910 and is said to have visited often prior to World War I. Ethel and Russell named their first child Samuel, known as Sammy, to honor his grandfather and great uncle. It is said that while at camp, Ethel loved playing the piano but also took to the bowling. "Pin boys" were employed for the summer to retrieve and reset the pins.

Shortly after Colt died in 1921, his family stopped visiting the camps. In

1925 an Appalachian Mountain Club August Camp took place at the Colt facility and Roy Bradeen, then proprietor of the Kidney Pond Camps, helped make the encampment a success. In 1926, after extensive damage from a destructive gale, the Colt family sold the camp buildings to Bradeen. Several of the buildings were moved across the frozen pond and incorporated into the Kidney Pond Camps. The piano also made the journey across the pond that winter and was enjoyed for many years in the Kidney Pond Camps dining room. The bowling alleys were broken up and many of the boards stored at Kidney Pond Camps for some years; they were later used to build the dining room tables, and the fancy dining room lamps are from the bowling alley as well. One can also find there among the books on the bookshelves several of those unique backcountry wooden bowling balls.

Kidney Pond Camps

Irving O. Hunt (also known as "I.O.") and his brother Lyman began constructing Kidney Pond Camps on the northwest shore of the pond in 1899. The Hunts were the grandsons of William H. Hunt, who established the famed Hunt Farm along the Penobscot's East Branch in the early 1830s. Having built sporting camps on Millinocket Lake years earlier, they were drawn to the Nesowadnehunk country where they, along with another brother, had worked as guides and trappers as early as 1884. In the early 1890s, the brothers erected several rough-hewn camps, called "Camps Sourdnahunk," at Indian Pitch, near the mouth of Nesowadnehunk Stream. However, by the late 1890s, the Hunts thought their "sports" would be attracted to the fishing and hunting opportunities around Kidney Pond. They had originally hoped to set up camps at Daicey Pond, but Maurice York had already established himself there. Instead they chose the northwest shore of Kidney Pond, just far enough from the neighboring Colt Camp. The Kidney Pond location was ideal, commanding a stunning view of nearby Katahdin.

The brothers originally named the camps "Hunt's Camps—Sourdnahunk Stream and Pond" to lure people to the stream's famed fishing waters as well as the pond. It was not long before the simpler name "Kidney Pond Camps" prevailed. Guests named the first main lodge "The Temple" or "Solomon's Temple" because of two huge log pillars flanking the front entrance. During the first few years of their new venture, the Hunts maintained the old camp buildings at Indian Pitch, which they used as outlying camps for fishing parties out of Kidney Pond.

**Irving O. Hunt, at left, on Katahdin's summit with unidentified companion.
Circa 1920s.** Courtesy, Mrs. Jeanette York.

I.O. was a bit of a character and a fantastic guide. Sometimes referred to
as the "Old Eagle of Katahdin," he was famous for using a birch bark horn
to call moose. Irving attended several Sportmen's Shows in New York City
and once took a live bear with him to the first Boston Sportmen's Show. He
guided many great men, including movie producer Cecil B. DeMille, the

president of Johnson and Johnson Company, and an attorney general. He was still guiding into his 80s.

By 1900, the Hunt brothers realized the merit of having a trail to Katahdin's summit for their guests, and that year I.O. cut a trail via the Southwest Spur, making Kidney Pond Camps a favored destination for many years. At one time the Hunts boasted that as many as 23 trout ponds were easily reachable from the camps, each of which retained canoes and boats to convey guests to the best fishing places.

In 1903, two important guests arrived at the camps—James Phinney Baxter of Portland and his 27-year-old son Percival. Percival's first visit to the region left an indelible mark on his life. He never forgot that fishing trip or the views of Katahdin and the surrounding mountains. Percival devoted the later years of his life to preserving the whole Katahdin area for future generations.

The Hunts gave many of the ponds surrounding Kidney Pond their names, most of which are still used today. When asked once how he named Lost Pond, I.O. replied:

> I'd heard there was a pond in that region from which some wonderful trout had been taken . . . but nobody seemed able to tell me just where it was. I took a day off and scoured the locality but couldn't find it. It seemed to have disappeared completely. In my next attempt I found it and named it Lost Pond, which it has been ever since.[3]

Over the years, Kidney Pond Camps had several outlying camps, small rough cabins or shelters to which guests could be guided for an overnight and extended fishing. Food for such outings was supplied by the main camp, the guide always serving as cook. If the fishing trip were for only a day, a noon dinner might be provided at the outlying site. Kidney Pond Camps had an outlying camp on the south side of the Penobscot West Branch right across from the mouth of Nesowadnehunk Stream, reached, of course, by canoe. It is a private camp today but still commands a striking view of the mouth of the stream across the river. Later, Kidney Pond Camps acquired the Rainbow Lake Camps' outlying cabin located upstream on the West Branch. The cabin was near the well-known Horserace section of the river. At Slaughter Pond several large tents and later a well-built log cabin were extremely popular with the guests for overnight stays.

Hikers in front of Slaughter Pond outlying cabin maintained for the guests of Kidney Pond Camps. Courtesy, Dexter Historical Society (Bert L. Call Collection).

Getting to Kidney Pond Camps

As for getting to the Kidney Pond Camps from the outside world, a promotional booklet circa 1916/1918 recommended taking the sleeper train from Boston to Norcross to meet with Captain Pearl S. Willey, proprietor of the South Twin House, and changing into camping clothes. From Norcross, guests would board a 10 A.M. steamer bound for Camp Wellington, a sporting camp at the head of Ambajejus. There they would meet Mr. Hunt, who would, after a hearty lunch, take the guests by canoe up the West Branch to Pockwockamus Deadwater. After a brief stop at Davis Camps (later Fred Pitman's Katahdin View Camps) the canoes continued to the mouth of Sourdnahunk Stream. From there, the guests walked three miles along an old tote road to Kidney Pond. It was an all-day excursion that ended with royal treatment at the camps and a sumptuous evening meal.[4]

A clever variation of West Branch canoe travel evolved over the years. The proprietors of the sporting camps on Daicey, Kidney, and Nesowadnehunk often left one canoe at the top of each river carry and one at the bottom. That enabled the guide and guests to lug only their personal "wangen" (luggage) across the carry without shouldering the canoe as well. With good planning, there was always a fresh canoe awaiting them on the other side of the carry. A guide could go all the way to Ambajejus Lake and back without ever having to put a shoulder to a canoe.

For many years, the guides left the sporting camp canoes at a small clearing at the mouth of Nesowadnehunk Stream. This may well have been the same area known as Gibson's Clearing in the early logging days. Once sporting camps had become well established, guides brought guests from the clearing by buckboard upstream to Kidney, Twin Pines, and Phoenix. Someone set up a simple horse corral where the animals were kept safely. In 1900, arrangements also could be made to have the horses drag canoes along the ancient carry around dangerous Nesowadnehunk Falls. The site later served as a fine camping location for river travelers for many years.

As log-hauling roads penetrated deeper and deeper into the Nesowadnehunk region, steamboat access declined. In the 1920s, a major log-hauling road from Greenville to Nesowadnehunk Field allowed guests to visit the camps by buckboard from the north. Kidney Pond Camps and Twin Pine Camps at Daicey shared a cabin at Nesowadnehunk Field to accommodate guests for a night before they went to the main camps the next morning. No one who traveled along the log-hauling road forgot the rollicking, bumpy

Horse-drawn rig operated by Kidney Pond Camps crossing Nesowadnehunk Stream. Doubletop Mountain is in the distance. Courtesy, Dexter Historical Society (Bert L. Call Collection).

ride down the Nesowadnehunk Valley. The trail stayed close to the stream, crossing it as many as sixteen times as it cut through the narrow gap between Doubletop and The Brothers. Some said that the buckboard's wheel spokes drank mud and careened from boulder to rut like a lumberjack returning from the settlement. "Jake" Day and Lester F. Hall followed the buckboard ruts from the Sourdnahunk Tote Road to Daicey Pond on their 1928 trip.

Kidney Pond Camps Changes Hands

During the winter of 1924–25, Roy Bradeen and Fred Clifford acquired the camp lease from I.O. Hunt, who some say lost the lease in a poker game.* By then the camps offered running water and generator electricity. I.O. became a guide at York's Twin Pine Camps on Daicey Pond.

After only a few years, Clifford left the partnership to establish Rainbow

---

* An unsubstantiated claim that has become part of apocryphal Katahdin lore.

Lake Camps, and by 1928 Roy and Laura Bradeen were the sole proprietors of Kidney Pond Camps. Around that time, the outlying camp on the river became known as "Bradeen's West Branch Camp." Bradeen also restored the outlying camp at Slaughter Pond for overnight fishing parties. Guests such as U.S. Supreme Court Justice William O. Douglas looked forward to staying at the camps, and he and Bradeen became good friends. In 1936 the cost of staying at one of "Bradeen's Camps" was $5 per day, all meals included, plus a small charge for canoe use. The fee of the guide was always extra, usually another $5 per day.

In 1937 Roy Bradeen drowned when his canoe capsized on the pond. His wife managed the camps until Marshall W. Doxsee and his son Arthur bought the lease in 1945.

In 1941 Governor Baxter purchased the land in that area from the Garfield Land Company, allowing the camp leases to continue. During the time the Doxsees ran the camps the land was formally conveyed by Baxter to the state of Maine. In 1950 the lease was transferred to Donald D. and Valle Ewing Kennedy, who operated the camps until 1960 when Charles J. and Betty Lipscomb bought the lease.

The Lipscombs had an excellent reputation and added touches of class with Thursday night lobster and steak meals cooked on an outdoor grill, table flowers, and a printed menu. Kidney Pond Camps were a bit more formal than Twin Pine Camps. Sometimes overnight visitors were even discouraged from entering the kitchen and from fraternizing with the help.

In 1967, Baxter State Park bought the Lipscomb buildings and other assets, and in 1968 Charles and Ruth Norris began leasing the land and buildings. In 1987, Baxter State Park assumed control of the campground and did not receive guests until 1990, first under the temporary management of several new leasers and later by park personnel.

The Kidney Pond Camps scrapbook, housed in the Baxter State Park Archives, is filled with interesting stories. Rev. B. Janney Rudderow (known as "The Parson") and his wife Mary, along with their family members, made the long trip to Kidney Pond from Philadelphia every season for more than 56 years. Cabins at both Kidney and Daicey were named for them. Rudderow was noted for leading groups up the Sentinel Mountain Trail on Sundays. The Episcopal clergyman preached and led worship on a prominent rock outcrop on the west side of the summit loop trail. Today the site is known by the name he gave it—"Pulpit Rock."

Another scrapbook story describes the years before and after World War II when a man named Duncan Hines published an inn and restaurant rating system, which was much appreciated by the traveling public. The publication, which listed as many as 1,700 vacation sites in North America, the Caribbean, and Bermuda, recommended Kidney Ponds Camps. The scrapbook contains some effusive lines of poetry in recognition of the recommendation, while one guest expressed concern over whether or not the listing might spoil the place. A countering opinion averred that wilderness would ultimately win the day and the essence of the beloved camps would prevail.

A third story is about two men whose names will always be associated with Kidney Pond Camps—John Winthrop Worthington and H.M. Knickerbocker. Worthington, a regular September guest at Kidney Pond Camps from 1942 to 1962, graduated from Harvard and practiced law in Boston. Knickerbocker, also a long-time September guest, first came to the camps in 1910. He and Worthington maintained trails in the area and even built the first trail up OJI Mountain. The two men may have also been involved in reopening some of the Doubletop trails. Both were avid hikers and loved working outdoors while staying at the camps. It is said that Worthington's favorite drink was rum but on the trail it was strictly tea.

In 1943, the two men collaborated to map the camp area and the surrounding mountains, ponds, and trails. Worthington did extensive research on Thoreau's 1846 route to Katahdin and published an essay on it in the Appalachian Mountain Club's journal *Appalachia* in 1946. He visited the remote Klondike area in 1900 or 1901 when he was 28 years old, a remarkable feat at that time. He did not, however, climb to Katahdin's summit until 1949, at age 76. Worthington took it upon himself one year to build a simple sapling pole bench at "Moose Lookout," near the site of Samuel Colt's camp on Kidney Pond. The site is now known as Colt's Point, and the tradition of keeping a bench there of the same design as Worthington's continues. The view of Katahdin and the surrounding mountains from that bench is astounding, one of the truly special places in the region.

Twin Pine Camps at Daicey Pond

Daicey Pond was known as Daisy or Daisey Pond as far back as 1900. Despite the variations, the pond's name was always pronounced "Day-cee," which explains the evolution from Daisey to Daicey. A 1921 advertisement carried by *In the Maine Woods* reads: "Daicey Pond or Daisey Pond, it makes no difference how you spell it, is the place for you. . . ."[5] The pond was likely named after the Daiseys, a family who worked in the woods in that area at the turn of the twentieth century. Charles Daisey bought the Phoenix Sporting Camps on Nesowadnehunk Lake in 1904, and probably named the pond for his father, George.

Maurice (pronounced "Morris") York, a former logger in the area, established the sporting camps on Daicey Pond. Some say that York established his claim by "squatting" on the shore of the pond where a state-mandated "Public School Lot" had been set aside by the Great Northern Paper Company. Because he could not be evicted from a public lot, York soon got approval for a lease and began building his log camps around 1899, the same year that the Hunts began building their camps on Kidney Pond.

With the area's timber already harvested, York used several abandoned lumber camp buildings in a field below the pond for his fledgling business and later moved into the newer buildings. The new camps sat near the shore under the shade of two giant white pine trees that gave rise to the name of the camps—Twin Pine Camps.* The camps boasted easy access to Sourdnahunk waters and ten ponds for fishing and canoeing, nearby hunting, year-round accommodations, and a trail (Hunt's Trail) that led to the summit of Katahdin.

In 1920 or 1921, Everett L. York, a cousin to Maurice, and Everett's wife, Vesta, were brought into the operation under an agreement that the one (Everett or Maurice) to survive the death of the other would be the sole owner. During the 1920s, as the tote road from Greenville to Nesowadnehunk Field (only eight miles from Daicey Pond) progressed, the camps expanded from five to twelve cabins. In 1921, rates were $3 a day, meals included, with free canoes at the nearby ponds. About this time, I.O. Hunt, former owner of the Kidney Ponds Camps, became a guide out of Twin Pine Camps.

When Maurice died in 1927, Everett and Vesta took over the camp operations. The couple was often referred to as "Uncle Everett" and "Mother York." Everett playfully referred to one of the peaks west of Katahdin as Mount Everett, a reference to the emerging prominence of Mount Everest in Nepal. He might have had fun telling his guests this during the years of the famous Everest Reconnaissance Expeditions in the late 1920s and early 1930s, but the name never took hold. One report suggests that it was so named because

---

* The two pines are still standing at Baxter State Park's Daicey Pond Campground.

the mountain "looked like Everett York laying down with his belt all pulled in."[6] The tote road system continued to progress from Millinocket, and by the early 1930s it was possible to drive to both Daicey and Kidney.

In 1932, Everett and Vesta turned the camp buildings over to their son Earle and daughter-in-law Maribel. The elder Yorks moved to Nesowadne-hunk Field to what they called "York's Tavern," the cabin that had accom-modated guests on their way from Greenville to the camps. In the early 1940s, the Twin Pine cabins, previously at the center of the site, were hauled back from the edge of the pond. After Earle's death in 1945, his son Earle Jr., known as "Junior," and his wife Jeanette joined Maribel as partners and continued to manage the camps.

In the mid-1930s, the Appalachian Trail from Georgia to Katahdin was completed, and it passed right through the sporting camp's center. Both the Appalachian Trail Conference* and the Maine Appalachian Trail Club had formed to maintain and manage the trail. In August 1939, to celebrate the trail's completion and the effort to extend the Appalachian Trail from Mount Washington to Katahdin, the Appalachian Trail Conservancy held its Bien-nial Conference at Daicey Pond. The meeting became a kind of pilgrimage to Katahdin for those who had worked so hard to make the Appalachian Trail a reality.

There were about 150 delegates, the largest gathering of any voluntary conservation group to meet in Maine. Speakers included Lore B. Rogers, Myron Avery, Roy Dudley, and many state leaders. The delegates were much interested in the story of Donn Fendler, lost on the mountain earlier that summer. They visited the newly completed cable bridge across the West Branch and placed a marker on the summit of Katahdin, commemmorating the start (or end) of the Appalachian Trail. They heard some of Roy Dudley's stories while they camped at Chimney Pond.

To accommodate the large number of people, the Yorks erected tents and a large dining area at the old lumber camp site near the bank of the Nesowadnehunk Stream.[7] It was indeed a historic meeting in the Katahdin region.

Junior and Jeanette were associated with the camps from 1945 to 1969, and their management became legendary. Jeanette was the cook and general overseer of the daily operations, including the help, while Junior maintained

---

* Now the Appalachian Trail Conservancy.

the buildings and did most of the guiding. Like many other sporting camps in the region, Twin Pine Camps also had an outlying camp. "River Camp," as it was called, was built in 1943 on the West Branch's north bank between the mouths of Abol and Nesowadnehunk Streams. Guides took guests there to fish along the West Branch and nearby ponds. The guides typically brought hearty food from the main camp and treated their "sports" to the best fishing spots.

During Junior and Jeanette's tenure, many distinguished guests visited the camp—artists James Fitzgerald and Helen Marshall; Leland Goodrich, who helped author the United Nations Charter; an attorney general under President Harding; a Harvard College president; a member of the John Philip Sousa Band; a number of leaders of the Maine Appalachian Trail Club; and Governor Percival P. Baxter (who loved Jeanette's cooking). Parson Rudderow and wife Mary actually visited Daicey more than Kidney, lured by Junior's legendary guiding skills and Jeanette's celebrated cooking. They often came for four to six weeks at a time. Their daughter, Betsy, learned canoeing and fishing skills from Junior, and Rudderow and Junior became good friends.

Betsy's husband, Rev. Hobart Heistand, recalled his first visit to the camps at Daicey when he was courting Betsy, who worked in the kitchen for several seasons. Junior was concerned that his guests' daughter marry a good man. One day, Heistand helped Junior remove trees that were blocking the road after a flood; he worked hard and made a favorable impression. As the two men wearily trudged back to the camps, Junior patted him on the back and said, with typical Yankee simplicity, "You'll do."

Junior was an eager raconteur, and guests took great delight in hearing his many Nesowadnehunk valley memories and adventures. Junior grew up at the camps and knew every trail, pond, and fishing spot for miles around. He said that he often took trout out of Grassy Pond, an excellent spawning place, and released them into other ponds in the area—his own private stocking operation. He knew where the fish spawned in every pond and was always fascinated by spawning bed activity. Junior boasted that Twin Pines had a more informal, down-home spirit. Primarily a fisherman in the flatlands, he was known for saying, "Only damn fools and paid guides climb Katahdin."

Junior's typical pack for guiding his "sports" for a day or an overnight included a full set of dishes and silverware, pans, steaks and chops, onions, boiled potatoes, canned vegetables, cooking oil, fresh baked bread, and the essential ax and fishing gear. A pint of spirits was not an unusual addition. The pack must have weighed between 70 and 80 pounds.

Junior always returned during winter with friends to cut ice from the pond for the next season. He then returned in early spring to split and stack the wood for the great iron kitchen stove and the library fireplace. It was a hard life, but the Yorks and other sporting camp proprietors loved the independence and freedom their lifestyle gave them. It was also a steady livelihood and an opportunity to meet interesting and diverse people.

In 1954, Junior and Jeanette became the sole owners of the lease. In 1969 the state took over the property amid some controversy. When the Yorks left Daicey Pond, they ended an unequaled 70-year, three-generation family association with Twin Pines.

At Daicey, the great mountain always dominated the view from the pond. After hiking more than 2,000 miles from Georgia, Appalachian Trail thru-hikers standing at the edge of the pond finally saw the object of their quest—Katahdin.

Camp Phoenix

By the 1890s rough logging roads traveled farther up Nesowadnehunk Stream, and a dam at the outlet of Nesowadnehunk Lake impounded enough water for the spring log drive. At the same time rough roads extended from Patten to Matagamon and up the Trout Brook watershed nearly to Nesowadnehunk Lake from the east.

During this time Albert McLain, his son Will, and two brothers by the surname of Hall recognized an opportunity to establish a sporting camp on Nesowadnehunk Lake, a beautiful wilderness oasis in the midst of the vast forest. The McLains, who had hunted and trapped nearby, knew the region well. Before building Camp Phoenix, the McLains and their friend Henry Priest built a rough trapper's cabin near the lake but it burned shortly after it was built. Undeterred, the McLains joined the Hall brothers in leasing land in 1896 to build a set of permanent log buildings at the shore of Nesowadnehunk Lake, near the old Palmer Depot Camp. They named this Camp Phoenix, for the bird of Egyptian legend, which from the ashes of its death was reborn to new life.

Early promotional ads from the turn of the century describe the way to reach the camps from two different Bangor and Aroostook Railroad stations.

From Norcross, a guest could take the steamer to Camp Wellington at the head of Ambajejus Lake, then travel by canoe up the West Branch, by foot or buckboard to Hunt's Camps on Kidney Pond, and finally to Sourdnahunk Lake. Alternatively, from Patten a guest could travel by buckboard from Matagamon up Trout Brook and through the old McCarty Depot Camp. The Patten route was the most popular in those early years. A 1902 ad boasted that "the rare hunting and phenomenal fishing in this region make this the gilt-edge resort of the Maine wilderness for sportsmen." The cost of the camp was $1.50 a day, with meals included. Guides could be engaged for an additional $3 a day.

After 1899, Will McLain and the Hall brothers managed the camps until they sold the lease in 1904 to Charles A. Daisey (pronounced "Day-cee"), who had been a guide for the McLains and Halls. The camps were often referred to as Daisey's Camps on many of the old maps. Daisey's parents had settled in Norcross after moving from Medway, and he had worked in various timber-cutting jobs before becoming a guide at Camp Phoenix. Because Daisey used Norcross as his base of operations, the river route became the primary way to reach Camp Phoenix. He and his wife, Minnie, ran the camps together until Minnie's tragic death in 1913 when a train struck her buckboard. Daisey soon married Minnie's sister, Sarah. This was an important transitional time in Camp Phoenix's history. During Daisey's ownership, both the tote road from Greenville (1916) and the tote road from Millinocket (1922) reached Nesowadnehunk Field, making access to the lake far easier than ever before. In October 1931, after Daisey's son, Arnold, became a partner in the business, a fire in the main lodge completely burned the lodge along with the dining room and kitchen complex. Fortunately, the fire did not spread to other outlying buildings, and repairs followed quickly. The camps were ready for business by spring. It was a second rising of the phoenix from the ashes.

When the road from Greenville finally reached Nesowadnehunk Field, where the Great Northern Paper Company developed its large depot, guests could drive within five miles of Camp Phoenix. A telephone line allowed arriving guests to arrange for pickup by buckboard. Several old lumber camp buildings served as garages during the summer season and could hold as many as ten to twelve cars. Later, Daisey used an old army ten-passenger command vehicle to transport guests. By the 1930s, the CCC had so improved the tote road from Millinocket that automobiles could drive to the camps.

In 1937, Charles Daisey bought the land around the camps, which freed him from the uncertainty of arranging lease renewals and spared Camp Phoenix from Governor Baxter's sweeping acquisitions in the 1930s and 1940s. Daisey and Arnold enjoyed a positive reputation, a result of their effective management of the camps. Arnold rebuilt and replaced many of the original buildings from the McLain-Hall era. Together they built a winter camp and a large main lodge, and placed new individual guest cabins farther apart along the shore of the lake. They also maintained an outlying camp on the West Branch above Nesowadnehunk Falls.

In 1942, Charles passed the lease to Arnold. By then the region was so accessible, the family knew that their once isolated camps would never be the same. As Dr. William Horner put it in his history of Camp Phoenix:

> From the Daisey perspective, things were not the same. "Everything changed when the chain came down," said Ella [Arnold's half-sister], a bit wistfully. Clearly, an era had passed. An emerging middle class had found and gotten access to Sourdnahunk Lake. Motorboats came in, new logging roads increased public access to the outlying ponds, and a "public landing" was established between the dam and Camp Phoenix. And, of course, Baxter State Park was becoming a very large and close neighbor. Arnold Daisey was ready to sell.[8]

After an amazing 51 years, the Daisey family sold the camps in 1955 to George and Beryl Emerson. The Emersons managed the camps quite successfully for another sixteen seasons. George leased from Great Northern Paper Company additional land next to the outlet dam around 1959. He set up a store and a camping area with tent sites and shelters, which he named Nesowadnehunk Lake Wilderness Camps or simply Sourdnahunk Camps. It is still open for public use.

When George Emerson sold Camp Phoenix in 1971, the camp began an era of short-lived ownerships by Irving and Claire Salley, Bud Burbank, and James "Dick" LeDuc. In the early 1990s, Holland and Merrill, two developers, worked out a joint ownership venture with individual cabins under private ownership and some shared facilities for all.

There were several very complicated boundary disputes over the property dating back to the 1940s that were not resolved until the 1990s. The present cooperative Camp Phoenix Owners Association has a much more cordial relationship with Baxter State Park and other landowners in the region. The association has retained much of the flavor of the original sporting camp site—the broad sweep of open field to the lake, the boat dock area, and the old lodge. The view of the surrounding mountains, the beauty of the lake, and the sense of being removed from the busy world have not changed.

Ambajejus Camps (a.k.a., Camp Wellington or Cypher's Camps)

The Ambajejus Camps sit just west of where the Penobscot West Branch flows across Ambajejus Falls and enters Ambajejus Lake. Here, the narrow river becomes a broader flow across the lakes. Native American artifacts have been found close by, giving rise to speculation that native peoples commonly camped here.

During West Branch log drives, the giant rocks and the nearby island were utilized to collect logs coming down the river. They would then be towed across the lake system in huge boom enclosures for later release into the lower West Branch, which led to the great Penobscot Boom at Pea Cove in Old Town. The Boom House, now on the National Register of Historic Places, housed the boom workers for many years and is still standing on the island opposite the site of the camps.

Shortly after the railroad reached Norcross and the steamboat businesses began to thrive, Seldon J. McPheters from Norcross built a sporting camp, named Camp Wellington, just west of where the Penobscot West Branch flows across Ambajejus Falls and enters Ambajejus Lake. Camp Wellington's location was excellent—it was the end of the line for the steamboats after they had stopped at other lakeshore sporting camps. At Wellington the steamboats discharged the last of the passengers, often those who were heading farther up the river for various wilderness camping or sporting experiences. The boat landing was located on the shore of a huge eddy at the foot of the falls right beside the camp buildings.

The camps offered many amenities—spring beds, a telephone connection to Norcross, pure spring water running directly into the main lodge, and Mrs. McPheters' fine cooking. However, Camp Wellington's most significant draw was its access to daily steamers. The camp was an ideal meeting place for upriver sporting camp proprietors, who met their "sports" there to take them the rest of the way by canoe. George Witherle, who explored the Katahdin region late in the nineteenth century, came to Camp Wellington on the steamer Gypsie in 1899 and had dinner there before continuing his ascent of the river toward the Abol side of Katahdin. He returned in 1901 and dined with the McPheterses before continuing up the West Branch. In 1902, a small Appalachian Mountain Club party reported visiting the camp in time for a fabulous supper of trout.

By 1907, the lease had been transferred from McPheters to Frank E. Tuck and W.H. Davis of Norcross. The cost was then $1.50 per day, meals included. Camp Wellington was for a time known as "Lakeside Camps on the West Branch at the Head of Ambajejus" and continued to serve West Branch travelers. In 1916, the lease was transferred to A.E. Chadbourne of Millinocket, and the camp was renamed "The Ambajejus House." An outlying cabin was built on an island in the middle of Hurd Pond.

In 1924, Harry L. Cypher acquired the camp's lease and renamed it "Cypher's Camps," a name that stuck until the 1940s. In his promotional ads, Cypher boasted that he owned a huge generator that could keep sewing machines, refrigerators, and even freezers running. By this time steamboat activity had started to decline, and access by car from Millinocket to Spencer Cove, where Cypher met guests with his boat, became more popular. Cypher offered a blanket box in every cabin, a telephone, a fine bathhouse with separate sides for men and women, a woodshed, horse hovels, cabins, bunkhouses, a lakeside gazebo, a workshop, an icehouse, a central hall, a large root cellar, along with an assortment of cows, pigs, and sheep. The last promotional ad for Cypher's Camp appeared in 1932. Very little is known about the camps between 1933 and 1947. Cypher probably continued running the camps, at least for a time. Some have suggested that he ran it as a boys' summer camp for a few years, but there is no evidence. It was still referred to on maps as "Cypher's" until the early 1940s. An old map from the 1950s refers to the site as "Robinson's Camps," so named by its proprietor Harry D. Robinson.

By 1947 or 1948 the lease was held by Messrs. Taylor, Buckley, Meinhold, and Draper, all of Massachusetts. Buckley named it Ambajejus Lake Camps, and it is so named today. For a short time they ran it as a boys' camp but later used it as a gathering place for friends and family. They had a powerboat and met guests at Spencer Cove for transport to the camps. Renowned Maine sports writer Bud Leavitt and world heavyweight boxing champion Rocky Marciano were guests during this period. Sometime in the 1950s the camps began a slow decline.

Around 1972 the lease was transferred to Charles Coffin, who had been a friend of the previous leasers and a frequent visitor. Today, Al and Cheryl Barden, Coffin's daughter and son-in-law, hold the lease. The family still uses the site and a few of the old buildings.

Passagamoc Carry Camps

In the early 1900s two well-known area guides, George T. Graham and J.W. Cripps, built a set of sporting camps consisting of two cabins at the carrying place around Passamagamet Falls. The falls were then known as Passcomgomac and the "resort" was named Camp Pleasant. In 1904, Graham bought out Cripps, built several more cabins, and over the years became a very popular proprietor. The camps boasted of having a direct telephone line to Millinocket.

While Eugene Hall of Norcross was proprietor in the early 1920s, he advertised the camps in *In the Maine Woods*. Like other West Branch sporting camps, the steamboat transportation system on the lakes downriver from Ambajejus Falls brought guests to the camps. Guests could use a well-built outlying camp on Rainbow Lake for fishing those popular waters. Nothing is known of these camps after 1924.

Debsconeag Fish and Game Club (Debsconeag Outing Camps)

In 1899, Charles C. Garland organized the private Debsconeag Fish and Game Club, located on a high bluff on the north shore of First Debsconeag Lake. A group of prominent gentlemen from all over New England and New York City provided an initial $10,000 capital stock investment in support of the new club. Garland, whose brainchild it was, became treasurer and managing director. A graduate of the University of Maine, Garland had once headed west to enter the business world. However, when his health broke down, his physicians recommended that he return to Maine to pursue a healthier outdoor occupation. Shortly after returning to his native state, Garland leased land on First Debsconeag Lake, which he had visited as a student, and began to organize and promote his club.

Members of the club contributed at least $50 for one share. Although there were no dues at first, early literature suggests possibly imposing them later. After arranging the financing, Garland erected a number of sturdy cedar-log buildings and by the 1901 season was receiving guests. At first only a rather luxurious clubhouse accommodated members and their families; later individual cabins and maintenance buildings were added. The site,

150 feet above the lakeshore, offered spring beds, lovely views, great fishing, and two lakeshore beaches. Members always had first choice of accommodations, of course, and paid $1 per day with meals. If there were openings, non-members could stay for $2 per day.

Within a few years, the club established three outlying camps—one on Hurd Pond, only a mile or so away, and two on the West Branch near the mouth of Abol Stream. Later an additional outlying camp was built on Rainbow Lake, but it was soon sold to become the start of the separate Rainbow Lake Camps. In addition, Garland built a cabin he named "Ktaadn Camp" partway up the Abol Slide to accommodate guests wanting to climb Katahdin. Garland laced his promotional material with bold superlatives about climbing to the summit:

> Many persons who have climbed most of the high mountains of the world say that Ktaadn is not only the most interesting but that no finer and more extended view can be obtained from it than from any other mountain on this continent, if not in the world.[9]

An eager businessman, Garland set up a post office named "Debsconeag, Piscataquis County," which he promoted in ads. His "mail run" traveled by canoe and steamer between Norcross and the camps three times a week. Debsconeag Fish and Game Club was named an official United States Weather Bureau Station, a designation that probably required Garland to relay weather information over the crude telephone arrangement he had set up.

Within a few years, the camp operation had evolved from a private club to a public accommodation, though the original investors retained certain privileges. Around 1905, the camps, known as Debsconeag Outing Camps or Garland's Camps, operated as a public resort. Garland maintained a very high standard and produced a lengthy brochure for prospective guests who were "tired and worn out from business cares, recovering from pneumonia, having nervous prostration, bronchial or catarrhal [sic] troubles, insomnia, constipation, stomach troubles, hay fever (unknown at Debsconeag), pleurisy, or needing a change. . . ."[10] Garland offered healthy food, air of unprecedented healing quality, along with other extravagant, likely true, claims on behalf of his beloved camps. In 1910, the short Garland era ended. Herbert M. Howes of Millinocket acquired the lease and renamed the camps

Howes' Debsconeag Camps. Howes gave Debsconeag as his mailing address from May 1 to December 1 and advertised for at least three or four years. For whatever reasons, the lease passed into private hands.

Joe Francis Camps

The Joe Francis Camps sat on the north shore of the Debsconeag Deadwater below Debsconeag Falls. Joe Francis, a former governor of the Penobscot tribe and West Branch lumber camp and river drive boss, was a highly respected guide when he established the camps. He was one of the best storytellers in the region and could keep a party entertained for hours. The commodious camps may have existed as early as 1890 at the site of an old lumber camp near the foot of the falls. Perhaps it was the very lumber camp Joe Francis bossed. A 1901 promotional ad identifies the camps as "Debsconeag Camp" and Francis as the proprietor. However, the name quickly changed. Francis' son-in-law, Joe Dennis, had his own camp home nearby and probably helped run the business. There is no record of a lease in the files of the Great Northern Paper Company, but in those days company officials often had only informal arrangements with native peoples for such matters.

The camps made a convenient stop at the necessary carry around the falls. A 1905 account of a trip down the West Branch reveals that a party stopped for dinner at the camps and may have also stayed for the night. The camps appear on maps of the 1940s and early 1950s, but there is no indication that they were receiving guests that recently. Some remains of the camps are visible at the site, and there are those who still refer to the river near the camps as the Joe Francis Deadwater. It may well be that those camps were among the earliest of all the camps in the Katahdin region.

Katahdin View Camps (Pitman's Camps)

The Katahdin View Camps rested on a high bluff on the south bank of the West Branch, about a half-mile upriver of Debsconeag Falls. The location was ideal for drawing river travelers, bound for upriver sporting camps, who had carried around Debsconeag Falls and were ascending Pockwockamus Deadwater.

Information about the camps' founding is scant. However, in 1899, B.C. Harris held the lease. Around 1914, the Katahdin View Camps, named so because of the bluff's spectacular mountain view, were transferred to two new leasers—W.H. Davis, an earlier Camp Wellington leaseholder, and his

View of the West Branch of the Penobscot from the porches of Fred Pitman's Katahdin View Camps. Courtesy, Dexter Historical Society (Bert L. Call Collection).

son, both of Norcross. But by 1916, Fred Pitman, also of Norcross, was the camps' proprietor. Pitman, who had been a logger, a river man, and a guide in the West Branch country for some years, knew the area well. He wanted to settle down to make a living doing what he loved best.

In his promotions, Pitman arranged transportation to Katahdin View Camps from Ambajejus Lake, where the steamer ended its run at Camp Wellington. He established outlying camps for fishing at Foss-Knowlton Pond and First Debsconeag Lake. He also maintained a garage on the north side of the river (near where the road to the Baxter State Park's Togue Pond

Gate turns off the original river tote road). Pitman canoed from the camps to the garage, where he kept his boats and automobiles. The camps were known by several names across the years—Katahdin View Camps, Pitman's Camps, Pitman's Katahdin View Camps, and sometimes just "Pitman's."

Sadly, in 1934, a major forest fire south of the river destroyed the camps and put Pitman out of business. Instead of rebuilding, he accepted employment at the new Baxter State Park and was assigned to what is today Katahdin Stream Campground.* Today at the site of the old Katahdin View Camps one might find some evidence of old stoves and bottles from that early era, but very little is left, mute reminders of a special sporting camp destination.

WASSATAQUOIK VALLEY SPORTING CAMPS

In the Wassataquoik Stream watershed, several sporting camps were important to the history of the Katahdin region. In the mid-nineteenth century, logging infrastructure such as roads made it possible for more people to visit the region to climb Katahdin, fish the remote ponds, and hunt. However, the Wassataquoik Valley was never quite as accessible as the West Branch, and sporting camp development remained minimal.

Lang and Jones Camps

In 1874, Messrs. Lang and Jones (their first names are unknown) cut a trail from the lower Wassataquoik Valley to Katahdin Lake and the Great Basin. Known as the Lang and Jones Trail, it was the first trail to reach the Great Basin and the second to reach Katahdin. Between 1874 and 1879, Lang and Jones established their sporting camps on the southwest shore of Katahdin Lake, slightly west of the present Katahdin Lake Wilderness Camps. The two entrepreneurs were simply taking advantage of the time-honored tradition of accommodating the needs of those wanting a fairly comfortable place to stay on their way to Katahdin. The camps were not profitable and may have closed by the early 1880s.

---

* In its early days, this park campground was sometimes called "Pitman's Camps," a reference to the popular tenure of Fred Pitman and his wife.

Katahdin Lake Camps

The Katahdin Lake Camps sat on the south shore of Katahdin Lake. Out-doorspeople heading to Katahdin from the Wassataquoik Stream valley in the 1840s found the easiest and most scenic approach was by way of Katahdin Lake and the Southeast Spur (Keep Ridge). The spectacular views of the mountain from the lake's southeastern shore made the route most rewarding. Except for those who occasionally ventured up the Wassataquoik to climb the mountain from the Russell Pond side, this was the preferred route for most of the second half of the century.

In the late 1880s, John F. Cushman and Madison M. Tracy established the Katahdin Lake Camps just east of the Lang and Jones Camps. At first they used the old 1887 Appalachian Trail to reach the northern head of the lake and brought guests the rest of the way across the lake to the camps by boat. Cushman and Tracy spent a week carrying an iron cook stove, a barrel of flour, and canoes into the camps. Just a few years later Tracy sold out to Cushman, and the camps became known as Cushman's Sporting Camps, Cushman's Camps, and sometimes Katahdin View Camps. In those early years, Cushman tried to establish the camps as a prime location for hunting moose, bear, and caribou.

Cushman ran a simple yet very successful operation for almost 25 years. He was well known in the region and in Eastern Seaboard cities, where so many of his guests lived. However, the 1918 decision by Maine's legislature to ban moose hunting dealt a very serious blow to his business. Cushman's disappointment over the action and his belief that fishing alone was not enough of a draw prompted him to sell the camps to a man named Spear in 1919. Spear, who had been one of Cushman's faithful "sports," did not reopen the camps immediately, and the disrepair and deterioration that had set in during the late Cushman period continued. The account of the famous 1920 trip to Katahdin by a party that included State Senate President Percival P. Baxter reported that the camps were not in use that season. However, people were camping at the site on their way to Katahdin. In the fall of 1920 Spear began to repair the facilities. In a 1921 speech before the state legislature it was noted that the camps had been repaired and enlarged to accommodate sportspeople who wished to visit the region's wonders.

Ralph E. Dorr is listed as proprietor from 1922 to 1925, but it is possible that Dorr only managed the camps for Spear. Dorr was a well-respected guide in the area, later much in demand as a guide out of Russell Pond Camps. He was also quite a storyteller, whose stories improved each year. He took great delight recounting the year that beavers built a dam and flooded out some of his trap lines near his old cabin. He often had to go in and break out the dam to lower the water level. On one such occasion he discovered that the beavers had installed the cabin's stovepipe at the dam, using the damper to control the water flow. The same story has been attributed to several others in the region; it may have been one of those generic yarns that made the rounds of the sporting camps.

In 1925, perhaps led by Spear himself, the camps became the privately owned Katahdin Lake Club. The club continued serving the public when not being used by its owners. Oliver R. "Bud" Cobb from Shinn Pond in the Patten area managed the new enterprise. The lease was transferred to a group of men from New York to be run as a private fishing lodge, an arrangement already well established in the Adirondack region. The group arranged for exclusive fishing rights to a surrounding 12,000 acres, later known as the Katahdin Lake Hunting Region. This acreage was actually one-half of an entire township as laid out by the surveyors a hundred or so years earlier. Many later old maps show the township divided in half, although there are no known references to the particular arrangements that were made with the Katahdin Lake Club.* Club rates were $5 per person, meals included. With the owners' permission, Cobb opened the camps to the public during the hunting season.

By 1931, the idea of an exclusive club had run its course. Due to the Great Depression, such a venture was no longer economically feasible. That year, perhaps because of back wages owed to him during the Depression, Cobb acquired the lease. Cobb immediately reopened the camps to the public after seven years as a private club. With his wife Della as the cook, he remained the proprietor for the next 32 years. The Cobbs substantially rebuilt and modernized the camps, often employing the help of out-of-work loggers. The outhouses were so nice that people referred to them as "chateaux." During Cobb's ownership, the camps became known as Cobb's Katahdin Lake Camps or simply Katahdin Lake Camps. Cobb brought his "sports" to the camps from the end of the Sandy Stream Tote Road by buckboard. He

---

* Timber companies often welcomed the sporting camp folk, allowing such a lease arrangement in exchange for having people protect the property from any lumbering encroachment by an abutting landowner. It was most likely a verbal arrangement only.

maintained an old logging-era, single-wire telephone line from Avalanche Field so people could request the buckboard service. In the 1940s, the Cobbs used a windmill to recharge their radio batteries. Cobb had strict fishing rules, allowing only fly-fishing. He sometimes stocked Twin Ponds up toward Turner Mountain with trout fingerlings taken out of Katahdin Lake.

A number of well-known artists were attracted to Katahdin Lake, some staying at the camps. Frederic E. Church first visited Katahdin Lake in 1855 before any camps had been built. Marsden Hartley stayed at the camps and painted there in 1939. James Fitzgerald came every year in the 1950s and 1960s, mostly in the fall, and even visited during winter in the late 1960s.

Bud Cobb died in 1963, and Della tried valiantly to make the camps available to old friends and guests, but the task proved too difficult. In 1965, she ended a 40-year labor of love and transferred the lease to Clarence Hilliard, whose wife Glenda became the cook. Hilliard built a tower with an observation platform at the far end of the camp yard so guests would have a better view of the mountain. Most of the guests arrived by horses and donkeys, many flew in, and a few hiked in on their own. The Hilliards gave up their lease five years later when Glenda took ill.

In 1970, Embert Stevens acquired the lease. His wife Josephine took on the traditional role of cook. Sadly, after Embert broke his back from being thrown by a horse, it became more and more difficult for the Stevenses to continue running the camps. Because the Stevenses' daughter, Suzan Cooper, and her husband, Al, had helped operate the camps for several years, the lease was formally transferred to them between 1975 and 1976. They continued to operate under the name Katahdin Lake Wilderness Camps.

The Coopers have tried to faithfully maintain the remoteness of the camps. Even today one can drive no nearer than three and a half miles to the camps. From Avalanche Field on Roaring Brook Road, hikers can arrive by packhorse; guests also still arrive by plane. This beautiful lake, once a bustling center of logging and hiking activity, has now quietly returned to its pristine state. According to Al Cooper, without the sporting camp to watch over and protect it, the lake would not retain its remote and unmarred character. Because it lies outside Baxter State Park's protective boundary, Katahdin Lake is more vulnerable to non-wilderness commercial use. Though still managed by the Coopers, the lease was sold in 2005 to Charles FitzGerald, who is equally committed to preserving the charm of this special place.

SANDY STREAM SPORTING CAMPS

The Sandy Stream watershed flows off the dramatic east side of Katahdin from Basin Ponds, Sandy Stream Pond, and Upper and Lower Togue Ponds. This major system flows into Millinocket Lake, by Millinocket Stream, and into the Penobscot West Branch. The Sandy Stream region was the scene of several large logging operations in the late nineteenth and early twentieth centuries and gave rise to the Togue Pond Camps and Millinocket Lake Camps.

Togue Pond Camps

What are today Upper and Lower Togue Ponds were originally one pond, named Katahdin Pond, with a narrow point of land in the middle jutting from one shore almost to the other. In the 1920s, when the Great Northern Paper Company extended a tote road from Millinocket toward the base of Katahdin, the builders laid the road across the pond by filling in the narrow passage and installing a culvert under the new road to accommodate the natural flow of water from both sides. The road eventually reached to Nesowadnehunk Field and became known as the Greenville-Millinocket Road. It would play a major role in the history of the Katahdin region.

Attracted to the striking view of Katahdin from Upper Togue's eastern shore and the direct access to Millinocket, W.H. St. John and Henry N. Walls of Millinocket saw an opportunity to provide accommodations near the mountain and the area's large number of smaller ponds. Their first ads stressed how easy it was to reach their sporting camp, only eighteen miles from Millinocket by automobile, a special bragging point not yet enjoyed by other camps in the region. Almost immediately after building the camps in 1924, St. John and Walls re-cleared the old trail up to the Keep Ridge (known earlier as Keep Path) and named it the St. John Trail. The trail branched off from the Sandy Stream Tote Road near Windey Pitch. They erected a lean-to at the ancient birch grove discovered years before by Rev. Marcus Keep at the foot of the avalanche. The men boasted that they not only had their own trail to the summit, but also the shortest. St. John and Walls developed a network of trails linking Abol Pond, Round Pond, Oak Hill, Trout Pond, Tea Pond, and others. Their trails stretched as far as Abol Stream and Pockwockamus and made twenty ponds within easy walking distance. These trails were the predecessors of the inter-pond trail network in that area today.

At some point St. John bought out Walls but operated the camps alone for only a year or two. In 1928 the lease was transferred to Reginald H. and Ina Crawford, proprietors for the next 14 years. The Crawfords offered all the amenities usually associated with sporting camps of that era. They maintained a telephone service and took trips into town several times a week. The base cost was then $28 per week, meals included. During the 1934 season, Crawford leased from the Great Northern Paper Company and managed several outlying camps—one at Basin Ponds for climbers on their way to Chimney Pond, one above Nesowadnehunk Falls known as Crawford's Camp, and one on Katahdin Stream, still in private use.

It is likely that the decline in guests caused by the onset of World War II discouraged Crawford from continuing the camps. In 1949, the lease transferred from Crawford to two New York ladies, Dr. Mildred Van Riper and Marjorie Winfield. Although the timing was less than ideal, the ladies had great dreams for the camps. They wanted to get away from the city and make their livelihood in the wilderness. Though they had little experience, their determined work ethic earned them the grudging respect of the locals. The ladies employed guides in the summer but did most of the hard work of management themselves. By 1952, their interest had waned, and the lease was transferred again, this time to Jerome Smart and Bernard Rush.

Smart and Rush also found the going very tough, and in 1953 the lease went to Joe and Clara Bartlett. Joe loved the woods and the camps dearly. Though Clara, a teacher in Millinocket, was not very involved with the camp operation, she wrote a book of poems about some of her experiences at Togue Pond. The Bartletts established an extension campsite at Pine Point on Upper Togue for the possible overflow of guests. The couple survived the burning of the main lodge and one cabin and operated the camps for a total of 22 years.

Around 1966, Joe Van Dyne acquired the lease but never opened the camps because of a heart attack. The lease passed through a number of hands until it reached Laurant "Lonnie" Pingree and his brother. The brothers had great expectations and extensively modernized and rebuilt the camps. However, their tenure was short-lived. Joe Bartlett reacquired the lease in the late 1960s, but the camps never regained their former luster and were finally sold to Baxter State Park in 1982. The park later razed the rapidly deteriorating lodge and cabins. Today the park's Visitors Center sits at the edge of the property, and the site is being restored and re-vegetated.

Millinocket Lake Camps

Irving O. Hunt and his brother Lyman built some rough camps on Millinocket Lake before they became interested in the Nesowadnehunk Stream region. Whether or not their old camps were at the same site as the present camps on Millinocket Lake we do not know.

The Millinocket Lake Camps, known today as Big Moose Inn, are located on a narrow spit of land separating Ambajejus Lake and Millinocket Lake. Before a dam controlled Ambajejus' water level, it was possible to pole up the short stream from Millinocket Lake into Ambajejus.

Fred Spencer built the camps, originally named Camp Eureka, in 1899 or 1900 and ran them with his brother. With the founding of Millinocket only a few years earlier and lumbering roads nearing Katahdin, the two lakes became more easily accessible. Camp Eureka was advertised as the only camp reachable by both boat (from Norcross) and road (from Millinocket). In 1905, the rate was $1.50 per day, meals included. Spencer also claimed the lakes had no flies or mosquitoes during spring and summer—a phenomenon caused by the way winds blow across the lakes, which makes it difficult for insects to gain a foothold.

The camps' name changed to Camp Spencer and later to Spencer's Camps.* Around 1929 the lease was transferred to Elmer Woodworth, who lived with his wife on a nearby island while they operated the camps. Elmer, a well-known guide, trapped over the winter, and his wife served as the camp cook. The couple soon renamed the camps Millinocket Lake Camps and Trading Post. They also maintained an outlying camp on Sandy Stream for their guests. In 1941, a major fire broke out in the area. The Woodworths saved the camps by wetting them down, but lost their island home when a stray spark jumped the cove. There is some evidence that, for a short time, a gentleman named Johnny Given either held the lease or managed the camps for the Woodworths. Except for that brief change the Woodworths operated the camps for many years until they passed the lease on to their son Ray, who ran them with his wife Muriel.

In 1977, the lease was transferred to Bob and Frederica ("Teddy") Boynton, who in 1981 sold the trading post to Erwin and Maureen Bacon. The Boyntons retained the sporting camp operation and later added a public

---

* Though the camps are gone, the nearby Ambajejus Lake inlet is still known as Spencer Cove.

restaurant. Teddy renamed the camps Big Moose Inn. Bob and his son Bruce made many renovations to the camps, while Teddy decorated and furnished them. The Boynton family has remained involved in the success of the inn and restaurant. After Teddy's death in 1991, management passed to Bruce and his sister Laurie, but Bob and other family members are still very involved. The dam separates the flowages of the two lakes. Millinocket Lake is about eight feet above its original level, and Ambajejus is now some 21 feet above its original level. Today several West Branch rafting companies make the inn their seasonal center of operations.

Lunksoos Camps

Around 1832, Hiram Dacey settled the site of today's Lunksoos Camps when he built a farmhouse on the bank of the Penobscot's East Branch, just one mile upriver from the mouth of Wassataquoik Stream and two miles upriver from William Hunt's farm, established about the same time. Legend has it that Dacey built his log house without using a single iron nail. Sensing opportunity, Dacey came to the region from the Skowhegan area to provide accommodation and supplies for loggers, woodsmen, and later for hikers entering the Wassataquoik Valley to climb Katahdin. In addition to Hunt's ford, Dacey operated a ferry service just below his farm to transport loggers and hikers across the river.

In the late 1870s, the clearing and buildings began to deteriorate with disuse. In 1880, C.R. Patterson, who had owned and operated the Hunt Farm's inn, bought the old Dacey Farm and built a new house for guests, named the Patterson House. Business boomed until 1891, when Fred W. Ayer and Luther B. Rogers leased the facility and made it the headquarters for their lumber operation up the valley. The two continued to operate Patterson House as a public facility but renamed it the East Branch House. They regularly met . the morning train at the Stacyville railroad station and brought the arriving guests into the camps by buckboard. Ayer and Rogers continued to ferry guests across the river aboard a scow attached to a steel cable between trees at both banks. The ferry operated at least until the late 1920s. A portion of the steel cable still encircles an old tree on the east bank. In 1895, Rogers and his son tore down Dacey's original farmhouse and erected an elaborate log sporting camp, which they named Lunksoos Camp (sometimes spelled and always pronounced as "Lunkasoo"). The name refers to a wild beast similar to the panther that terrorized the early native peoples.

In 1898, George C. Witherle stayed at Lunksoos Camps during one of his explorations of the Katahdin region. In 1902, proprietor Edwin Rogers developed and promoted a saddle horse trail to the Great Basin from the East Branch and named it Rogers Trail. He boasted that it was the only saddle trail to Katahdin. In 1903, artist George C. Hallowell found refuge at Lunksoos after narrowly escaping the great fire that swept through the Wassataquoik valley that year. By 1918, the Rogers family began promoting the Lunksoos Trail, which ran from the camps to the Great Basin.

In 1920, Edward B. Draper, another lumber operation owner, owned the lease. That August, the camps welcomed a party of distinguished state politicians and officials, among them Percival P. Baxter. The party was beginning its trip into the Great Basin and to Katahdin. The trip was Baxter's first ascent of the mountain and was destined to be one of the major influences that led him to embark on his "magnificent obsession"—acquiring Katahdin and the region surrounding it for the people of Maine. Arthur Staples described the group's arrival at Lunksoos Camps:

> I wander on and watch the tints of brilliant light change to mauve and gold and jade. This is going to Lunkasoo! Lovely name. The partridges drum up from the thicket or scurry thru the trees. The moments fly. The feet, unaccustomed to walking, begin to tire but are buoyant yet. The hours pass away and lo, as the hour strikes six in Patten we are in a clearing, and the East Branch of the Penobscot rolls away at our feet, and we are in a valley on a hillside and there is a fair domain, with mountains stretching far away to the eye, and the river curving to the hills that come down to meet them.
>
> On the edge of the hill sit Draper camps. . . . At one side is the trim little ivy-covered camp of the care-taker, Mike O'Leary, an original woodsman with a brogue that is enriched by frequent applications of the Blarney-stone and with stories of the woods until you can't sleep. Mike and his dog rush out to meet us. . . .
>
> That night we sat on the wide veranda after supper and looked at the mountains. Mike O'Leary told his stories of Ezra Robar and his dog "Kelly," a mighty man of that country! And Ed Parker matched him fish or man, and Burt Howe came across with yarns that savored of the days of the drive and that are passing all too soon. It was a wonderful night, warm and starlit. Afar hooted an owl. Mike's dear and loving dog nestled in Percy Baxter's arms. We brought our mattresses down to the floor of the camp and lay there. I

could not sleep. The surroundings were weird: The late cigars and pipes of the teamsters glowed on the veranda. The morrow held out too many expectations. Finally I dropped into slumber.[11]

The next morning, after Mrs. O'Leary served the group a sumptuous breakfast, Mike transported the party across the river in bateaux and they were on their way.

Not long after this significant moment in Lunksoos' history, Harry P. Rodgerson became the proprietor. Wanting to capitalize on the sweet waters of that spring, he boasted in promotional ads, "You should drink from our boiling spring. It will prolong your life." He continued to call the camps "Lunkasoo," but it was not long before the traditional spelling prevailed.

In the late 1930s, Nelson McMoarn held the lease, which remained in the McMoarn family until the mid-1950s. It was McMoarn who in 1939 spotted and rescued the emaciated, ghost-like figure of Donn Fendler on the bank of the river opposite the camps. Fendler had been lost on Katahdin and had wandered for nine days down the valley of the Wassataquoik.

The lease finally passed to new owners in the mid-1950s. They, in turn, burned the old camp buildings to make way for new construction. Since then, there has been a succession of owners. The camps are still reachable by rough logging roads and continue to operate for the benefit of fishermen, hunters, canoeists, and others seeking the wilderness experience of the traditional sporting camps.

BY THE 1940S AND 1950S, ONLY A FEW SPORTING CAMPS REMAINED in private hands—Big Moose Inn, Katahdin Lake Wilderness Camps, and Lunksoos Camps. The others have either closed or have been incorporated into Baxter State Park and operate quite differently from their predecessors. Camp Phoenix, now operated by a private association, is an exception to that rule.

What brought the change? Certainly the coming of the automobile had a profound influence. The onset of World War II interrupted many traditional patterns of vacation and recreation, and people never returned to past practices in the same numbers as before. When Baxter State Park took over some of the camps and converted them to overnight campsites, it discouraged certain sportspersons from coming into the region. The changing preferences for outdoor recreation enthusiasts may have also taken its toll.

Whatever the cause of the sporting camp decline, it is enriching to look back on the unique way of life that the camps offered, to meet the people who operated them, and to remember those who came to stay as guests in the shadow of Katahdin.*

---

* Today, some sporting camps operate in areas adjacent to Baxter State Park, and a stay at one of them will evoke the rustic days when city dwellers came as far as Katahdin to live as out-doorspeople, if only for a week or month. South of the immediate Katahdin region, in the 100-Mile Wilderness, the Appalachian Mountain Club owns and runs Little Lyford Pond Camps, originally established in 1872, and offers traditional sporting camp hospitality for hikers, skiers, anglers, and families. For more information, go to www.outdoors.org/lodging.

PART III

Footpaths and Campsites

THE SOUTH AND EAST SIDES

From the Penobscot Branches to the Summit

> There is an old saying in the Middle East: with a trail, the best way to keep it
> alive is to walk on it, because every time you walk on it, you create it again.
> —Bruce Feiler, *Walking the Bible*[1]

THE LURE OF THE WALKING TRAIL IS UNIVERSAL. SOME MAY WISH
to follow pathways of religious pilgrimage, others the trails to mountain
heights. Some follow the paths linking villages; others seek the ridgelines
of vast mountain ranges. Some may follow ancient native trails, game trails,
trails of history, or trails leading to the discovery of one's cultural heritage.
Some follow the paths of roads long abandoned, trails to natural wonders,
or a footpath alongside a lovely watercourse.

At the very core of the Katahdin experience are the foot trails that through
the years have enabled the hiker to discover and appreciate the treasures the
mountain offers. While a hiking trail's purpose is to allow the hiker to get
from one place to another, the reward is not always reaching the destination—it can be in the journey itself.

Some of Katahdin's trails were built in one deliberate effort; others
evolved over time. Some are in places never before accessible; others follow
older trails used by those who lived before the visitor arrived. Each trail has
its distinctive purpose and character and spirit. There are trails to the summit of Katahdin, to remarkable geological features, to noteworthy bodies of
water, to places historically and culturally significant, to neighboring and
outlying mountains, to awe-inspiring streams, waterfalls, and rivers. Each

of these trails is unique. Each has an interesting story to tell. Each is a joy to walk.

TRAIL MAINTENANCE

Katahdin's trails have been maintained and cared for in a variety of ways across the years. In the early days, interested individuals as well as members of the Appalachian Mountain Club (AMC) managed the trail system. The relatively new Baxter State Park signed an agreement in 1941 with the AMC to maintain 185 miles of trail at and around Katahdin itself. That agreement remained intact until the park staff assumed responsibility for trail maintenance in the 1950s.

In the early years of Baxter State Park's existence, the campground rangers maintained the trails and even built many of the new trails. Sometimes the trails were not well cared for because of lumbering activity or the lack of personnel; the latter was especially true during World War II. Even as late as 1950, the Maine Appalachian Trail Club guidebook warned hikers that trails near Katahdin not maintained by the AMC were inconsistently cared for and to use them with caution. As management of the park matured, it fielded a trail crew, well trained and supervised, that today provides a high standard of basic trail maintenance and has the means to deal with major trail erosion problems. The crew's specialized effort, along with that of volunteers, allows hikers to make their journey safely, in proper conditions that protect the surrounding land.

WEST BRANCH TRAIL HISTORIES

Although the first formally constructed and marked trail, the Keep Path, was on the Penobscot East Branch side of the mountain, the earliest explorers and adventurers climbed Katahdin from the south. The popularity of the south side was due to the location of the West Branch of the Penobscot River, which flows southeasterly near the base of Katahdin. The river was a major highway for Native Americans and later for explorers, scientists, and recreational visitors.

For a time in the mid-eighteenth century, the rough, undeveloped south side trails languished as the Aroostook and Military Roads made the east side more accessible. In the century's waning days, the building of the

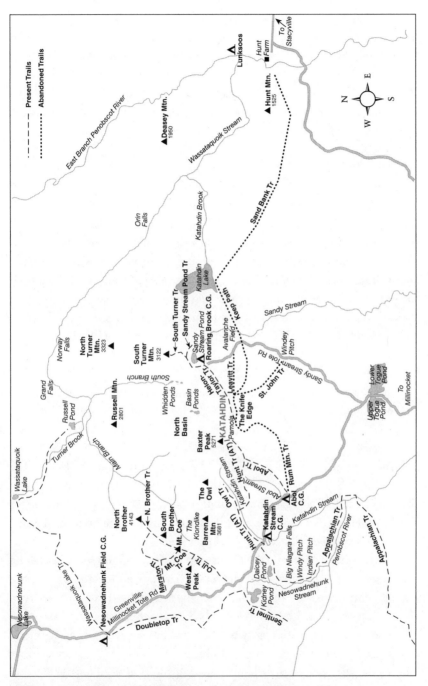

Trails and campsites on Katahdin's south and east sides.

Bangor and Aroostook Railroad to Norcross and Millinocket allowed easier access to both the south and east sides. This access stimulated the creation of sporting camps along the West Branch and on the ponds and streams that flowed into it. New trails were built to the mountain. In the 1920s and 1930s the Great Northern Paper Company built major tote roads from Togue Pond and along the river at the very base of the mountain, making access to trails easier still.

Abol Trail

Although not a formally marked trail until the twentieth century, the Abol Trail, which, in its early days, ascended Abol Stream from the West Branch and then the Abol Slide to Katahdin's Tableland, was the easiest way to reach the summit. Depending on one's point of view, that is still true. Most of the early explorers and climbers approached the Abol Deadwater along the West Branch and camped at the ancient Native American site at the mouth of Abol Stream, where they began their climb. From that site a stunning view of the Katahdin massif caught their attention and provided sleepless anticipation the night before their ascent began. Fannie Hardy Eckstorm described the view from Abol as:

> That glorious revelation of Katahdin which bursts upon you above Abol, that marvelous picture of the giant towering in majestic isolation, with its white slide ascending like a ladder to the heavens.[2]

The traveler did not always follow the same footpath to the base of the avalanche, but the goal was always the Abol Slide. From the time the avalanche opened a giant gash on Katahdin's flank in 1816, it was a prominent landmark. It was known at first as the South Slide or the Southwest Slide, but soon the designation "Abol Slide" prevailed.

Charles Turner Jr. made the first ascent of Katahdin in 1804, likely along the Southwest Spur (now the Hunt Trail). There is no record of any other ascents until 1819, a full three years after the avalanche. That year a party of British surveyors, led by Colin Campbell, made the first known ascent of the Abol Slide. Campbell's party built a crude hut shelter on a terrace along the slide. The hut was discovered and used the very next year by another surveying party and may well have been the site later used for the location of a fire warden's cabin.

Throughout the nineteenth century, most of Katahdin's visitors hiked the slide from the West Branch side. They took various routes from the river to the slide's foot, but most followed the slide for the rest of the way. Thoreau, on his celebrated climb of 1846, camped at the mouth of Abol Stream like so many others but then bypassed the slide on his route to the mountain. He did not reach the summit but experienced the great cliffs and precipitous rock walls of the West Branch side's upper portion. Thoreau could have climbed to the summit if he had followed the well-worn paths at the lower elevations.

J.W. and Joseph Sewall's 1881 survey map of Old Town identified a path along Abol Stream to the slide and summit as "Ktaadn Path." That name appears on other early maps, but when the trail was formally cut later it was given the name Abol Trail. In August 1889, when Eckstorm and her father canoed down the West Branch and climbed Katahdin via the slide, she reported finding a small crude sign near the mouth of Abol Stream with "Path to Katahdin 4 mi." carved on it.

By 1882 a rough lean-to known as Camp Comfort sat on the east side of the Abol Slide. In 1901, George C. Witherle, wishing to camp at the site, found it occupied and instead decided to set up his camp at the slide's base. When he later discovered that the occupants had departed, Witherle and his party collected their belongings and equipment, climbed back up the slide, and settled into Camp Comfort for the night. While the lean-to's exact location is unknown, it probably occupied the same terrace used earlier by the 1819 Campbell party and later by the fire warden. Witherle, in his travels in 1899, actually refers to a "Green Island," a patch of green grass beside the avalanche. He himself built a slightly more substantial lean-to shelter at the foot of the slide. This became the camping site of choice for Witherle during his visits in 1883, 1899, and 1901, but others used the same site before and following the Witherle years.

In 1901 or 1902, Clinton C. Garland built Ktaadn Camp (later also referred to as the Garland Camp) on the west side of the slide, about 300 feet off the trail at an elevation of 2,300 feet, not far from the foot of the slide. Garland was manager of Debsconeag Outing Camps, established in 1900 on First Debsconeag Lake by a group of investors. Ktaadn Camp could accommodate eight persons and was used by "sports" whom Garland led from the main camps up the West Branch and Abol Stream to the slide and the camp.

Around 1912, the Maine Forest Service established a forest fire lookout on Katahdin. Frank Sewall was the watchman for this effort and was expected to construct his own housing on the mountain. In 1913 he built a log cabin on the terrace that was the site of the earlier crude lean-tos near 3,000 feet. At age 67 Sewall carried everything up to the site by hand, including two bedsprings and a sheet iron cook-stove. The cabin was a relatively spacious eighteen-by-sixteen-foot room made of peeled spruce logs, with white cedar splits for the roof and hemlock planks for the floor. All of this he cut and hauled from the woods below the foot of the slide. A wide roof overhang in the front of the cabin afforded protection from the wind and the rain. Full fire observation likely began in early 1914.

There never was a summit tower, but near the cabin on the slide itself, a simple wooden, probably roofless, platform gave Sewall an unobstructed view of the entire country from the southeast to the southwest. In his story of a 1924 Katahdin climb, Walter Pritchard Eaton reported that after a hearty dinner at the Sewall site:

> We went out on Frank Sewall's observation platform to look down on the wilderness under the moon, and to look up the white scar of the slide above us till it met the pinnacle rocks, which seemed phosphorescent in the moonlight. It was a surprisingly warm and still night for late September, so instead of sleeping in the cabin I rolled up in my blanket on a bed of boughs some recent camper had made near by. But at two o'clock I woke chilled, and rose to stir up my fire. Once up, I felt curiously wide awake, and went out on the lookout. There was a slight murmur of wind along the towering mountainside, and no other sound in all the world. A white, silvered mist was forming over the lakes far below me, like streaks of pale snow. The moon rode high above the forest, and old Orion, a stranger since last winter, was striding up the sky. I felt a lonely atom in an immensity of wilderness.[3]

Every week Sewall made his way down the recently constructed and still very rough Sourdnahunk-Millinocket Tote Road to Millinocket for kerosene, food, and other supplies. The fire lookout effort ceased at the end of the 1919 season, after only seven years. Sewall, then 73, retired, and the slide returned to its formerly uninhabited state. The lookout station was simply too high for convenient access, and the view was too often obscured by clouds, mists, and rain.

While Sewall was on active duty he welcomed hikers and climbers to "Sewall's Camp" or the "Firewarden's Camp" to stay in the cabin or to tent

Fire Warden Frank Sewall in front of the cabin he built in 1913 for the Maine Forest Service a short distance from the Abol Slide near the 3,000 foot level. Courtesy, Dexter Historical Society (Bert L. Call Callection).

on the terrace. Visitors continued to use the cabin after the Forest Service abandoned it. During the Eaton climb of Katahdin in 1924, the party swapped stories around a campfire and reveled in the experience of climbing Katahdin. Their guide, in a reminiscent mood, told the group that he had once given Katahdin away:

"I give it to a woman from Buffalo," he said. "I was taking her down the West Branch, and when we come opposite Pitman's [a sporting camp along the river] it was one of those nice, clear days when it [Katahdin] stood up there big and handsome, and she says: 'My goodness, I never seen nothing so beautiful; I wish I had it in my back yard at home!' I was feeling sort of generous that morning, so I said: 'Lady, take it right along. It's the biggest pile o' rocks we got in Maine, but if you want it you can have it. We boys'll get together this fall and pile up another one.'"

He poked his pipe. "She's been kinder dilatory about takin' it," he added.[4]

Walter Leavitt* reported finding the cabin greatly deteriorated in 1934.[5] Although the Civilian Conservation Corps repaired it in 1935, the cabin continued to deteriorate and was finally abandoned when use of the Abol Trail was suspended in the mid- to late-1930s due to large-scale lumber operations. The CCC crew ironically gave the Abol Trail its first blue blazes, just before the trail closed in 1934. By 1938, a guidebook reported that the Sewall cabin was no longer available and extensive lumbering had rendered the Abol Slide route to the mountain unusable. A 1942 guidebook reported the route abandoned and the Sewall cabin torn down; it was the end of a remarkable era on the West Branch side of Katahdin.

After years of neglect, a crew from the AMC reopened the Abol Trail around 1949. Closed in 1963 because of serious fire danger from slash left by a major storm,** the trail deteriorated once again. In 1965, it was reopened again. The present trail does not begin at the Abol Stream mouth, but follows portions of the path used by the early explorers and adventurers. At the top of the famous slide, the trail climbs through huge boulders and finally gains the Tableland. After crossing that expanse for a quarter-mile, it joins the Hunt Trail (the Appalachian Trail) at Thoreau Spring. This undependable

* Author of the remarkable book *Katahdin Skylines*, which describes Katahdin's pre-World War II trails.
** This is the same storm that claimed the life of ranger Ralph Heath during his attempt to rescue a woman who had fallen off the Knife Edge.

source of water was at one time known as Governor's Spring, so named in honor of Governor Ralph Owen Brewster who visited it in 1925. In 1933, Governor Baxter renamed it to honor Thoreau.

Today the Abol Trail is one of the popular climbs in Baxter State Park, providing, with the Hunt Trail, a dramatic circuit trail and the most direct access to Katahdin's Tableland and summit. Its fascinating history adds much to the climbing experience. The scree and granite sand still slide down the avalanche course toward the river, making the trail a challenge for hikers.

Rum Mountain Trail
South of Katahdin's South Peak is Rum Mountain, a small, gently rounded wooded peak. The nearly mile-high Katahdin massif so dwarfs the peak that one hardly notices it at 3,361 feet. In 1962, the Intercollegiate Outing Club Association, representing outing clubs from many New England colleges, proposed building a trail from Baxter State Park's four-year-old Abol Campground, across Rum Mountain and up Katahdin's south flank, to South Peak. With the proposal accepted, Gardner Perry III, the association's leader, and ranger Rodney Sargent began laying out the trail. Work began in the summer of 1963, but the same devastating storm that closed down the Abol Trail that fall delayed the effort. The association and the rangers completed the work in 1966. By 1967, the trail was placed on the park's official list of trails. Unfortunately, frequent blowdowns below treeline and creeping rock above made maintenance almost impossible. The trail was finally abandoned and its use discouraged. Although the AMC's 1968 *Maine Mountain Guide* recommended the trail without reservation, the 1971 edition specifically discouraged taking the trail.*

There are some who claim that Thoreau may have climbed to Katahdin's South Peak by this general route. Though he may have passed near this route early his first day, it is more likely he eventually veered farther west.

---

* In 1967 I had the good fortune to climb this route. I remember to this day passing areas of blowdown through which the trail had been cut; the scrubby col between Rum Mountain and Katahdin's boulders; the sight of the bold precipitous south flank of Katahdin; and the exhilarating climb up the abrupt ridge to South Peak where the trail joined the Knife Edge. It was a spectacular trail experience and made a rewarding circuit climb with the Abol and Hunt Trails. The first 0.8 mile is still in use as the trail from Abol Campground to Little Abol Falls.

Hunt Trail (Appalachian Trail)

The heart and soul of the Hunt Trail is at its beginning, the Katahdin Stream Campground field. In the early 1930s four shelters were built where the Hunt Trail crossed the Sourdnahunk-Millinocket Tote Road, thus establishing Baxter State Park's Katahdin Stream Campground (then named Baxter Field). The Hunt Trail was relocated to the west side of Katahdin Stream because of lumber activity. Here, as one gazes up to see Katahdin in all its glory, one can follow the location of the trail clear to the Tableland. That view has inspired Appalachian Trail thru-hikers and day hikers for generations, ever since Irving Hunt's vision became reality in 1900.

A professor of geology at Harvard and frequent explorer of the Katahdin area, Charles E. Hamlin, was likely the first to suggest building a trail up the Southwest Spur to the Tableland. Inspired by his own 1869 ascent of the spur, he wrote in 1881:

> The slopes of the spur are less abrupt than those of the slide, and would therefore be easier of ascent were it not for a belt of spruce scrub, which at its highest part becomes impenetrable, and can be passed only by walking upon the tops of the interlacing shrubs. If a path were cut for a short distance through this troublesome growth, travel would no doubt be largely deflected to it, though the Southwest Slide should be climbed by the tourist at least once, as being one of the grandest features of the mountain.[6]

An 1881 map by the J.W. and Joseph Sewall Company in Old Town shows a trail labeled "Proposed Path to Katahdin" along Katahdin Stream and up the spur. Until that time, all who visited Katahdin from the West Branch side had followed Abol Stream to the Abol Slide and on to the Tableland. An alternate route was unnecessary because the slide route offered the most direct access to the higher elevations.

It is likely that the Southwest Spur was Charles Turner Jr.'s route as he made the first recorded ascent of the mountain in 1804. Through most of the nineteenth century, the Abol Slide was the preferred route for those visiting the mountain. That is, until Irving Hunt came along and entertained other ideas. When Hunt built the trail in 1900, he and his brother Lyman were the proprietors of the newly established (1899) Kidney Pond Camps. In a 1936 interview, Hunt described his motivation for and intense effort in building what was then being called "Hunt's Trail":

I built that trail in 1900 . . . partly because some of my campers wanted to climb Katahdin and it was pretty hard to take them up without any trail; and partly because I thought a trail was needed on the west side of the mountain. As I saw it, this was the easiest side to climb, and I believed that a good many people would prefer to climb it from this side if they had a trail. . . .

. . . I made the trail all alone, without anyone's help—not even a boy's. It took me about a year. . . . I had to do quite a little survey work before I found what suited me, for I was looking for an easy trail to the peak and you know it isn't very easy to get a trail thru such a rough country. Then it had to be cleared out and the roughest places fixed up. I understand the Appalachian Trail makers have fixed it up some more and built camps at Baxter Field [Katahdin Stream Campground].[7]

Hunt's Trail began at his own Kidney Pond Camps, skirted Daicey Pond and York's sporting camps, passed between Elbow and Grassy Ponds, and crossed overland to Katahdin Stream. There the trail crossed to the east side of the stream and began ascending the mountain by Katahdin Falls to the Southwest Spur. Although there have been a number of minor relocations due mostly to lumbering activity, the present-day Hunt Trail closely follows the original route. Hunt first advertised his new trail in a 1902 sporting camp ad and promoted it for a number of years.

In 1906, Hunt added a new twist by providing burros to carry supplies for guests on overnight trips to Katahdin's summit. He quickly dropped the idea because of the difficulty in carrying out such a bold plan above treeline and did not advertise the scheme again. However, Hunt was a creative and versatile entrepreneur and quickly devised another plan to accommodate his guests on their climb. He established a canvas tent shelter site near what is now called O Joy Brook, not far below treeline. His Kidney Pond guests tramped to and spent the night at the campsite on the first day. On the following day they climbed to the summit, spent a second night at the campsite, and returned to Kidney Pond on the third day. Hunt called the site his Katahdin Camp, and the idea proved enormously popular. By 1913 it was referred to as a lean-to and later as Hunt's Shelter but appears to have remained a tenting experience. The site was a very scenic spot on a wooded knoll with views off to the south and west. Hunt kept the shelter well equipped and maintained. Walter Leavitt reported that Clarence E. Holt, a Portland dentist, gave the O Joy Brook its name, which he wrote was "simply an impression the little stream made on me when it was first visited."[8]

Beyond the shelter the trail climbs steeply, passing a large cave just below treeline. Above treeline begins the exciting climb of the great boulders. In later years, iron bars were attached to some of the more difficult boulders to serve as hand holds. Passing through "The Gateway," the trail reaches the southeastern edge of Katahdin's magnificent Tableland.

The trail finally reaches the summit, originally named Monument Peak but renamed Baxter Peak in 1932 to honor the man whose vision and commitment resulted in the setting aside of Katahdin and the region around it to be "forever wild." From 1946 through the early 1960s, the Appalachian Mountain Club kept a register in a metal canister in a niche in the summit cairn where people could record their ascent.

The campsite at O Joy Brook continued to be used for many years. In 1934 the CCC crew improved the Hunt Trail and built a three-sided Adirondack-style log lean-to, which they named the Hunt Spur Lean-to. The lean-to was near Hunt's tent shelter and accommodated five to six people. The sturdy log lean-to at O Joy Brook burned in July of 1948, apparently the result of carelessness. Fortunately, an all-night rain following the fire protected the surrounding area, and the fire did not spread. The shelter was never rebuilt. There are still some remains to be found, mute reminders of a camping experience high on Katahdin's slopes.

On August 19, 1933 Myron H. Avery, J.F. Schairer, A.H. Jackman, and Shailer S. Philbrick stood on the summit of Katahdin. They had in their possession a bicycle wheel, which served as a trail mileage marker, paint buckets and brushes, blue and white paint, and diamond-shaped galvanized iron Appalachian Trail (AT) markers. Their aim was to begin the enormous task of painting the white blazes of the newly declared Appalachian Trail from Katahdin across Maine and into New Hampshire. The original planners of the AT had placed its northern terminus at Mount Washington, but Myron Avery, a native of Lubec, Maine and a key official of the Appalachian Trail Conference (now the Appalachian Trail Conservancy) in Washington, D.C., convinced the planners that the trail should be built through the wilderness of Maine to Katahdin.

As these men painted white blazes along the popular Hunt Trail, they became a part of an historic effort to establish the AT, the continuous long-distance trail from Maine to Georgia. Spending the night in wilderness sporting camps along the way, this crew and others like them painted close to 118 miles of the AT from Katahdin to Blanchard in a two-week period

Myron H. Avery, center, and friends gather at the summit in 1933 to begin cutting and marking the Appalachian Trail south across Maine. Note the bicycle wheel used to accurately measure trail distances. Courtesy, Maine State Library, Myron H. Avery Collection.

before Labor Day that year—an astonishing achievement. Founded in 1935, the Maine Appalachian Trail Club (MATC) began to regularly maintain the AT, including the Hunt Trail, throughout Maine. After operating under an informal verbal understanding, the MATC negotiated a written agreement with Baxter State Park in the early 1980s that is still in effect.

If one looks carefully at the eastern side of the Southwest Spur just below the open ridge and before the Gateway, the image of a skeleton-like face on the side of the mountain can be seen. Likely caused by minor rockslides, the sight of this gaunt, hollowed-eyed old man's face lends an aura of mystery to the fascinating history of this fine trail.

Appalachian Trail, South of Katahdin Stream Campground

Below the present-day Katahdin Stream Campground, the Appalachian Trail briefly follows Baxter State Park's tote road before skirting Tracy and Elbow Ponds and reaches the Daicey Pond Campground. From Daicey Pond the Appalachian Trail follows down Nesowadnehunk Stream. When first cleared, the trail crossed Nesowadnehunk Stream below the pond at the old timber toll dam built in 1879. The trail then followed an old tote road south to Nesowadnehunk Falls on the Penobscot West Branch, where the Great Northern Paper Company had built a large dam in 1903. The 1936 *Guide to the Appalachian Trail in Maine* described the trail as a:

> Worn old road along Nesowadnehunk Stream to the West Branch of the Penobscot, a dark rushing torrent gathering momentum for its leap over Nesowadnehunk Falls, with the ominous roar which some distance back on the trail had warned of the river. A bridge built across the old dam piers by the CCC has supplanted the former uncertain canoe crossing here after the old dam was destroyed a few years ago.[9]

When the Appalachian Trail was first envisioned, some people hoped that it would be possible to cross the West Branch on the old dam itself. Hikers in the early 1920s had reported that the dam needed repairs but was crossable. However, the dam was "blown out" by high water in 1932 and, although repaired in 1934, crossing the dam was not safe.

There were a number of alternative arrangements for crossing the West Branch at the head of the carry where the water was more placid. Sometimes the watchman at the dam ferried people across the river. He often left his shack at the dam unlocked to provide shelter for hikers. Old photographs show that both canoes and bateaux were used for the ferrying. The river was sometimes filled with logs, so the crossing could be a very tricky and dangerous affair. One of the dam's sluice gates bore the inscription "Frank Sevoy drowned here July 5, 1917."

In September 1934 a party of Appalachian Trail hikers heading south from Katahdin had some difficulty crossing the West Branch. Later, Ron Gower, a long-time member and officer of the Appalachian Mountain Club, wrote that the watchman at the dam was no longer there. If the hikers had used the Twin Pine Camps canoe, it would have taken too long to carry this large a party across. However, they convinced some nearby loggers to ferry them across in a bateau. The water was at a dangerously high level but they all finally arrived safely on the opposite bank of the river.[10]

Without a safe way to cross the West Branch above the falls over the Nesowadnehunk Dam, it became increasingly more difficult to reach the far shore. As he had done many times before, Avery came to the rescue.

Avery's career had taken him to Washington, D.C., where he served as a maritime (admiralty) lawyer. Using his connections, Avery arranged to have a 200-foot suspension footbridge across the West Branch added to the list of Civilian Conservation Corps projects. He arranged for the financing and formal approval for the project. The Patten, Maine, CCC group began work on the bridge in 1935 and completed it in 1936. Faint evidence of the old dam abutments, used to build the new bridge, are still visible just above the falls. Early pictures of the bridge show the old dam's massive, though deteriorating, cribwork.

Cable bridge built in 1936 to allow Appalachian Trail hikers to cross the West Branch of the Penobscot just above Nesowadnehunk Falls. Courtesy, Maine State Library, Myron H. Avery Collection.

The cable bridge became one of the most notable features of Maine's Appalachian Trail, and many flocked to cross it. Because of World War II neglect, the expense of repairs, and the lack of clear responsibility for its maintenance, the bridge was in serious need of repairs by 1949. A portion of the foot-tread had actually given way by that time. Much of the late damage had resulted from a major storm that occurred during the winter of 1948–49. The damage was so great that hikers had to once again make arrangements through the folks at Daicey Pond Camps to be ferried across.

In 1950 the MATC, led again by Myron Avery, arranged for the Maine Highway Department to repair the bridge; the Appalachian Trail Conservancy, the MATC, and the Great Northern Paper Company shared the costs. The Maine Forest Service coordinated the project with the paper company and provided heavy equipment. Maine Highway Department rebuilt the entire bridge, excepting the towers, and the bridge re-opened on June 7, 1950. The MATC placed a wooden sign on the bridge to acknowledge its original date of erection (1936) and the date of the rebuilding (1950).

During its early existence, the Appalachian Trail followed the West Branch upriver after crossing it. In 1935 a CCC crew built an open-front log lean-to about a quarter of a mile from the bridge on the south bank. Named the West Branch Lean-to, the structure could accommodate about eight hikers. A fire in 1942 may have destroyed the lean-to, and the site became a tent site for a time until the trail was relocated away from the river.

Further upriver, the Appalachian Trail passed a cabin, which served as an outlying fishing and hunting camp for Fred Clifford's Rainbow Lake Sporting Camps. Here, where Horserace Brook enters the West Branch, the Appalachian Trail turned abruptly south up the brook and crossed a height-of-land before descending to Rainbow Lake. Although no longer a part of the Appalachian Trail, the trail to Rainbow Lake from that point still provides access to several remote ponds and streams. The old outlying camp still exists, providing seasonal shelter for the Maine's West Branch Corridor Warden.

The cable bridge served hikers until the mid-1950s when it received fatal damage from the weight of winter snow and ice. It finally collapsed in 1963. This normally would have caused a serious interruption for those hiking, but around 1953 the Great Northern Paper Company built a road bridge, known as Abol Bridge, across the West Branch just below the mouth of Abol

Stream. In 1956 the MATC began to relocate the Appalachian Trail in order to cross the river on the new bridge. Utilizing old tote toads, the trail followed down the east side of Nesowadnehunk Stream and continued along the north bank of the West Branch to Abol Bridge. After crossing the bridge, the trail turned into the woods and, as it still does today, headed for Rainbow Lake, by way of Hurd Brook and Rainbow Ledges, and on to Georgia.

Owl Trail

The Owl, at 3,736 feet, is a prominent rounded peak north of Katahdin's Southwest Spur and the Hunt Trail. Its sheer easterly face is one of the most conspicuous features as one ascends Katahdin. Walter Leavitt wrote:

> If . . . The Owl . . . were standing away by itself instead of being practically engulfed between the westerly cliffs of Katahdin and Barren Mountain, it would attract the admiration and respect of mountain climbers. In its sheltered location with no trail to its summit, it remains unvisited and unpraised. Its interesting summit has probably been visited by only a limited few, and its attractions have been described by only one or two explorers, foremost of whom was the late George C. Witherle of Castine, Maine. Many isolated mountains in elevation much inferior to The Owl are generally known and praised.[11]

During the 1965 and 1966 summer seasons, Stephen Clark,* his family, and members of a Scout troop built the Owl Trail, which runs from the Hunt Trail to The Owl's summit. The trail departs from the Hunt Trail just before Katahdin Falls and ascends northwesterly before climbing the rocky summit from the west. The outstanding views from the top, especially into the steep Witherle Ravine, make this little-used trail a real gem.

OJI Trail

At 3,410 feet, OJI, looming north of the Nesowadnehunk Valley, does not appear to have had a name before an act of nature provided one. Sometime before the 1930s a series of rock slides on its southern slope created a formation that resembled the letters "O," "J," and "I" against the dark surrounding

---

* Clark, a member and officer of the Appalachian Trail Conservancy and the Maine Appalachian Trail Club, is the editor of *Katahdin: A Guide to Baxter State Park and Katahdin.*

spruce. Subsequent rock slides in 1932, 1954, and 1963 altered the letters' shape so that they are no longer as obvious as before.

A trail to the summit was built in the 1930s after the Sourdnahunk-Millinocket Tote Road was extended, but it was not maintained and languished. In 1944, H.M. Knickerbocker, J.W. Worthington, and other Kidney Pond Camps guests marked and built a new trail to the summit. They used sections of the slides, which proved extremely dangerous and led to recent relocations. Two trails to OJI and a link to the Mount Coe Trail make possible a number of rewarding circuit climbs from the valley.

Marston Trail

Marston Trail allows access to North and South Brother from the Nesowadnehunk Valley. Spectacular views from both peaks await those who climb these peaks, which form a western wall to the Klondike, the Northwest Basin, and the upper valley of Wassataquoik Stream.

In 1953 James L. and Philip Marston of Worcester, Massachusetts received permission from Baxter State Park to build a trail from the Sourdnahunk-Millinocket Tote Road at the slide dam to the summit of North Brother. With the aid of a group of Explorer Scouts, the trail took two years to build and was likely finished in 1955. This trail, along with a link trail to South Brother, offers dramatic access to many of the peaks of the Katahdinaughuoh, the Native American name for the range of mountains west of Katahdin.

Mount Coe Trail

Commanding excellent views of the Klondike and other mountains in the region, Mount Coe is an open rocky peak north of OJI. Mount Coe was likely named for the prominent Bangor lumberman Ebenezer S. Coe, whom Alfred Hempstead in his *Penobscot Boom* identifies as one of the first trustees of the famous Penobscot Lumbering Association, which represented the interests of the lumbermen using the log boom in Old Town. A civil engineer by training, Coe was hired in 1842 by David Pingree, who acquired ownership of huge tracts of land in Maine for timber harvesting. Coe was Pingree's agent in the field, especially in the Allagash region, where he was responsible for building in 1846 the famous Chamberlain Farm, which supported the harvesting effort in that area. Eventually Coe became a landowner himself and owned part of the township in which Mount Coe rests. We do not know who built the trail or when the work was done.

Doubletop Trails

Once identified by Myron Avery as Maine's most perfect mountain, Doubletop was a prominent landmark for those who first explored the West Branch and the Nesowadnehunk Valley. Named for its twin peaks, Doubletop is prominent from the valley and from Katahdin's trails. The shape of the mountain, however, is quite different when viewed from along the West Branch below Abol. In 1836 Jacob Whitman Bailey named this mountain Sugarloaf because it reminded him of a cone-shaped loaf of unrefined sugar.

In 1913 the Maine Forest Service cut a trail from the lumber road coming in from Greenville to allow access to a wooden fire lookout tower it built on the north peak. A 48-foot steel tower replaced the old wooden tower in 1918. When the Forest Service finally abandoned the fire tower in the mid-1930s, the trail began to deteriorate. Use of an old trail up the south side of the mountain, probably built to accommodate Kidney Pond Camps guests, also lapsed.

In 1955 guests at Kidney Pond Camps reopened the south side trail but it was only marginally maintained. In the late 1960s, park personnel cut and reopened the trail on the north side. Great slides have fallen from Doubletop's eastern face to the Nesowadnehunk Valley below. Although some believe those slides dammed Nesowadnehunk Stream at one time, the damming was the result of slides from the other side of the valley.

The fire tower, often the victim of lightning strikes, later posed a hazard after it fell on its side. Park personnel, the Maine Forest Service, and the Maine National Guard removed it in 2000.

Wassataquoik Lake Trail

First built in 1975 by Baxter State Park personnel and relocated several times since then, Wassataquoik Lake Trail offers unique access to the interior of the Katahdin region from the Nesowadnehunk Valley. It begins from the Tote Road at Nesowadnehunk Field Campground and ranger station. This lengthy trail passes lovely Little Wassataquoik Lake, Wassataquoik Lake, and spectacular Russell Pond deep in the park's central region.

Sentinel Mountain Trail

This low-lying mountain southwest of Kidney Pond has been referred to at times as "The Sentinel" because of the way it seems to stand watch over the Penobscot West Branch. As late as 1934, the mountain was also known as

"Roosevelt Mountain" by some who mistakenly claimed that Teddy Roosevelt had climbed Sentinel with Bill Sewall. Roosevelt, it turns out, only visited the east side of Katahdin, and so the name did not stick.

The trail begins at Kidney Pond and, after gaining the spacious summit area, offers outstanding views of the western side of Katahdin. Although there is no record, Irving Hunt likely built the trail in the early 1900s after establishing the Kidney Pond Camps. An old, perhaps original, route was relocated around 1938 by Earle W. "Junior" York, when his father and mother were proprietors of the Daicey Pond Camps.

Rev. B. Janney Rudderow, known as "The Parson," and his wife Mary were frequent visitors to Kidney Pond Camps. Each Sunday morning he was in residence, Parson Rudderow led a group to the summit of Sentinel. There he conducted worship, preaching sermons from a stunning lookout to the west now named "Pulpit Rock" or "Parson's Pulpit." Cabins were named in his honor at the sporting camps on both Kidney and Daicey Ponds, and a picture of Rudderow still graces the wall of the Kidney Pond Campground library.

Inter-Pond Trail Systems

A series of trails connect many of the small ponds in the Kidney-Daicey area and the Togue Pond area. The Kidney-Daicey area trails that connect Lily Pad Pond, Grassy Pond, Little Beaver Pond, Celia Pond, Jackson Pond, Draper Pond, Slaughter Pond, Polly Pond, Rocky Pond, and Windy Pitch Ponds are among the oldest and most beautiful in the park. Most of these trails date back to the early twentieth century when the sporting camps first opened. The more recent Togue Pond area trails that connect Rum Pond, Kettle Pond, Cranberry Pond, Abol Ponds, and the recently named Caverly Pond offer outstanding low-country hiking.

WEST BRANCH CAMPSITE HISTORY

Katahdin Stream Campground

Developed in 1934, Katahdin Stream Campground is one of Baxter State Park's oldest campgrounds, second only to Chimney Pond. That year the CCC crew constructed four Adirondack-style lean-tos at a gravel-washed field where a lumber camp once stood and where the historic Hunt Trail and

Katahdin Stream crossed the Sourdnahunk-Millinocket Tote Road. They also built a parking area, picnic tables, a log cabin for the Forest Service rangers, and a dam across Katahdin Stream to create a pool they named Mirror Lake. The dam was rebuilt between 1954 and 1955, again in 1964, and replaced in the early 1970s. In 1939 Richard Holmes became the first park ranger at the campground, which served as park headquarters for a time. The Maine Forest Service added four more lean-tos in 1959. Some of the apple trees from the early days of the lumber camp are still there.

The campground was formally named Camp Baxter in 1939, but it was also known as Baxter Field and later (informally) as Pitman Campground or Campsite well into the 1950s. Fred Pitman at one time ran a sporting camp operation along the West Branch and after the camps burned in the mid-1930s he served as Baxter State Park ranger at Camp Baxter from 1941 to 1955. Pitman, who also had experience as a Forest Service warden, ran a little store at the campground to serve hikers, lumbermen, and the occasional visitors by automobile using the relatively new tote road.

Katahdin Stream Campground remains one of Baxter State Park's most popular campgrounds. It continues to have special significance to the Appalachian Trail thru-hikers who begin or end their long-distance hiking odyssey at Katahdin.

Abol Campground
Established by Baxter State Park in 1958 to relieve overcrowding at Katahdin Stream Campground, Abol Campground is one of the newer park campgrounds. Located where many of the various trails to Abol Slide crossed the Sourdnahunk-Millinocket Tote Road, the campground was designed to be small and more private than other campgrounds in the region.

One of the most noteworthy moments in the campground's history occurred in April 1976 when a group of Maine Native Americans of the Wabanaki Federation, representing the Penobscot, Passamaquoddy, Micmac, and Maliseet people, "occupied" the campground. They talked briefly of establishing a permanent settlement at the site to dramatize their claim that the Katahdin area was a sacred location for their people. After considerable discussion and negotiations among all parties, the Native Americans discontinued their occupation. Their action, however, has remained an important symbol of Native American reverence of Katahdin.

Foster Field Campsite

Foster Field, located near Nesowadnehunk Stream and a few miles north of Katahdin Stream Campground, was the site of a large timber cutting operation that took place as the Sourdnahunk-Millinocket Tote Road extended northwest of Katahdin in the 1930s. Some say Foster Field got its name from Chuck Foster, a lumberman and likely the boss of the operation that utilized the field. At an early time it was known as Foster's Field or Foster's Storehouse. In the late 1930s, after the CCC used the site as one of its side camps, most of the buildings were razed. One white building, the home of the scaler who monitored the timber, was given to the York family at Twin Pine Camps and, after many renovations, still serves as the ranger's cabin at Daicey Pond. It was at the edge of this field that the park, before the Pack In and Pack Out philosophy took hold, had a trash and garbage dump for many years. It became a favorite place for overnight campers in the area to gather at dusk to view the bears who came to paw through the leftovers.

Nesowadnehunk Field Campground

Now a Baxter State Park campground, Nesowdnehunk Field was once a major depot lumber camp field (some two to three hundred acres) for the Great Northern Paper Company. Here the Sourdnahunk-Millinocket Tote Road and an earlier tote road from Greenville met, making the field a very important junction for the lumbering industry in the early twentieth century. From Nesowdnehunk Field, the main tote road continued northeast and linked with the tote road that by the 1950s had been extended from the Patten region into the forest north of Katahdin. Charles Daisey, who took over the Phoenix Camps on Nesowadnehunk Lake in 1904, brought guests up the West Branch of the Penobscot and Nesowadnehunk Stream to this huge field. After 1916 the Camp Phoenix owners met those arriving by car at the field and took them the rest of the way to the camps by buckboard.

The Yorks, who operated the Twin Pine Camps on Daicey Pond, kept a small cabin, known as York's Tavern, at the field where guests, arriving from Greenville, spent the night before being taken down Nesowadnehunk Stream to the camps.

In 1952 the park campground opened, and by 1953 a ranger cabin and two lean-tos had been built. At one time a nearby gate into Baxter State Park provided access from Greenville, but it closed in 1988. Today the campground offers primitive camping in a remote and quiet area of the park.

EAST BRANCH TRAIL HISTORIES

On Katahdin's south side the Penobscot's West Branch acted as the central highway by which Native Americans and the early non-native explorers accessed the mountain. In contrast, the East Branch never became a major thoroughfare, and the east side remained, except for Native American trails and early timber cruising, untouched until the early 1830s.

Around that time the newly built Military Road, which linked Mattawamkeag and Houlton, connected Maine's coastal communities with the northern St. John River valley farmlands in the event that military action was needed to protect them. It did not take long for villages and livelihoods to spring up along the new road. Almost immediately the timber industry cast a covetous eye toward the prime forest in the vast valley of Wassataquoik Stream and its tributaries and the flanks of Katahdin itself.

In the early 1830s William Hunt constructed a rough road from Stacyville that crossed the East Branch at a ford just above Whetstone Falls. He built a substantial farm at the ford crossing to accommodate the many travelers and lumbermen he felt confident would arrive. And arrive they did, journeying in great numbers to the Hunt Farm and up the Wassataquoik in the years to follow.

From the East Branch crossing there were two routes to Katahdin. The first route continued up Wassataquoik Stream to its tributaries and ascended the mountain from the stream's two major branches, which join just southeast of Russell Pond. The second route headed west at Katahdin Brook to Katahdin Lake and traveled straight to Katahdin's Southeast Spur (Keep Ridge).

Lumber roads continued to penetrate this wilderness during the middle part of the nineteenth century, and the trails to Katahdin were frequently relocated as timber cutting operations swept through. The great lumbering activities in the Wassataquoik Valley were both a blessing and a curse in that they allowed hikers greater access to the mountain but made it difficult to establish dependable trail locations. In the midst of this confusion the Wassataquoik or Stacyville Tote Road along the stream's northern bank remained unchanged, providing primary access to the region until the early years of the twentieth century.

Keep Path

In 1848, Rev. Marcus Keep, aided by John Stacy, cut and marked the first formal trail to the mountain. (Some hikers and many explorers had ascended earlier to the Tableland by the Abol Slide on the south side, but the many approaches to the foot of the slide were informal and unmarked until the twentieth century.)

On his two previous trips to the ridge, Keep had traveled to Katahdin Lake from the rough Wassataquoik Tote Road. He began cutting his new trail from that road and directed it toward the lake, which he had found so striking during his previous visits. From the lake the trail led west until it crossed Avalanche Brook and began its ascent toward the Southeast Spur, which was later known as the East Spur, Parson Keep's Ridge, and Keep Ridge. The trail then climbed an avalanche (variously known as Avalanche Slide, the East Slide, the East Avalanche, Old Man's Slide, and St. John's Slide) on the ridge's south side and headed toward Pamola Peak.

Between 1849 and 1861 Keep guided parties along his trail. The trail was relocated at times because of lumbering activity, but the Keep Path remained in steady use until the late 1870s when lumbering almost obliterated it. In 1897 Dr. George Kennedy and a party from Boston re-cut the path but lumbering continued to interfere. In 1903 Lore Rogers, a local guide, re-cut the trail but by that time other trails were in use to reach the more popular Great Basin. The Keep Path was never restored, though the final half-mile of today's Helon Taylor Trail follows the original Keep Path as it nears Pamola.

St. John Trail (Avalanche Trail)

During the twentieth century, trail use shifted from Wassataquoik Stream and Katahdin Lake to the Great Northern Paper Company's new Sandy Stream Tote Road, which ran up the west side of Sandy Stream from Togue Pond. By 1925 the road had reached Windey Pitch but did not extend to Avalanche and Roaring Brooks until the mid-1930s. The extension of Sandy Stream Tote Road from Great Northern's Greenville-Millinocket Tote Road made possible the establishment of Togue Pond Camps by W.H. St. John and H.N. Walls of Millinocket. Shortly after opening their camps in 1924, the two re-cleared the Keep Path route from Avalanche Brook toward Pamola for their guests. From the start of the trail at the tote road it was only five miles to Pamola.

At the foot of the avalanche St. John and Walls constructed a crude log lean-to for use by their "sports" on climbs. St. John and Walls wrote glowingly in their ads about this feature of life at their sporting camps, including word of the sparkling ice-cold water available at the campsite.

The trail continued to be a popular route to Pamola and the Knife Edge for some years until it also fell into disuse because of lumbering operations. Lester F. Hall, known as "Sawdust," describes a 1938 hike along this trail, just before its demise:

> I am very glad that I walked this path, for it is one of the most beautiful woods trails that I have ever seen in this region. Huge birches are in abundance for a long way up along Spring Brook, and after the trail leaves it one enters a solid white birch forest which continues way up to the headwaters of Avalanche brook, right under the slide on the mountain. There is an old camp ground here in a beautiful setting by the bank of the brook and the little stream bubbles merrily along among the myriad of small trout that are striving to grow up and fortify themselves for the rigors of a life among their larger fellows in Sandy Stream and Millinocket Lake. I'd like to have a little camp, even a leanto, right here. From the brook one looks way up to the top of Pamola, and the trail starts steeply up the mountain almost from the farther bank.[12]

The lumber cuttings that occurred between 1939 and 1941 destroyed the trail, and the route was abandoned by 1950—the near legendary birch grove having been cut over in 1946. A memorable feature of this trail was a wind-carved rock formation at the point where the trail reached the Keep Ridge. From the right angle, the rock looked like a sea lion and was dubbed the Guardian of the Avalanche.

Leavitt Trail

Over a period of four days in August of 1933, H. Walter Leavitt, a civil engineering professor at the University of Maine and author of *Katahdin Skylines*, his son Lawrence, and friend Winfield S. Gilmore scouted out and blazed a trail intended as a scenic circuit to Pamola when combined with a return by way of the St. John Trail and the avalanche back to the tote road. From Windey Pitch, the trail headed almost due west toward Keep Ridge where it joined the St. John Trail, a half-mile below Pamola. Just below that junction is an area where the wind whips up in a powerful whirlwind fashion.

Leavitt re-blazed his trail in 1934 with the help of his son again and Professor H.D. Chase. Orono Boy Scout Troop 47 and others made further improvements in the next couple of years. Unfortunately, increased lumber operations in the late 1930s and 1940s once again interfered with trail use and the trail was little used after its early years.

Helon Taylor Trail

The Helon Taylor Trail was named in honor of the man who served as superintendent of Baxter State Park from 1950 to 1967 and did so much to establish the park in its formative early years. The trail begins at Roaring Brook Campground and ascends the Keep Ridge to Pamola. The trail has a number of historical roots in Katahdin history. Along its lower portions it follows the older Leavitt Trail, and in its upper portions it follows the old Keep Path.

In 1952 Ed Werler, ranger of Roaring Brook, cut a trail to a scenic rocky overlook dubbed Ed's Lookout. The ridge's lower end had burned over earlier, opening up clear vistas. Werler himself remembers waking one morning to the smell of smoke. He climbed to the Lookout, discovered the location of a woods fire, and radioed the Forest Service, who extinguished the fire before it did any extensive damage.

In 1963 Millinocket Boy Scouts, under the direction of Monroe Robinson, opened the new Taylor Trail, which continued up the ridge beyond the Lookout. Baxter State Park rangers later improved and marked the trail, which was formally opened in 1963 by Governor Percival P. Baxter himself. Today the Taylor Trail offers a spectacular approach along the Keep Ridge to Pamola, the Knife Edge, and the high peaks beyond.

Sandy Stream Pond Trail

The short Sandy Stream Pond Trail, which runs from Roaring Brook Campground, allows access to the headwaters of Sandy Stream. A lovely pond at the foot of South Turner Mountain provides a remarkable view of the Katahdin massif. Sandy Stream Pond was once considered as a public facilities site. In a 1916 *Appalachia* article, William Dawson extolled the pond's beauty and asserted that it was the "perfect site for a permanent camp of considerable size" as long as the buildings were "in harmony with the landscape, that is, in the style of the Swiss chalets or, better still, substantial log cabins."[13] However, nothing further was ever heard of this plan.

Edwin Rogers may have built a small temporary lumber camp on the shore of the pond. In the 1920s there is mention of a stone fireplace at the pond for cooking and enjoying the unprecedented view from the shore. Thankfully, with the exception of bordering trails, the pond has been spared human encroachment.

South Turner Mountain Trail

Located about four miles northeast of Katahdin, South Turner's 3,122-foot summit seems to pale in the shadow of Katahdin's grandeur. Leavitt suggests that the mountain has been "neglected because of its proximity to Katahdin."[14] Many who visit the region, however, believe that the South Turner summit offers one of the most spectacular views of the Katahdin massif (relative to the effort of the climb). The mountain was not named for Charles Turner Jr. but for a lumberman who likely ran the area's lumber operations and whose full name and identity have been unfortunately forgotten over the years.

Legend has it that after the gods had used all of the rocks they needed in making Katahdin, they dumped them in a nearby pile and thus created the Turner Mountains. A rough trail to South Turner's summit existed during the lumbering era but eventually suffered from disuse and became overgrown. Early in 1955 Baxter State Park rangers Ed Werler and Ralph Dolley laid out the South Turner Mountain Trail. That August five Harvard geology students staying at Roaring Brook constructed the trail under Werler's supervision. A five-member crew from the AMC completed the trail in the spring of 1956, and the trail was ready for public use.

Sand Bank Trail

The largely forgotten Sand Bank Trail followed old Draper Operation roads up Sand Bank Stream and provided a direct footpath from just below the Hunt Farm on the East Branch to the site of Katahdin Lake Camps. It was blazed in 1920 at the instigation of Madison Tracy and other Stacyville citizens at a time when there was speculation over the establishment of a park in the Katahdin area. Folks in the Stacyville area wanted a scenic entry from the Hunt Farm ford into such a park. The Sand Bank Trail offered an appealing alternative to the tote road route to Katahdin Lake. Lumber operations continued to obscure the trail, and it never became a point of entry into the Katahdin area.

Sand Bank Trail appeared on trail maps between the mid-1920s and 1950s. Though CCC crew members reopened and blazed the trail in 1936, it was usually referred to as "obscure" during most of those years and as "obliterated" on a 1950 map.

EAST BRANCH CAMPSITE HISTORY

Roaring Brook Campground

Completed in 1935, the Great Northern Paper Company Tote Road ran along Sandy Stream to a depot camp on the banks of Roaring Brook. The open field site was an important starting point for climbs to Pamola and the Great Basin. The improvements the CCC crew made on the road in 1935 allowed comfortable automobile access to Roaring Brook and resulted in increased hiking and camping activity. In order to establish minimal control over those growing demands, the park built a campground at Roaring Brook. Construction began in August 1949, and before winter, a garage and a ranger's cabin had already been erected. The parking lot and six lean-to campsites had been cleared and the lean-tos were finished in the spring of 1950. Roaring Brook was officially opened in 1950 and soon became the central point of control for Russell Pond, and the interior wilderness, as well as the Great Basin and Chimney Pond Campground.

Avalanche Field Campsite

The site of one of Great Northern Paper Company's depot camps, Avalanche Field Campsite is located where several old lumber roads converged and where Avalanche Brook crosses the tote road that leads to Roaring Brook. In the early- to mid-1930s it was a CCC side camp, but most of the buildings were razed in the late 1930s. Today the field is used for group tenting and serves as the wagon road access point for the Katahdin Wilderness Lake Camps on Katahdin Lake.

THE GREAT BASIN 7

The Heart of Katahdin

TO STAND AT THE FLOOR OF KATAHDIN'S GREAT BASIN AND LOOK in awe to the surrounding sheer heights that rise some 2,000 feet is to experience the majesty of this "greatest mountain." Carved out during the Ice Age when a massive glacier covering New England began to recede, the basin inspires wonder and veneration. To one's left Pamola rises abruptly from the basin floor, and from that dramatic peak one's eye can follow the jagged and craggy spine of the Knife Edge to South Peak and finally to Katahdin's rounded summit. To one's right three great rock pinnacles identify the steep Cathedral Trail as it rises from the basin floor. In the near distance one can see the steep western ramparts of the Great Basin, capped by Hamlin Peak.

Pamola thus crowns the east side of this giant glacial cirque and Hamlin Peak the west. Between those two promontories are some of the most spectacular hiking opportunities anywhere in the country. The Great Basin itself is divided, to a lesser degree, by the Cathedral Ridge or Ledges, causing the more dramatic basin at Chimney Pond to be known simply as the South Basin. The Great Basin has been called "a volcanic caldron," "a meteorological whirlpool," and "the birthplace of storms."[1]

These persistent phenomena are abetted, no doubt, by Pamola's notorious anger. It can also be a place of incomparable beauty.

There are two additional basins at Katahdin and these we will deal with in due time. One is the trail-less North Basin, and the other the spectacular Northwest Basin. All of these geological wonders have contributed much to the spell and fascination of Katahdin across the years. Geologists have been especially drawn to these impressive mountain sites to study their rich treasures.[2]

FIRST VISITORS

Native Americans would have found the Great Basin as they explored the headwaters of rivers and streams after the Ice Age. Many of the stories handed down from generation to generation refer to this special place. Their respect for these sacred ridges and peaks, reflected in story, was surely developed after generations of experience with its fierce terrain and weather.

The first visit recorded in writing was relatively recent: Rev. Marcus Keep entered the Great Basin in October 1847. Keep had made his second ascent of Pamola from the east in September of that year, and was inspired again by the view from Pamola of the basin and its lovely pond. He was determined to reach the basin as soon as he could gather a group to make the trip, which had to be made without the benefit of any trails. The experience made a deep impression upon him, and the account of his entry into the basin is a stirring one. This was to be but one of many visits there by Keep across the years.

Earlier that summer, members of Dr. Aaron Young Jr.'s Botanical Expedition to Mount Katahdin, although not reaching the basin, reached the summit, and as they gazed into the basin far below, named the pond they saw there Norris Pond in honor of Joseph Norris, the Monument Line surveyor. The name did not stick. There is some evidence that the name "Basin Pond" was also given to it by members of the Appalachian Mountain Club, but those designations soon gave way to the name Chimney Pond, and the name Basin Ponds was then used to identify the ponds found at the base of the moraine.

No further visits are recorded until 1858 when a survey team from the J.W. Sewall Company of Old Town, Maine, employed by Shephard Boody, came to begin its survey for a proposed road from the Aroostook Road all the way to Chimney Pond, with a connecting bridle path to the summit of

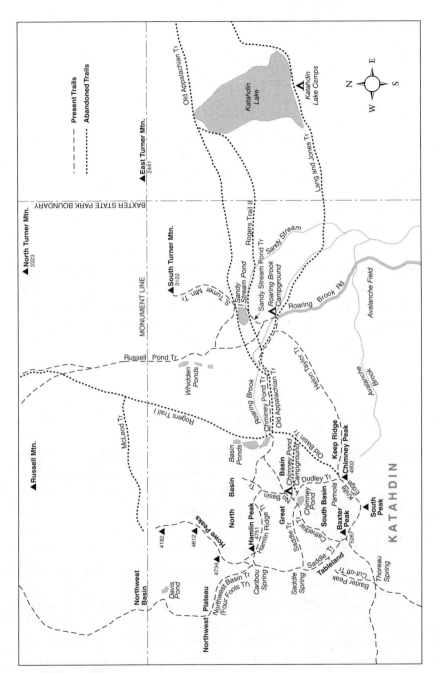

Great Basin trails.

Katahdin via the saddle between Hamlin Peak and Katahdin's Monument Peak. Because the pond in the Great Basin is named "Chimney Pond" in the field notes for this survey, the name had obviously received wide usage by that time. A year later in 1859 the first recorded woman visitor, Harriet Scribner, came to the Great Basin.

The 1860s and 1870s saw the first development of rough trails into the Great Basin area from the Wassataquoik Valley. These trails, their locations constantly shifting because of timber cutting, provided for the slowly increasing numbers of visitors to the basin. Frederic E. Church, the great Hudson River School landscape artist, visited in 1877 and again in 1886, making a number of sketches and drawings. Some of his drawings indicate that avalanches fell toward the pond between the years of his visits.[3]

In 1879 Theodore Roosevelt hiked into the basin and climbed to the summit with friends and relatives. In 1881 Charles E. Hamlin was guided into the basin by Marcus Keep himself in what was to be the 65-year-old Keep's final visit to Katahdin. It was on this trip that Hamlin recorded his own dream that a road be built to the Great Basin, a hotel erected there, and a smooth bridle path developed to the summit.

CAMPING AND CRUDE SHELTERS

The year 1887 was a special transitional year at the Great Basin. Inspired, no doubt, by the writings of Charles E. Hamlin, a large group of Appalachian Mountain Club members came to the basin for a lengthy spell of camping and hiking. They had engaged a local guide, Clarence Peavey, the year before to help an advance party of five members of the Appalachian Mountain Club (AMC) to scout and rough out a trail to the basin and to build some temporary shelters there and at Katahdin Lake. This trail would become known for many years as the Appalachian Trail, not to be confused with the present-day Appalachian Trail on the southwest side of the mountain.

The AMC presence in the Great Basin that year, and again several years following, gave rise to an increasing number of visitors both for scientific exploration as well as recreational hiking and climbing. Later in the early twentieth century there were other AMC encampments. An account from one of those early visits tells of the joy of preparing for the night and then gathering around the evening campfire at the shore of Chimney Pond:

Heavy brush was cleared and the grounds laid with a double thatch of balsam. Here after supper we sang songs and listened to stories of Ktaadn. This is unquestionably the most inspiring camp site in all New England.[4]

During those two trips into the Great Basin the AMCers cut rough trails into the North Basin and up Pamola, erected signs, and improved some of the very rough informal trails below treeline.

When the Bangor and Aroostook Railroad reached the lake country west of Millinocket in 1894 and continued north to Stacyville not far from the Penobscot East Branch, a new era began for the Katahdin area. More and more accessible to hikers, the Great Basin became a major destination point, overshadowing the trails on Katahdin's south side and even those up along the Keep Ridge. Though the dream of some that a resort hotel be built at Chimney Pond never materialized, people still came to see this remarkable glacial phenomenon and were awed and invigorated.

In 1900 a rough 20-foot-square log cabin was built near the pond by Dr. Lore Rogers for use by two Harvard botanists, Dr. George G. Kennedy and Dr. B.H. Dutcher. The cabin, named "Camp Kennedy" by Rogers, was built of unpeeled spruce logs and believe it or not, had a chimney of green spruce bark that directed the smoke from it. No fire code had been established at the basin to that point! There was a south-facing door and even a glass window. Unfortunately, the cabin caught fire on several occasions that summer and proved to be a somewhat dangerous place. The roof collapsed the very next winter so the cabin never became a fixture at the basin. In the 1930s Roy Dudley pointed out its location to Myron Avery; the stone base of that questionably engineered chimney could still be seen. Although this was a heroic start to providing enclosed protection at the Great Basin, only a few rough lean-tos were built in subsequent years to provide simple refuge for those visiting the basin. It would not be until 1924 that any kind of substantial shelter was constructed there.

A 1904 ad for the Lunksoos House Sporting Camp on the East Branch boasted that the only saddle (horseback) trail to the Great Basin started at the Lunksoos House and ended at Chimney Pond where a "comfortable cabin is located." It is difficult to discern to what this refers. Camp Kennedy might have been repaired or some other enclosed shelter erected. There is evidence that a canvas-covered lean-to was soon built next to Camp Kennedy utilizing one of its walls for support. Whether or not any of these structures could be termed "comfortable" is, of course, anyone's guess, but in the early years of the century they might have been deemed so by the most hearty.

In 1916 the Appalachian Mountain Club's interest in the Great Basin strengthened and the club engaged Madison Tracy to clear a trail into the basin for some of its members and to build some temporary shelters next to the pond for its August Camp. The AMC returned in 1923 when some in the group were called upon to help extinguish a huge fire in the Basin Pond area.

KNICKERS, PIPE IN MOUTH, AND STORYTELLING (THE ROY DUDLEY YEARS)

Recognizing the need in the Great Basin for some kind of oversight and management of the resource, the state of Maine decided in 1924 to build a more substantial cabin at Chimney Pond and employ a warden there during the recreational season. The charge to him was to oversee the Katahdin Park Game Preserve, as it was then known. Mark Leroy Dudley of Stacyville was initially named Deputy Warden and assigned to the basin. From that time on, until his untimely death in 1942, Roy Dudley and Chimney Pond would be identified almost as one. Dudley was born June 4, 1873, in Wesley, Maine, and moved to Stacyville as a child. At the age of fourteen he took a job cooking for lumberjacks, and that brought him into the Katahdin region for the first time. Beginning at the age of eighteen when he started guiding people into the Great Basin, he learned to love the mountain with a special passion that was to last throughout his life.

One of his first clients was James H. Emerton, an entomologist seeking unique spider specimens on the mountain. In due time, Dudley discovered that the scientist had a few mighty strange ideas about how to keep a backpack light while still providing for the nutritional needs required for such a rough trip. Dudley was a little mystified about the lightness of Emerton's pack as they started out, but he assumed that the man knew what he was doing. Over the course of several days spent camping at Chimney Pond and climbing around on the Tableland and reaching the summit, the scientist provided nothing more than some of kind of dark liquid concoction and a mess of pills he claimed contained all the energy that would be needed for their entire trip. After a few days, poor Dudley was so hungry that he spent much of his time desperately trying to find wild berries to eat. When the two finally reached the Patterson Place, an inn on the East Branch where Dudley knew a hearty dinner awaited, he noticed that his client was wolfing down his meal with obvious delight. The man finally conceded to Dudley that neither the liquid nor the pills had provided proper nourishment for such vigorous mountain climbing.[5]

Sometime before 1917, after many years of guiding "sports" to the basin, Dudley built himself a very rough three-person, open-front lean-to near a huge overhanging rock on the south side of Chimney Pond in the very shadow of the cliffs leading to the summit of Katahdin. It was so crowded there that in 1917 he built a similar but slightly larger lean-to near the present ranger's cabin on the north side of the pond. This he dubbed Dudley's Den and it was so named by a great many hikers who for many years found shelter there, even after the state cabin was built.

In 1924, Dudley, assisted by Alex "Sandy" Mullin, erected the State Fish and Game Department cabin just up from the pond. It was built of peeled logs harvested in the Basin Pond area and had a porch (or piazza, as it was then known), a stove, and four double bunks. Those who worked on the cabin that season stayed in the nearby Dudley's Den and the AMC lean-to shelter, which had been built the year before. In subsequent years additional

State cabin built in 1924 at Chimney Pond. Game Warden Roy Dudley is at the left, on the porch. "Dudley's Den" is on the left. Courtesy, Maine State Library, Myron H. Avery Collection.

lean-tos and shelters were built at the location, as the area became more and more a favored destination. The area around the pond had largely remained wild and untamed, but with the increase in camping accommodations the virginal terrain commenced a very slow but steady decline and would never be the same again.

In mid-August of 1925, two parties converged at the summit. One party was led by Maine's Governor Ralph Owen Brewster and included Roy Dudley as the guide, several state officials, and friends. They had spent a night at Togue Pond Camps and then climbed to Chimney Pond where they enjoyed biscuits and hot coffee with Roy at the new state cabin. The next morning was clear and the party reached the summit where a most unusual occurrence was about to unfold.

The second party consisted of several gentlemen from Houlton who arrived at the summit armed with a carrier pigeon cage. Inside was Joan, who had already gained a reputation among homing pigeon aficionados as well as the public. With great ceremony Joan was released from the summit at 11:00 A.M., allowing her to return to her home in Houlton nearly 60 miles away as the pigeon flies, so to speak. Though there was fear that the hawks that hung around the Great Basin might interfere, Joan circled the summit several times and, with a final flap of her wings, headed straight for Houlton. Joan's handlers learned later that she had made it back home in one hour and twenty minutes.

In the meantime, members of the governor's party were so touched by their time at the summit they decided to spend the night there. Though Dudley and the wardens present hiked down to Chimney Pond and returned with blankets, the decision was not a wise one. A storm set in at midnight, and the group finally retreated down the Saddle Trail at four in the morning amid rain, wind, and thick clouds. They were restored to a reasonable level of comfort by the hot breakfast the wardens served them in the state cabin kitchen. Further restoration was provided by a swim followed by dinner back at Togue Pond Camps before the group returned to Augusta the next day. It would appear that Joan's trip home was a good deal easier than the governor's!

During the 1920s and 1930s Dudley continued to serve as the state's fish and game warden and fire warden. Perhaps of greater significance, however, he and his wife became gracious hosts and friends to all who visited the basin. Dudley became justly famous for the legendary stories and tales he shared with all who would listen. He loved to explain, for instance why he had so many frying pans on the wall of his cabin:

One day a man blew into camp and he told me he was writing a book concerning Mt. Katahdin. He asked me if I'd tell him something about the mountain. I told him I'd tell him all I knew and it wouldn't take me long to do it. So he stayed around and explored and evenings we talked about the mountain. . . .

After he'd been here about a week and I'd been telling him all about the mountain, he was standing in front of the stove one night, and he noticed all the fry pans hanging up back of the stove. He asked me, "Where'd you get all them fry pans?"

I says, "You wunt believe me if I tell you."

Says he, "I don't know. I been believing a lot of the stuff you been tellin me!"

"Well," I says, "a party come up here one time, climb the mountain and cruised around. One day, whilst they was out cruising they caught a partridge and brought it into camp. They thought it would make a nice pet and to keep it from flying away whilst they was up climbing the mountain, they took their frying pan and tied it to its leg. They had him three or four days, and they thought he was gettin real tame.

"Then one night they come in after a hard day's climb and they commenced to look for their bird so's to feed him his supper. They hunted high and low but they couldn't find him. By that time their vacation was up and they had to start for home. I hunted for the bird for a while after they'd gone, but I couldn't find it. Finally summer was gone and I bid goodbye to Chimney Pond till the next spring.

"The following summer I wanted a straight pole to fix up around the camp so I went out in the woods to cruise for one and I run onto a flock of partidge, about fifteen of them. And judge my surprise when I found each one with a fry pan on his leg!

"After I had taken the fry pan off the first two, the others seemed so rejoiced that they come right to me and held their feet up for me to take the fry pans off! Instead of getting the pole I went after, I picked up an armful of fry pans and lugged them into camp. They's right here now to show for themselves."[6]

Sometimes Dudley would tell his stories around the evening campfires; sometimes he would gather a crowd around him in front of the cabin piazza, after the chores of the day were finished. There, as the sun set behind Cathedral Ridge and the shadows of the night descended, he would look up and point out the domain of Pamola, the central figure in many of his tales. In addition to Pamola other fascinating characters were included in his stories: Sukey Guildersleeves (one of his lady friends), Pamola and Sukey's son, Sukey's brother Charles Idolphus Guildersleeves, and an assortment of other odd Chimney Pond visitors including the Growler, A Man Named Egypt, the Fat Man from Boston, the Man with the Green Hat, and the Widow-Woman from Portland.

He loved to tell how he made friends with Pamola:

Well, I'm going to tell you how I made friends with old Pamola. Now I used to have to make my rounds regular over to Daicey Pond and Kidney pond, visiting York's and Bradeen's camps over on the west side of Katahdin. Well, one time it was getting quite late and looking like rain. I thought I better be getting back to Chimney Pond before nightfall. But when I got on top of the mountain the wind come up and the rain come down in sheets.

So I arrived at the cabin just a little after dark, cooked my supper and done the dishes. Then I got out an old Western novel and sat down by the table to read a while by candlelight. The storm was raging something terrific outside. I could hear the wind whistling around Pamola Peak and the Knife Edge and over towards the Chimney, making a groaning noise like so many dying people. I sat there reading. The great big fir trees were bending, their tops lashing together, and hail struck on the roof as big as hen's eggs. I could hear the roofing flopping back and forth and the boards slamming back. I was expecting every moment to hear the roof go off the camp and be left there sitting in the rain.

All of a sudden I heard something strike the ground awful heavy out in the yard. I thought it was one of the big trees had blowed down, so I paid little attention to it. I kept on at the book, and first thing I heard was an awful groan and sat still for a minute, staring at the window. Soon it was followed by another groan. I listened and I says, "That sounds funny. I'll see what that is."

So I got up and went into the back room and got my revolver. I rolled the cylinder around to see that it was full of new cartridges. Then I took the flashlight and stepped to the door. About that time there come another groan and when I threw open the door, such a sight met my gaze I shall never forget! For lying on his back, stretched out full length in the yard lay old Pamola with both hands grasping his stomach.

I says, "What is the trouble, Pamola?"

He says, "I went down to Sandy Stream pond and killed a tough old cow moose and ate the whole of her and I think I overdone the thing a little bit!" U-U-UGH-H-M-M-M-M! Then came another awful groan.

I says, "I'll see what I can do to help you." I didn't have much stuff for doctoring indigestion, but I couldn't see Pamola lie there and suffer so.

I went into the camp. I had a bucket of water there, still on the stove and hot, so I put in about two pounds of sugar, to sweeten it up good, and put in a pound of black pepper. I stirred it up well, took it out and gave it to Pamola. He drank it at one big GULLUP. He commenced to rub his stomach. Soon he straightened up and says, "I'm feeling better." He got up, stretched himself and says, "You've taken the cramp out of my stomach! I'll be a true, honest, faithful friend to you as long as I live. I'll never do anything more to harm ye!"

He flopped his wings and flew towards his den, and Pamola and I have been the best of friends ever since. And I always keep a good supply of Pepper Tea in camp, for I don't know when I might want to use it.[7]

He also took great delight in telling how the porcupines would build their nests in Pamola's ears and then Roy would have to remove them. Some of the rangers remember Roy telling about the boy from Bangor who came to Chimney Pond wearing a brilliant scarlet sweater. He ate so many apricots and drank so much water that he finally exploded, scattering pieces of the sweater across the Tableland. Those bright pieces became lovely red flowers and were enjoyed by hikers as they ascended the mountain.

Dudley was indeed a born storyteller. He once related how his father, as a child, actually heard old Governor John Neptune of the Penobscot tribe tell of his hair-raising encounter with the fury of Pamola at Chimney Pond.[8] Dudley's memory of that story surely inspired him to add to the legend of Pamola in his own way through the years. Though not "discovered" until recent years many of Dudley's stories have been remarkably preserved and have now been published.[9]

Having heard Dudley tell of his relationship with Pamola on one or more previous visits to the Great Basin, a hiking party of four ladies arrived at Chimney Pond early in 1939 and were moved to write the following letter to Dudley, leaving it tacked on the door of the state cabin:

Dear Mr. Dudley,

We the undersigned have a very serious complaint to make. On May 28, 1939, we arrived at Baxter State Park Cabin, cold, hungry and WET after a fearful swim through roaring brooks, fully expecting to see the usual welcoming sign of smoke coming from your cabin. Much to our horror and dismay it was empty. We accepted your absent hospitality however and started our supper which was stale.

Suddenly we heard terrific noise, rocks rumbling, boulders rolling, then a whir from a mighty pair of wings. Of course, we knew at once it was Pamola. We looked up to see a pair of eyes staring at us from the window, eyes as big as lights of an automobile. We were able to eat by the light. With a roar, a snort, and a burst of flames we heard a bellow "Consarn females, nothing but consarn females, where's Roy!" and with that he flew back.[10]

On one of my visits to Chimney Pond in the mid-1990s, I learned from the ranger that Jane Thomas, who knew Dudley when she was a child and who helped to collect and publish his stories, was staying at the campground. Thomas was and is still a frequent visitor to Chimney Pond and is often asked to tell some of the Dudley stories in the evenings at the edge of the pond. She has tried through the years to faithfully tell the stories as Dudley would have told them. She agreed to my invitation to tell some that night as my companions and I sat on the lean-to deacon seat and looked up toward Pamola's cave and the precipitous Knife Edge. It was a magic moment our little group will never forget. It was bitter cold that late August night, but we were surrounded by the warmth of memory and imagination and a deep appreciation for Roy Dudley and this remarkable mountain place.

Ralph Robinson, who later became a ranger at Chimney Pond, remembers the first time he visited the Great Basin in 1933. He hitchhiked from his home in Millinocket to Millinocket Lake. He then hiked to Windey Pitch and along Roaring Brook to the Basin Ponds and on to Chimney Pond. Ralph's mother and father knew Dudley; he often stayed with the Robinsons in Millinocket when he was in town for supplies. Ralph and his younger brother Wilmot "Wiggie" Robinson were allowed to sleep that summer in Dudley's Den. They helped campers find firewood or provide for their other needs and sometimes did chores for Dudley and his wife. In return, they often received left-over food from campers to supplement the fish they caught in nearby ponds. As they grew older they did some guiding as well. They loved it there and looked forward to their summer sojourns as teenagers in the shadow of Katahdin.

Almost from the start of his tenure at Chimney Pond Dudley took it upon himself to more firmly establish the trails to and out of the basin. At least one source tells that Dudley put a notch in one of the cabin beams each time he climbed the mountain. We know that by 1920 he had climbed to the summit at least 38 times. In 1926 a party reported that he had by then climbed it an astounding 170 times. Were there really that many notches in the beam?

In 1927 the big event on the mountain was the August marriage of Roy and Abby Dudley on the summit of Katahdin. Members of an Appalachian Mountain Club group staying at York's Twin Pond Camps that year recalled seeing a significant amount of rice among the rocks when they reached the summit a day or two later. Abby did not know much about primitive woods life until she married Roy, but after some trips with him, she came to love the forest and the mountain and later became a licensed guide herself. She presided over the cabin and the campground with grace and tact, always cheerful and helpful, especially to those visiting the Great Basin for the first time. She even took the lead on some rescue efforts when Roy was away from the basin. Sadly, Abby died in 1935.

Dudley often wore knickers and sometimes even a tie while at Chimney Pond. He was also noted for a legendary strong tea he brewed to offer folks during the day and after they had completed their climb at the end of the day. It is said that as the teapot emptied more tea and water were simply added. His pay was usually minimal, but the Dudleys were allowed to rent out blankets and sell wood and minor supplies on their own and keep the proceeds. Abby also cooked at times for camping groups for a small fee. Known by many as the Dean of Katahdin, and usually found with a pipe in his mouth, Dudley left a lasting mark upon the history and lore of Katahdin and especially the Great Basin. He will not be forgotten as long as stories and tales are told around Katahdin's campfires.

Roy Dudley died in a tragic accident on February 15, 1942. He had been given a ride on a long-log hauler truck to a remote area so he could check a trapline. As he descended from the truck he slipped on the ice and slid under its wheels as it got underway again. He lived only a few minutes. Dudley was deeply mourned by his many friends and associates. Ron Gower of the Appalachian Mountain Club wrote, "To his many friends the moaning of the great winds across the Knife Edge will always be the grieving of the Spirit of Pamola."[11]

On an August Sunday in 1949, 50 friends and relatives gathered near the site of Dudley's Den to dedicate a memorial tablet in his honor. The tablet reads:

1874   Leroy Dudley   1942
Katahdin's Warden And Guide
For Nearly Fifty Years
Whose General Philosophy,
Kindly Ways And Droll Tales
Endeared Him To All.
He Loved This Mountain

Erected By Friends In The
Appalachian Mountain Club
1949

LIFE AT THE GREAT BASIN

The campground at Chimney Pond has always been a popular place to camp and to start one's climb to the summit. At various times lean-tos and bunk-houses were built to accommodate the public. In 1935 a National Park Service consultant made an unusual series of proposals. Among them was one calling for a major development at Chimney Pond, including construction of a main lodge and store, along the lines of a Hudson's Bay Company post, where campers could purchase supplies and swap yarns in the evening. Also included were plans for a ranger's cabin and a number of lean-tos as well as individual cabins for less hardy visitors. Water was to be piped from Cleftrock Pool or a spring along the Dudley Trail. These proposals are still on paper in the file; fortunately they were never carried out.

There are many interesting notes that appear on the pages of an old Chimney Pond Register maintained for years at the state cabin.[12] Here is a sampling:

September 12, 1936—An entry signed by members of the 1130th Company of the Civilian Conservation Corps.

July 3, 1938—Four people hiked up from Roaring Brook with two quarts of ice cream for their enjoyment at Chimney Pond.

July 25, 1939—"Lost boy found by three fishermen on E. Branch near Hunt Farm—alive but very weak. Clothing all torn off and badly cut and scratched by bushes. Search started Monday night (July 17) with over 200 men."[*]

September 9, 1939—"My fourth visit to Roy Dudley and Chimney Pond (1920, 1933, 1936, 1939) with great respect to Pamola and asking his blessing for the years to come." [Signed] "Percival P. Baxter, Portland."

September 9, 1941—"Seen in a Register of the Swiss Alpine Club. Fits here!
   First it rained, and then it blew
   And then it friz and then it snew
   And then it fogged and then it thew
   And very shortly after then it rained and blew and fogged again."
   [Signed] "University of Maine Class of 1944"

Another interesting aspect of life at the Great Basin in the late 1930s was the naming of the paths around the campground. Such names as Katahdin Square (the bunkhouse area), Pamola and Boulder Avenues, Pamola Court, Exchange, Central, and Main Streets became fixtures for a time in those years. One might be assigned, for instance, to a lean-to at 2 Pamola Avenue for the night. An unfinished new log bunkhouse was dubbed "Hotel Debunk" for a time in the early 1940s.

As World War II enveloped the country with uncertainty and fear in 1941, the Baxter State Park campgrounds were mostly deserted and solemn. The ranger cabin at Chimney Pond, which had been Roy Dudley's home for so many years, was boarded up because the position could not be filled after his sudden death. It was wartime and the park was not, as yet, well established. Trail maintenance was neglected. Myron Avery of the Maine Appalachian Trail Club had been an outspoken critic of the overuse that was taking place in the park in the 1930s, especially in the Great Basin. He

---

[*] This is the famous incident when Donn Fendler was lost near the summit while descending the Hunt Trail and the entry might have been written by Roy Dudley himself after taking a prominent part in the search.

later welcomed the low use during the war, declaring it an opportunity for the resource to recover.

An amusing report appeared shortly before the end of the war. A January 1945 article in the *Appalachian Trail Conference Newsletter* boasted that one could be taken by taxi from Millinocket all the way to Chimney Pond for $15. A letter to the editor later had fun with that assertion and suggested that Paul Bunyan must run the taxi service. To go that far (and not end the fare at the end of the road at Roaring Brook) would be a real bargain.[13]

After World War II the Great Basin area came under Baxter State Park jurisdiction and Ralph Robinson became the ranger there in 1946, coordinating the entire northern side of the mountain while Fred Pitman managed the southern side. Robinson was looking for post-war work and ended up with the job because he had spent so much time in the Great Basin as a young man. He recalls that his salary was $32 a week though he was allowed to supplement that by selling candy and postcards at the ranger's cabin. What he assumed would be a temporary position became a five-year assignment.

For many years there was a packhorse operation that served clients coming into Chimney Pond from Avalanche Field. Jack Grant began the service in the mid- to late-1930s while he was a Forest Ranger in the area. He had a string of horses housed in an old CCC building at Avalanche Field, which at that time was the termination point for automobile travel for those heading to the Keep Ridge or Chimney Pond. For a short time, consideration was given to establishing a major Baxter State Park campground at that site, but later that facility was built at Roaring Brook. Grant had worked out a trail system to Roaring Brook and on to Basin Ponds and Chimney Pond, a second trail branching off to follow the north side of the South Branch of Wassataquoik Stream to Russell Pond. All of this was still on private land at the time.

Jack Grant apparently was a real character. He stayed in a cabin at the old Great Northern Paper Company depot camp at Avalanche Field where he took care of his animals in a nearby shed. He often shared his cabin with his clients. In 1941 he was still operating the business out of the last building from the lumbering era at the depot camp, offering to take anyone anywhere a horse could travel. It is said that he never packed an animal into Chimney Pond until he had led it himself at least two or three times so the horse could get acquainted with the trail. Later he led the animals past Blacksmith Brook as far as the junction where the trail into the Wassataquoik Valley branched off to the north. Once past the junction he let them go at their own pace to Chimney Pond. When they reached the Great Basin they grazed in the field there or at Dry Pond until Jack caught up to them and unloaded. He also packed visitors into Russell Pond.

He was very affectionate with the animals, talking to them constantly, sometimes using stronger language in the face of inevitable stubbornness. Jane Thomas recalls that her mother spoke of the air "turning blue" at times when Jack spoke to them but that it was a "soft blue."[14] Grant discontinued the operation during World War II when the number of clients dropped sharply.

After the war, in 1947, Harold Dyer, Baxter Park Supervisor, and Ralph Robinson, the ranger at Chimney Pond, bought two burros, Jack and Nancy, to haul supplies and equipment back and forth to Chimney Pond. In the beginning the role of the burros was confined to that mission. In 1950, when Ed Werler became the ranger at Chimney Pond, Dyer and Robinson sold the two animals to him for $200, and the burros continued hauling supplies and gear. Later, after he was reassigned to Roaring Brook Campground, Werler asked for and received permission to use the animals to haul supplies for park visitors who wished to camp at remote sites. A fee ($6 per hundred pounds in 1956) was charged for this service, and the burros were housed at Avalanche Field or at Roaring Brook Campground. Clients were taken each summer to Chimney Pond, Russell Pond and even as far as Wassataquoik Lake. There was not a lot of care needed to maintain the animals, but they ate almost anything, including cardboard boxes, and one time, several of Ed's T-shirts off the laundry line. One of the animals was of mixed burro and pony ancestry. Her name was Nancy, and she became known far and wide for her strength and endurance. Werler recalls that Nancy was a resourceful animal as well. On at least one occasion she got loose at Avalanche Field and, on her own, headed along an old tote road all the way to Katahdin Lake Camps, a distance of nearly three miles. There she raided proprietor Bud Cobb's oats supply, much to Bud's great displeasure. Nancy lived to the ripe old age of 40, long after her service in the park ended.

During the winters of 1959 and 1960 Ed and Ralph Dolley, the ranger at Russell Pond Campground, arranged for clients to snowshoe into Roaring Brook and fan out from there on day trips to Chimney Pond, the Turners, and other locations. At first, they had supplies flown into Sandy Stream Pond but later brought the supplies in themselves with the help of an old Polaris

Baxter State Park Ranger Ed Werler loading up his burro to take guests to Chimney Pond in the 1950s. Courtesy, Edward Werler.

Sno Machine. All of these operations apparently ceased when Werler left the employ of Baxter State Park in 1960.

Another unusual aspect of Chimney Pond history was the unsuccessful attempt to close the Great Basin to camping and relocate the campground to the Basin Pond area in 1970. The slow but steady increase in the number of persons allowed to camp at Chimney Pond each night caused an accompanying loss of forest cover and more erosion in the years after World War II. Systematic planning to address such problems was lacking during the early years of park management as it sought to establish itself even while Governor Baxter continued to add to the land base.

Finally in 1969, the Baxter State Park Authority, after years of discussion, decided to close Chimney Pond Campground completely and build a new campground at Basin Ponds. Sites were selected and several shelters were actually built during the summer of 1970. Before the campsite was ready for occupation in 1971, however, natural elements dramatically intervened. That winter severe storm winds toppled several of the new lean-tos. With a new understanding and appreciation of the ferocity of the winter winds at the South Basin location it was decided to keep the campground at Chimney Pond after all.

The increased erosion there had to be addressed, however, and over the years there has been a tightening up of the rules governing that camp-site—banning wood fires, increasing education, limiting the number of res-ervations, careful planning of the surrounding trails, and much more. These measures have contributed to a significant restoration of the forest cover and the reduction of erosion at this spectacular location. Baxter State Park is to be commended for its enlightened management of the Great Basin.

Charles Hubbard wrote of his experience standing at the edge of Chim-ney Pond, opening himself to what the moment had to offer. Nothing, he felt, could compete with the spirit voice that spoke to his inner soul:

The scene now becomes sublime. The vast area is hemmed in on three sides by rock walls, the jagged skyline of the Knife Edge lying before us, the for-bidding flanks of Pamola on the left while to the right those breath-taking Cathedral Cliffs soar ever upward toward Baxter Peak, and still farther to the north rise the steep walls of Hamlin Ridge. One may search in vain through-out all New England for such impressive exposures of rock. The forest climbs and ever climbs, utilizing every interval between the gigantic ledges to main-tain a hold and still the massive cliffs rise above, up to the very verge of the great Katahdin Tableland.

In the midst of all this grandeur, close to the foot of the mighty Pamola lies that tiny glacial lake known as Chimney Pond. Surrounded by wood-ed areas of spruce and fir and birch with branches contorted into fantastic shapes by the weight of a thousand icestorms, this forest forms an appropri-ate border to the pond lying like a jewel in its gigantuan granite setting.

But of the many moods made manifest through this age-scarred visage, who shall presume to command adequate description? I have seen it one all-encommpassing, peaceful summer morning, a latter-day Eden unsaddened by the world's woes. I have seen it wrapped in early morning's silvery mists with the first rose tints of sunrise touching its highest overhanging crags. I have seen it in the stillness of nightfall when mountain and forest and evening star found in it their perfect reflections. I have seen it when wild cloud masses came rolling over the peaks in endless ranks, swirling in and out among the pinnacles, the vast concave depressed in gloom; and I have seen it when waking on a wondrous night, a snowy cloud rested above the peak like a white veil and the moon was round.

Here are seen the effects of those titanic forces which have formed the world, and here we have come in admiration of this gem, this tiny offspring of the great continental ice-sheet, this shrine of beauty, this mirror of God.[15]

EARLY TRAILS

The enduring popularity of the Great Basin has resulted in the construction of many trails. The locations of some of the more recent trails are rather simple to identify; others, especially those built long ago, are far more complex and difficult to uncover. In the early years there were trails leading to the Great Basin from the Wassataquoik Valley as far as Roaring Brook. From Roaring Brook to the Basin Ponds they all followed much the same line of approach along that brook. Beyond Basin Ponds there were two ways to cross the glacial moraine into the basin itself.

The confusing location of the trails from the valley to Roaring Brook is due primarily to the constant shifting of timber cutting, which regularly obscured established trails. A portion of trail could thus be rendered useless until a few dedicated and enterprising hikers went to work to blaze and cut a new trail or trails to make the trip once again feasible. Sometimes part of an old trail was reopened after the timber had been cut. Roads built to transport logs to the streams and rivers were often utilized as well.

For example, although there is no recorded evidence that he did so, Rev. Marcus Keep likely marked a trail from the Wassataquoik Valley to the Great Basin the year after his first visit there in 1847. He returned a number of times as a guide for other parties, and marking the trail would have rendered his trips easier. In 1861 a major geological survey team led by Maine State Geologist Charles Hitchcock, with Keep as a guide, followed a roughly spotted line out of the Great Basin toward the valley. Also, not long after the Civil War, perhaps in the late 1860s, two men had spotted a very rough trail so they could guide clients into the Great Basin from the valley. (These were the same two men who later more formally cut what was to become known as the Lang and Jones Trail.)

Chimney Pond Trail

The Chimney Pond Trail we know today follows, to a considerable extent, the historic trails into the Great Basin. All the trails from the Wassataquoik Valley ended at Roaring Brook and all of them, like moving into a giant funnel, followed Roaring Brook itself the rest of the way to Basin Ponds. The footpath has remained much the same across the years, shifting only to address serious matters of erosion or to accommodate the work of the lumber industry in the region.

A 1933 Katahdin guidebook records that just after it crossed through the old depot camp at Roaring Brook this trail passed an abandoned blacksmith shop where one could still seek shelter long after it had ceased operating. The brook that empties at that point into Roaring Brook was and is still named Blacksmith Brook.

Beyond Basin Ponds there were two major trails cut to reach the Great Basin. One took a line toward Pamola Peak and then, staying on elevation, turned toward Chimney Pond. We will describe the history of that trail shortly. The other trail, the present Chimney Pond Trail, skirts the shore of the lower or more southerly of the Basin Ponds, and then sharply ascends the glacial moraine to Chimney Pond in the South Basin. This portion of the trail was likely cut by Roy Dudley about the time he was named the Maine Deputy Fish and Game Warden for the Great Basin and built the state cabin there in 1924. The trail soon became the preferred way to reach the Great Basin and, in tandem with the new Dudley Trail to Pamola, the preferred way to reach Katahdin's summit by way of the Knife Edge. It has been so ever since.

Lang and Jones Trail

Shortly after the Civil War these two gentlemen whose first names are unknown initiated a stagecoach line from Mattawamkeag to Patten along the old Military Road. As they carried their passengers past the Stacyville area they must have looked at Katahdin in the distance and felt a strong urge to explore that wild and uninhabited place. At the same time word was filtering back to the villages along the stagecoach road of the beauties and wonders of the remarkable Great Basin itself. The adventuresome and entrepreneurial spirits of these two men got the best of them, and they began to guide hiking parties toward the mountain. To do that with some degree of comfort, they had to do two things. One, they had to develop a clear trail to get folks there. Two, they had to provide accommodations for them between the Hunt Farm and the Great Basin.

At first, Lang and Jones cleared only a rough trail, but later, during the season of 1874, they cut an improved trail from the lower Wassataquoik Valley to Katahdin Lake. From there, the trail headed to the Great Basin by way of Reed's Upper Dam along Sandy Stream, up Roaring Brook, and on to Chimney Pond. The trail was thus the second established trail to Katahdin, the Keep Path being the first. It was, however, the first trail to reach all the way into the Great Basin. The trail followed lumbering roads when possible and was improved later and at times relocated. In fact, improvements allowed one to reach Katahdin Lake by buckboard with a fair amount of ease by 1882.

By 1879 or 1880 Lang and Jones had established the region's first sporting camps on the southwest shore of Katahdin Lake, slightly west of the present Katahdin Lake Wilderness Camps. The cabins were of crude log construction but provided a modicum of shelter for the clients the two were guiding to Chimney Pond. Their sporting camp business was not particularly profitable, and the buildings were later abandoned, the two men disappearing from the scene by mid-1880s. Because many clients wished to go only as far as the camps, the trail to Katahdin Lake was used far more often than the trail beyond that point toward the mountain.

Frederic E. Church, the renowned painter of the Hudson River School of landscape painting, used the Lang and Jones Trail when he visited the Great Basin in 1877. This was also the likely route that young Teddy Roosevelt took to climb the mountain with his friend Bill Sewall in 1879. Both Professor Charles E. Hamlin and George C. Witherle utilized the route during their later explorations of the Katahdin region. Marcus Keep accompanied Professor Hamlin into the Great Basin along the trail in 1881 in what turned out to be Keep's last visit to his beloved mountain.

By the mid-1880s a massive fire in the Wassataquoik Valley, along with major blowdowns, had so obscured much of the Lang and Jones Trail that a new trail was needed to reach the Great Basin. The arrival of the Appalachian Mountain Club in 1887 for its large encampment at the Great Basin provided the impetus for developing such an alternative.

The Original Appalachian Trail

Those who claim that the Appalachian Trail was created in the 1930s when a 2,160-mile trail between Katahdin and Mount Oglethorpe in Georgia was blazed and constructed may be unaware that an Appalachian Trail already existed in the Katahdin wilderness. When members of the Appalachian Trail Conference (ATC) began to lay out the present Appalachian Trail from the summit of Katahdin in 1933, heading south along the Hunt Trail, they preempted a trail name that had already been a part of Katahdin's history for almost 50 years.

The story of this major trail system leading to the Great Basin began in 1886. Prompted by the writings of Charles E. Hamlin, Harvard professor and active club member, the Boston-based Appalachian Mountain Club decided to bring a large group of its members to the basin in 1887 and engaged Clarence Peavey of Patten to be their guide. The year before, in 1886, Peavey was asked to spot and begin to clear a trail between Wassataquoik Stream and the Great Basin in preparation for their visit. Although Peavey may have had time to scout and mark his route that year he was not able to do much work on it until early in the 1887 season. Rosewell B. Lawrence of the AMC, reporting on the 1886 reconnaissance trip he and others took into the region, tells how important this new trail was to the hiking community:

> The route via Ktaadn Lake, the one recommended by Professor Hamlin, was, however, badly obscured by "blowdowns" a few years ago; and the path over the northern summits, taken by several Club members in 1886, is very long, and does not, without much labor, enable one to camp in the Basin. In order to take a Club party to the mountains in 1887, it seemed necessary to open a new route, and the great success of the excursion proved the wisdom of undertaking the work.[16]

Irving O. Hunt, the man who laid out and built the Hunt Trail on the southwest side of Katahdin, once recalled that his father Oliver Hunt and one or two of his uncles helped Peavey build the old Appalachian Trail toward Chimney Pond.

Beginning at the Upper Katahdin Crossing along Wassataquoik Stream, Peavey's trail linked together some of the lumber roads already in existence and some sections of his own making. The great fire of 1884 had caused extensive damage in the valley so he had to take that into consideration as well.

One could follow the trail by buckboard to Katahdin Lake, where a shelter of spruce logs with a birch bark roof was constructed to accommodate the AMCers. From the north end of Katahdin Lake the foot trail headed nearly due west toward the Roaring Brook-South Turner Mountain area and followed the old Lang and Jones route to Basin Ponds. It then headed for Chimney Pond by climbing directly toward Pamola before veering off to the Great Basin roughly at the same elevation. At Chimney Pond Peavey built another shelter, which later the AMCers named "Ktaadn Basin Camp." This trail became the third formal trail to Katahdin and the second into the Great Basin.

When the AMC group of nearly 50 arrived in August 1887, its members marveled at the trail and the preparations that had been made for them. They came armed with tools for further trail work and a number of signs to erect, especially above treeline. Their sojourn was such a success they returned to the Great Basin the following year to make more trail improvements and to experience the beauties of this remarkable place.

For many years this Appalachian Trail was used as the principal path to the Great Basin. The shifting activities of timber cutting caused persistent problems, of course, but that was a never-ending feature of life in this remote region where lumbering was still king. After a portion of the trail was cut over or burned, someone would simply relocate it or cut a new path through the brush.

With the establishment of a new sporting camp facility on Katahdin Lake by John Cushman and Madison M. Tracy in the late 1880s, use of the old Appalachian Trail was revived and the trail was better maintained. But not for long. A visitor in 1896 related the "Appalachian Path" was so overgrown it was somewhat difficult to follow. Gradually people traveling to the Great Basin from the east would trek to Katahdin Lake Camps then head over to Great Northern Paper Company's Sandy Stream Tote Road, and the original Appalachian Trail route between Katahdin Lake and Roaring Brook was neglected and finally abandoned.

The McLeod Trail and the Rogers Trail I
When the firm of Ayer and Rogers began its timber cutting operations in 1891, the owners established their headquarters at the so-called Patterson House along the Penobscot East Branch. They soon changed the name to the East Branch House, and it later came to be known as the Lunksoos Camps.

During the course of their cutting they utilized a rough road that had been cut south from the Bell Dam along the South Branch of the Wassataquoik to a site where a substantial stream flowed into the South Branch. The McLeod Camp, named after the boss of the lumber camp, was built there.

That same year or soon after, perhaps in 1892, Rogers cut two hiking trails from the McLeod Camp. One of the trails, the McLeod Trail, followed a westerly course directly up to the higher elevations of the Katahdin massif and its spectacular Tableland. The trail eventually linked into the relatively new Tracy and Love Trail (now the North Peaks Trail) that had been cut in 1885–86. A high country lean-to shelter was built just below treeline at the 4,000-foot level near a prominent open knob. This was most likely the highest shelter ever built on Katahdin.

All this activity was, for the most part, to accommodate members of the lumber operation who wanted to climb the northern peaks of Katahdin and to allow hunters access to prime caribou feeding grounds above treeline. Unfortunately, the great fire of 1903 burned the McLeod Camp to the ground and obliterated the McLeod Trail. It appeared on only a few of the early maps, but it must have been spectacular to ascend to treeline on this trail and cross the northern peaks of the Katahdin range.

The second trail Rogers cut also originated from the McLeod Camp and was named the Rogers Trail, not to be confused with the Rogers Trail built later from Katahdin Lake to Basin Ponds. With the McLeod Camp located a mere three miles from the Great Basin, Edwin Rogers, son of Colonel Luther B. Rogers and brother to Dr. Lore A. Rogers, cut the trail in 1894 to provide direct access to the Great Basin from the upper Wassataquoik Valley. The trail followed the north shore of the South Branch of the Wassataquoik, cut through a stand of virgin pine, and linked into the old Appalachian Trail in the Basin Ponds area.

Shortly after it was cut, Lore Rogers took a party into the Great Basin by this route, and George C. Witherle utilized it in 1898 during one of his exploration trips. Two Harvard botanists, George C. Kennedy and B.H. Dutcher, for whom a crude log cabin was built in the Great Basin in 1900, traveled this route, guided by Edwin Rogers. Lore Rogers is said to have built the cabin. Members of the Rogers family often used the route while hiking with friends and clients. The massive fire of 1903 that obliterated the McLeod Camp and Trail obliterated this path as well and rendered useless the tote road along the South Branch.

Rogers Trail II

In 1902 Edwin Rogers, then proprietor of the Lunksoos Sporting Camp on the Penobscot East Branch, accompanied by an employee of the John Ross timber operation, cut a new trail from Katahdin Lake to Roaring Brook and up along Roaring Brook nearly to Basin Ponds. It was designed to be on more level ground to accommodate his packhorse teams. A 1904 ad carried by *In the Maine Woods* boasts that the "only saddle trail into Katahdin starts from the Lunksoos House, following the Wassataquoik Valley, passing Katahdin Lake and the south end of Turner Mountain, crossing Sandy Stream, rounding the head of Sandy Pond and then climbing up Roaring Brook to the South Basin where a comfortable camp is located."[17]

This trail paralleled the old Appalachian Trail from Katahdin Lake to Roaring Brook and then coincided with it to Basin Ponds. On one of his exploration trips Professor LeRoy H. Harvey described the route. Although the trail is shown on several 1927 and 1928 maps, there appears little evidence of its use at that time and no record of use after that period.

Basin Ponds Area

Today, Chimney Pond Trail takes a slight bend to the left and unless one is alert, the short side trail to the shore of Basin Ponds might be missed altogether. That few hundred yards leads to one of the most remarkable views in the Katahdin region. With the blue waters of a pristine mountain pond at one's feet, one gazes up to take in, on a clear day, the whole panorama of the Katahdin massif from Pamola at one's left, across the Knife Edge to South Peak, to Katahdin's summit, and on to the Saddle, Hamlin Peak and the glory of the Howe Peaks. As one's gaze lowers, one begins to see into the Great Basin, above its glacial moraine, as well as the dramatic Cathedral and Hamlin Ridges and the striking North Basin.

What is little known is just how important the location around this magnificent view was to the history of the region and the Great Basin. From the earliest days it was recognized that the best way into the Great Basin was to follow Roaring Brook to this very spot where a brook flows out of Basin Ponds and begins its tortuous, rock-strewn journey down to Sandy Stream. Thus all the trails to the Great Basin came to this magnificent view—and that is still true today. The only way to ascend to the Great Basin is to pass the Basin Ponds.

We have traced some of the history of the trails leading into Basin Ponds from the Wassataquoik Valley east of Katahdin during the nineteenth century. Eventually all those trails were abandoned. In addition to the persistent encroachment of timber cutting along the valley, the most important effect on trails into the Great Basin was the slow northward march of Great Northern Paper Company's Sandy Stream Tote Road in the early years of the twentieth century.

Timber operations began along Sandy Stream as early as 1874 and utilized the stream for driving logs down to the West Branch. The old Hersey-Reed operation was generally unprofitable and most of the work eventually ceased. In 1901 another charter was granted for cutting in the Sandy Stream watershed, and a road along the west side of the stream began to make its way north, first to Avalanche Field where a depot camp was built and then to Roaring Brook, the site of a smaller lumber camp. This is now Baxter State Park's Roaring Brook Road.

By 1921 the tote road was completed by Great Northern all the way to Basin Ponds, and cutting began in a considerable area north and east of the Great Basin. That road followed the route originally cut for the Appalachian Mountain Club in 1887 and subsequently used by a number of other trail systems. In further preparation for its massive timber operation in the shadow of Katahdin, Great Northern built a spacious camp building right at the site of the magnificent view previously mentioned. The lumbermen housed there at the outlet into Roaring Brook helped facilitate the flow of logs down the stream. The Basin Ponds Camp, as it came to be known, was built in 1921 and became the center of this major cutting into the late 1920s. The camp building had enough double bunks for the 70 to 80 men who worked there. A large number of horses were also kept at the camp.

The main building and accompanying sheds became known also as Whalen's Camp No. 3, named to honor Patrick E. Whalen, the Superintendent of Great Northern Paper Company at the time. Fred Gilbert, who once headed the Penobscot Log Driving Company on the West Branch, was also associated with this operation, and one of the smaller buildings was named the Gilbert Camp. He later became Superintendent of Great Northern for a short time and was an outspoken opponent of Governor Baxter's effort to purchase land in the area to fulfill his dream of preserving the Katahdin region. A smaller lumber camp was established on Little Basin Pond, resulting in that pond being referred to at times as Depot Pond. There was also a Camp 4 high on the side of the mountain. The Basin Pond operation was a major timber cutting effort.

An article in the Great Northern newsletter, recounting a 1923 winter visit to the Basin Pond Depot Camp, tells the story of this operation and includes pictures of enormous piles of 4-foot logs at the very edge of Roaring Brook waiting for the spring runoff when they were to begin their journey down the watershed to the Millinocket mills.

> Camp No. 3 which is located at the foot of Basin Pond, right in the old trail from Katahdin Lake to Chimney Pond [the old Appalachian Trail] is approached by a road leading from the depot [at Avalanche Field], a distance of four miles, almost entirely up hill. Some of it is very much up hill!
>
> At No. 3 or the South Basin Camp, we found a jolly crew of seventy men, under the boss of Frank Sullivan, just waiting for their Sunday dinner. They put off the dinner long enough to pose for the camera. Sixteen horses were stamping and calling restlessly for their dinner. The South Basin Pond was already piled with pulp wood. . . .
>
> The business of getting pulpwood off the sides of Mount Katahdin is not a job for the tenderfoot. The hill and rocks are a continual hindrance. The rocks must be blasted out to clear a way for the road. To anyone who has ever made the trip over the trail from Katahdin Lake to Chimney Pond, the recollections of that rocky climb must come back. Well, the pulpwood is taken part of the way over that same trail. But it is not the same, for the great rocks have been blasted out and the holes filled in until, with its snow covering, it is smooth and even. Down those grades the sled loads of wood are eased with snubbing machines. But they get it down. Roaring Brook is piled high with it for miles—so it seemed to us. . . . The brook is completely hidden at points by the wood it is expected to float off with the spring freshet. It will go all right when the snow gets to melting on the mountain side.[18]

On August 19, 1923, a major disaster was averted when a fire that had broken out in the area was contained by the crew before it spread out of control. Their efforts were aided by an Appalachian Mountain Club group camping at Chimney Pond at the time. Fortunately, AMC food and equipment and many Great Northern supplies stored at the camp building were spared. Although damage had been limited the scars were visible from Katahdin's peaks for a number of years.

Through the 1920s the Great Northern Paper Company was generous in allowing use of some of the camp buildings by summer hikers who wished to stay there on their way into the Great Basin. By the late 1920s, after the area had been cut over and the operation closed down, the camps were left open for year-round recreational use. In 1933 and again in 1934 Reggie Crawford, proprietor of the Togue Pond Camps, leased the buildings and operated them as a part of his sporting camp operation. He advertised that he could accommodate a limited number at the Gilbert Camp and could offer five double beds with springs; food and blankets were not included.[19] A caretaker stayed there for several seasons to oversee this arrangement.

A 1936 guidebook reported that the Basin Pond Camps were leased by Colonel Harry Ross, who was one of several granted the Sandy Stream Dam and Improvement Company charter in 1901 and the son of John Ross, renowned boss of many of the old West Branch river drives. By that time the main building had slowly deteriorated. We do not know much about Ross' intentions for the Basin Pond area, but the buildings accidentally caught fire and were burned to the ground that same year, and the Basin Ponds area began a slow but inevitable recovery toward its long-lost primitive character. Even the short-lived proposal in 1969 to close Baxter State Park's Chimney Pond Campground and open a campground at Basin Ponds did not halt this natural process of recovery, the results of which we are privileged to witness today.

As one stands now at the end of that short side trail and looks out to the vast panorama of pond and forest and mountain, it is difficult to imagine all the boisterous activity that took place there in the past. Only a few relics covered by thicket remain. Remnants of the wooden outlet dam that controlled the water for Basin Ponds can still be seen. They are but mute reminders of a storied past that have now given way to the grandeur of that extraordinary view.

Old Basin Trail
The story of this little known trail has two episodes. The first centers on the lower section of the trail, which was laid out in 1887 for the use of the folks from the Appalachian Mountain Club going to the Great Basin for their first August encampment. It was, therefore, an integral part of the old Appalachian Trail for many years and was the only way into the Great Basin until

the present trail leading directly up the glacial moraine was cut by Roy Dudley in the early 1920s. From the southeast corner of Lower Basin Pond the Old Basin Trail ascended directly toward Pamola Peak. Near the 2,900-foot level, at several large prominent open boulders, the trail veered to the right and generally followed that contour line west to Chimney Pond.

The second episode of the story begins in 1924 when the trail was extended from that prominent boulder junction straight on up to Pamola. The purpose of this action may have been to provide more direct access to Pamola for those then beginning to use the Great Northern Paper Company Tote Road that had been built to Basin Ponds. What apparently was not foreseen was the growing popularity of the Dudley Trail built by Roy Dudley just the year before in 1923 and which also ascended Pamola from Chimney Pond. The Old Basin Trail reached that summit just slightly to the east of Dudley's Trail. This new trail-building activity from Chimney Pond, coupled with the building of the trail directly up the moraine about the same year, rendered the Old Basin Trail nearly obsolete shortly after it was cut. Walter Leavitt descended it in 1924 and found it well marked and easy to follow. When he returned in 1929 to try it again he was hardly able to find the trail through the scrub. It had obviously not been maintained because of the increasing popularity of the Dudley Trail. By 1934 it was reported that the old trail was no longer used to reach Chimney Pond. The trail was included in Walter Leavitt's *Katahdin Skylines* profiles in 1942, but perhaps that was a tip of Leavitt's hat to a venerable old trail used by many early climbers to reach the Great Basin. The trail was totally abandoned and the cairns removed by 1939. The trail was known by a number of names through the years—Old Basin Trail, Basin Ponds Trail, Old Pamola Trail, and the Basin Ponds-Pamola Trail.

MODERN TRAILS

Hikers had frequented the Great Basin since 1847, and one way or another they had ascended to the Tableland, the Knife Edge, and Katahdin's summit without clearly delineated or marked trails. There can be little doubt that across the years rough trails were cut or worn through the scrub and even some simple cairns placed above the treeline to guide the way. It was not, however, until Roy Dudley took up permanent seasonal residence in the Great Basin in 1924 that the trails out of the basin were formally located, cut and marked. Most of those trails were built in the 1920s, as we shall see, and they largely remain the same today.

The Dudley Trail and the Knife Edge

It was natural for early visitors to the Great Basin to see the possibilities for reaching Pamola and the Knife Edge by ascending the slopes that rose so sharply from the eastern shore of Chimney Pond. During the first Appalachian Mountain Club trip to Katahdin in 1887 its members climbed many of Katahdin's peaks, built trail cairns to some of them, and even erected signs to help those who followed them. As there were not many alternative routes up those steep slopes, the trails must have followed generally the route of the present Dudley Trail. According to the 1907 *Guide to Paths in the White Mountains and Adjacent Regions*, the first edition of what is now known as the AMC's *White Mountain Guide*, a very rough path and a few cairns showed the way between Chimney Pond and Pamola. No name is given for this obviously crude but passable path.

During the season of 1922 Roy Dudley, then a private guide operating out of Chimney Pond, began to consider a location for a safe and clear path from the pond up the steep slopes to the peak of Pamola. He may have even located some of the route that summer as well. No doubt Dudley was eager to return in 1923 to put the finishing touches on his "new" trail. When, later that summer, Marjorie Lee, a Millinocket school teacher, came to climb the mountain, Roy was excited about the prospect of showing off his handiwork. Ms. Lee had been guided to the Great Basin from the Penobscot East Branch side by a good friend of Dudley, and the two of them did everything they could to make their client comfortable.

The day after their arrival the two guides and Ms. Lee climbed to the summit by either the Cathedral Ridge or the Saddle and then crossed the Knife Edge. As they descended from Pamola Peak to Chimney Pond, Dudley was delighted to guide them down his new trail, asking for their evaluation and inviting suggestions for improvement. As a result of their experience that day several relocations were, indeed, later carried out by Dudley.[20] At first the new trail was named Dudley's Trail but soon the simpler Dudley Trail name prevailed.

In the course of his earlier explorations Dudley discovered massive caves on the north slope of Pamola. He called them Pamola's Caves and, in 1927, he cut a side trail to them from the by then well-established Dudley Trail.

He often referred to the caves in his legendary stories about Pamola, declaring that it was through those caves that Pamola gained access to the interior of the mountain. When one climbs the Dudley Trail today one is closest to Pamola's domain and may sense his presence, especially on a day when the clouds and mists roll in or when thunder suddenly overtakes the mountain.

On the upper part of the trail one passes close to a major landmark. Index Rock is a huge pointed boulder that protrudes in lonely splendor from the boulder-strewn slope. It can be seen from a number of other trails. Climb with me as we complete this historic route and stand together on Pamola Peak. Look back down Dudley Trail to Chimney Pond far below and the great glacial moraine that holds back its sparkling waters. Gaze down the boulder strewn Keep Ridge and thrill to the wilderness country to the east. Turn southwest and experience the majesty of the Knife Edge, which begins here. Glance across the Great Basin to Katahdin's summit and the ridges and open rock plateaus to the west. Know the profound reward offered in payment to all who make the effort to stand in this remarkable place.

The Knife Edge has been known by many names across the years—Knife's Edge, The Saw Teeth, The Narrows (in an AMC 1887 account), and Knife Blade (in a 1925 account)—all seeking to convey a sense of its unusual and remarkable characteristics. The mile-long Knife Edge Trail is an exhilarating traverse from Pamola to Katahdin's summit. The trail is at times only a few feet wide, sheer cliffs falling at the side, at times sharply and at other times more gradually, providing spectacular views in all directions. One crosses this chaotic assembly of granite boulders and scree marveling at the great natural forces that shaped it. When one finally stands on the summit of Katahdin it is almost anticlimactic.

Cathedral Trail

It is quite obvious as one stands on the shore of Chimney Pond that the prominent Cathedral Ridge was utilized to reach the summit long before any formal trail existed there. Among the most conspicuous features of this ridge are three majestic rock formations that rise steeply from the ridgeline. At first sight the ridge is so steep that it appears to be insurmountable except with technical climbing equipment. Yet miraculously, ways were found to climb this spectacular ridge safely, and it has always been one of the most rewarding routes to the summit. It happens to be the shortest way from the basin as well, no small reward for one's effort. Because of its steepness it is generally recommended that one ascend it only and descend another way.

Roy Dudley formally marked the trail in 1923, and the first users were reported to be members of an AMC August Camp group, guided by Dudley himself. The trail leaves Chimney Pond and, after passing a small pond known today as Cleftrock Pool, but known in the past as "Cathedral Pool" and even "Dudley's Bathtub," begins its ascent of the ridge. On the way one passes by or around those three cathedral-like boulder formations, finally climbing talus slopes and boulder fields to the summit. Despite relocations at the higher elevations, the trail remains much the same as it was when Roy Dudley finished marking it so long ago.

Saddle Trail

The Saddle Trail ascends the very prominent Saddle Slide, an avalanche at the far western end of the Great Basin that gave way during the winter of 1898–99. This is actually a "new" avalanche and was first reported in June of 1899 by Dr. Lore A. Rogers when he was traveling to the Great Basin by way of the short-lived McLeod Trail to the northern peaks and down to the saddle between the summit of Katahdin and Hamlin Peak. For years a much earlier avalanche slide slightly north of the present one was used to reach the saddle. One can still see the old slide when standing at the edge of the saddle or from the floor of the basin. Several early explorers tell of descending the then-named "Basin Slide" to Chimney Pond. In 1887 the Appalachian Mountain Club August encampment marked a route up the old slide just a few years before the new one tumbled into the basin. After the new slide came down, people seeking to climb the mountain in the early years of the twentieth century simply picked their way through the more recent avalanche rubble to the saddle.

In 1927 Roy Dudley finally marked and constructed a formal trail through the scrub and the slide debris. For a time the trail was known as the New Saddle Trail and was even named the New Dudley Trail for a short time by federal and state geologists. It was also known for some years as the Parsons Trail, an attempt to honor Willis Parsons who, as the Commissioner of Inland Fisheries and Game for the state of Maine at that time, had a major role in creating the Katahdin Park Game Preserve in 1921. That Preserve designation proved to be an important step toward the establishment of Baxter State Park. Parsons also accompanied Governor Baxter and others on their historic visit to the Great Basin and climb of Katahdin in August of 1920. That trail name would have been a most appropriate one, but it did not prevail, and it was not long before it became known by its present name.

The Saddle Trail is one of the most popular trails to Baxter Peak because, though steep in some places and not having the most stable footing, it is the easiest path to the summit from Chimney Pond and offers spectacular views, especially once one reaches the storied Tableland.

In 1934 a blue-blazed side trail was marked on the Tableland between the Saddle Slide and Thoreau Spring to provide an alternative route if needed in threatening weather. For a time in the 1930s some folks intending to spend the night on or near the summit picked pine boughs in the scrub area at the saddle and carried them to the summit. A 1942 guidebook reports that this practice had trampled and denuded the area around the Saddle Spring, a short distance from the top of the slide, and warned against continuing such behavior. Spending a night on Katahdin is not allowed today by the rules of Baxter State Park. Across the years there have been frequent relocations to the Saddle Trail, all designed to make it safer and less prone to erosion. Although it is discomfiting in some places to climb on the loose scree of the avalanche, this historic path is still one of the most popular trails for climbing to the Tableland and Baxter Peak.

Hamlin Ridge Trail

This dramatic ridgeline descending from Hamlin Peak toward Basin Ponds forms the southern flank of the North Basin and divides it from the Great Basin. Though there may have been an undeveloped trail earlier, Roy Dudley cut the trail in 1925 utilizing the Chimney Pond Trail for a short distance below the Great Basin and thence across what is now the North Basin Trail to the base of the ridge which the trail then ascends. An Appalachian Mountain Club group improved the trail in the 1930s. The ridge is a spectacular boulder-strewn climb with expansive views of the little-visited North Basin, the Great Basin, the Knife Edge, and Katahdin's summit. The ridge and the peak were named for Dr. Charles E. Hamlin, Professor of Chemistry and Natural History at Colby College, later Professor of Geology and Geography at Harvard College. Hamlin's many exploration trips beginning in 1869 revealed for the first time to the outside world the complex physical characteristics of this remarkable area.

North Basin Trail

This trail leads off the Chimney Pond Trail not far below the Great Basin and ascends gradually to Blueberry Knoll at the top of the North Basin glacial moraine. There one can see the whole panorama of the impressive North Basin, one of the best glacial cirques in New England. Though there were certainly a few early explorers who must have entered the North Basin, no trails, even rough ones, were cut into this remote area for many years. A very rudimentary trail was cut and used extensively by some of the members of that famous 1887 August encampment of the Appalachian Mountain Club, but it was apparently never well maintained. A 1917 AMC guidebook indicates that one is entirely on one's own if a visit to the North Basin is contemplated.

It is difficult to find a firm date, but there is evidence that sometime in 1930 or 1931 Roy Dudley saw the wisdom of continuing the trail he had cut to the base of Hamlin Ridge so that one could visit Blueberry Knoll less than a mile beyond where the Hamlin Ridge Trail begins its ascent of Hamlin Peak.

Sometime in the mid-1940s Wendell Taber, co-author with Ralph Palmer of an *Appalachia* article on Katahdin's birds and a frequent Chimney Pond visitor, scouted and marked with cairns a trail from Blueberry Knoll across the floor of the North Basin. The trail continued on up the basin wall where it linked in with the North Peaks Trail (then known as the Howe Peaks Trail) not far from Caribou Spring. The route was known for a very short time as the Taber Route, but it was soon abandoned completely because of the dangerously unstable steep walls of the North Basin. Permission to climb in this area is no longer granted. And for good reason!

Blueberry Knoll is, however, a most pleasant place with remarkable views into the North Basin, the Great Basin, and out across the interior wilderness of Baxter State Park to the north. At the right season, one always finds there a praise-worthy profusion of mountain cranberries and, of course, the blueberries that give the knoll its name. Some have even sung such praises in song. The source of this little song is uncertain, but it is a unique commentary on the reputation of the fruit of the genus *vaccinium*:

> I stopped on the trail over Blueberry Knoll,
> My bucket was empty, my stomach a hole,
> I gathered some berries and went on my way,
> If I'd known who would meet me I'd have stayed home that day.
>
> Chorus:
> On Chimney Pond Trail I was hiking along
> With a pail full of berries I was singing a song,

When I met with a scrounge from the Vassar O.C.*
Can't go back to camp 'cause I lost my berries.

Her name it was Dugan, she looked at my pail,
She started to mooch it, she knew she'd not fail,
She offered to bake me a blueberry pie;
I gave her the berries, God only knows why.
[Chorus]
I chopped up her firewood, I cleaned out her pot.
She rolled out the pie crust right there on the spot.
She threw in the berries and started to sing,
I knew at that moment I'd lost the whole thing.
[Chorus]
The pie came out flaky, a rich golden brown;
She cut it in pieces, folks gathered around.
My mouth started drooling, I reached for my share,
But when Dugan had finished, the plate it was bare.[21]

The Four Fools Trail

As the number of trail systems out of the Great Basin grew and more and more visitors came to camp there, Roy Dudley and others felt by the late 1920s that it was time to provide a way for hikers to visit the spectacular yet still remote and little-visited Northwest Basin and Davis Pond, the lovely mountain tarn at its base. Preliminary exploration of a possible route was done in 1929 by Grace Butcher and other members of an AMC group. Apparently no work was done in 1930, but in the spring of 1931 Grace and Frank Butcher, along with their son and Roy Dudley, explored a possible route down to the basin from Harvey Ridge. They camped in the basin, returning to the Northwest Plateau along a route that was deemed a better location for the trail. Dudley began to tag the trail through the scrub, and in September another AMC group started to clear the trail.

After that season they decided to begin the trail at the top of the Saddle Trail and follow the already well-worn trail up the slope of Hamlin Peak to Caribou Spring where it connected with the Hamlin Ridge Trail not far from the summit of Hamlin Peak. From there the new trail would follow in

* Refers to the Vassar College Outing Club.

a northwesterly direction across the open spaces of the Northwest Plateau (part of Katahdin's vast Tableland) and, after reaching the far end of that plateau, descend sharply into the Northwest Basin. They also began to lay plans for a shelter at the foot of the basin.

In mid-June of 1932 Dudley, his wife Abby, and their son Verdie, along with their now close personal friends, Frank and Grace Butcher, began the shelter construction. First, they built a rough temporary shelter so they would have a safe place to stay while they finished work on the permanent shelter and on the toughest trail section from the plateau, down to the pond. Next, they cut and peeled logs for the permanent shelter. They got the log shelter up three logs high that spring before time ran out and they had to leave.

In mid-June of 1933 the Dudleys, their two sons, and the Butchers returned amid a terrible black fly infestation and completed the shelter. Lester "Sawdust" F. Hall and Jake Day had difficulty finding their way across the Tableland and down into the basin that season, but in the summer of 1934 Dudley and the Butchers erected cairns across the Tableland and the trail was completed. The original foursome of the Dudleys and the Butchers had named themselves the Four Fools, hence the affectionate name given to the trail for several years. In 1936 Governor Baxter suggested it be named the "Burton Howe Trail" in honor of his dear friend who had introduced Baxter to the wonders of the Katahdin region. Although both names appeared briefly in guidebooks, the trail eventually became a part of the Northwest Basin Trail that now follows all the way from Russell Pond to the Saddle Trail. Baxter later got his wish to honor his friend, however, when the peaks north of Hamlin Peak were named the Howe Peaks.

At first the Four Fools Trail began at Chimney Pond and ended at Davis Pond, but in 1937 Lester F. Hall of Damariscotta Mills, Maine, and Clayton Hall cut a new trail from Davis Pond northward toward the Wassataquoik Tote Road, thereby linking the Wassataquoik Valley with the Northwest Basin. The section of the Four Fools Trail from the plateau to the pond was improved by the AMC in 1941 and its location has remained largely the same since that time except for changes to improve safety and prevent erosion of the footpath.

THE NORTH SIDE

8

Russell Pond and the Interior Wilderness

To hike into the expansive wilderness north of Katahdin is to enter a world far different from anything found nearer to the mountain. On the Penobscot West Branch side, with Katahdin nearby, there are many more trails and campgrounds, along with the visitors who use them. The Penobscot East Branch side has been nearly abandoned and is rarely visited. On the west side, the commanding presence of less accessible, outlying mountains has resulted in there being few trails or visitors. On the other hand, the wild Russell Pond side of Katahdin is a unique and incomparable realm. Though there are many mute reminders of the old lumbering days, those are no longer as visible as they once were. Three branches of Wassataquoik Stream roar down from the higher elevations and, after joining as one, make their way through boulder and forest to rendezvous with the East Branch of the Penobscot River. Remnants of the old Wassataquoik Stream Tote Road can hardly be seen now unless one is alert to the signs. There are dozens of wilderness ponds, some often visited, and others rarely. There are mountains, of course, but they seem dwarfed by Katahdin.

It is a storied region and appeals to those willing and eager to find the solitude and simplicity not always found "on the mountain." The center of this region is the Russell Pond Campground, reached only after a full seven miles of backpacking from the nearest parking lot at Roaring Brook. Though Russell Pond is the natural "hub," there are many spokes that lead to outlying treasures: Wassataquoik and Little Wassataquoik Lakes and their remote campsites, dank and mossy Greene Falls, the Northwest Basin's remarkable glacial cirque, the Howe Peaks, the celebrated Grand Falls of the Wassataquoik, remote Pogy Pond, and the always enchanting South Branch Ponds.

The stark beauty of this interior expanse has a strong association with the great lumbering era. There are still reminders of the great fires that swept through the region in 1884, 1903, and 1915. Many of the trails follow, at least in part, the roads that were once used to reach remote depot camps. Many of the campsites are located at or near some of the camps that housed the lumberjacks and their equipment. The region is very special, indeed.

NORTH PEAKS TRAIL (THE HISTORIC TRACY TRAIL)

Though the path itself became known as the North Peaks Trail, the rocky peaks north of Katahdin it crosses were, by an act of Maine's legislature in 1937, named Howe Peaks.

The trail was not formally constructed until 1885, but there were a number of early explorers who climbed Katahdin roughly along the same line. Their motivation was to ascend from the Wassataquoik Valley to the Tableland and the high peaks. They usually took the Middle (or Main) Branch of the Wassataquoik, veering off to climb through a ravine between Russell Mountain and Tip Top. This brought them to a spectacular series of peaks leading finally to Hamlin Peak.

Edward Everett Hale and his Harvard friend, William Francis Channing, climbed along this route when they made one of the earliest recreational visits to Katahdin in 1846. They had followed the tote road along the Wassataquoik, which was opened up by lumbering interests in 1841. Eventually they had to make the final climb to the northern peaks on their own because timber cutting had not yet reached that point. Two years later, in 1848, members of the Aaron Young Botanical Survey also climbed to the northern peaks along this route.

Both of these parties were certainly aware that this track, although considerably longer, offered a more gradual way to reach the high peaks, especially since approaches to the Keep Ridge and the Great Basin were

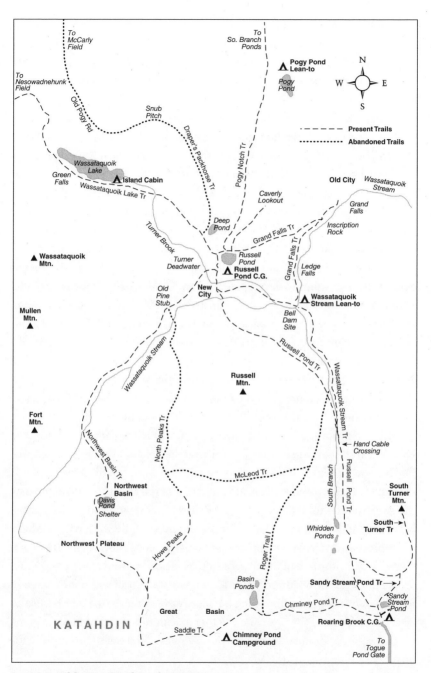

Interior wilderness trails and campsites.

still limited at this time. Later, the greater accessibility of those other routes would divert people from the Upper Wassataquoik Stream routes for many years. There are very few references to anyone climbing Katahdin along this path again until the 1880s, though it is likely that lumbermen wishing to make the climb would have kept open a very rough path.

A major change took place in the early 1880s when the first spruce loggers began to penetrate the upper Wassataquoik Valley beyond the New City Depot Camps near Russell Pond. The Tracy and Love lumber operation began in 1883, named for its managers Foster J. Tracy and his son-in-law Hugh Love. As their road system slowly made its way up the valley of the main branch of the Wassataquoik, it became much easier for climbers to reach the high peaks north of Katahdin.

Despite having to contend with a major cyclonic wind that devastated the valley in 1883 and a major fire that did extensive damage in 1884, members of the Tracy family developed a scheme to construct a formal trail to Katahdin in 1885. The plan was to construct a bridle trail from the lumber road system, up the ravine between Russell Mountain and Tip Top to the timberline, thence along the northern peaks to Hamlin Peak, and eventually to Katahdin's summit. The hope was to entice tourists to stay at the Tracy and Love Depot Camp at New City during the summer season and take them on a thrilling journey to the high peaks by guides and packhorses. (At this point, the cabins at Russell Pond cabins had not been built.)

The two proprietors of the Lang and Jones sporting camps on Katahdin Lake heard about the scheme and, realizing the benefit of such an adventure for their own clients, offered $100 toward the cost of building the trail. Although the trail may have been laid out and marked as early as 1884, most of the construction took place in 1885. Madison Tracy, who shortly thereafter helped found the Katahdin Lake Camps, did most of the work with the help of employees of the Tracy and Love operation along with members of his own family. By the end of the 1885 season Madison boasted of having taken a saddle horse to the northern peaks to prove that the trail was not only ready to be used by the public for hiking but also ready to receive packhorse use as well. The dreams of the Tracy family then began to expand to include plans for a resort development on the northern slopes of the Katahdin massif with buckboard access along the Wassataquoik.

The very next year, in 1886, George C. Witherle came through on one of his exploration treks and followed the new trail, expressing great enthusiasm and praise for the quality experience it offered. Witherle on several occasions called it "Katahdin Path" but the trail soon became known as the "Tracy Trail." A party of fourteen, including Mrs. Luther B. Rogers of Patten, also made a trip that year along the route, riding buckboard to the end of the road and climbing the rest of the way to Katahdin.

The inexorable movement of lumber operations up the main branch of the Wassataquoik and several major fires in the region eventually had a negative effect on the new trail, and it became difficult to keep it open. The resort dream faded as people failed to respond to the Tracy offer of somewhat primitive lumber camp accommodations. Perhaps the mixing of recreational climbing with the mess left by a typical timber cutting operation did not suit the needs of the tourists they had hoped to draw to the region. At the same time people had discovered and were becoming more and more enamored by the unforgettable Great Basin. Another factor that led to the public's departure from the interior for a time was that sporting camps had sprung up along the West Branch and its tributaries as well as on the Keep Ridge side of the mountain. By the end of the century people were coming to these camps in large numbers.

Within ten years Witherle could hardly find the Tracy Trail during another of his exploration trips, this one in 1895, and even referred to it as the "Old Katahdin Path." All indications are that it may have actually passed out of use altogether for the ensuing 35 years or so. Major timber cuttings along that part of the Wassataquoik were taking place throughout the early part of the twentieth century and certainly made access to the trail a nightmare. Myron Avery found parts of it still visible in 1924 but barely so at best. After the Draper operation ceased cutting in 1914 people more or less abandoned the valley.

However, in 1927 a new era began for the upper Wassataquoik Valley. Timber cutting had finally come to an end after the disastrous fire in 1915, allowing the forest to begin its slow recovery. In the early 1920s William F. Tracy, a nephew of Foster J. Tracy, purchased the lease on a set of sporting camps along the Penobscot East Branch and began to bring his guests to a small outlying camp he built on the shore of Russell Pond. The outlying camp there became so popular that he steadily expanded that part of his operation.

Realizing the desire of some of his clients to do more than fish and hunt, he decided to reopen the old Tracy Trail so his "sports" could climb the mountain. Tracy did the work in 1927 with help from other members of the family. Within a few years Tracy included a sentence about "our own trail to Mt. Katahdin" in his ads in the Bangor and Aroostook Railroad publication *In the Maine Woods*. Despite his good intentions, however, Tracy found that maintaining such a trail took tremendous effort. Extensive maintenance work was done on "Tracy's Trail" by his uncle Foster J. Tracy, in 1930. It was once again re-blazed and worked on in 1939 by Henri Soucie, a guide at the now well-established Russell Pond Camps. Of special note was the broken stub of a huge old pine that for many years marked the place where the Tracy Trail left the Wassataquoik Tote Road and headed for the high peaks.

As the interior wilderness area became more accessible in the 1940s, the trail received more use and was eventually identified as Howe Peaks Trail (or Howe Trail) in honor of Burton Howe, who introduced Percival Baxter to the Katahdin region. Today it is known as North Peaks Trail. The trail never has had extensive use and sometimes has become obscure, but it is truly one of the most historic and scenic trails of Katahdin. A small but faithful group of hiking enthusiasts remained loyal to hiking this trail over the years. At the time of this writing the trail has been closed by Baxter State Park for a number of reasons, but there are those who hope for its return someday to the park's trail system.

NORTHWEST BASIN TRAIL

The Northwest Basin is one of the most beautiful places anywhere in the Katahdin region. It is, like the Great Basin, a huge glacial cirque left behind by the retreating ice sheet that once lay over New England. Because it takes such effort to reach it, little has changed in the basin through the years except the natural changes that normally occur. There are still only two trails into the basin, one from the Wassataquoik Valley and the other from the Northwest Plateau. There is only one small shelter into which only one party of no more than four can be booked on any given night. It is, indeed, a magical place and leaves impressions that last a lifetime.

We cannot know for certain if Native Americans visited the basin but it is likely, as they usually explored to the headwaters of the streams and rivers they used for transport and livelihood. We do know that the first non-native visitors were members of the Monument Line Survey of 1833. The basin had been seen but not entered by earlier survey teams. It was then apparently forgotten for more than 50 years. George C. Witherle saw the basin from North Brother on his exploration trip of 1884, but he did not descend into it. He called it the West Basin and described it more fully after a later trip. It was thoroughly explored for the first time in 1901 or 1902 by Dr. LeRoy H. Harvey, Professor of Natural History at the University of Maine in Orono. It was he who named it the Northwest Basin. Harvey also designated the cirque's two bodies of water Lake Cowles and Davis Pond, but we do not know why he chose those names.

In 1927 Myron Avery and Henry Buck tried to visit but failed in the attempt. They came back the next year and finally reached the basin successfully, making a very thorough exploration and finding some of the old monument cairns that had been erected almost 100 years before. They extolled its many wonders in their report to members of the Appalachian Mountain Club. There were still no trails in or out of the basin but that was soon to change.

In 1929 an Appalachian Mountain Club group descended into the Northwest Basin from the Northwest Plateau (part of Katahdin's Tableland) and saw the possibilities for an outstanding path from the Saddle Trail to the Northwest Basin by the route they had followed. We have already recounted the building of that trail beginning in 1931 by the self-styled "Four Fools" (Roy and Abby Dudley, and Frank and Grace Butcher). Because of their efforts the trail was known as the Four Fools Trail for several years.

In order to expedite the building of the trail a rough temporary shelter was built in the basin by the Dudleys and the Butchers. It was quickly recognized that a more substantial shelter was needed and over the next two years, while the trail was being completed and formally marked, the "four fools" went about constructing a shelter that would withstand the rigors of such a location. They started in 1932 and completed it in 1933. The men cut the logs while the women peeled them, and construction was completed in a relatively short time that second year.

Members of the Intercollegiate Outing Club Association enlarged the shelter in 1938, but the roof collapsed during the winter of 1939–40. Because this was a time of impending war preparations, the shelter was not at first replaced, but in 1942 the Appalachian Mountain Club was able to put together a crew, and a new enclosed log shelter was built under the leadership of Vern Sampson of Whitefield, New Hampshire. The group journeyed to Avalanche Field and then north with the help of Jack Grant's packhorses along the South Branch of the Wassataquoik. They then followed the old tote road up the Main Branch toward the basin. They were not able to bring the packhorses any nearer than two miles of the basin so everything had to be lugged by packframe the rest of the way. It took four or five days to construct a shelter that was patterned after one the club had built earlier in the Great Gulf Wilderness in New Hampshire. It had an open door in front with enough bunk space on both sides of the entrance to accommodate twelve persons. It even had a fireplace—such luxury, indeed![1] AMC groups used it frequently when they came to do trail maintenance on Katahdin, and it was also available to others at no fee. Few, of course, came during the war years but traffic began to increase in the late 1940s.

Though the shelter was maintained well for many years, by 1962 its condition had deteriorated so badly that Baxter State Park administrators decided to tear it down and erect a new one. A new open-faced Adirondack-style lean-to was finally finished by park ranger Owen Grant in 1964, the logs having been cut and peeled the year before.

There have been times in recent years when serious consideration was given to making the Northwest Basin shelter-free. The location is far away from resident campground rangers, making maintenance and management difficult. There is also the problem of managing human waste in such a remote and fragile zone. In addition, if fire broke out in such a place, it would be almost impossible to check its spread under dry conditions.

Even taking into consideration those legitimate concerns, Baxter State Park officials have recognized first, the desirability of a shelter there for emergency purposes at the least, and second, the awesome experience awaiting the serious backpacker who spends a night there. A number of limitations have wisely been put in place for all those who camp in the Northwest Basin. It is still and shall remain one of the most memorable places in or around Katahdin.

IN THE YEARS IMMEDIATELY AFTER THE BUILDING OF THAT FIRST shelter in the basin it was noted that there was a need for a trail from the Northwest Basin directly north to connect with the Wassataquoik Tote Road. Though from 1911 to 1912, E.B. Draper had cut a rough logging road from the basin north to and then along Wassataquoik Stream, it was very difficult to follow. Members of the Appalachian Mountain Club were likely involved in preliminary scouting for such a trail, but it was Lester F. Hall of Damariscotta Mills, Maine, and Clayton Hall (no relation) who in 1937 laid out and began to cut this trail with the blessing of Chimney Pond ranger/ warden Roy Dudley. Lester had visited Davis Pond the year before and while there began to dream of marking and cutting such a trail. The two Halls set the trail from Davis Pond down its outlet stream in order for it to link into the Tracy Trail along the valley tote road. For a few years it was known as the Hall Trail, but the name did not last and its present name, Northwest Basin Trail, emerged in more common usage and it is so named today.

There were not many visitors to the basin in those early years from any direction so the trail was at times neglected only to be improved again, usually by an ever-faithful AMC crew. In 1941, for instance, there were several major relocations made by an AMC trail crew to improve the trail, and further improvements were made through the 1940s and 1950s. Most of those improvements were made to the upper end of the trail, the lower end continuing to simply follow the old tote road along the west bank of the Wassataquoik. Even today it is quite obvious to the hiker that the lower portion still follows the old road almost to where the trail crosses the Wassataquoik and heads up the steep slopes of the moraine and into the basin. In fact, a hiker may still find evidence of the old logging operations along the way.

Hall Trail (now Northwest Basin Trail) and Tracy Trail (now North Peaks Trail) joined at a point along the tote road where there was for many years a huge dead pine tree stub. It was so large and so visible that it served as an important landmark for visitors using those trails. The stub was visible from both trails whether ascending or descending. During a 1932 trip to the Northwest Basin, AMC member Ron Gower measured the butt of the old stub as 4 feet in diameter at a height of 5 feet off the ground. He goes on to say that this "grand old relic of a vanished race must have been a tall tree in its day. What is left is about 50 feet high."[2] Old photographs support that estimate. One photograph also tells the story of why the tree was originally cut so high off the ground. Because the bases of many of those large trees were often hollow, the lumberjack needed to get farther up the tree to make his cut. To do that he would chip out a series of wedge-cuts up the trunk. Into each of those wedge-cuts he would jam a slab of wood so he could put his weight on it. Using the slabs alternatively just like stairway steps the cutter could climb right up the trunk of the tree. When he reached the desired height he went to work, with good footing, and felled the tree while standing on the last slab step, being kept from falling by a big leather strap around both the tree and his waist. It was dangerous business, to be sure, but an ingenious way to accomplish a desired aim. It is likely that the great height of this landmark pine stub was the result of this old lumberjack technique; a careful study of the old photograph reveals clear evidence of a series of such notches being cut into the trunk. The stub has long since fallen and rotted but the mounded earthen area of the great base of the trunk is still clearly seen at the present junction of the two trails.

WASSATAQUOIK STREAM TRAIL

This trail was the first trail between Roaring Brook and Russell Pond. From the Roaring Brook area it skirted Sandy Stream Pond and the Whidden Ponds, descending into the valley of the Wassataquoik South Branch. The trail then followed an old tote road along the South Branch to the present site of the Wassataquoik Stream Lean-tos. This was the site of Bell Dam, an important component in the management of the Wassataquoik for driving logs. It is also near the confluence of the three major branches of that stream: the South Branch, the Main Branch, and Turner Brook. From Bell Dam, the trail crosses the stream, follows the old Wassataquoik Tote Road through the site of the New City lumber camp (once called "Russell Camp" in honor of one of Tracy and Love's timber bosses) and ascends slightly to Russell Pond.

Though a rough logging trail was pushed through in the early 1900s from Bell Dam to Roaring Brook for logging purposes, it was William F. Tracy who, in 1927, reopened the road as a trail for recreational use by his Russell Pond cabin guests who wanted to reach Roaring Brook and the Great Basin. Because of this special use by Tracy and later by Jack Grant and Ed Werler to bring people to Russell Pond, the trail was referred to as the Tracy Horse Trail (or Tracy Packhorse Trail), and even today it is sometimes referred to as the Tracy Trail. As automobile access into the region got closer and closer to Roaring Brook this trail became the way to reach Russell Pond, a welcome alternative to taking the long and arduous trip up along Wassataquoik Stream from the East Branch.

It is said that Bill Tracy himself hiked each spring from Russell Pond to the Bell Dam site to maneuver large boulders into the stream so his guests could cross without getting wet. Because natural forces were strong and the water ran swiftly there, he had to repeat his efforts each year. The open-field site of the New City Camps was, and still is, a unique place. There were at one time as many as ten or twelve buildings along with a schoolhouse, a blacksmith shop and plenty of horses and oxen. Some relics of this era can be seen today along the side of the trail.

In the early 1950s several significant changes took place in the area. The first was the building of a new trail in 1952 from the valley of the South Branch across a shoulder of Russell Mountain to provide a more direct route to Russell Pond. This became part of the present Russell Pond Trail, and the old trail by way of Bell Dam became the Tracy Horse Trail. The traffic was thus reduced along the old trail as the years went by.

The second was Ed Werler's decision to open his pack burro business in 1950, when he became the Baxter State Park ranger at Roaring Brook. The old Tracy Packhorse Trail had been neglected, so Werler and fellow ranger Ralph Dolley reopened it, and Ed began to pack people into Russell Pond that way. Werler takes delight in telling a story about an experience during one of those trips. He was leading his burros on a pack trip to Russell Pond and was having difficulty getting the stubborn animals across Roaring Brook just beyond the ranger's cabin. He cajoled and shouted at them, and was beginning to lose patience but did not wish to be cruel to them. It happened that Helon Taylor, the Superintendent of Baxter State Park, had just arrived at Roaring Brook for a visit and came across Ed struggling with the burros.

Taylor was a big man, and he stood by for a time watching the proceedings with great interest. He finally said, "Ed, step aside for a moment. I think I can persuade them to cooperate." With that he went over to the edge of the woods and broke off a huge tree pole some 3 or 4 inches in diameter, trunk and all, and approached the burros with fire in his eye, waving the big pole in a threatening way. They took one look at this big man waving that menacing stick at them and decided to cross without further incident.[3]

This trail is a most pleasant one, affording access to the remote lean-tos at the site of the Bell Dam as well as other special features of this historic interior area.

RUSSELL POND TRAIL

The present trail leaves Roaring Brook and skirts the Whidden Ponds before descending into the valley of the South Branch of the Wassataquoik. After crossing the South Banch and passing Halfway Rock, a huge glacial boulder, the trail climbs over a shoulder of Russell Mountain before descending to cross in quick succession the Main Branch of the Wassataquoik and Turner Brook, finally reaching the shores of Russell Pond. In 1939 the trail was diverted from the shores of Sandy Stream to allow a shorter route to Whidden Ponds. In the nineteenth century there had been a number of old logging roads up along the Wassataquoik and its tributaries, and the route follows some of those old roads along the way. The trail from Roaring Brook to the Wassataquoik South Branch was already in existence in 1952 when Russell Pond Ranger Ralph Dolley relocated the trail beyond that point to higher ground, and in so doing shortened the distance between the two campgrounds.

It was early recognized that crossing the South and Main Branches of the Wassataquoik was difficult and, at high water periods, even downright dangerous. To address this situation it was decided in 1960 to install a pulley and cable system to get people safely across. Some old-timers still recall with great fondness that heart-thumping crossing with a full pack on one's back, pulling on the cable, all the while sitting in a crouched position on top of the two-by-six stud attached to the cable. It was great fun, especially when one was out over mid-stream with the water raging below, to hear one's companion exclaim with obvious delight and a veiled snicker, "Oops! I think the cable is stuck!" Sometimes one was reduced to blatant bribery in order to get one's companion to resume pulling the contraption the rest of the way across the roiling white water below.

Irvin "Buzz" Caverly, retired Director of Baxter State Park, remembers installing this remarkable attraction back in 1961. During the park's 1960 season it was determined by Park Supervisor Helon Taylor that the South and Main Branches needed the cable bridge system for the sake of hiker safety. During the winter of 1960–61 preparations were made and the equipment was assembled at Roaring Brook. Using an old Polaris snowmobile whose stability was somewhat questionable, Taylor, along with Merle Scott who was serving as a year-round ranger at the time, delivered to the South Branch crossing site the equipment needed to set up the two cable bridges the next season. Apparently it was quite an adventure accomplishing even this first part of the operation, especially trying to keep the snow machine upright in rough winter terrain.

In the spring Buzz and his younger brother Tim went in and strung a single cable across the South Branch on which the two pulleys that held up the four-foot plank would run. Holes were drilled through trees on each side through which the cable was strung and a come-along was used to tighten the whole system.

A hiker with full pack on could move the plank he or she was seated on by slowly pulling on a rope line strung alongside the cable. Of course, if there were more than one hiker the task of pulling themselves across could be shared. After the cable was strung across the South Branch, Buzz and Tim had to lug the remaining cable and support equipment another three miles on foot to the site of the trail's crossing of the Main Branch, no small task with the black flies out in full force.

Gradually through the years the cables rusted, and in 1968, the South Branch cable broke while someone was crossing. Fortunately, no one was seriously injured, but both cable systems were removed for obvious safety reasons in 1969. Wooden bridges were built across both branches, but they were very difficult to maintain due to the force of the stream flow against the piers. They were finally abandoned. Today there are no bridges, and hikers are left on their own to cross the streams in any manner they deem safe.[4]

LOOKOUT TRAIL

This short trail leads to the ledges overlooking the countryside, to the south of Russell Pond. Ralph Dolley, then ranger at Russell Pond Campground, built it in the 1950s. The lookout itself was named Caverly Lookout in 2005 to honor Irvin "Buzz" Caverly, retired director of Baxter State Park.

GRAND FALLS TRAIL

This trail allows a pleasant hike from Russell Pond to view the spectacular Grand Falls of the Wassataquoik. When standing at the foot of the falls it is not difficult to imagine the flow of long logs and later 4-foot pulp logs tumbling through these cascading falls. To avoid a curve in the river that often created a logjam, the loggers at one time blasted a new course for the falls. If one explores the site carefully one may still find relics of the great logging era. Ralph Dolley built the trail in the 1950s not long after the Russell Pond Campground was established.

WASSATAQUOIK LAKE TRAIL

The west end of this trail was covered in our chapter on trail histories on the West Branch side of Katahdin. The east end of the trail from Russell Pond to Little Wassataquoik Lake originally followed an old logging road at the edge of the Turner Deadwater to Wassataquoik Lake, the first mile following Draper's Packhorse Trail. William F. Tracy, proprietor of the sporting camps at Russell Pond, improved the trail in 1927 for hiking and packhorse use by those who wanted to reach remote fishing locations. Baxter State Park rangers then relocated the trail in 1960 to avoid the wet areas along the old tote road in the Turner Deadwater area. This beautiful hike to lovely Wassataquoik Lake has been immensely popular across the years. In the 1800s the lake was known to loggers as "Big Pond" or "Big Lake."

Another recent relocation along the west shore of Wassataquoik Lake in 1994 protects the lake's fragile west shoreline. The new trail is set back from the shore and provides a delightful tramp past Greene Falls and on to Little Wassataquoik Lake.

LEDGE FALLS TRAIL

This short 1.5-mile trail leads from the Wassataquoik Stream Trail across from the lean-tos to Grand Falls. It follows the historic Wassataquoik (or Stacyville) Tote Road, which brought large numbers of loggers into the valley beginning in the 1830s. For almost a century the tote road was the major artery to the timber operations that eventually reached to Katahdin's flanks. The road was made prominent in later years when young Donn Fendler followed it to safety after being lost on Katahdin's Tableland in 1939. Fendler came across the old tote road in his wanderings downstream and followed it to the site of his eventual rescue on the banks of the Penobscot East Branch.

The trail generally follows the Wassataquoik past Ledge Falls, ending at the Grand Falls Trail. At this junction one can see near the shore of the stream Inscription Rock, a remarkable boulder landmark from the great lumbering era.

The clearing of a portion of the old tote road for this trail was done around 1980 by Bernard Crabtree, a ranger at Russell Pond Campground, with the help of his wife Alice and several of their friends. There are no Baxter State Park trails east of Grand Falls, and, therefore, no longer any access from that side into the interior wilderness.

POGY NOTCH TRAIL TO SOUTH BRANCH POND

This trail provides a footpath link between the north and the south ends of Baxter State Park. Following in some places old logging roads the trail was cut around 1951 by Ralph Dolley, Baxter State Park ranger at Russell Pond, with the help of other rangers. After skirting Pogy Pond with its lovely views back to the Turners, the trail moves north through Pogy Notch and then, after skirting both Upper and Lower South Branch Ponds, it ends at the Baxter State Park campground on Lower South Branch Pond.

After the Pogy Notch Trail leaves Russell Pond heading north it follows some of the original location of the old Draper's Packhorse Trail, which was cleared around 1910 to 1914 to accommodate the E.B. Draper logging operation in that area. The packhorse trail had been cut to link the New City Depot Camp along the Wassataquoik with the Pogy Trail coming in from the McCarty Field Depot Camp northwest of Russell Pond.

At one point the park considered a trail from South Branch Pond east through Traveler Gap, skirting Traveler Pond, and ending along the Penobscot East Branch. A rough trail was brushed out but never formally accepted or maintained.

OLD POGY ROAD AND DRAPERS PACKHORSE TRAIL

From 1910 to 1914 the Draper logging operation sought to connect the New City Camps on the Wassataquoik Stream to the Eastern Corporation's McCarty Field operation along the Trout Brook watershed. The now long-abandoned Pogy Trail followed that road. The trail went from Russell Pond to Deep Pond, crossed the outlet of that pond and started its ascent of South Pogy Mountain. A logging camp was set up on the south slope of Pogy Mountain near the site of the "old well," a landmark for many years for those who walked the trail. The camp became the hub of this virgin spruce logging activity on both North and South Pogy Mountains. The logs cut at higher elevations were sent down a huge, completely enclosed 1,600-foot sluice, which was curved slightly upward at the bottom so the logs would rocket out into Wassataquoik Lake. A story is told of the tragic death of a Russian logger who got caught in the sluice and was killed instantly. Earlier, near the head of Wassataquoik Lake, a small mill was installed to cut long logs into 4-foot lengths in order that they could more easily make their way down the roiling Wassataquoik Stream to the East Branch. Later a similar sawmill was

Remote Wassataquoik Lake from the top of South Pogy scree slope. Note the long, narrow island snaking toward the center of the lake. Courtesy, John W. Neff.

set up at a higher elevation to saw the logs into four-foot lengths before their trip down the sluice. There were also several snub pitches used off this road to ease long logs down to the valley.

In 1915, after Draper had completed his cuttings in this area another disastrous fire swept across both North and South Pogy. This left the whole region abandoned and the trail from McCarty Field to New City no longer used. The Pogy Trail was thus left to old lumbermen and adventurous hikers to negotiate as the years went by. Myron Avery followed the trail after a 1927 trip into the Allagash region and again in the mid-1930s, referring to it in his account as a "new" trail to Katahdin. Considering the age and state of the old road, it was new to some degree, but it was never used much by the hiking community, perhaps because of the great difficulty in reaching McCarty Field at that time. The 1950 Katahdin Section of the *Guide to the Appalachian Trail in Maine* warned that the trail data printed there was based on 1937 information and could not be trusted.

Now and again lumber continued to be cut across the Pogys but that finally ceased with the Baxter purchase. Ranger Ralph Dolley tried to keep the trail open for a time but few were using it, so those efforts were not of high priority. Although it was still listed as an official park trail as late as 1967 it had already become obscure and was eventually abandoned altogether.

FORT MOUNTAIN

Charles Turner Jr., the first non-native to ascend Katahdin, referred to this peak in 1804 as English Fort Mountain. The name suggests the way this open rocky summit appears to guard the northwest flank of the Tableland that Turner and his companions saw from the summit of Katahdin that day.

This short-lived trail to the summit of Fort Mountain left the Northwest Basin Trail after that trail crossed Annis Brook. It then likely followed some of the old logging roads of the early twentieth century, heading west to ascend the mountain. It was never a well-developed trail and only used by a few who knew about it. Some have speculated that it was first cut to enable rescuers to reach the wreckage of an Army Air Force C-54 cargo plane that crashed into the mountain in 1944 during a World War II training mission. The crash site was not far below the summit. Seven crew members and the pilot were killed. However, we now know that a rough path was cut from the Millinocket-Greenville Tote Road into the site for the rescue teams, and they did not try to reach the plane from the north.

It is, however, probable that Ralph Dolley, long-time ranger at Russell Pond, later roughed out the trail so it afforded a view of the wreckage, as well as the scenic summit in the bargain. He and others who knew and used this somewhat dangerous trail kept it open in a minimal way. The trail came out of the woods near the northwest knob of Fort Mountain where one could then scramble over the ledges and rocks to the summit.

The trail was so hazardous it was never used much. With the constant encroachment of blow downs it was eventually abandoned, not even making it into the guidebooks.

POGY POND LEAN-TO

Built on the northeast side of the pond around 1976, this shelter is but a short distance from the Pogy Notch Trail and offers fine views of North and South Turner Mountains. The site was relocated and a new lean-to built in the late 1990s.

RUSSELL POND CAMPGROUND

Although the pond was near several important logging roads—primarily Draper's Packhorse Trail and the Wassataquoik Stream (Stacyville) Tote Road—there is no evidence of anyone building on its shores until the 1920s.

Madison Tracy had cut a trail to the northern peaks of Katahdin in 1885 from the Wassataquoik Tote Road he was using for the family logging operation. His hope was to have folks come from the Penobscot East Branch, stay in one of his lumber camp buildings, and ride horseback along his bridle path to the Katahdin high country. When few responded to his promotions, his dream collapsed.

By 1901, Ed Whitehouse of Sherman and Frank C. Cram of Stacyville had established sporting camps along the East Branch 10 miles above the old Hunt Farm site. The camps were named Little Spring Brook Camps because they were located just downstream from the mouth of that brook where it flows into the East Branch. Charles E. McDonald became proprietor in 1902 and later, likely in the early 1920s, William F. Tracy and P.A. Tracy of Stacyville bought the camps and began to operate them year round, renaming them the Hathorn Pond Camps (Little Spring Brook flows out of Hathorn Pond). Although later they became the Wassataquoik and Hathorn Pond Camps they were always referred to affectionately as "Tracy's Camps," as would the camps on Russell Pond as well. Bill Tracy's wife became the cook and established quite a reputation in her own right across many years.

Bill Tracy began to run packhorse trips from Little Spring Brook over to the Wasstaquoik Stream Valley and on to Russell Pond. The trail followed old logging roads that ascended Little Spring Brook toward Hathorn Pond, then headed southwest and, after skirting Little Hathorn and Robar Ponds, followed the latter's outlet brook to the Wassataquoik Tote Road. From there, Tracy gained access to the whole interior area at a time when logging had ceased and interest in sporting camps was on the rise. In the record of a 1925 trip along this route a guest speaks of the great granite boulders seen all along the way. Also seen were blanched stumps and the trunks of burned and fallen trees. In appearance, the region was desolate.

By 1926 Tracy was the sole proprietor of the camps and had already built several log buildings on Russell Pond to accommodate his guests who were looking for unusual and interesting fishing locations. He continued to improve the site over several years. The establishment of the Katahdin Park Game Preserve in 1921 made hunting off limits in that area so Tracy promoted Little Spring Brook camps for fishing and hunting and Russell Pond for fishing only. At one time a sign at the shore of the pond read "Trout Limit—25 a day." His packhorse string would bring guests into the Wassataquoik region for several overnights at the outlying camps on Russell Pond.

A moose ventures into Russell Pond at daybreak. North and South Turner Mountains are in the distance. Courtesy, John W. Neff.

In 1927 Bill Tracy brushed out the old logging road trail up the South Branch of the Wassataquoik to Roaring Brook, another to Wasstaquoik Lake, as well as the old trail to the northern peaks of Katahdin. His intention was to provide his guests access to his Russell Pond Camps as well as a variety of hiking opportunities to remote ponds and streams for fishing. Obviously 1927 was a mighty busy year for this man. His was for a very long time the only presence in the whole interior region, and it was, of course, a constant challenge to keep all those trails open, though he did receive help at times from Appalachian Mountain Club members who came to camp and hike in the region.

The name of the camps remained the same into the early 1930s when they began to be referred to as the Russell Pond Camps. Russell had been one of the Tracy and Love lumber bosses who had worked in the area much earlier. The camps were also referred to informally as "W.F. Tracy's Camps" or simply "Tracy's Camps" in some mid-1930s and later guidebooks and maps.

Over the years more buildings were erected, all located at the south end of Russell Pond. The camps were known in those days for the great personal service and excellent food provided. Mildred Carter, a niece of William Tracy, was a waitress at the camps in 1939 and remembers her experience fondly. Other than the guides who came and went there were only three of them in residence—Bill Tracy, his wife who was the cook, and Mildred. Bill took care of the buildings and the equipment and often guided when needed. Ralph Dorr, a later proprietor of the Katahdin Lake Camps, was a highly respected guide at Russell Pond for some years. Five cabins for sleeping at that time accommodated fifteen to twenty guests. Throughout the 1920s and 1930s the Tracys maintained both the Russell Pond Camps and the ones at Little Spring Brook, and continued to provide packhorse trips between them. Eventually Tracy packed people to and from Roaring Brook along the South Branch of the Wassataquoik. The horses were kept at the former New City Depot Camps where there were still some usable sheds and also plenty of grazing areas. Bill even maintained a small sawmill at New City to cut whatever lumber was needed at the camps. His highly prized garden in the vast field provided fresh food for the table.

One year, Mildred remembers, a large AMC group of nearly a hundred camped at or near the pond and had their meals at the camps. It was quite a challenge but they managed. Of course, at times, providing supplies for the camps was difficult; sometimes family members hiked over to the Turner Deadwater to catch enough trout for dinner as well as some extra to stock Russell Pond. Each year Bill came to the pond in the winter to cut ice for use during the summer; most of the sporting camps of that time did the same in their locations. In addition, a large root cellar dug deep into the ground kept vegetables and other food fresh. Bill also had his own well in the field in front of the cabins. The old hand-pump mechanism is still there.

These were the only private sporting camps in the whole Katahdin region that remained under one owner (W.F. Tracy) throughout their entire existence. The camps remained under Tracy's lease until 1941 when Governor Baxter bought the land for inclusion in the new Baxter State Park, and Bill was compensated by the state for the buildings. This transfer of the camps from the Tracy lease to Baxter ownership was not a happy one; most of the camp buildings were razed and only limited camping was allowed there for several years. In 1950 the site became the Baxter State Park Russell Pond Campground and Ralph Dolley was assigned as the ranger there. Bill Tracy's home cabin became the ranger's cabin and a nearby building was retained as a bunkhouse. Dolley remained for ten years and was responsible for reopening or building many of the trails in the interior.

Across the years there have been lean-tos built, rebuilt, or replaced. A few new tentsites have been established and a new ranger's cabin was built between 1973 and 1974. The basic capacity of the campground has not been increased much through the years, and the sense of beauty and remoteness has remained largely the same.

One curious sight at Russell Pond is the image of a moose and calf painted years ago on the face of a giant glacial boulder at the edge of the old camp field and visible just as one arrives at the site from the south. There are a number of stories about its origin, but the one that seems to be the most credible is that a member of the park trail crew, Connie Stockley, first painted the image in the mid-1960s. Beyond that basic information little else is known.

All of these are treasured memories of a long-ago era, deep in the Maine Woods in the shadow of Katahdin.

WASSATAQUOIK LAKE CABIN AND LITTLE WASSATAQUOIK LEAN-TO

When Bill Tracy opened up the old logging trail to Wassataquoik Lake in 1927 he wanted to make that exquisite wilderness lake available to his Russell Pond clients. His trail made possible an overnight tenting experience on a long finger-shaped island near the lake's outlet. Later in the 1930s a rough lean-to was built on the island for the use of visitors and for emergency purposes.

In 1942 a New Jersey couple by the name of Kahler began camping on the island each year with the permission of the park. They grew to love the site and eventually suggested that a cabin be built on the island. Helon Taylor, park supervisor at that time, approved the idea. Of course, the whole notion was made a bit more palatable by an offer from the Kahlers to cover the cost. Ralph Dolley built the cabin between 1954 and 1955. The floor and the sides were built of wood, but the roof was left open to be entirely covered by canvas for the recreational season. It was rented for 25 cents per night. What an incredible bargain! At the end of the season the three sections of the canvas covering were taken down and lugged back to Russell Pond for safe winter storage. Irvin "Buzz" Caverly, who was at one time a ranger at Russell Pond, remembers all too well how heavy the canvas load became during the 2.5-mile trek back to Russell Pond. In the 1950s, Ed Werler's packhorses often brought people into this campsite and they loved it.

By 1972 the years had taken their toll on the cabin, and the old frame had greatly deteriorated. That year Barry MacArthur, then Russell Pond ranger, rebuilt it, and a permanent roof replaced the old frame that held up the heavy canvas covering.

This island campsite is one of the most enchanting places in the Katahdin region. The island itself snakes out toward the middle of the long narrow lake, and blueberries grow there in profusion. To experience a beautiful sunset while seated in the evening at the western tip of the island is to know a deep and abiding joy along with gratitude for the wonders of creation.

For some years prior to 1969 a rough built lean-to on Little Wassataquoik Lake served those who wished an even more remote experience. Then in 1969 or 1970 Baxter State Park personnel built an Adirondack-style lean-to at the site.

WASSATAQUOIK STREAM LEAN-TOS

These lean-tos are located on the south bank of the Wassataquoik just downstream from where its three branches converge. It is also the site of the old Bell Dam and depot camp of the Tracy and Love logging operation. Across the years consideration was given now and then to abandoning the campground at Russell Pond and building a new one at this site. As early as 1946, park administrators suggested that facilities for hikers and fishermen be built at the Bell Dam site instead of Russell Pond. This never took place, and in 1969 a few open lean-tos were finally built there; the site is now a much appreciated stop for backpackers who visit the region. The overuse problems at Russell Pond were later resolved with careful planning, and it was decided to keep two lean-tos at the Bell Dam site. They are out of sight of each other, thus enhancing the wilderness experience at each site.

THE KLONDIKE

The Klondike is a vast scrub fir and spruce bog area about 2,500 feet between the Katahdin massif and the Katahdinauguoh Mountain barrier to the west. It is a place of great mystery because of how difficult it has been across the years to reach it and move through it. There are no trails in the Klondike, only dwarf timber, deadwaters, and dense undergrowth. Legend has it that Joe Francis of the Penobscot tribe hunted moose in the area and at one time built a cabin or lean-to on a pond at its western edge. At first, he named it Teapot Pond because he often boiled tea there, but later he gave the pond and the whole area its present name, a reminder of the immense Alaskan wilderness by that name.

The area was first observed by the Monument Line surveyors in the late 1820s, but was not described until visited by George C. Witherle of Castine, Maine in 1886. Not until 1901 was it visited again, this time by Dr. Lore A. Rogers who named the pond on the western side "Merrill Pond" in honor of a University of Maine botanist who earlier made a number of scientific visits to the Katahdin region.

It is said that John Winthrop Worthington, a Boston lawyer, visited the Klondike in 1900 or 1901, but there is no account of that visit. In 1901 or 1902 Dr. LeRoy H. Harvey, Professor of Natural History at the University of Maine in Orono, investigated the Klondike and published several reports on his findings. He referred to his expedition to this remote area as an "ecological excursion to Mt. Katahdin."

In 1921 the Klondike was "rediscovered" by Ludwig K. Moorehead of New York City, and he asserted the trout he found there were sweeter than any he had tasted elsewhere. Moorehead's father, a famed archaeologist, had explored Katahdin earlier, and his son was now carrying on that tradition. He named its tarn "Mayo Pond" in honor of his guide Ernest Mayo, who was operating out of York's Twin Pine Camps at Daicey Pond, though there is some evidence that it may have been known by that name a few years earlier. Mayo did most of his guiding on the Penobscot West Branch side of the mountain, but once he learned about the Klondike, he often guided there as well. Obviously these pond names never quite took hold, and its present name Klondike Pond has prevailed.

In 1929, botanist Judson Ewer and Amherst College Librarian E. Porter Dickinson explored the Klondike and the Northwest Basin. In 1932 Ronald Gower of the Appalachian Mountain Club led a small group into the Klondike and explored over several days, finding it almost impenetrable in most places.

During the 1940s, perhaps also earlier, the guidebooks describe a trail from the Northwest Plateau over to the edge of the Tableland, then descending an avalanche slide that had come down in a small glacial cirque on the side of that plateau. They also tell of several good locations for camping at the pond. This trail has long been abandoned, and the park no longer allows visitors into the Klondike, choosing to allow the area to remain at peace in its natural state.

THREE PROPOSED TRAILS

Brief mention should be made of three trails once proposed but never built. The first is Myron Avery's informal proposal in 1928 to extend the Appalachian Trail from the summit of Katahdin down to Roaring Brook Campground and then across both the Turner and Traveler Ranges to the north end of what is now Baxter State Park. He described this idea as one easy to accomplish with a few signs and some reroutes of old logging roads. No action was taken.

The second is the Ralph Heath Trail to honor the Baxter State Park ranger who lost his life in 1963 while trying to rescue a lady caught by a major October snowstorm while trying to hike directly from the Knife Edge to Chimney Pond. The proposal, made by Clarence LeBell in a 1965 edition of the Appalachian Mountain Club's journal *Appalachia*, suggested the trail follow the same path Avery had earlier proposed across the Turners and the Travelers but then continue on north to Estcourt, Quebec, at the Maine-Canada border. The plan was to continue the trail to James and Hudson Bays. Someone actually hiked the proposed uncut route in 1965 to promote the idea, but there is no evidence of any trail cutting. These two proposals may surely be considered forerunners to the present International Appalachian Trail, which today links Katahdin to Cap Gaspé, Quebec.

The third is a 1941 proposal for a Donn Fendler Trail, utilizing portions of the way Fendler traveled after being lost on Katahdin in 1939. The trail was to begin at the point where the Saddle Trail reaches the Tableland, cross over Hamlin Peak and the Howe Peaks and then descend the North Peaks Trail to the old Wassataquoik Tote Road, which it would follow to the Penobscot East Branch. An elaborate map was drawn but the idea was never implemented nor heard of again.

PART IV

Inspiration and Interpretation

THOREAU'S PILGRIMAGE

The Poet Meets the Mountain

9

IN THE SUMMER OF 1846, HENRY DAVID THOREAU TRAVELED UP the Penobscot West Branch and attempted to climb Katahdin from the south side—the typical itinerary at that time. His visit to Katahdin was a formative experience in the development of his philosophy as well as in the mountain's history. Although quite a number of explorers, surveyors, and scientists had already visited the region, very few people had come to recreate and commune with nature, as Thoreau was doing.

In 1848, Thoreau published an account of his expedition in the *Union Magazine* of New York in an installment titled "Ktaadn and the Maine Woods." That installment was later joined with the accounts of the two other sojourns Thoreau made to the northern forest wilderness of Maine. The magazine installments reached a vast readership for whom the notion of untamed wilderness was remote, romantic, and wild. These accounts were finally published together as *The Maine Woods*.

When he came to Katahdin in 1846, Thoreau had lived at Walden Pond for one year, and he would write the first draft of *Walden* the year following that visit. Thoreau's encounter with Katahdin was a powerful experience, helping to shape his unique relationship to nature and perspective on wilderness, which he would so successfully share with the world. As part of his conclusion to *Walden*, Thoreau wrote:

At the same time that we are earnest to learn and explore all things, we require that all things should be mysterious and unexplorable by us, that land and sea be infinitely wild, unsurveyed and unfathomed by us. We can never have enough of nature. We must be refreshed by the sight of inexhaustible vigor, vast features and titanic—the sea coast with its wrecks, the wilderness with its living and its decaying trees—the thunder cloud—and rain that lasts three weeks and produces freshets. We need to witness our own limits transgressed, and some life pasturing freely where we never wander.[1]

Thoreau had likely heard about Katahdin from several sources. Having a scientific interest in nature, he probably knew of the 1830s expeditions, especially the one led by Charles Jackson, the brother-in-law of his friend Ralph Waldo Emerson. Thoreau knew of Edward Everett Hale's 1845 expedition, as by 1848, Thoreau and Hale were members of the same literary circle. Hale and William Francis Channing's accounts of their challenging venture to the Wassataquoik Valley and Katahdin's northern slopes may have prompted young Thoreau to consider such an excursion for himself. In his own Katahdin journey accounts, Thoreau refers to the "two young men from Boston" who had climbed Katahdin in 1845.

Inspired, Thoreau set out on the overnight steamer from Boston on August 31, 1846, accompanied by his relative, George Augustus Thatcher, and two other men, all from Bangor. At Old Town they visited Indian Island and watched residents build a bateau. In Lincoln, they engaged Penobscot guide Louis Neptune. Neptune had accompanied Jackson nine years before and knew the region well. Unfortunately, he did not show up at the appointed rendezvous upriver, and Thoreau and Thatcher began their journey without a guide. Thoreau probably chose the West Branch approach because it had been Jackson's and the intended Hale-Channing route.

The party stayed several nights at George McCauslin's farm (just west of what is now East Millinocket). McCauslin was known as "Uncle George" to his friends and had spent years on the West Branch log drives; he was at that time running a farm to supply the loggers and to accommodate recreational river travelers.

McCauslin knew the river well, and Thoreau persuaded him to accompany them as their guide. McCauslin suggested that they enlist the help of young Tom Fowler Jr., whose farm was upriver at the mouth of Millinocket Stream, as a second guide. McCauslin felt that Tom would be adept at maneuvering their bateau along the river's more challenging sections. When they reached the Fowler farm, Tom readily agreed to accompany them.

The men poled their way up Millinocket Stream to Tom Fowler Sr.'s farm, the last before entering the West Branch wilderness. From there, they began an important portage to Quakish Lake that enabled travelers to avoid the dangerous Grand Falls. As they ascended the river, they saw evidence of the famed West Branch log drive—lumber camps, dams, sluices, and booms. They finally

Henry David Thoreau.

had their first view of "Katahdin, its summit veiled in clouds, like a dark isthmus in that quarter, connecting the heavens with the earth."[2] The party continued their journey, poling, rowing, and portaging across lakes, falls, and deadwaters—until they reached Ambajejus Lake. From there, Thoreau observed that the summit of the mountain had a "singularly flat table-land appearance, like a short highway, where a demigod might be let down to take a turn or two in the afternoon, to settle his dinner."[3]

Seven days later, the six-person party finally reached the "Sowadnehunk Deadwater" (Abol Deadwater). According to Thoreau, they stopped at the mouth of Aboljacknagesic, known to earlier travelers as Sandy Brook and today as Abol Stream. There they camped on high ground on the south side of the river, at an ancient Native American campsite that commanded a spectacular view of Katahdin. The next morning, they headed toward the summit:

> Seen from this point, a bare ridge at the extremity of the open land, Ktaadn presented a different aspect from any mountain I have seen, there being a greater proportion of naked rock rising abruptly from the forest; and we looked up at this blue barrier as if it were some fragment of a wall which anciently bounded the earth in that direction.[4]

The path Thoreau chose for his climb is not entirely clear. Although he was aware of the route along the Abol Slide from Charles T. Jackson and Jacob W. Bailey's accounts, he chose not to follow it. McCauslin and Fowler knew the route up the avalanche, and Fowler may have actually climbed part of it. However, Thoreau, a non-conformist, shunned the path others had trod, preferring to explore a new route.

Using a compass bearing from the mouth of Abol Stream toward the highest visible peak Thoreau followed an almost straight line to South Peak, passing northwest of Rum Mountain and just east of the Abol Slide. His observation of the Tableland the next day suggests that Thoreau likely reached or nearly reached the ridge between the summit and the South Peak.

Thoreau actually climbed to the mountain's higher reaches without his companions. On two occasions, the first evening before setting up camp just below treeline and again the next day, Thoreau experienced the mountain alone. That likely did not happen by accident but by Thoreau's own design.

> While my companions were seeking a suitable spot for [our campsite], I improved the little daylight that was left in climbing the mountain alone.
>
> . . . Leaving this at last, I began to work my way . . . up the nearest, though not the highest peak. At first scrambling on all fours over the tops of ancient black spruce-trees (*Abies nigra*), old as the flood. . . .
>
> . . . This brought me to the skirt of a cloud, and bounded my walk that night. But I had already seen that Maine country when I turned about, waving, flowing, rippling, down below.[5]

After what must have been a restless night, members of the party arose early and made their plans to climb to the summit. Thoreau, ever sensitive to the enormity of the natural forces present around him, tells of that singular day in his life.

> The tops of mountains are among the unfinished parts of the globe, whither it is a slight insult to the gods to climb and pry into their secrets, and try their effect on our humanity. Only daring and insolent men, perchance, go there. Simple races . . . do not climb mountains,—their tops are sacred and mysterious tracts never visited by them. Pomola [sic] is always angry with those who climb to the summit of Ktaadn.[6]

Thoreau's musings become a comparison of the land he once considered so pastoral—rural Massachusetts—and the territory he began to understand as truly rustic.

From this elevation, just on the skirts of the clouds, we could overlook the country, west and south, for a hundred miles. There it was, the State of Maine, which we had seen on the map, but not much like that,—immeasurable forest for the sun to shine on, that eastern *stuff* we hear of in Massachusetts. No clearing, no house. It did not look as if a solitary traveler had cut so much as a walking-stick here.[7]

The author's final reflections are proof of the degree to which his journey through the Katahdin region affected his point of view:

It is difficult to conceive of a region uninhabited by man. We habitually presume his presence and influence everywhere. And yet we have not seen pure nature, unless we have seen her thus vast and drear and inhuman....Nature was here something savage and awful, though beautiful. I looked with awe at the ground I trod on, to see what the Powers had made there, the form and fashion and material of their work. This was that Earth of which we have heard, made out of Chaos and Old Night. Here was no man's garden, but the unhandseled* globe.[8]

Prior to Thoreau's extraordinary Katahdin experience, he had encountered nature that was more pastoral, gentle, bevevolent—not far from habitation and civilization. Now he views nature as uninhabited, grim and drear, wild and untamed, primitive and powerful.

At Katahdin, Thoreau's dramatic encounter with the divine spirit led him to reconsider elemental human questions. He began to believe that humans cannot always control nature and so must live in harmony with it. Robert D. Richardson says of the poet's experience:

Nature may indeed smile on man in the valley, but there are places where man is not welcome. In short, there are limits. Man is still very much a part of nature, but he is only one part; he is not everything. Nature will support and nourish him, but only if he respects and acknowledges the limits.[9]

The party reached their bateau by two in the afternoon and two hours later were threading their way down river toward Bangor and home. Thoreau

---

* Pure, fresh

returned to the Maine woods twice, in 1853 and 1857. During the last trip, Thoreau intended to climb Katahdin by way of the Wassataquoik Valley route. He was thwarted in this, however, when one of his companions, Edward Hoar, had some foot problems and they decided not to undertake the climb. Although Thoreau does not comment on this turn of events, it meant he would never reach the summit.

In the ensuing years Thoreau's works greatly influenced the American public's perspective on wilderness. As new attitudes toward nature made wilderness seem less terrible and more accessible, Katahdin's treasures became more familiar, and would emerge in the twentieth century as the penultimate symbol of wild beauty in the Northern Forest.

Capturing Katahdin on Canvas and Film

FREDERIC E. CHURCH

Twenty-seven-year-old Frederic Edwin Church thoughtfully studied the incomplete canvas on the easel before him. An aspiring artist, he struggled to convey a message through the large emerging oil painting. On that wintry day, Church debated over which colors to choose and what techniques to employ. Seeking inspiration, he gazed out the window of his studio at the Art Union Building in New York City. He could clearly see through the swirling snow a three-day-old sign in a store window that read "Welcome 1853." The New Year had barely begun.

Breaking from his reverie, Church carefully reviewed his sketches from the summer before, when he had visited the remote Maine wilderness. Going over the sketches brought back the ebullience he had experienced that summer when he first traveled north and became acquainted with the landscape around Katahdin. Although lumbering activity was creeping closer and closer to the mountain's flanks, the region's largely untouched wilderness and Katahdin itself had deeply moved Church.

After weeks of steady and earnest concentration, Church at last completed the painting he would title, simply, *Mt. Katahdin*.[1] In so doing, Church, one of America's greatest landscape artists, began a love affair with Katahdin and the surrounding region that would last his entire life.

BORN IN CONNECTICUT IN 1826, CHURCH DEMONSTRATED HIS talent at an early age. By the time he was eighteen he had become a pupil of Thomas Cole, the father of the Hudson River School of painting. At the age of 23 he was elected a full member of the prestigious National Academy of Design.

The Hudson River School artists found inspiration in the American wilderness (many used the Hudson River Valley as the subject of their romantic scenes). Under Cole's tutelage, Church sharpened his natural technical skills and developed his own distinctively heroic style. His early success as a painter brought him fame and wealth. By the close of the 1840s Church was already the most famous painter in America and recognized as the leader of the American Landscape School.[2]

In the summer, Church traveled up the Hudson River Valley and sometimes west to Niagara Falls, and other times east to New England. During the winter months, he returned to his New York City studio with sketches from his journeys and there completed his grand paintings. A self-assured and audacious young man, his creative drive lasted throughout his life. He was deeply moved by dramatic landscapes and passionate about his grand subjects.

THE PURSUIT OF WILD LANDSCAPES BY MANY NINETEENTH-CENTURY American painters made the "discovery" of mostly inaccessible Katahdin inevitable. Church had read of Hale and Channing's 1845 ascent of Katahdin and likely read or heard of Thoreau's 1846 visit. The transcendental philosophy with which Thoreau is identified greatly influenced the Hudson River School artists—their paintings reflect the Transcendentalists' God in the raw, untouched, and primal wilderness.

Before he visited Katahdin, Church had spent at least two summers at Mount Desert Island with several artist friends. The rugged Maine coast drew many artists, including Thomas Cole and marine artist Fitz Hugh Lane. Church was inspired by the wild Atlantic shore's beauty and grandeur, but after completing several paintings there, he found himself wanting something more. While most of the artists working in Maine at that time did not stray far from the coast, Church was drawn inland to the remote woods surrounding Katahdin.

While visiting Mount Desert Island in the summer of 1852, the young

Illustration by Frederic E. Church for an 1871 *Scribner's Magazine* account of an expedition he and other artists took to the Great Basin.

artist journeyed into the interior to climb Katahdin—at the time, still quite a rigorous and uncommon endeavor that required considerable planning and support. He returned to the island for some weeks, only to turn around and return to the interior to sketch the autumnal landscape surrounding the mountain. Church likely visited Katahdin Lake and left with a lasting impression of the view from there.

CHURCH'S NAME IS WELL-LINKED TO KATAHDIN, BUT HE WASN'T the first artist to visit the region. John James Audubon, the distinguished ornithologist and artist, sketched the flora and fauna of the region when he traveled down the East Branch in 1832. Charles T. Jackson arrived in 1837, and made a number of lithographs of Katahdin and other landmarks. Many other artists' travels remained unrecorded. However, Church's visits did the most to introduce Maine as a subject to the art world and as a uniquely American landscape to the public. Church's reputation grew during the 1850s and the public embraced his exotically styled paintings of New England, especially those depicting Katahdin and the coast of Maine.

Church visited the Katahdin region again in 1855. With his friend, Charles Tracey, and several others, he canoed down the East Branch and stayed at the Hunt Farm on the way to Katahdin Lake (and possibly on up the wild Wassataquoik Valley). Thomas Wentworth Higginson stayed at the farm a few days later and lamented that their paths had not crossed. Unfortunately, there are no other recorded details about Church's 1855 trip. Certainly Church created more studies and sketches that he would later paint, once back in New York.

Church returned to Katahdin the next year for a major adventure with several companions, including a distinguished friend and colleague, Theodore Winthrop, a descendant of both John Winthrop, the first Governor of Massachusetts, as well as Jonathan Edwards, the fiery preacher of the Great Awakening. The group traveled a long and circuitous route from New York City to Albany, through the Adirondacks to Lake Champlain. From there they made their way across Vermont to New Hampshire via Dixville Notch, and then across Lake Umbagog to the Rangeley Lakes region of Maine. They reached Moosehead Lake, crossed it by steamer to Northeast Carry, and canoed down the Penobscot West Branch. They climbed Katahdin from the south side before continuing downriver to Bangor and returning to New York City. Winthrop's account of the 1856 expedition appears in his *Life in the Open Air*, where he exuberantly recounts this adventure in the northern wilderness. In the account, Winthrop refers to Church as "Iglesias," the Spanish word for "church." Winthrop wrote:

> We needed to see Katahdin,—the distinctest mountain to be found on this side of the continent. Katahdin was known to Iglesias. He had scuffled up its eastern land-slides with a squad of lumbermen. He had birched it down to Lake Chesuncook in bygone summers, to see Katahdin distant. Now, in a birch we would slide down the Penobscot, along its line of lakes, camp at Katahdin, climb it, and speed down the river to tidewater. . . .
>
> Next morning, when we awoke, just before the gray of dawn, the sky was

clear and scintillating; but there was a white cotton night-cap on the head of Katahdin. As we inspected him, he drew his night-cap down farther, hinting that he did not wish to see the sun that day. When a mountain is thus in the sulks after a storm, it is as well not to disturb him: he will not offer the prize of a view. . . .

Besides sky, Katahdin's view contains only the two primal necessities of wood and water. Nowhere have I seen such breadth of solemn forest, gloomy, were it not for the cheerful interruption of many fair lakes, and bright ways of river linking them. . . .

We stayed studying the pleasant solitude and dreamy breadth of Katahdin's panorama for a long time, and every moment the mystery of the mist above grew more enticing. Pride also was awakened. We turned from sunshine and Cosmos into fog and chaos. We clambered up into Nowhere, into a great, white, ghostly void. We saw nothing but the rough surfaces we trod. . . . Up we went,—nothing but granite and gray dimness. Where we arrived we know not. It was a top, certainly: that was proved by the fact that there was nothing within sight. We cannot claim that it was the topmost top . . . except for one instant, when a kind-hearted sunbeam gave us a vanishing glimpse of a white lake and breadth of forest far in the unknown toward Canada. . . .

The first thing, when we touched *terra firma*, was to look back regretfully toward the mountain. Regret changed to wrath, when we perceived its summit all clear and mistless, smiling warmly to the low summer's sun. The rascal evidently had only waited until we were out of sight in the woods to throw away his night-cap.[3]

Winthrop described what was very probably Church's inspiration for his painting *Sunset*, dated later that year.[4]

Just before sunset, from beneath a belt of clouds evanescing over the summit, an inconceivably tender, brilliant flow of rosy violet mantled downward, filling all the valley. Then the violet purpled richer and richer, and darkened slowly to solemn blue, that blended with the gloom of the pines and shadowy channelled gorges down the steep. The peak was still in sunlight, and suddenly, half-way down, a band of roseate clouds, twining and changing like a choir of Bacchantes, soared around the western edge and hung poised above the unillumined forests at the mountain base; light as air they came and went and faded away, ghostly, after their work of momentary beauty was done.

One slight maple, prematurely ripened to crimson and heralding the pomp of autumn, repeated the bright cloud-color amid the vivid verdure of a little island, and its image wavering in the water sent the flame floating nearly to our feet.

Such are the transcendent moments of Nature, unseen and disbelieved by the untaught. The poetic soul lays hold of every such tender pageant of beauty and keeps it forever. Iglesias, having an additional method of preservation, did not fail to pencil rapidly the wondrous scene. . . .[5]

It is also likely the sketches Church made on this trip resulted in his small painting *Mount Katahdin*, dated 1856.[6] More significantly, the trip may have inspired Church's great Maine masterpiece, *Twilight in the Wilderness*, dated 1860.[7]

In 1860, Church married Isabel Carnes. Over the next decade, the artist purchased land in Hudson, New York, where he designed the Moorish-style estate "Olana." Built at the crest of the hill above the river, Olana still offers a commanding view of the countryside and insight into the mind and soul of Frederic E. Church and his family.

By the late 1860s, the onset of rheumatism began to cripple Church's right hand, forcing him to learn how to paint with his left. Despite the loss of his technical skills and diminished reputation, Church continued to travel and paint, and devoted much of his creative energy to the building and landscaping of Olana. There is no record of Church visiting Katahdin between 1856 and 1869 and only a few references to visits between 1869 and 1875. However, Maine was likely never very far away from Church's mind and heart, and there may have been a number of unrecorded visits. Beginning in the mid-1870s, Church returned to the Katahdin area almost annually, usually in the fall.

In early September 1876, Church again canoed the Penobscot's West Branch accompanied by noted photographer James C. Stodder and Frederick S. Davenport, both of Bangor. Having already made a number of trips to Katahdin, Davenport guided the party down the West Branch and perhaps on a climb to Katahdin. Stodder's photographs from that trip constitute a classic collection and offer a remarkable record of travel along the West Branch.

A much more publicized trip to the region took place the next September. This time, Church organized the expedition, and brought three of his landscape artist friends—Sanford R. Gifford, H.W. Robbins, and Lockwood

Photograph taken by James C. Stodder during his 1876 canoe trip with Frederic E. Church and others down the West Branch of the Penobscot. Courtesy, Special Collections, Bangor Public Library.

de Forest, all noted artists who, along with Church, comprised the core of the American Landscape School. M. La Rose and A.L. Holley also accompanied the group. Holley later wrote a stirring account of the trip that appeared in 1878 in *Scribner's Magazine*. In the account, Holley referenced the travelers by pseudonyms: Don Cathedra (Church), Don Gifaro (Gifford), Herr Rubens (Robbins), M. de Woods (de Forest), and Mr. Arbor Ilex (Holley). The group traveled by train to Mattawamkeag and by wagon to the Hunt Farm. After several days camping at Katahdin Lake, the men hiked along the short-lived Lang and Jones Trail to the Great Basin, to sketch and paint.

The published account included dramatic and vivid sketches that revealed rustic camping life and invigorating visits to the mountain. Holley's account stated:

I had the opportunity—an interesting experience—of seeing Don Cathedra make many of his sketches, of observing the bold and rapid manner in which he caught all the characteristic colors and effects of the landscape.

But our life, pleasant as was its routine by day, was not mere sketching, fishing, and tramping. The evening meal, with its liberal fare and its rousing appetites, its jokes and its relation of the day's experiences, and then the lying at ease before the glowing camp-fire, with its pipes, and punch, and stories, and the dropping off of one and another in sweet, healthful sleep, without the formality of "retiring"—these are scenes of which the memories will last like those of Ktaadn itself.[8]

After this grand expedition of the American Landscape School artists, Church began several major works, including *The Great Basin* (1877), *Katahdin from Upper Togue Lake* (1877–78), and *Katahdin from the Lake* (1878).

In September 1878, while sketching and painting in the region again, Church purchased the 400-acre Stevens Farm on the southern shore of Millinocket Lake. He and Isabel had decided to build a simple log cabin for use when visiting the area. They named the cabin "Camp Rhodora" after the shrub found throughout the northeastern wilds. The cabin provided a spectacular view of Katahdin, which would bring joy and inspiration to Church for many years to come.

In the spring of 1879, Thomas Sedgewick Steele stopped at the Hunt Farm on his way down the Penobscot's East Branch. He reported that a 28-foot canoe (which he overestimated as weighing close to 300 pounds!) had just been built for Frederic E. Church at the farm and was ready for delivery. Steele and his party also observed that a team of men was leaving for Millinocket Lake the next morning to build several log buildings on the Church site.[9] During the 1880s and 1890s, Church visited the cabin as frequently as he could, always in the fall, to relax and sketch. In a Katahdin-themed exhibition's program notes, artist Chris Huntington observed:

It was Katahdin that moved [Church] to ponder the immensity of the American experience and the profundity of human existence.[10]

Church's deteriorating health gradually restricted his ability to make the difficult trip to his cabin. The extension of railroad to Norcross in the 1890s allowed Church to reach Millinocket Lake via steamboat across Ambajejus Lake; even so, the trip became more difficult for him each year.

In 1895, Church completed his last dated painting: *Katahdin from Millinocket Camp.*[11] He had started the painting in 1891. It was one of his favorites, and upon its completion, he presented it as a birthday gift to his beloved Isabel. The painting represents the view from Camp Rhodora's front porch and included the artist canoeing in the foreground. Church included the following endearing note with his gift:

> I am happy in the belief that owing to your generous, unselfish and cheerful nature the Autumn of your life will be beautiful in its brightness and color. Your old guide is paddling his canoe in the shadow, but he knows that the glories of the Heavens and the earth are seen more appreciatively when the observer rests in the shade.[12]

In 1898, two years before Church's death, he and his youngest son, Louis, had the original cabin torn down and a new, two-story camp built at the Millinocket Lake site. The new main cabin included a huge stone fireplace in the living room area, a front porch, a dining room–kitchen–pantry area, two bedrooms, and considerable storage space. Two separate sleeping cabins were later added. There was also a boathouse, an ice house, guide's quarters, a spring house, a workshop shed, and a stable. Later, a bedroom was added to the main cabin for the cook. Except for the boathouse, all of the buildings were constructed of large, peeled logs, a style that would define sporting camps into the next century.

Due to his poor health, Church likely did not visit this expanded wilderness haven. When he died in 1900, he bequeathed the property to Louis, who spent each summer at the camp until 1924. In the mid-1950s, Elmer Woodworth, the proprietor of the nearby Millinocket Lake Camps, bought the complex. He had been employed to care for the property for many years and knew the Church family well. Mr. Woodworth would later bequeath it to his son, Ray. Through the years the site became known as Church Cove. Shortly after his death, one admirer described Church as the "best example of the old school of American painters, a man of lofty and original ideas, who sees far above his head into the ether and among the great elevations of mountains as no other painter in our time sees."[13]

Later that year New York's Metropolitan Museum mounted an exhibition of ten of his most important paintings. Its catalog was written by Church's friend Charles Dudley Warner. In it, Warner wrote:

> We can scarcely overestimate the debt of America to Mr. Church in teaching it to appreciate the grandeur and beauty of its own scenery, and by his work at home and in tropical lands in inculcating a taste and arousing an enthusiasm for landscape art—that is, landscape art as an expression of the majesty and beauty of the divine manifestation in nature. . . . He aspired to interpret nature in its higher spiritual and aesthetic meaning. No other American painter of Church's generation held higher aspirations, and none equaled his powerful and original vision of landscape. For three decades in the middle of the nineteenth century, when landscape spoke to the nation with an unrivaled authority and clarity, Church . . . stood alone.[14]

OTHER NINETEENTH-CENTURY ARTISTS

Many artists who painted in the Katahdin region in Church's era were his friends or students. Both Sanford R. Gifford and Jervis McKentee accompanied Church on his inaugural 1879 trip to Camp Rhodora. Gifford, who studied at the National Academy of Design, had accompanied Church on his well-documented 1877 expedition to Katahdin. McEntee, Church's dedicated pupil and friend, accompanied Church on some of his trips to Mount Desert Island and the Katahdin region. McEntee was a well-known landscape artist. Two of his paintings are in the permanent collection at the Farnsworth Museum in Rockland, Maine and one in the Portland (Maine) Museum of Art.

Landscape artist Alden Partridge visited the Katahdin region in the mid-1880s to paint an unspoiled American wilderness paradise. Landscape and portrait painter Richard W. Hubbard traveled widely in New England and upstate New York and produced the well-known 1874 oil painting *Mount Katahdin*. Virgil Williams, also a landscape and portrait painter, visited the region in the late 1860s and produced his *West Branch of the Penobscot* featuring Katahdin, which is in the permanent collection of the Corcoran Gallery of Art in Washington, D.C.

Throughout the 1800s, Katahdin remained remote and largely inaccessible, reachable only by mounting a substantial expedition. Church and his associates opened the way for a much greater influx of artists in the early years of the twentieth century.

TWENTIETH-CENTURY ARTISTS

George Hawley Hallowell

As the new century began, George Hallowell, a young Boston artist and photographer, journeyed to the Katahdin region in search of recuperation and rest. What he found was the inspiration to paint and photograph the world around him.

Born in 1871, Hallowell was exposed at an early age to the arts. His father was an architect and his mother a painter and musician. After studying at Boston's School of the Museum of Fine Arts, he pursued a number of artistic ventures before traveling to Maine. In Maine, Hallowell grew especially interested in the long-log river drives and the rugged characteristics of the lumbermen that he met. He spent the winter of 1900–01 with the Ayer and Rogers logging operation and followed the spring drive down Wassataquoik Stream to the East Branch. According to Myron Avery:

> There are views of the forests in winter, then the cutting, the hauling, the yarding, and innumerable pictures of the labor of the river drivers on the Wassataquoik. This stream was reported to be the most difficult stream for long-log driving in Maine. The labor and hardships of river driving apparently fascinated Hallowell, for the major emphasis in this photographic collection is devoted to picking off logs and the breaking of log jams.[15]

In 1902, Hallowell and several others hiked into the Great Basin where they likely climbed to Pamola and across the Knife Edge to the summit. His sketches and photographs from that and a later trip formed the basis of his striking painting *Knife's Edge* (1915).[16]

In 1903, Hallowell engaged Charles MacDonald as his guide, and together they followed the Wassataquoik Stream log drive to the Penobscot East Branch. During this trip, Hallowell took many photographs and later painted one of his most stirring works, *Wassataquoik River Drive*, which is in the permanent collection of the Corcoran Gallery of Art, Washington, D.C.

While Hallowell took photographs and sketched in the Wassataquoik Stream area that summer, a devastating fire broke out in the Traveler Mountain area and roared through the region. Trapped by the approaching fire, Hallowell and his companions took refuge in the stream. Many of his later photographs show the aftermath of that fire. Hallowell's work never received wide acclaim. Most of his paintings were left to his sister and remained un-known for many years. The collection was auctioned in 1949 and bought for only $600 by Myron Avery and a Boston art gallery. Avery later donated his share to the Maine State Library. Some of the larger works are on display there and a large number of smaller paintings are a part of the library's My-ron H. Avery Collection.

Charles Daniel Hubbard

Between 1910 and 1930, American Impressionist Charles D. Hubbard visited the Katahdin region on several occasions to paint. Unlike most of the other artists who visited the area in the first half of the twentieth century, Hub-bard spent a great deal of time on or very near the mountain rather than paint from a distance. In search of inspiration, he often scaled the summit.

Hubbard was born in 1876 and lived most of his life in Guilford, Con-necticut. A graduate of the Yale School of Fine Arts, he spent a good part of his life as an art teacher. Hubbard painted a set of striking murals that form the backdrop for the wildlife exhibits at the Good Will School of Hinkley, Maine, which was founded by his friend Rev. George W. Hinkley. Though Hubbard never aspired to wide recognition, his works make up an impor-tant part of the Katahdin region's artistic history.

Marsden Hartley

Born in 1877 in Lewiston, Maine, to English immigrants, Marsden Hartley left his native state as a young man to study at the Cleveland School of Art. He traveled and painted throughout the county and overseas. He frequently returned to Maine, painting at Georgetown, Vinalhaven, Lovell, Ogunquit, Mount Desert Island, and Corea but had no real home. His itinerant lifestyle influenced his painting and contributed to his distinctive modern style.

Over the years, Hartley began to lose the creative edge that had sus-tained his work as a young artist. His work lacked a central focus, and as his physical and mental health waned, he sought a new creative impetus. In 1937, while painting along the coast of Maine and Nova Scotia, Hart-ley realized that mountains were a constant theme throughout his work. He had painted the western mountains of Maine, the mountains of Mexico and New Mexico, the towering spires of the Bavarian Alps, and even Mont Sainte-Victoire, the rocky hill in Provence that had so moved Cezanne.

During his two years back in Maine, Hartley read Thoreau, Theodore

Winthrop, and Fannie Hardy Eckstorm and studied Church, who had been so richly influenced by the northern wilderness and especially Katahdin. The artist resolved to visit and paint Katahdin himself. Hartley moved to Bangor and, at fellow artist Carl Sprinchorn's suggestion, engaged Caleb Scribner, not only a Maine Fish and Game Warden but also an amateur artist, to take him to Katahdin Lake.

At Katahdin Lake, Scribner introduced Hartley to Bud and Della Cobb, the proprietors of the Katahdin Lake Sporting Camps. Hartley spent a week at the camp, where he obsessively sketched, painted, and took notes. He had found his Mont Sainte-Victoire in the great northern woods. Hartley was determined for his career to culminate in being recognized as the "official portrait painter" of Katahdin. He was sure that whatever fame or success he achieved would come out of what he did during that sojourn. Hartley returned to Bangor and eventually New York City. He painted feverishly from the sketches he made at Katahdin Lake. During the next several years, Hartley produced between twelve to eighteen paintings of Katahdin. During that time, new fire and energy entered his life. He wrote to one friend that he "had seen God for the first time" and that he earnestly hoped his name would always be associated with Katahdin. In her biography of Hartley, Jeanne Hokin wrote:

> Throughout his career, he had searched for stability and permanence in a world of impermanence. . . . Instinctively. . . he had always known that he would find the source of his strength and his spiritual center in his beloved mountain and in himself. The mountain became the essential icon of his personal existence: his mother, his father, his Creator, and in a profound sense the mirror of his own inner resources and durability.[17]

Marsden Hartley died in 1943 and is now recognized as one of Maine's most important artists and one of the finest American modernist painters.

Carl Sprinchorn

Carl Sprinchorn's association with the Katahdin region was notably different from that of his friend Hartley. Sprinchorn returned again and again to the area over a period of nearly twenty years. While Hartley tried to capture Katahdin's essence, Sprinchorn seldom painted the mountain and concentrated instead on other features of the wilderness region: the lumberjacks, the forest, the rivers and streams, and the winter sky. Born in Sweden in 1887, Sprinchorn moved to New York City where he studied with the artist Robert Henri. Henri saw such promise in the young artist that he soon named him the manager of his Robert Henri School of Art. Henri, who frequently visited Monhegan and the Boothbay region, probably introduced Sprinchorn to Maine.

His first visit to Maine in 1907 captivated Sprinchorn. From 1911 to 1914, he lived and painted at Monson's Swedish Colony. During that time, Sprinchorn created some of his best work. In 1917, Sprinchorn began making extended visits to northern Maine. His favorite place was Shin Pond, a remote lake west of Patten and northeast of Katahdin. There he painted local landscapes, hunted with friends and one year accompanied the log drive down the Seboeis River.

In the fall of 1944, Sprinchorn spent time in an old log camp on the banks of the Penobscot's East Branch, near where the Hunt Farm and later the Matagamon House hotel once stood. Sprinchorn's friend Caleb Scribner suggested that the artist stay at the camp. Nat Turner, a local carpenter, trapper, and woodsman, agreed to fix up the place and stay with the artist to take care of the supplies and chores, freeing Sprinchorn to paint. They arrived from Patten by way of Happy Corner, past the Lunksoos Sporting Camps and down the East Branch by boat. Sprinchorn painted and sketched constantly, reveling in his fall/winter wilderness experience until they left in January 1945. The artist had "found his muse in the wooded landscape of Maine."[18] His works from this time are among his finest. Although he returned to stay at Turner's camp in 1951, Sprinchorn came to Maine less often as he grew older. He died in 1971, never having achieved wide recognition outside of a small and faithful cadre of admirers.

Maurice "Jake" Day

Maurice "Jake" Day was born in 1892 in Damariscotta, Maine. After graduating from the School of the Museum of Fine Arts in Boston, he served in the military during World War I. After the war he became an illustrator of children's books and a commercial artist in Boston, where his reputation flourished. A California exhibition of his drawings attracted the attention of a company doing animation film work, and in 1936 he was invited to join their stable of artists. By 1938 he had joined the staff of the Walt Disney Studio, which was making a feature-length animated film based on the book

Bambi. Day lobbied for the star of the film to bear the likeness of the white-tailed deer that roamed the great North Woods of Maine. The studio liked the idea and dispatched Day to his home state in 1938 to produce the sketches and drawings for the film.

Day knew that the best place to find white-tailed deer was Baxter State Park. He convinced his good friend Lester F. Hall from Damariscotta Mills to go with him. He then engaged Caleb Scribner to guide them into the region. Day also enlisted his sons Mac and Dick to help haul supplies and equipment into the park. The state of Maine agreed to support the effort as needed. Day and Hall spent almost a month near Katahdin gathering material for the film. They even had two fawns shipped to California to serve as models for further drawings in the course of the filmmaking.

At first, they set up their base camp along Sandy Stream near the old Hersey Dam. From there the two thoroughly explored the region. Lester fished while Jake sketched. Both were thrilled by the flora and fauna that surrounded them at every turn. Jake had brought along the *Bambi* script, and they read and reread it around the campfire.

One of their tasks was to search for a location that might represent the glade or glen where Bambi was born and where he would later gather with his woodland friends to play and visit. During one backpacking trip Jake and Lester hiked to Chimney Pond, up across the Tableland to Davis Pond in the remote Northwest Basin. They descended the Wassataquoik Valley to Russell Pond where they spent several days. As they returned to their Sandy Stream base camp they came to the old lumber camp clearing named New City. In his journal, Hall wrote:

> As we came out into the New City Clearing and paused to look out over the meadow towards the wooded slopes of Russell Mountain, the thought came to us at once—"This is Bambi's birthplace. Here is the clearing where the forest creatures came for food and play. Here is the edge of the forest where they disappeared when danger threatened. And here is the little knoll from which the elder deer could keep an eye on their offspring." It was perfect.[19]

Day soon returned to California to work on the film but felt increasingly homesick, a condition, no doubt, fueled by his journey to Katahdin. In 1944, after the completion of *Bambi*, Day and his family moved back to Maine, where he painted landscapes of nearby coastal areas and whittled forest creatures and scenes. Day's love for the Katahdin area and all of the North Woods intensified as he and his friends began taking hunting and fishing trips there. Bound closely by their outings, the group of friends dubbed themselves "Jake's Rangers" in the 1950s. They wore arm patches designed by Day, the group's "Colonel." U.S. Supreme Court Justice William O. Douglas was made an honorary member after asking the group of outdoor devotees to accompany him on several trips into Katahdin's interior. During one trip to the park, a reporter radioed Ranger Ed Werler to get a quote from Douglas. Justice Douglas responded: "I have known Katahdin for over a quarter-century. It is for me my favorite mountain the world around. It is not high as mountains go, but one who looks up for four or five thousand feet to see the clouds playing over it sees a mountain peak in all its splendor. There are trails to climb, cliffs to scale, meadows to explore, and lakes to fish. Moose, deer, and bear adorn the area. This is a place for quiet relaxation and soul searching."[20] A local newspaper featured his words in a write-up a few days later.

During these ranger trips, Day created numerous renderings, which were the basis for a large body of work on Katahdin-area subjects—the old logging dams, ponds and lakes, the Great Basin, the north end of Baxter State Park, the Wassataquoik Valley, and even whimsical depictions of Roy Dudley telling his famous tales or conversing with Pamola, the legendary spirit said to reside on the mountain. Day gave many of these paintings as gifts to Baxter State Park, Baxter State Park Authority members, and to a few park rangers and supervisors.

In the early 1970s, Day designed the logo that is still used by the park. Because of his considerable contributions to preserving its history, Baxter State Park named him Honorary Artist-in-Residence, the only artist ever to be so named. Day always toasted Pamola and asked for his blessing as he and his rangers entered Baxter State Park. According to Mac Day, the one year the group members forgot to perform the toast, all sorts of problems ensued during their time in the park.

Day continued to visit the Katahdin region for many years. In 1968, at the age of 77, Governor Kenneth M. Curtis invited him to climb Katahdin with a large party. In his record of the trip, Curtis refers to Day as a "friend and historian." The group ascended the Hunt Trail and descended the Saddle Trail to Roaring Brook. Even in his late seventies, Day held his own alongside many younger than he. He once said that he passed up climbing Katahdin at age 80 only because the black flies were bad that year.

Author Edmund Ware Smith, one of Day's rangers, would immortalize Day and his rangers in his beloved stories "Jake's Rangers vs. Spring Fever" and "Jake's Rangers vs. the United States Supreme Court."[21]

James Fitzgerald

James Fitzgerald was born in South Boston in 1899. Encouraged by his family, he attended both the Massachusetts College of Art and the School of the Museum of Fine Arts in Boston. After a season sailing on a Grand Banks schooner, Fitzgerald traveled to Monterey, California, where he built a studio on the Pacific shoreline. There his career and reputation steadily developed. However, after only three years, Fitzgerald felt the tug of New England and headed east in 1938. Over the next three decades, he spent his summers at Monhegan Island, where an artist colony was emerging, and October at the Katahdin Lake Sporting Camps. Although he sometimes stayed at Daicey Pond Campground, Fitzgerald's first love was Katahdin Lake with its stunning view of the mountain.

Fitzgerald would observe the mountain for hours. Other times he sketched and painted. At other times the artist remained in his cabin for a number of days, waiting for the weather to clear, so he could see his subject in "her many moods."

These fall visits were spiritual pilgrimages for Fitzgerald as he sought to express the mountain's sacred nature on canvas. Like Church and Hartley, Fitzgerald felt driven to express himself through painting Katahdin and its wilderness. Fitzgerald reportedly painted as many as 100 images of Katahdin, more than any other artist. Through the years, a deep and abiding friendship grew between Fitzgerald and the camps' proprietors Bud and Della Cobb. Fitzgerald often sketched Bud Cobb and his horse Tex, who appear in some of his paintings.

Fitzgerald pioneered the modernism movement, which simultaneously explored abstraction and realism. After initially falling ill in Millinocket, where he was trying to finish some of his earlier Katahdin works and several new winter paintings, Fitzgerald returned to Ireland where he died in 1971.

Fitzgerald left his estate and entire collection to his Monhegan friends, Ed and Anne Hubert, who had often helped him through the difficult times. Under their careful stewardship before their deaths, Fitzgerald's reputation grew. His legacy has endured, and his collection now rests at the Monhegan Historical and Cultural Museum.

Photographers

James C. Stodder was born in New York City in 1838. After graduating from Rensselaer Polytechnic Institute in 1859, he moved to Bangor. He took up the wet-plate method of photography and frequently journeyed into the forest north of Bangor to take photos while his brother painted. As an amateur photographer, Stodder accompanied Church on his 1876 expedition down the Penobscot's West Branch. Stodder's photographic record of that journey has become a classic collection of early Katahdin-area photography. This remarkable collection remained in Church's family until after his death. Church's son Louis gave the photographs to Albert F. Fowler, who was later convinced by Myron Avery to give the collection to the Appalachian Trail Conservancy. The Conservancy subsequently donated the collection to the Bangor Public Library where it can now be seen.

Amos L. Hinds, of Benton, Maine, graduated from Colby College in 1858. Between 1865 and 1870, he owned photography businesses in Portland and Boston but decided to return to his hometown where he continued doing amateur photography. He produced a three-set series of stereo views of Casco Bay, Katahdin, and the Penobscot River. Some of these are among the earliest photographs taken of Katahdin. They are considered among the finest examples of nineteenth-century Maine landscape photography.

Fannie Hardy Eckstorm and her brother F.W. Hardy made noteworthy photographic and artistic contributions. During trips along the West Branch and at Katahdin, Hardy took stereopticon views of the Katahdin area, and Eckstorm also took many photographs. A photo taken by Hardy of the Hunt Farm in 1873 has become a bit of a classic in Katahdin archives. At one time, Hardy had a photography studio at the Kenduskeag Block in Bangor.

Lore A. Rogers, son of Luther B. Rogers of the Ayer and Rogers lumbering operation in the Wassataquoik Valley, was the first man to photograph some areas of the Katahdin region, including Chimney Pond and the Great Basin. As a young man, Rogers roamed the area taking pictures. In 1894, he accompanied Professor Lucius H. Merrill of the University of Maine into the Great Basin where Merrill took many photographs.

As photographic techniques and equipment improved in the twentieth century, there was an increasing line of illustrious and distinguished photographers who were inspired by Katahdin and sought to make their own record of its wonders. Samuel Merrill concentrated on pictures of moose in his 1907 photographic collection. William F. Dawson, of Lynn, Massachusetts, and a prominent member of the Appalachian Mountain Club, hiked all over the Katahdin region taking pictures. He was particularly noted for a set of 1915 photographs of the Great Basin. These were undoubtedly used to illustrate his frequent lectures in support of Governor Baxter's drive to set aside the Katahdin area for permanent preservation.

Albert Lincoln "Bert" Call, a gifted photographer in Dexter, Maine, incorporated his career and his great love of the outdoors. He took camping trips into the remote northern Maine forest areas, always toting his cumbersome photographic equipment. Call provided photographs of the Maine wilderness for many publications, especially for the Bangor and Aroostook Railroad annual booklet *In the Maine Woods* and state publicity pieces. In the process, he fell hopelessly in love with the Katahdin area and returned there year after year. He took great delight in photographing the spectacular scenery from valley to summit and captured unique views of life at the sporting camps below Katahdin. The Special Collections Room of the Fogler Library at the University of Maine in Orono preserves Call's collection of negatives. Many of the original prints were given to and are now preserved by the Dexter Historical Society.

Sam E. Connor, reporter and photographer for the *Lewiston Journal* of Maine, produced a memorable photographic record of Percival Baxter's famous 1920 expedition to Katahdin. Myron H. Avery, long-time president of the Appalachian Trail Conservancy, was a prolific photographer whose photographs give a remarkable record of the Katahdin area between the 1930s and 1950s. A major portion of his collection is at the Maine State Library, and the rest is in the possession of the Maine Appalachian Trail Club.

Katahdin in Film

Three outstanding recent films feature Katahdin and Baxter State Park. The first, entitled *The Story of Baxter State Park: Nature at Peace*, was produced by P.S. Hemingway Productions in 1998. Bill Silliker Jr. was the photographer and Steve Pulos the videographer. Special music was provided by Tim Janis.

The second, titled *Katahdin: The Mountain of the People*, was produced by Jeff Dobbs Productions, Bar Harbor, in 2000. Photographers were Bing Miller and Jeff Dobbs and the narrator, Jack Perkins. Original music was composed by John Cooper and Catherine Russell wrote the script. Both of these videos have been aired on the Maine Public Broadcasting television system in recent years.

The third, *Wilderness and Spirit: A Mountain Called Katahdin*, was produced by Huey Films (James Coleman) of Portland, Maine, and was released in 2002. It is a feature-length film headlining outstanding footage of Katahdin and the nearby region, the spiritual aspects of Native American culture and their unique relationship with the mountain, stories of some of the early explorers and artists who were influenced by the mountain, and the amazing story of Governor Baxter's efforts to preserve and protect the area that it might remain "forever wild." Original music was written by Tom Myron. It is a stunning film.

KATAHDIN CONTINUES TO INSPIRE ARTISTS AND LIKELY ALWAYS WILL. Contemporary artists and photographers hail from across the region and include Chris Huntington, Abbot Meader, Thomas Paquette, Marguerite Robichaud, Paul Knaut Jr., Connie Baxter Marlowe (a grandniece of Percival P. Baxter), Robert Villani, the late Bill Silliker Jr., and many others. These artists constitute a community that inherited Church's legacy, which they pass on to future artists through their own interpretation of the mountain.

PART V

The Twentieth Century

FOREVER WILD

11

Governor Baxter's Legacy

AN IMPORTANT DRAMA UNFOLDS

In June of 1920, in a moving railroad smoking-car somewhere between Chicago and Portland, Maine, a group of politicians returning from the 1920 Republican National Convention in Chicago discussed an expedition to climb Katahdin. With this discussion, a drama that would greatly impact the State of Maine and the wilderness of the Katahdin area started to unfold. The state delegates present were Burton W. Howe, a Patten lumberman and politician; Charles P. Barnes, Republican member of the Maine House of Representatives; Arthur S. Staples, influential editor of the *Lewiston Journal*; and, of course, Percival P. Baxter of Portland, member of the Maine House of Representatives, a first-time convention delegate, and a declared candidate for State Senate.

After the usual national convention post-mortem conversations ran their course, one of the delegates, Burt Howe, suggested that the group arrange an expedition to climb Katahdin that summer. It was reported later that the suggestion was made after the train had crossed the Niagara River and its occupants had viewed the mighty Niagara Falls from the train window. That awesome sight caused Howe to remind his colleagues that Maine had a mountain in its remote northern forest that was certainly the rival of the great falls they had just beheld. Before the train reached Portland, Howe had offered to make the arrangements for such a trip and the group had agreed to assemble at his home in Patten on August 5 to begin a five-day excursion to Chimney Pond and to climb to the summit of Katahdin.

After Howe's return home to Patten from Chicago, he contacted Roy Dudley, one of the most respected and sought-after guides in the area. Dudley had been leading parties into the Great Basin for years and was the right man for this important assignment. He went to work immediately planning the details and making the necessary purchases of food and equipment.

When the long-anticipated day of departure arrived, the group, then fourteen or more in number, gathered in Patten with much excitement, their expectations high and their enthusiasm unbridled. For one in their number there was a special sense of excitement—Percival P. Baxter had first seen Katahdin from a distance seventeen years earlier, but this would be his first visit to the mountain. The journey was for him much more than a simple recreational adventure. He and his "cronies" viewed this as an opportunity to strengthen the efforts already underway to preserve and protect Katahdin and its surrounding woodlands. He had become the leading legislative proponent for preserving this jewel of the northern forest, and now he had the perfect occasion to journey to the heart of Katahdin and experience first-hand the wonders of this matchless place.

ONE OF THE MOST REMARKABLE ACHIEVEMENTS OF THE AMERICAN wilderness conservation movement of the early twentieth century can be attributed to the persistent dedication of this man. When a number of legislative proposals failed to permanently preserve Katahdin and the extraordinary lands around it, Baxter realized that he had to do it on his own, using his considerable personal wealth and influence as currency. He made his first purchase of land in 1930 and his final in 1962, a span of 32 years of singular commitment and focused dedication to a monumental task.

The Baxter story is well known not only across the state of Maine but also beyond its borders, especially among backcountry enthusiasts. The staff of the park that today bears his name manages the more than 200,000 acres Baxter gave to the state, a gift to the people of Maine and all who love the wild places of the earth. The park's creation is unique among the world's public parks. The tale is known by many, but new generations should hear the story and learn the vision of a preserved wilderness that inspired a sometimes lonely but always unwavering effort.

Fortunately, there are many exceptional resources that ably tell the story of the Baxter odyssey and the history of Baxter State Park. Therefore, this book does not seek to tell it again in great detail. What follows is a brief recounting of the salient moments of that history, with special attention given to a few of the more human-oriented stories, delightful tales that should be passed on and remembered. Many personal memories about Governor Baxter and those who guided the park in its early years would be lost if not recorded now. The story must live on and be retold so its lessons remain fresh, especially when the wilderness values of Baxter State Park, and wilderness elsewhere, can be so easily threatened.

HERITAGE AND FAMILY

Percival Proctor Baxter was born on November 22, 1876, the middle of the three children of James Phinney and Mehitabel Proctor Cummings Baxter. His father came from a venerable New England family that traced its roots back to England. His mother also had New England roots; her family was from the Salem/Peabody area of Massachusetts. An ancestor, John Proctor, had the dubious distinction of being hanged during the witch trial events in Salem in the 1690s.

Intending at first to pursue a career in law, James Phinney Baxter became instead a businessman in Portland where he and "Hetty" made their home. After success in a downtown hardware business, he and a friend, William G. Davis, founded what soon became a profitable dry goods business. They were, however, soon caught up in a whole new venture. The canning industry was sweeping the country at that time, and they and several other partners organized the Portland Packing Company during a period of great prosperity. The company became one of the largest food packing firms in the world, requiring James to do a considerable amount of traveling across the country. The partners never wavered in their commitment to products of high quality, and their fortunes continued to grow.

Sadness visited James' life in 1872 when his first wife, Sarah, whom he had married in 1854, died during childbirth while the family was residing at a farm in Gorham for the year. She had given birth already to Florence who died at two years of age, Hartley Clinton, Eugene ("Genie"), James Phinney,

Alba ("Dolly"), and Rupert; the last child Mabel lived only a few months. To this sadness was added the death later in 1872 of his only grown daughter, Dolly, who had been injured in an accident and never recovered.

During Dolly's illness, James' life was touched by the devoted care given his daughter by a Mrs. Perkins, a woman from Massachusetts. He soon realized his attraction for her, and they began to correspond and visit back and forth. The relationship blossomed and he and Hetty were married in April 1873 and moved to 61 Deering Street in Portland, where they lived for the rest of their lives.

Governor Percival P. Baxter. Courtesy, Maine State Library, Baxter Collection.

Three children would result from this happy union. Emily was born in 1874 and Madeline in 1879. In between the two girls, Percival Proctor Baxter was born in 1876. James' business ventures continued to expand and his personal wealth grew. He had become one of Portland's wealthiest and most prominent citizens.

In the early 1880s after a lengthy illness, James decided to retire in order to devote more time to his many personal pastimes. He sold his interest in the packing business to his three oldest sons and turned to managing his personal wealth through a number of investments. Freed now from the pressures of the day-to-day responsibilities of a successful and growing business, James began to invest his considerable personal wealth and energy in a variety of remarkable ways. He pursued his artistic talent as an artist. He delved into English and Maine history, publishing several historical studies. He wrote and published a number of literary works. He and the family traveled widely to England and Europe and, closer to home, took long sojourns to the Mount Washington Valley in New Hampshire and to the Rangeley Lakes region in Maine. He loved the outdoors.

James Phinney Baxter also gave himself to a great many civic projects in Portland and left a number of lasting legacies to that city: a new library, strong leadership in many community organizations, six terms as mayor, protection of the Eastern and Western Promenades from development, construction of the downtown Baxter Block, purchase of what later became Baxter Woods, and a vision for park and public land use in Portland, including today's Back Cove and Baxter Boulevard. Many of the father's interests and accomplishments were later reflected in the son's life: a love of the outdoors, a compelling commitment to public service, a desire to travel, an interest in history, and a dedication to using his own personal wealth for the benefit of the people of Maine.

EARLY LIFE AND POLITICAL CAREER

Young Percy grew up entirely in Portland except for two years when he and his parents lived in England, where he attended a private school. He graduated from Portland High School in 1894; from Bowdoin College, with honors, in 1898; and from Harvard Law School in 1901. Members of the Baxter family, including Percy himself, often told the following story that reveals something of his character development. This version is related by Neil Rolde:

> It happened while he was fishing with his father on a family trip to the [Rangeley Lakes]. They were out on Oquossoc Lake and the fish weren't biting. Seven-year-old Percy was growing restless. To quiet him, James Phinney made the boy an offer. For every trout he caught weighing more than five pounds he would be paid $10 a pound. "I was just a small boy, sitting in the middle of the boat, holding onto a short stubby rod with both hands," Percy later related. Suddenly, he had a strike. Fighting the fish all by himself, he finally landed an eight-pound beauty of an eastern square-tailed brook trout. At $10 a pound this meant a fortune for him—$80.
>
> The boy's character and upbringing were revealed that same evening. In the Oquossoc Club lounge, the gentlemen anglers present teased the lad about his winnings. What was he going to do with them? "Bank 'em," he instantly retorted, no doubt coaxing amused smiles and nods of approval from these business-minded folks. Bank them, Percy did. The nest egg was left for almost half a century until the original $80 had compounded to more than $1,000. Only then did he spend it. Or, rather, he gave it away, as he did with so much of his money, in this case donating it to a fund to teach children about wildlife.[1]

Upon completing his studies at Harvard Law School in 1901 Percy returned to Portland and apprenticed at a local law firm. His father was then
70 years old, had been retired for twenty years, and was in need of someone
to take over some of the responsibility for his complex investment and civic
interests. Percy was ready and willing to do that, and he gave himself primarily to that task until his father's death in 1921, which happened during
Percy's first term as governor of Maine. Because his brothers were well cared
for by their own business ventures and because of the unique relationship/
partnership between father and son, Percy was to become the principal heir
to the Baxter fortune, a fact significant, of course, to the Katahdin story.

It was not long before the promising young Portland businessman entered politics. Baxter managed his father's successful campaign for mayor
of Portland in 1904 and later that year was elected himself to Maine's House
of Representatives in Augusta for the 1905–06 session. Though he lost his
re-election bid he was later elected to the State Senate in 1908 at the age of
32. There he lost a brash bid to become president of the Senate in his very
first term. Again he lost his re-election bid in 1910, a victim of a Democratic
landslide throughout the state. Six years later, in 1916, two years after the
death of his mother, he decided to re-enter politics and seek a seat in the
Maine House of Representatives. He was successful and was re-elected two
years later when his brother Rupert was also elected to the State Senate
from Sagadahoc County. Repeating his bold political expectations Baxter
decided to seek election as Speaker of the House of Representatives. The
reaction of his fellow House members to this impulsive political move may
have been predictable, and he was defeated in his bid for the eminent post.
Despite that setback, Baxter had a very productive 1917–18 legislative session, and his stature grew as he mastered the political processes.

Baxter went on to win re-election to the House of Representatives in 1918
and gained stature in statewide circles of the Republican Party. Those were
productive years for him, and he finally began to win some of the political
battles he had waged against great odds: seeking more public involvement
and control over the state's waterpower resources, supporting women's suf-
frage in Maine (a struggle not easily won), working to pass strong anti-Ku
Klux Klan legislation, working toward animal rights anti-vivisection legislation, and supporting a number of anti-war causes he espoused.

One outcome of his growing success was his election as a delegate to the
Republican National Convention in Chicago in the early summer of 1920.
It was returning home on the train from this convention that the idea was

hatched for Burton Howe of Patten to plan a trek to Katahdin for a group of prominent Mainers interested in the preservation of the Katahdin region.

THE 1920 CLIMB—A TURNING POINT

When the 44-year-old Percival P. Baxter arrived in Patten on August 5 to begin his hike to Katahdin's summit, he carried with him a growing conviction that this mountain and the land around it must be permanently protected. He had accompanied his father on a fishing trip to Kidney Pond in 1903 when he was 27 years old, likely staying at Irving O. Hunt's newly established sporting camps there.[2] There is little doubt that Baxter was deeply moved by the stunning view of Katahdin from the camps and the magnificent panorama of the Nesowadnehunk Valley mountains from a point of land across from the camps, known today as Colt's Point. Found at times in the Katahdin literature is an unsubstantiated but believable story that Baxter stood that same year on a ridge in Stacyville and, upon gazing at Katahdin's eastern and northern flanks in the distance, declared that Katahdin should belong to the people of Maine.

It is also said that on this occasion he was in the company of two of his close friends, Lore Rogers and Caleb Scribner. Rogers, the son of Colonel Luther B. Rogers, first climbed Katahdin in 1887, and after a career in lumbering co-founded the popular Lumberman's Museum in Patten. Scribner, also from Patten and Maine's Game Warden for Penobscot County for a considerable time, accompanied Baxter on several trips to the Allagash region and around Katahdin. He was the other co-founder of the museum.

Whatever might have been the circumstances of his first visit to the Katahdin area in 1903, it was only one year later that Percy was elected to his first term in the Maine House of Representatives. Whether or not he foresaw his own destiny in preserving Katahdin at that time we do not know, but his own Katahdin visit prompted him to support several public actions that built on efforts made earlier by others.

As early as 1895, Katahdin became more accessible when the Bangor and Aroostook Railroad laid its tracks not far from the shadow of Katahdin's southeastern and eastern flanks. That same year the Maine Hotel Proprietors Association urged the creation of a huge 900-square-mile state park with Katahdin at the center. It was hoped that such action would be taken before the area was devastated by lumbering, fires, and even squatters.

About that time the mayor of Bangor, Dr. Augustus Hamlin, advanced the idea of a game preserve in the region. This was followed in 1896 by the Maine Sportsmen's Fish and Game Association's advocacy for preservation. The Maine Federation of Women's Clubs joined the effort and began to advocate for state ownership of Katahdin, arranging for the introduction of a legislative petition in 1905 that would achieve just this. It met early defeat, but several major newspapers began to join the chorus of voices in favor of some kind of preservation. State Forest Commissioners, the Bangor and Aroostook Railroad annual publication, *In the Maine Woods*, the state Board of Trade, and many Maine Fish and Game Commissioners joined the preservation effort as well. The idea was gaining slow but steady momentum. Conservation and protection was in the air.

In 1910 U.S. Congressman Frank E. Guernsey, from Dover-Foxcroft, introduced a bill in the United States House of Representatives calling for federal purchase of land in the White Mountains as well as Katahdin. Though this effort failed, the Weeks Act of 1911 succeeded in authorizing the creation of a United States National Forest Preserve Commission to purchase or receive, through donations, eastern lands for stream-flow protection, and to maintain the acquired lands as national forests. In 1913 Representative Guernsey re-introduced congressional legislation, this time calling for the creation of a National Park and National Forest Reserve at Katahdin. He followed that with an address entitled "Mount Katahdin as a National Park" to the Bangor Historical Society in 1915. That and a subsequent congressional effort in 1916 failed.

During these years Baxter began to champion the protection of the mountain, the sight of which had so moved him in 1903. He was encouraged in his convictions by the emergence of the modern American conservation movement, spurred by President Theodore Roosevelt's great effort to expand the acreage of protected land across the country. After his presidency, Roosevelt visited Portland in the spring of 1918 to address the State Republican Convention. Baxter was there and certainly conferred with Roosevelt about their mutual preservationist convictions. Significantly, Roosevelt's commitment to the protection of wilderness places in large part grew out of his own climb of Katahdin in 1879 with his good friend Bill Sewall of Island Falls, Maine. Now Baxter was approaching the time when his commitment to preserving Katahdin would be energized by a similar climb to Chimney Pond and the summit 41 years after Roosevelt had been so invigorated.

A ringing speech by Appalachian Mountain Club member William F. Dawson to a January 20, 1920, meeting of the Maine Sportsmen's Fish and Game Association strongly urged public preservation for Katahdin. Though Baxter supported all of these early preservation attempts, he began to take leadership in the effort after 1916. Never convinced of the appropriateness of federal ownership, he concentrated his efforts in the direction of state ownership. He introduced legislation in 1919 to buy as many as 15,000 acres of land at and around Katahdin to be set aside as a preserve. The timber owners were much opposed to such an idea and, with their clout in the state legislature very strong, the going was tough for anyone in support of the measure. While Baxter's efforts failed, a substitute bill allowed for private gifts of land to the state for designation as reserved lands. Perhaps Baxter's ultimate personal destiny began to unfold with the successful passage of that legislation.

As Baxter's stature grew in Maine GOP circles he was emboldened to lead the effort to preserve Katahdin. Following the defeat of his legislation in 1919 there were a number of initiatives in and outside the legislature. Though not mentioning Katahdin specifically, Baxter did manage to include a plank in the Maine Republican Party platform advocating state purchase of land for recreational and wildlife preserves. The effort now became a central part of his personal goals and aspirations.

With all this as prelude, it is clear why Baxter may have been one of the prime movers of that journey to Katahdin in the summer of 1920. One can imagine Baxter thinking on the train from Chicago: "I must go and stand on the summit of Katahdin myself if I am to continue to lead this important effort. I must see for myself that treasure for which we are contending. Seeing it from Kidney Pond is not enough."

THE GROUP GATHERED AT BURTON HOWE'S HOME IN PATTEN ON August 5, 1920, most of them arriving by train from Bangor. Howe had made all the preparations, including the equipment and provisions. Besides Baxter the following were present as the party headed down the road toward the East Branch of the Penobscot River:

- Burton W. Howe, a Patten lumberman, active in state politics, who knew the Katahdin area well and had climbed Katahdin a number of times. He had long advocated for its protection.

- Roy Dudley, renowned guide to Chimney Pond, who had helped Howe with the trip planning.
- Charles P. Barnes of Houlton, member of the Maine House of Representatives and a strong supporter of Katahdin-area preservation. He would be elected Speaker of the House of Representatives at its next session and in 1924 become a Justice of the State Supreme Court.
- Arthur G. Staples, editor of the *Lewiston Journal.*
- Sam E. Connor, a reporter and photographer for the *Lewiston Journal.*
- Charles H. Fogg, editor of the *Houlton Times.*
- George M. Houghton, General Passenger Agent for the Bangor and Aroostook Railroad, and the man responsible for the railroad's annual publication, *In the Maine Woods*, which had become so influential among those who visited Katahdin and the North Woods.
- Willis E. Parsons, Maine's Fish and Game Commissioner.
- Howard Wood, Maine's Chief Game Warden.
- John T. Mitchell, District Fire Warden.
- Nathaniel "Nat" Howe of Ashland, a cousin to Burton Howe.
- Elroy J. "Ed" Parker, a prominent Patten potato farmer who provided horses for the early part of the journey.
- Oscar Smith, a school teacher, Parker's son-in-law, and a trip teamster.
- An additional number who were to pack in supplies and do the cooking.

For an era when small private parties were the rule of the day, this group of more than fourteen was indeed a formidable one. Howe had done well to engage Roy Dudley as guide for the group. Dudley was known widely for his knowledge of the Katahdin area, especially the Chimney Pond side. Just a few years after this trip, the Katahdin Game Preserve was formally established, and Dudley, after being named Deputy Game Warden, took up seasonal residence at Chimney Pond. He and Baxter became friends on this trip, and they were to remain friends for more than twenty years until Dudley's untimely death.

The significance of that particular year, 1920, was not lost on those who started out that day from the Howe homestead. It was 100 years earlier, in 1820, that Maine had become a state. Unlike the Monument Line surveyors who in 1820 traveled up the West Branch in canoes and bateaux to get anywhere near Katahdin, most of these men traveled to Patten in the comfort of a train.

The group set out in the mid-day sun first by automobile to Six Corners and then by foot to the Lunksoos Sporting Camps where they spent the night. Their baggage and equipment reached the camps by buckboard. Lunksoos was then operated by Edward B. Draper, who had earlier managed the Draper lumber operation in the Wassataquoik Valley. Mike O'Leary, Draper's caretaker, greeted the group and provided for its needs. Early the next morning after a sumptuous breakfast, they were ferried across the Penobscot East Branch by bateaux. A memorable picture of some in the party crossing the river shows Baxter wearing a dark shirt and a light-colored tie. The man surely had style!

Soon the party was ascending gradually toward Katahdin along the old Wassataquoik Tote Road. Arthur Staples reports in his account of the trip:

> The lure of the woods soon began to get me. I love the woods and I have never been slow to express it. The mighty dimness; the aisles slanting with the sunlight; the winds in the tree-tops; the loneliness and the mystery; the religion of them, speaking sweetly to the soul in all gentleness and kindness get me. And so after a while the old jubilance returned; the laziness departed; the town was rubbed off; the disappointment passed. I found myself leaping into the footprints of the man ahead; heard my voice in joke and song; laughed at the cramps in the ball of my right foot. . . .
>
> Ah! The woods! God made them! Man alone can desecrate and destroy them. The State or the Nation that willfully neglects to preserve them robs— aye robs—his children and his children's children; despoils the fair earth and is guilty of a sin past all reparation. Here is the hospital; here the sanatorium of man! Let's preserve it![3]

They had lunch at "Halfway Camp," named by lumbermen to note progress along the old tote road between the East Branch and the New City Depot Camp. It was also the site of the rough-hewn cabin of Israel Robar who, along with his dog Kelley, lived there as a squatter/hermit for a time in the 1880s and was much admired for the stories he told around the evening campfires of those who camped there.

That second night they camped on the shore of Katahdin Lake, at the site of the recently sold Katahdin Lake Camps which were not operating that season (the camps were renovated later that summer and reopened the next year).

Members of a 1920 expedition to Katahdin crossing the East Branch of the Penobscot in a bateau. Percival P. Baxter and Arthur S. Staples are in the bow, both wearing ties. Courtesy, Maine State Library, Myron H. Avery Collection.

The next morning the group had another long day's journey to Sandy Stream Pond, from there along Roaring Brook to Basin Pond, and finally along the old Appalachian Trail* to Chimney Pond. How their hearts must have been moved by the view from the pond, looking up to the great northern ramparts of the Great Basin. Staples described what it was like to stay at Chimney Pond:

> Around you rise the silent spruce! Above you roar the winds. In front is the proscenium [arch] of the mightiest stage ever set. At your feet the little mountain pond, gleaming white with waters like crystal. Over beyond it so near that it seemed as tho one could touch it with one's hand, is Katahdin— not a solitary peak, but two, three, connected by knife-edged [ridges], and

---

* Not to be confused with the twentieth-century Appalachian Trail that runs from Katahdin to Georgia.

sort of circling around this little pond in its basin. You feel in the centre of an auditorium of wonders. You face a picture that time cannot dim. It is primordial, strange, weird, mystic.[4]

The conversation around the campfire that evening inevitably turned to preservation efforts.

The next morning before their climb to the summit, the men decided to divide into two groups. One group ascended the Saddle Slide by an as-yet-unmarked but worn trail up avalanche debris to the Tableland and on to the summit from the west. The other group, including Baxter, Roy Dudley, George Houghton, Charles Barnes, Charles Fogg, Ed Parker, John Mitchell, and Oscar Smith ascended the steeper route to Pamola Peak, also without benefit of a formally marked trail. Dudley, however, knew the route well; the account reported that this was to be Dudley's 38th ascent of Katahdin. It was an exciting day for everyone. The group that hiked the Knife Edge recalled later crawling in many places to avoid falling over the cliffsides. They were exhausted when they finally reached the summit. Baxter is said to have remarked at that exhilarating moment, "I wouldn't go through that experience again if someone offered me a million dollars, but I wouldn't have missed this wonderful scenic view for a million. This is the hardest thing I ever undertook."

The two groups finally met on the summit. There, according to Staples, after soaking in the awesome beauty of the forest, the lakes, the rivers below them in the distance, and the great granite crags of the mountain at their feet, they talked again of creating a Mount Katahdin State Park in order to ensure the continued protection of this sacred space. They even began to lay out a specific strategy for such an effort.

Staples would later reflect on the experience:

Today, some weeks after coming from this trip as I write these words, I can feel yet the spell of Katahdin. I expect never to escape it. I hope never to escape it. I have seen other mountains; climbed a few here and there; but none is like this. It is solitary, wild, titanic—speaking a varied language to the heart and to the emotions. It is an old giant, battered and torn in a northern wild.[5]

Baxter would later describe his feelings:

A few months ago I stood spellbound upon the top of Mount Katahdin, and looked across the great forest areas of northeastern Maine. Hundreds of thousands of acres of the finest timberland in the world lay at my feet, and the black growth of the evergreens, patched with the lighter growth of hard woods, stretched forth in every direction.

Here and there the bright waters of the rivers threaded their way through the woods on their long journey to the sea, and the foam of the waterfalls and rapids, catching the rays of the sun, spanned these waters with glistening bands. I was in the heart of Maine, on the highest peak of land within the State. Standing there all alone, I was carried away by the prospect before me. To me Maine seemed to be nothing but forests.

The memory of the busy cities and towns faded from my mind. I forgot about our great institutions, our farms and our seashore resorts; for Maine was a State of the Woods.

I felt a certain fellowship with the wild life about me, and when my companions called me to return to camp, I took a final survey of the panorama, and impressed it indelibly on my mind.[6]

In that moment, Baxter reaffirmed his resolve to make a major contribution to the preservation of this sacred place for all time. Jack Perkins, in his narration for a video on Katahdin, put it this way: "It is said that men cannot move mountains but a mountain can, indeed, move a man."

The adventurers reluctantly left the summit and, after exploring the Tableland, descended by the Saddle Slide. They spent another wondrous night at Chimney Pond, recounting the events and experiences of the day, and continuing to identify the strategies they would follow to bring the protection effort to a successful conclusion. The next morning the party uneventfully descended to Katahdin Lake and finally back to Patten. They had covered 73 miles in five days.

This adventure made an enduring impression on Baxter. Though already committed to its preservation as a public park, Baxter's effort now took on the flavor of a personal crusade. The die was cast. The effort would become one of the central themes of his political and personal agenda. Eleven years later he wrote in this regard:

While I was there that day I said to myself, "This shall belong to Maine if I live. I have never lost sight of [that intent]."[7]

The presence in that party of several prominent newspapermen, highly placed political activists, and professional state leaders ensured extensive media coverage for the trip; that kept the matter very much alive as an issue. The trip participants began to refer to themselves as The Katahdin Club, and they became active in the effort to preserve this special place for the people of Maine. Burton Howe's prominent role in organizing the trip resulted in Baxter's later declaration that Howe was the one who first introduced him to the great treasures of the region. Although Baxter was unsuccessful in having a trail permanently named after his friend, the range of peaks north of Hamlin Peak are today known as the Howe Peaks.

Baxter had already announced that he would leave his seat in the House of Representatives to again seek election to the State Senate. He also boldly announced his candidacy for the position of Senate president. His daring bid was successful this time. He was elected in November in a GOP land-slide and subsequently elected by his colleagues as president of the Senate in January 1921. Much of the support he received was due to his continued mastery of the political processes of governing effectively. He began his ten-ure as Senate president with high hopes that the protection of Katahdin and other issues of interest to him could be advanced and receive support in a GOP-controlled Senate.

An invitation to address the members of the Maine Sportsmen's Fish and Game Association on January 27, 1921, gave Baxter the public platform he needed to launch this new and more formidable effort to protect Katahdin. Titled "Mount Katahdin State Park," the address is a stirring plea for the preservation of this remarkable place deep in the northern forest. In the years to follow many of the ideas and views espoused that day were heard again and again in the "stump speeches" Baxter gave whenever he had the opportunity. Here are some key excerpts from that landmark address:

Mount Katahdin is located in the very heart of the great timberlands of Maine, the "wild lands" as they usually are called, and in view of this it is fitting that in my remarks I should outline to you the history of these wild lands, in which we are now beginning to take an interest. The history of these is fascinating. It is a story of violent speculation in which fortunes were lost and men's reputations ruined, and in which fortunes were won and great timber-owning families were established, and made wealthy for generations to come. It is a story of intrigue and corruption, where powerful and selfish men often took that to which they had no right, from those too weak to defend themselves and their property. It is a story in which the rights of the people in a princely inheritance were given away or bartered for a song, for the folly of which future generations forever will pay. . . .

These facts are of the past; they are incidents of a by-gone day, and regrets are fruitless. Today it is necessary for us to face the situation as it now exists, so that we may plan to build for future generations better than our ancestors built for us. . . .

Having in mind the fact that the people of Maine once owned these great areas of timberland, is it not fitting that, upon payment of a fair price . . . the grandest and most beautiful portion of all this great area which the people of the State once possessed, should again become their property?

Baxter then describes in detail his own climb of Katahdin in 1920, continuing to praise the unique experience the mountain offers to any who visit it:

Today the conditions for the establishment of this park are ideal. . . . This park will prove a great attraction not only to the people of Maine who will frequent it, but also to those who come from without our State to enjoy the free life of the out of doors. The park will bring health and recreation to those who journey there, and the wild life of the woods will find refuge from their pursuers, for the park will be made a bird and game sanctuary for the protection of its forest inhabitants. Roads, trails, and camps will be built in the most favored locations, and the camps will be rented for nominal sums to those who wish to use them. For those who want hard mountain climbing, trails will be laid out over difficult routes to the top of the mountain, while easier trails will be provided for those who do not desire to make the supreme effort. Katahdin then will become a great recreation center for those who seek the woods that are unspoiled by fashionable hotels with liveried attendants, or by costly club houses frequented by the devotees of tennis and golf. . . .

Maine is famous for its 2,500 miles of seacoast, with its countless islands, for its myriad lakes and ponds, and for its forests and rivers, but Mount Katahdin Park will be the State's crowning glory, a worthy memorial to commemorate the end of the first and the beginning of the second century of Maine's statehood.[8]

It must have been a special experience to have been in the audience that day to hear this ringing address urging support for the preservation of Katahdin and the region nearby. There was no hint of the tumultuous events that were soon to follow.

Less than a week later, fate was to dramatically intervene to lead Baxter and other state officials in an entirely new and difficult direction. Frederick H. Parkhurst, a Bangor Republican, had been elected governor of Maine in November 1920 and subsequently inaugurated on January 6, 1921. Three and a half weeks later, on January 31, Parkhurst died suddenly from a serious infection, and, by the laws of the state, the new Senate president, Percival P. Baxter, succeeded him to the high office of governor.

A time of mourning naturally followed in Augusta and throughout the state, after which the legislature and the new Governor Baxter began to pursue once again the agenda that was before them. An important additional part of that agenda was the effort to preserve Katahdin as a fitting way to celebrate the Centennial of Maine statehood.

Some of the highlights of that effort included:

1. A strong call for protection in a prominent paragraph in Baxter's Inaugural Address as Governor, February 9, 1921.
2. Introduction of legislation in late February of that year to create a Mount Katahdin State Park. The bill was finally defeated in the House after lengthy hearings and major debates, along with strong opposition from the powerful timber owners and many newspapers. The Senate followed suit. Baxter openly decried those who opposed the park proposals.
3. Baxter's promise in an address in the spring of 1921, shortly after another bill was defeated, to re-introduce the proposal in the 1923–24 session of Maine's legislature.
4. Introduction of legislation in the United State Congress in 1921 to create a National Park at Katahdin. The measure was defeated.
5. Creation of a 90,000-acre Katahdin Park Game Preserve in August 1921, by Willis E. Parsons, Maine's inland fish and game commissioner, who had accompanied Baxter on his 1920 trip to Katahdin.
6. Another stirring, widely reported address in January 1922, this time to the Annual Meeting of the Maine Forestry Association. In that speech Baxter once again recalled his personal experience of climbing Katahdin in 1920 and repeated the urgency of protecting that treasure.

7. A much-publicized ascent of Katahdin in 1922 by Judge George C. Wing, Willis Parsons, Roy Dudley, and several game wardens. John Francis Sprague, a state senator, gave coverage of this expedition in his *Sprague's Journal of Maine History*, a publication very popular at that time. That coverage sparked wider interest in protection for Katahdin as a park. Sprague never climbed or even approached the mountain because of a severe deformity of the feet, but he became a strong, consistent, and spirited advocate in the effort to protect Katahdin even before Baxter entered the fray. He was the founder of the Maine Fish and Game Association, which also exerted strong pressure for protection. The courageous part he played in this effort needs also to be remembered.

8. Introduction in 1923, after Baxter had been re-elected Governor, of another state legislative proposal to create a Mount Katahdin State Park. This measure was also defeated, this time resoundingly.

9. Governor Baxter began, in 1923, to consider the idea of a National Forest Preserve, if all state park efforts proved unsuccessful. In the end, however, he rejected federal involvement.

10. The state completed the building of a cabin at Chimney Pond in 1924. Roy Dudley was named game warden and began his long tenure of providing seasonal supervision in the Great Basin.

11. After deciding not to seek re-election to a third term as governor, Baxter used his Farewell Address of 1925 to strongly urge the creation of a Mount Katahdin State Park. He said in part:

> The Mount Katahdin Forest Reserve or Park would be the State's greatest natural attraction. It would draw to us many people from beyond our borders, and would serve us as a place of resort for thousands of our own citizens. It could be developed at moderate expense, year by year, all the while contributing to the health and recreation of those who use it. . . . The establishment of a game preserve in that territory is a step forward, a feeble beginning.[9]

Baxter then warned of possible limitations and regulations governing access to the forest lands of Maine by the timber owners. He again urged the incoming legislature to enact the law establishing the park. Seeking to "put his money where his mouth was" he publicly offered the salary of his last two years as governor to offset the $10,000 needed to get this task done by purchase or condemnation. He outlined very clearly a number of conditions that had to be met before his offer could become a reality. The conditions were never met.

12. Introduction of yet another legislative bill in 1925 to create such a park. The measure was defeated once again.

13. Introduction of a bill to the United States Congress later in 1925 to create a national park at Katahdin. It was defeated.

14. A 1925 visit to Chimney Pond and the summit by then Governor Ralph Owen Brewster, a visit he used to give further publicity and support to Baxter's call for preservation of the area.

... MY LIFE'S WORK

After Baxter left the governor's mansion in January 1925, at the age of 49, he must have spent much time reflecting on his future in politics and especially on his vision for Katahdin. We know there were fewer legislative and other public proposals, and the energy for such preservation waned considerably in the immediate years following his years in office. After he stepped down as governor, Baxter's vision of personally purchasing the land at and surrounding Katahdin emerged and grew into a commitment that would define the rest of his life and help determine his legacy to his beloved state. Years later he often mentioned 1925 as the year he finally gave up on the effort to create a park by legislative action and decided the only way open was to buy the land himself and give it to the state.

Baxter had certainly read Henry David Thoreau's reflections on the need for national preserves to protect some lands:

The Kings of England formerly had their forests "to hold the king's game," for sport or food, sometimes destroying villages to create or extend them. . . . Why should not we, who have renounced the king's authority, have our national preserves, where no villages need be destroyed, in which the bear and panther, and some even of the hunter race, may still exist, and not be "civilized off the face of the earth,"—our forests, not to hold the king's game merely, but to hold and preserve the king himself also, the lord of creation,—not for idle sport or food, but for inspiration and our own true recreation? Or shall we, like the villains, grub them all up, poaching on our own national domains?[10]

Baxter agreed, later adding that such land should never be restricted to a few but be accessible to all the people.

Baxter was also influenced by Teddy Roosevelt's incredible commitment to preserve land for public use. Baxter had also developed a friendship with Gifford Pinchot and knew well of his dedicated service as director of the new United States Forest Service. Those influences plus his own experience on the summit of Katahdin in 1920 helped established Baxter's post-public office career.

It was not a carefully crafted wilderness philosophy that drove the early Baxter effort toward park legislation. It was more a preservation effort. In fact, the reader may have noticed already that Baxter, at the outset, harbored a few notions that tilted slightly toward tourist development. He said, for instance, on January 16, 1922:

> Katahdin to be developed as a resort, should be owned by the State and the developments there should be made by the State. Proper access to the park must be provided, camps and small hotels will be built at the most beautiful locations upon land leased to the builders by the State, and everything must be done to advertise the great natural attractions of that region.[11]

Those early ideas steadily gave way to a stronger commitment to go beyond preservation, to embrace a "forever wild" concept that would minimize human impact on the land and allow the region to become more primitive and wilder, thus allowing it to return to the way it was in the distant past.

An example of his later thinking can be found in this communication to the state legislature in 1945:

> I want no hard surfaced roads in this Park, my object being to have it remain as nearly as possible in its natural wild state, unimproved by man. . . .
>
> I seek to provide against commercial exploitation, against hunting, trapping and killing, against lumbering, hotels, advertising, hot-dog stands, motor vehicles, horse-drawn vehicles and other vehicles, air-craft, and the trappings of unpleasant civilization. Nor is the Park to be kept exclusively for professional mountain climbers; it is for everybody.
>
> Everything in connection with the park must be left simple and natural and must remain as nearly as possible as it was when only the Indians and the animals roamed at will through these areas. I want it made available to

persons of moderate means who with their boys and girls, with their packs of bedding and food, can tramp through the woods, cook a steak and make flapjacks by the lakes and brooks. Every section of this area is beautiful each in its own way. I do not want it locked up and made inaccessible; I want it used to the fullest extent but in the right unspoiled way.[12]

The land in question was certainly not an untouched wilderness when Baxter began his effort. It had been cut over widely since the 1830s. Any number of fires had burned and devastated the area. The establishment of a Game Preserve was a start but more action was needed. To his everlasting credit Baxter knew that this land, so abused in the past, would eventually recover and heal itself over the generations to come if it could be set aside in his day. He began to embrace the already established if not highly utilized idea of private purchases of the land. Such land purchases, later to be given to some government entity, had already occurred in California's redwood forests and even on coastal land on Maine's Mount Desert Island, later to become Acadia National Park.

And so it was in 1930 that, after reviewing all the options, Baxter, embarked on his personal odyssey to buy Katahdin and establish a governing entity to administer it for future generations. His endeavor was helped along ironically by the death in 1928 of Garrett Schenck, the tough-minded head of Great Northern Paper Company, and the forced retirement in 1929 of Schenck's successor Fred H. Gilbert. Both had fervently opposed Baxter's protection proposals, and their opposition was often extremely personal. New company management in the early 1930s, however, contributed to a more open attitude toward Baxter's overtures to the landowners around Katahdin.

Baxter's first purchase of nearly 6,000 acres, including Katahdin and most of the nearby peaks of the massif, occurred on November 12, 1930 in what became a rather complicated agreement for which he paid $25,000. Baxter's intention was to make the land a gift to the state under that 1919 state law allowing for such private gifts of land to the state. This he finally did in 1931, and the gift was formally accepted by the state in 1933, after some of the complications in the deal were resolved. The legislature then established Baxter State Park and renamed its summit Baxter Peak (known then as Monument Peak). Great energy was expended in completing the purchase of that first parcel of land, but finally it was accomplished. The dream was starting to become a reality.

On September 11, 1932, Baxter again hiked to the summit, by way of the Hunt Trail, to take part in the installation of a bronze plaque that was authorized by Maine's governor and its Executive Council. Though the text of the plaque is quite lengthy, it reminds all who reach the summit of the clear expectation that the Katahdin region will forever remain in its natural wild state and as a sanctuary for wildlife. The Baxter gift is acknowledged with deep gratitude, and some of the rules governing the park are clearly stated.

The occasion was a memorable one and the press widely reported the whole event. There were eighteen in the party, including Baxter, several key state officials, members of the Millinocket Chamber of Commerce, and personnel from the Great Northern Paper Company. Some of the latter lugged a compressor all the way up the mountain to drill holes in the rock for the bolts that would secure the sign. Ralph Dorr, a much respected guide in the Katahdin area, was the cook and it was reported that the dinner over which he presided at the end of the day at Katahdin Stream Campground was a masterpiece. This was Baxter's first visit to the summit since his 1920 climb and, as far as can be determined, his last.

This was, of course, only the beginning of the Baxter land purchases. There would be 28 separate acquisitions in all, culminating in the final tract bought in 1962, bringing the total protected land to more than 200,000 acres. In January 3, 1963, Baxter wrote a letter to then Governor John H. Reed and members of the legislature drawing attention to the fact that he had completed the park acquisitions. In that letter he made one of the great understatements of Maine history. He said, "This brings to an end an interesting incident in Maine history."

During those years there were several attempts to make the region a national park, but Baxter grew more suspicious of federal involvement and more strident in his opposition of such efforts. In most cases, the Deeds of Trust always included some kind of clear statement that the lands be kept in their natural wild state. Baxter stated in 1941 that he wanted to establish a clear precedent over a number of years so his wishes would be carried out faithfully, a trust that could never be broken.

John Hakola has painted a brief but insightful picture of Baxter's efforts across those significant years:

> [Baxter] showed amazing diligence and patience. In some cases, he pursued
> pieces of property for over two decades before reluctant owners would sell

to him. Fortunately, the tendency toward longevity in his family favored him and benefited the state, for the last land was acquired . . . when he was eighty-seven years old. After the attempt to create a national park in the 1930s, if not before, Baxter made the creation of a large state park in his memory his life's work. He was willing to be patient in acquiring land, willing to pay higher prices than the land would normally have brought in order to obtain it; and sometimes he purchased lands in outlying areas—often considerably better in quality than those he sought—in order to exchange them with owners who were fearful of losing production potential for wood needed in the papermaking process and persuade them to part with their land. He was not above using moderate pressures to coerce reluctant owners to sell, pressures such as the national park threat, with reminders that he had been primarily responsible for stopping its creation; finding common ties in family backgrounds, and similar stratagems. Though he did not like the idea, at times he was willing to make some rather important concessions in his ideals for the park to obtain property.[13]

The complex story of the Baxter acquisitions is told admirably by Hakola in his *Legacy of a Lifetime: The Story of Baxter State Park*. Baxter made many friends and not a few enemies during that 30-year period as he pursued his "magnificent obsession." His is a story of courage and perseverance, obstinacy and patience, idealism and pragmatism—a tale of the remarkable vision of one man who has left a matchless legacy to the people of his beloved state. Whenever he had the opportunity, Baxter noted that his gifts were meant to express his gratitude to the people of Maine who had given him the opportunity to serve them as a public servant.

Here in Baxter's own words, written in 1941, is the story of his "life's work":

As modern civilization with its trailers and gasoline fumes, its unsightly billboards, its radio and jazz encroaches on the Maine wilderness the time may yet come when only the Katahdin region remains undefiled by man. To acquire this Katahdin region for the people of Maine has been undertaken by me as my life's work, and I hope as the years roll on that the State Park will be enjoyed by Maine people and those who come to us from beyond our borders. . . .

Katahdin stands above the surrounding plain unique in grandeur and glory. The works of man are short lived. Monuments decay, buildings crumble, and wealth vanishes but Katahdin will forever remain the mountain of the people of Maine. Throughout the ages it will stand as an inspiration to the men and women of this State.[14]

A PARK FOR ALL THE PEOPLE

Though the history of this remarkable park has been laudably and comprehensively covered it is important to our journey to share some of its salient features. Baxter State Park became a formal entity in 1931 when the state of Maine accepted its first parcel of land from Baxter. Administrative responsibility for those initial nearly 6,000 acres was to be carried out by the state forest commissioner with whatever funds could be squeezed out of his department's regular budget. From the very start conditions were grim. There was little money available and no additional personnel. In short, no one was quite sure what to do with or how to manage Baxter's generous gift.

Realizing the need for some sort of central authority over the new park, the legislature authorized in 1933 a Baxter State Park Commission, consisting of the governor, the forest commissioner, the commissioner of Inland Fisheries and Game, and two public members at least one of whom had to be a resident of Millinocket or Greenville. Although there were still only meager funds, many state agencies pitched in to contribute time and equipment as they could. The commission did not meet very often, but it did function for six years as an important point of coordination as state and federal resources became available.

In the early 1930s, proposals to set aside the Katahdin area as a national park surfaced again. Those overtures soon faded, only to resurface in 1937 when U.S. Senator Ralph Owen Brewster, Baxter's successor as governor of Maine, introduced such a measure in the Senate. Baxter, by then convinced of his own ability to purchase the land and entrust it to state management, strongly opposed the whole idea of federal control and waged an aggressive campaign against it. It became a somewhat bitter battle and strong personal feelings and attitudes came into play with Baxter, the Appalachian Mountain Club, and other allies on one side, and Brewster and Myron Avery of the Appalachian Trail Conference on the other. Avery was also very critical of the lack of state care of the early Baxter purchases. Support for the measure finally faded in 1938 and the growing threat of war in Europe kept it from being reintroduced.

One positive result of the battle to avoid national park status was the recognition by the state of Maine that it could no longer neglect its responsibility to better manage the land Baxter was steadily acquiring. In order to sharpen the lines of responsibility, the state, at Baxter's request, replaced the old Baxter State Park Commission with a new Baxter State Park Authority to consist only of the attorney general, the commissioner of Inland Fisheries and Game, and the forestry commissioner. The legislation gave the authority greater powers and a clearer statement of its duties. The authority has stood the test of time and today remains the park's basic governing group to which the day-to-day professional staff is accountable.

The story of the Civilian Conservation Corps will be told in another chapter, but we must note here the important role it played in the early years of the park's life. Indeed, the CCC may have saved the park from the consequences of neglect in those early years. The development and improvement of the roads, the building of campgrounds, the construction of key trails, and other such assistance resulted in a much more acceptable level of management, long before the state began to provide even minimal funding for the park.

Though funds earmarked for Baxter State Park from the state's general fund finally began to flow to the park in 1945, the authority for years had to make special requests to the legislature for necessary capital improvements. Fortunately, General Fund appropriations slowly increased throughout the 1950s and 1960s.

Early in its existence the authority realized the wisdom of designating someone to be the supervisor of the park operation. Richard Holmes was hired in 1939 by the authority as the first paid ranger for the park, a full eight years after its creation. He was sent to live from June to November at Katahdin Stream Campground where the Forest Service maintained a telephone. A tent served as the ranger station. There was no vehicle, no badge, and no uniform. Holmes' duties included helping campers and hikers, visiting the sporting camps in the area, and being alert to emergencies.

In an extraordinary twist of fate one of Holmes' first tasks that summer was to help organize the hundreds who aided in the search for Donn Fendler, the young boy who lost his way on the mountain in a thick Tableland fog and was not found until he arrived nine days later on shore of the Penobscot East Branch. Having only been employed for the summer and fall seasons, Holmes left in November to pursue other career opportunities. The authority, realizing the need for a permanent presence in the park, named Harold Dyer to the position of full-time supervisor in 1940, and he began to preside over a slow expansion of the park and its facilities. Across the years there have been a number of outstanding administrators managing the day-to-day affairs of the park. They are:

Harold Dyer	1940–1950
Robert Dyer	1950
Helon Taylor	1950–1967
Irvin "Buzz" Caverly	1968–1969
Harry Kearney	1969–1971
Irvin "Buzz" Caverly	1971–1981
A. Lee Tibbs (Director)	1975–1981
Irvin "Buzz" Caverly (Director)	1981–2005*
Jensen Bissell	2005–Present

Of those park managers, three stand out as giants in the history of the park. Harold Dyer, the first superintendent, was a graduate of the University of Maine with a degree in forestry and wildlife. During his ten years as the administrator Dyer supervised its early growth, the important transition to a more centralized professional management, and an emerging clarity of mission.

Helon Taylor became superintendent in 1950 and made major contributions to the development of Baxter State Park, retiring in 1967. He enjoyed the strong support of Governor Baxter and a rich personal friendship developed between the two. Those post-World War II years of Taylor's management of the park were crucial for the park when campgrounds were built or refurbished, old trails stabilized, and new ones developed. Many major issues threatening the wilderness integrity of the park were faced courageously. Though they did not always agree, Taylor was willing to work closely with Governor Baxter on park matters. There had to be thoughtful response to the sharply increasing numbers of visitors in the post-World War II era and the resulting increase in personnel and infrastructure. Taylor used to say that during his first year the park took in $3,000 and in his last year $35,000. Taylor was a giant of a man in physical appearance, but he was also a man

---

* Note that Buzz Caverly served first of all as supervisor and later assumed the role of director when the latter title was adopted to identify the chief officer for the park.

with a giant and generous heart to match it, a man totally committed to this very special place and much respected by all who knew him.

The third of the superintendent/directors who have made remarkable contributions to the history of Baxter State Park is its recently retired director, Irvin "Buzz" Caverly. Throughout his many years as either superintendent or director, Caverly remained steadfast in his commitment to keep Baxter State Park "forever wild" in the spirit of Governor Baxter's intentions. One of the last of those who knew Baxter well, Caverly was a first-rate steward of the Baxter dream. That did not always endear him to those who have pressed for greater and greater access to the park, but it endeared him to those who believe that the wilderness values of this place should be protected and never compromised.

During his tenure, Caverly faced a number of major issues that confronted the park, presided over a time of stabilized financial support thanks to prudent investment and wise use of the Baxter Trust Funds, and wisely managed the infrastructure and personnel of the park. His love of the park and his commitment to keeping it as close as possible to its original wild state was apparent to all who met him. He was and continues to be a staunch friend to the park that nurtured his career.

Buzz Caverly's dedication and commitment to the wilderness values envisioned by Baxter have been deservedly recognized on a national level. In 1991 he received the Olaus and Margaret Murie Award from the prestigious Wilderness Society, in recognition of his career-long devotion to maintaining and enhancing the wilderness character of this very special park.

Governor Baxter provided a number of principles to guide the decision-making process of those who followed him. Those guidelines, however, are not always clear or consistent and require interpretation. The challenge of the future is to continue to identify a consistent philosophy of wilderness that will best reflect Baxter's wishes in our day.

THE MEASURE OF THE MAN

Many warm, personal stories about Baxter that reveal his innermost character have become a part of the Baxter legacy.

One story, from his years while serving as governor, reveals his legendary love of animals and especially his close relationship with his own Irish setters. One of them named Garry (Garryowen) faithfully followed his master each day to the governor's State Capitol office where he would remain for the day. When Garry felt the need to visit the grounds surrounding the state-house for his personal canine needs he scratched on the side of the door to the governor's inner office. The governor or an aide then responded to his call. Today a small plaque on the door of the office of the Senate president (formerly the governor's office) points out the reason for the woodwork scratches that can still be seen. It is a simple reminder of Baxter's love of animals and his special relationship with Garry.

The governor got into a heap of trouble while he was still in office when he ordered the statehouse flags be flown at half-mast at the time of Garry's death. Responding to several press attacks, Baxter publicly argued in an address before the legislature that such canine gentleness and faithfulness were as worthy of public recognition as that of any human. All of the Bax-ter dogs are buried in a special ground on Mackworth Island in Casco Bay, where Baxter helped establish the Baxter School for the Deaf.

Another Baxter animal story involves Helon Taylor's daughter, Doris, and her husband Myrle Scott, who was a Baxter State Park ranger at the time. Myrle had been assigned to Roaring Brook Campground in the 1950s, and when he and Doris arrived there to begin their service they had an Irish setter whose name was Clancy. The Scotts were green and inexperienced and were not yet aware of the consideration being given by Baxter and the park's administrators to banning domestic animals in the park—something Percival Baxter himself felt rather strongly about. When they learned about Baxter's views on the matter they agonized over what they should do be-cause they loved Clancy so much.

While they were still pondering this dilemma they were informed that Governor Baxter himself was on his way to the campground for one of his inspection visits. Afraid of what Baxter might do if he discovered they had a dog, they took Clancy off into the woods nearby and tied him to a tree to await the governor's departure.

As the governor arrived, Clancy decided he had had enough of his lonely imprisonment and began to bark. The governor heard it, paused, listened, and of course, asked sternly if he was hearing a dog. The Scotts admitted to their canine concealment attempt, and the governor asked darkly to see the dog. Myrle went into the woods feeling great sadness; he untied the dog to take him to the governor. Upon seeing that Clancy was an Irish setter, how-ever, Baxter's demeanor changed markedly, and he greeted Clancy with the same cordiality he would have given to one of his own beloved setters. No doubt Clancy returned the affection. Much to the Scotts delight and relief, Clancy was granted a special Baxter exemption from the efforts at that time to establish a no-pet regulation.[15]

Baxter's conservative approach to small financial matters, which could be said to border on stinginess, also became legendary. Helon Taylor remembered that Baxter occasionally showed up for one of his tours of the park with holes in his shoes. He came for several days at a time, driven from Portland to Millinocket by his chauffeur. Taylor met Baxter there, and they drove through the park so Baxter could be kept up-to-date on what was happening. The rangers remembered that he was very generous with Christmas bonuses for all on the staff and often brought oranges for their children. Baxter was not a strongly committed outdoorsman, but he loved "his" park and wanted to be sure others enjoyed it as well.

When Taylor first met Baxter he was prepared not to like him because he was a man of such great means, but Taylor quickly discovered that Baxter was a pleasant and likable man. Taylor never forgot that even in the 1950s Baxter was driving an old 1944 Cadillac and did not buy a new one for a long time after that.

On one occasion Baxter asked Taylor to fly down to Portland to drive him back in Baxter's car to Millinocket for his park inspection tour. Taylor arranged for his wife to drive out of the park to pick him up when he and Baxter reached Millinocket so they could be home for the evening together. The governor, however, insisted that Taylor take the Baxter car and drive home in order to avoid inconveniencing his wife. Taylor returned in the morning whereupon Baxter, much to Taylor's surprise, checked to be sure no extra mileage had been put on his beloved old "Caddy."

The following story involving former Baxter State Park director Buzz Caverly is told by Trudy Scee in her *In the Deeds We Trust*:

When Buzz and Jan Caverly planned their wedding in early 1963 they sent Governor Baxter an invitation. Although Baxter was unable to attend the ceremony he sent the young couple a check for fifty dollars as a wedding gift. Caverly was stationed at Russell Pond at the time. On his first off-duty day he wrote Baxter a thank-you note, addressed an envelope, and enclosed the letter. Not having a three cent stamp—all that was currently needed for a one ounce letter—Caverly placed a six cent stamp on the envelope. He then walked out to Taylor's cabin at Togue Pond and asked Taylor if he would mail the letter when he went to town. Taylor said he would mail the letter, but looking closely at it though his thick glasses noticed the six cent stamp and said, "Oh my, this will never do."

Taylor then started a steam kettle heating, steamed off the six cent stamp, walked to his desk, placed the six cent stamp in it, and placed a three cent stamp on the envelope. "You know," he said to Caverly, "Governor Baxter would give away thousands, but if he thought you were giving away a single cent to the federal government he'd never speak to you again." Generally a frugal man, Caverly seems to have learned his lesson.[16]

Though his frugality in some of the minute things and his cautious attitude toward federal largess may be legendary, Baxter's profound generosity to the park and its employees and to untold charitable interests throughout the state was equally legendary and will always be remembered with gratitude and affection.

Earle Shettleworth Jr., present director of the State of Maine Historic Preservation Commission, remembers when he was a sixth-grade student in Portland in the early 1960s, asking if he could visit Governor Baxter in connection with a school project. A little timid about the whole adventure, he went to see Baxter, then in his 80s, at his office in the Trelawney Building. To this impressionable young man, meeting and talking to the governor was an awesome and unforgettable experience. At one point in the interview Governor Baxter pointed to a picture of Katahdin on the wall of his office and asked, "Have you seen my mountain?" It was one more indication of the warm and humble pride that Baxter felt, having achieved his life's ambition to protect Katahdin forever for the people of Maine.

Whether from Maine or elsewhere, many feel deeply indebted to this man for his inestimable gift, a feeling that will last for generations. Hopefully, gratitude for his extraordinary gift will be expressed in the future in the ways we care for and preserve the park that bears his name.

No finer summation of Baxter's "magnificent obsession" can be found than in his own words, written in a communication to Governor Edmund S. Muskie and the members of the 97th state legislature, on January 11, 1955:

In 1917, I first proposed that the State make a beginning in creating a Park at Katahdin. From that date until now I have worked diligently and patiently upon this project and have seen it grow from small beginnings to its present ample proportions. In the years to come, when the Forests of our State have been cut off and disappeared, when civilization has encroached upon the land we now refer to as "Wild Land," this Park will give the people of succeeding generations a living example of what the State of Maine was "in the good old days," before the song of the woodsman's axe and the whine of the power saw was heard in the land. I am confident that the people of Maine, as time passes, will appreciate this Park and the State never will break these Trusts. I know the conscience and Soul of Maine. The word of this State as given in Acts passed by its Legislatures and signed by its Governors is as sacred a pledge and trust as Man can make.[17]

Finally, the opening line of a plaque honoring Baxter at the State Capitol in Augusta bears these simple but eloquent four words, expressing how the people of the state of Maine feel about this man:

"Among Men A Mountain"

The People and Places that Define the Mountain

IN THE TWENTIETH CENTURY, THOUSANDS CAME TO EMBRACE Katahdin and its environs as a place for hiking, camping, paddling, and quiet contemplation. Throughout the century, special people and events—from a precocious female historian, to a courageous boy lost on the mountain, to a rescue that ended in tragedy—would play roles in defining Katahdin's mystique. A mythical creature, a stirring elephant hunt, the work of the Civilian Conservation Corps (CCC), and a trail that would become a national treasure would all contribute to Katahdin's unique traditions. There are, of course, many more such stories, but perhaps the following will help the reader understand something of the character of this sacred ground.

THE REMARKABLE SURVIVAL OF DONN FENDLER

Few stories of the Katahdin region have stirred the public as much as that of the twelve-year-old Boy Scout from Rye, New York, who was lost on Katahdin's vast Tableland in July 1939. Separated from his father, his brothers, and several friends, Fendler began an extraordinary nine-day odyssey alone across the Tableland's rock-strewn wastes and down the valley of Wassataquoik Stream to the East Branch of the Penobscot River. It is a story of strong courage, constant fear, persistent loneliness, physical deprivation, and dogged determination. It is also a story of a boy possessed of a deep and abiding faith that he would return safely to his family.

The saga began when Donn and his friend Henry Condon crossed the Tableland on the Hunt Trail and neared the summit. Thick clouds quickly lowered, reducing visibility to nearly zero. Neither boy wanted to stay there long, but Henry was eager to wait and greet a hiker nearing the summit from the Knife Edge side. Donn, on the other hand, decided to head back down the trail to meet others in his party still ascending. In that breath of a moment Donn wandered off the trail and lost his way. He realized too late that he should have stopped and waited to be found. Instead, he kept going, thinking at any moment he would come upon his father and the others.

The clouds thickened, sleet began to fall, and the boy, eager to reach a lower elevation, kept steadfastly on. After wandering about the Tableland and passing near the head of the Saddle Slide, Donn finally realized he had to get off the Tableland and find a stream or tote road he could follow to safety. After he stumbled down through thick treeline scrub growth, the terrain began to level out. There he spent a frightening and uncomfortable night, the reality of his situation beginning to enter his consciousness.

In the morning, after overcoming a bout with hallucinations, he came across and followed an old abandoned tote road along one of the branches of Wassataquoik Stream. Later that morning he lost his sneakers, which had been ripped badly during his descent the day before through the unforgiving rocky terrain of the mountain.

Over the course of the ensuing week, Donn slept fitfully wherever he could find shelter at night and by day continued to follow along other Wassataquoik Stream branches, one in which he lost his dungarees. Through it all he found solace and inner strength in constant prayer and a strong reliance upon God taught him at home.

He endured swarms of black flies and mosquitoes, hallucinations and frightening dreams, and fits of crying when matters seemed unbearable. He found berries but was often hesitant to eat them unless he felt certain they were not poisonous. He came upon an old lumber cabin at one point in his journey, but it had been long abandoned and was not much use to him in his eagerness to keep moving forward to safety. Though often discouraged, his spirits were kept up by an expectation that he might come across a fisherman looking for a good trout pool along the stream.

As day followed day Donn lost all track of time. His legs took a frightful beating—he had scratches, sprains, bleeding, insect bites, clinging blood-suckers, and terrible swelling. On the sixth day he heard the sound of an air-plane, but he was too much under the forest canopy to be seen by what was likely a search plane. It became more and more difficult to move his legs but he gamely walked on, buoyed by the possibility of finding an inhabited cabin. He came to believe that he was never quite fully alone, that a guardian angel was present and watching over him.

Nearing the very end of his endurance, Donn reached the East Branch of the Penobscot near where the stream he had been following joins the river. When Donn looked across the river he could see the cabins of the Lunksoos Sporting Camps. His weak yells were finally heard by Nelson McMoarn, the shocked proprietor of the camps, who rushed across in a canoe to rescue the boy. The word quickly spread that Donn Fendler had been found alive.

The search and rescue attempts organized the first day of Donn's dis-appearance had been almost abandoned by the time he was found, but his family and thousands of people following the news reports had never given up hope. The adventure continues to inspire people who celebrate the strength of the human spirit in the face of what appears to be unbeatable odds. As for what immediately followed:

> National magazines, newspapers, and radio acclaimed his feat in the months to follow. Life magazine carried text and photographs of the emaciated boy's dramatic return by canoe down the East Branch of the Penobscot River to the arms of his mother. His tributes included a parade held in Augusta and a White House visit with President Franklin D. Roosevelt. The Congressional Record of August 10, 1939, contained an entry by Maine Congressman Ralph O. Brewster lauding Donn and stating that "American youth everywhere may well read the story of Donn Fendler and raise themselves to greater heights in the face of whatever difficulties and discouragement may seem to hold them back."[1]

Donn himself told the story of his extraordinary saga in *Lost on a Mountain in Maine*, which he wrote with the help of Joseph B. Egan, not long after his rescue. The book has become a classic of Katahdin and Maine litera-ture and continues to be read by adults and schoolchildren throughout New England and across the world.

Roy Dudley welcomes Donn Fendler to Chimney Pond in 1940, one year after Donn's remarkable wilderness odyssey. Courtesy, Donn Fendler.

In 1941, the National Park Service, as a part of a series of proposals it made for development at Katahdin, suggested that a Donn Fendler Trail be designated in Baxter State Park. The trail would follow closely the route of Fendler's astounding adventure as researched by Myron H. Avery. Many Boy Scout troops were naturally eager to help make such a trail possible. The trail was to begin at the Saddle Spring on the Tableland, ascend Hamlin Peak, cross the North Peaks (then named Howe Peaks), descend to Wassataquoik Stream and continue on the tote road along the stream to the East Branch of the Penobscot opposite the Lunksoos Sporting Camp. A map of the suggested trail is now in the Map Collection of the Maine State Library—but the idea never came to fruition.

Donn had become a national hero with magazine accounts of the adventure, personal appearances on the Walter Winchell and Lowell Thomas radio shows, and invitations to give speeches to many Boy Scout troops. Later, upon completing his high school education, he enlisted in the Navy and served with the Seabees in World War II. After the war he completed his college studies at the University of Maine and the University of Georgia. He then returned to military service, this time with the Army. He served in Vietnam as a Green Beret and later retired in 1978, having reached the rank of Lt. Colonel. He now lives in Maine and continues to be generous with his time, telling his story and sharing the lessons he learned with Scout troops and school children throughout Maine, all of whom continue to keep the legend alive.

A TRAGEDY ON THE KNIFE EDGE, 1963

One of the most notable and tragic search and rescue incidents occurred in October 1963. Although the park was officially closed, two women, Helen Mower and Margaret Ivusic, both from Massachusetts, received permission to climb Katahdin from Chimney Pond where they were camping. It was a beautiful, crisp autumn day, and everything went well as they ascended the Cathedral Trail, lunched on the summit, and started across the Knife Edge toward Pamola Peak.

For some reason Mrs. Ivusic chose to leave the Knife Edge, intending to descend to Chimney Pond more directly. Mrs. Mower, apprehensive of following such a course, chose to return on the marked trail to Pamola and down the Dudley Trail to the campground. At first the two maintained occasional voice contact and from that Mrs. Mower soon learned that her friend was trapped and could not go up or down. Mrs. Mower continued on to Chimney Pond to get help. When Ranger Ralph Heath returned after a day of trail work, he was also able to establish voice contact with Mrs. Ivusic from the edge of the pond. His original intention was to begin a rescue attempt at first light but a sudden change in the weather prompted him to try to reach her during the night.

After failing in that effort, Heath left again early the next morning with food and equipment (having already radioed for back-up assistance). Complicating matters was the onset of a severe snow storm that quickly accelerated to blizzard conditions. Now Heath, likely having reached Mrs. Ivusic, was trapped as well. The back-up rangers tried valiantly to reach the site but were driven back. Overwhelmed with sorrow, the rescuers finally abandoned their efforts after almost a week of worsening conditions and a number of rescue attempts.

In the spring when park personnel began the grim task of locating and evacuating the bodies they discovered that Ranger Heath had, indeed, reached Mrs. Ivusic and had been able to place her in warm clothing. We can't fully know what happened that day, as Heath died in his valiant attempt to save Mrs. Ivusic's life. Ralph Heath's willingness to sacrifice his own life for another's is still celebrated, and his memory is still held in deep respect by park personnel.

The Baxter State Park archives reveal that some years later a Ralph Heath Trail was proposed by Clarence LeBell. The trail was to begin at the summit of Katahdin, cross the Knife Edge, descend to Roaring Brook, ascend South Turner Mountain and then cross North Turner and the Traveler Range. From the north end of the park the trail was mapped out to cross Beetle Mountain, touch the shores of the Musquacook Lakes, then head north beyond Allagash Falls where it would cross the Quebec-Maine border at Estcourt. The trail was envisioned to continue to Riviere-du-Loup, the Parc des Laurentide and eventually to James and Hudson Bays. In Canada it was to be named the Northern Canada Trail. It was truly an ambitious dream. LeBell, though an active member of the Appalachian Mountain Club, apparently made the proposal on his own initiative. A great number of people bought into the idea, and some sections were actually constructed on land where permissions had been granted. After some initial interest the idea died a quiet death and nothing more was heard of it.[2] This idea could be considered a forerunner to the more recent establishment of an International Appalachian Trail.

There have been many other climbers who have looked down to Chimney Pond from the Knife Edge and been lured into thinking they could see an easy shortcut directly to the campground. Indeed there is no shortcut unless one is an experienced technical climber with a great deal of mountaineering training and the proper equipment.

FANNIE HARDY ECKSTORM

On June 18, 1865, two months after General Robert E. Lee surrendered to General Ulysses S. Grant to end the carnage of the Civil War, Fannie Pearson Hardy was born in Brewer, Maine, to Manly and Emeline Hardy. After attending public schools in Brewer and Abbott Academy in Andover, Massachusetts, she graduated from Smith College in 1888. She married the Rev. Jacob A. Eckstorm in 1893, and together they served churches in Eastport, Maine, as well as Providence, Rhode Island, and Portland, Oregon. Widowed in 1899, Fannie, by then known as Fannie Hardy Eckstorm, returned to Brewer where she became a teacher and took up residence in the family homestead until her death at age 85 in 1946.

A few years before her death Eckstorm wrote the following words in a Christmas message sent to her friends:

> There are but two kinds of people in the world, those who strive for what they
> can get out of it and those who strive to leave something in it.[3]

Eckstorm was definitely one of the latter. Her remarkably wide range of interests included natural history, especially ornithology; Maine history, especially the North Woods and the lumbering industry; Native American history and folklore; and the folk songs of Maine, especially those of the lumberjacks. Her books include *Indian Place-Names of the Penobscot Valley and the Maine Coast*, *Old John Neptune and Other Maine Shamans*, and *Minstrelsy in Maine: Folk Songs and Ballads of the Woods and Coast*, to name only a few. She wrote dozens of articles for periodicals and a number of small booklets on a variety of subjects.

Her father may have been the greatest influence in shaping Eckstorm's interest in the natural world. Manly Hardy was successful and well known in fur trading, a business that took him regularly into the wilderness areas of the northern forest. He knew and loved the ways of wilderness travel, and at a very early age Eckstorm began to accompany him on many of those trips. In 1888 she and her father canoed down the East Branch of the Penobscot River and climbed Katahdin by way of the Knife Edge. A year later they canoed down the West Branch from the Northeast Carry and climbed to the summit along the Abol Slide. She grew to love the forest and the people she met there. Her published accounts of those trips have provided invaluable information about the Katahdin area in the late 1800s and the early part of the twentieth century. Her brother became an artist and photographer but never responded to the lure of the wilderness places as did his sister.

Manly was noted for dealing fairly with the Native American fur traders and was highly respected among the tribes. They were fast friends, and native peoples often visited the Hardys in their Brewer home. That respect carried over into Eckstorm's lifelong interest in Native American history and folklore.

Eckstorm grew up near the banks of the Penobscot River at a time when the river near her home was choked with ships being loaded with lumber that had been cut at the Old Town, Orono, and Veazie sawmills and floated down to the waiting ships at Bangor and Brewer. She knew the river drivers personally and often visited them in the lumber camps along the West Branch. She wrote their stories to be sure they were preserved and to celebrate what she believed was a vocational art form. According to Eckstorm:

> These men were proud of their trades. They felt that they were artists and creators, working at something that was inspiring. Too late sometimes we realize that we have been moving among great events; when we are out of the woods we find that we did not see the forest because the trees were in the way. The era just past was a period in which bred men who were great in their grip of realities, who wrestled with unwilling circumstance until they compelled it to do their work for them. Hardly a greater story is there on record than this of a few common men, isolated in their location, many of them with neither capital nor education, taking hold of an engineer's problem of subduing a most unmanageable river and finally bitting and bridling it and training it to be their River, that brought their logs to market at their bidding.[4]

Eckstorm was a formidable woman both in physique and personality. She made up her own mind and had such confidence that she freely expressed her strong opinions, often in print. At the same time, she was careful to do her homework on issues and was always accurate in her research. Eckstorm was a unique, home-grown historian, and her work remains a significant part of the Katahdin story.

THE GREAT MAINE ELEPHANT HUNT

When neophyte "sports" from the city came to the old sporting camps for a wilderness experience, there were always some experienced fellows unable to resist the temptation to play tricks on them. These pranksters didn't lack for especially gullible victims who were fair game for their unique brand of good-natured fun.

During one group's stay at the Joe Francis Camps at the foot of Debsco-neag Falls on the Penobscot West Branch near the turn of the nineteenth century, the ultimate practical joke was played on an unsuspecting victim, and his group of friends enjoyed a heap of fun at his expense. During most of their week's stay the men deligently rose early each morning and, after enjoying a heaping breakfast, spent most of the day hunting for moose, the great monarchs of the North Woods. At the end of the day, after a hearty dinner back at the camp, they gathered around the great fireplace, warmed themselves in its glow and heat, and swapped stories of their adventures. Likely encouraged by the excitement of their adventures, each would, with all due modesty, seek to tell a taller tale. One of the group was especially eager in his zeal that year to land a moose in order to return home triumphantly to the awe-inspired cheers of his friends and neighbors. Unfortunately, this gentleman was so near-sighted that when he got within shooting distance of a moose he was unable to complete his mission. This combination of circumstances only encouraged his hunting buddies to decide that he was the obvious choice to be the victim of that year's prank.

As the fellows gathered that week around the blazing hearth, those who were in on the joke began to spread the rumor that glimpses had been caught of a huge gray moose not far from the camp, and that the mysterious creature had been able so far to thwart any attempt to shoot it. Each night another would tell of a sighting, each one reporting that the gigantic gray moose was approaching nearer and nearer to the sporting camp itself. Soon the near-sighted fellow's blood began to boil, and his desire to possess this enormous creature reached fever pitch. Finally one evening at dusk the other hunters encouraged the poor fellow to go out and try his luck since the moose might not be able to see his approach in the gathering darkness.

What the unsuspecting victim did not know was that one of their number had carefully smuggled into his trip supplies an immense paper elephant such as was often used for big city parades. Also included was a goodly supply of firecrackers. It is said that Joe Francis, the native Penobscot owner of the camps, entered into the caper with great enthusiasm and even volunteered to be the man's guide that evening. Led by the guide, our nearsighted hunter cautiously paddled along the Debsconeag Deadwater with his senses at full alert. Lingering behind in other canoes were his friends, waiting with much tittering for the unfolding of events. Suddenly the guide stopped paddling and asked for complete silence—not even a whisper—in order not to scare away the great moose. Shortly, as they drifted closer to shore, he motioned for the victim to prepare to shoot. One of his friends was to later report that "when the canoe stole softly up the shore, the very faint light of the moonless evening showed to his excited vision a monster which looked so enormous that [he might have been able to hit it even if] his gun was pointed the other way." All at once, the guide signaled that the moment to take action had arrived, and the man took aim and blazed away with one, two, and even three shots. To his astonishment the creature seemed to simply collapse. He quickly paddled to the shore, jumped from the canoe, and rushed forward to discover the paper elephant in a heap at his feet. At this startling discovery his friends set of the firecrackers from their canoes to celebrate their successful ruse. Such a serenade of sound had never before been heard in those regions and would not likely be again.

Amid much laughter and frivolity, the remnants of the "great gray moose" were taken back to the camp lodge and hung on the wall for posterity. Around the fire that evening the victim took it all with good humor and laughed as heartily as the others over this amazing climax to his week in the great North Woods. As the years went by the tale of the hunt for the monstrous gray moose never failed to entertain the guests as they gathered each evening before the blazing fire to tell their tall tales.[5]

THE SIDE-HILL GOUGER

After a long and tiring day of fishing or hiking or just plain "hanging out," the guests at Kidney Pond Campground often gathered on the porch of the dining room to swap stories and share adventures. Sometimes imaginations ran untamed. Here is a tall tale—an old lumberjack legend in form of a song. It tells of a mythical creature known as the Side-Hill Gouger, or sometimes, Side-Hill Winder.[6]

The Side-Hill Gouger's bid for fame
Is in his asymmetric frame.
The species has dimorphous form
And either kind may be the norm.
In one, the left legs longer grow
Than do the right, so he must go
Forever clockwise round and round
The hills, his only stamping ground.

The Gouger of the other sort
Suggests a chronic list to port
In that its left legs are the shorter,
(Or, right grow longer than they oughter)
And he, Right-sided to excess,
Has leftist leanings more or less.
It follows for his structural sins
This gouger must go widdershins.

In cirque, ravine or mountain bay
All gougers go the other way;
That is, left-siders go to left, perforce;
Right-siders take a right-hand course.
But none can walk on level ground
Like any common Valley-Hound.
The bias, it is evident,
Derives from the environment.

Some nature-fakers tell us that
The Gougers change their habitat:
The right-side with the left-side sort
Combine for mutual support.
Arm-in-arm, as one they say,
Across the plains they make their way—

An interesting sight to view,
It would be, were the story true.

The Gouger's figure might, perhaps,
Assist in using contour maps.
Sometimes when traversing a slab,
Or feeling for a hold to grab;
Or else, side-stepping on my ski,
Approximating chin to knee,
I would I might adopt the style
Of this lop-sided animile.

But then, in climbing, I have found
That sometimes I must turn around
Or, should there come a heavy rain,
I fain would back-track home again.
Such evolutions, one may see,
Conflict with the anatomy
Which, by hypothesis, is given
To every Gouger under heaven.

And should, by chance, a Gouger find
A girl-friend of the other kind,
Since they must travel face to face,
He cannot lead, or set the pace;
Nor can he join her for a stroll—
And so I think that, on the whole,
I'm glad, in spite of his renown,
That both my legs go all way down.

Bernie Crabtree, a retired Baxter State Park ranger, once showed me wood carvings of a Tree Squeak and a Side-Hill Gouger. He identified them as products of the imagination of the artist Jake Day. Yet after reading about the latter critter I have a lingering doubt; I am thus still hoping to sight this elusive member of Katahdin wildlife. Be on a sharp lookout for, and make a record of, any Gouger sightings while traveling in the region.

THE CCC AND NATARSWI

In a fortunate coincidence, the year Baxter State Park was formally created by the legislature of the state of Maine, a bill was passed in the United States Congress creating what would later be named the Civilian Conservation Corps. Though Governor Baxter long fought against any attempt to make the Katahdin area a national park, he grew to appreciate the federal New Deal program that provided teams of men—who otherwise might have been unemployed during difficult times—to do conservation work in many parts of the country.

Baxter made his first gift of land to the state in 1931, but it took a few years for the state to accept the gift. Almost before the ink was dry on the legislation accepting Baxter's gift, conservation projects were being mapped out for the Katahdin area, authorized by the U.S. Emergency Conservation Work Agency. Twelve camps were to be established in Maine. Some of the work had begun in 1933, and by 1934 Company 193 had settled in at a site in Millinocket and Company 159 in one at Patten. Later that first season side camps were established at the Great Northern Paper Company lumber camp facilities at Lower Togue Pond, Foster Field, and Avalanche Brook.

The purpose of these conservation teams was to build and improve the timber roads in the region as well as to open the area to recreational use by building and improving the trail systems and establishing campsites. An additional purpose was to help the National Park Service decide whether to establish another park in its system in the Katahdin region. This effort proved to be highly controversial and eventually was abandoned, largely because of Baxter's adamant opposition.

The CCC presence at Katahdin lasted for only a few years; a phasing out process began in 1936 and continued until all work ceased by 1940. During the time of their service, however, the CCC "boys," as they were known, accomplished many tasks that the state at that time had neither the will nor the funds to complete. Here is a partial list of the projects undertaken and largely completed:

1. Completion of the Nesowadnehunk-Millinocket Tote Road to its junction with the tote road coming in east from Greenville at Nesowadnehunk Field.

2. Start of construction of the tote road from Trout Brook Road west and southwest to Nesowadnehunk Field.

3. Completion of the road along Sandy Stream beyond Windey Pitch toward its terminus at what later became Roaring Brook Campground.
4. Fighting a number of forest fires in the region.
5. Development of the Katahdin Stream Campground at the site of an old Great Northern Paper Company lumber camp.
6. Improvements to the Hunt Trail, including the building of a wooden lean-to at O Joy Brook, general maintenance, painting of the traditional white blazes, and some minor relocations.
7. Other trail work including the Abol Trail and an early attempt to develop a horse trail from Roaring Brook to the top of Katahdin.
8. A suspension bridge to carry Appalachian Trail hikers across the West Branch of the Penobscot at Nesowadnehunk Falls.

As the program was being phased out in the late 1930s many of the old buildings at Foster Field and Avalanche Brook were razed. The Lower Togue Pond site was spared that fate when, after negotiations in 1935 and 1936, the site was leased in 1937 to the Abenaki Girl Scout Council for use by its Camp Natarswi program. Prior to this action their summer camp was held at Cold Stream Pond, but the council welcomed this turn of events, enabling it to occupy one of the most beautiful lakeside sites in Maine with its dramatic view of Katahdin across the pond. The name Natarswi comes from NAture, ARchery, and SWImming, three focal points of the camp's program at that time. The camp continued to lease the land from the Great Northern Paper Company until 1970 when it finally acquired the property outright. The camp is still operated today by the Girl Scouts.

The CCC era at Katahdin was one of great productivity in building infrastructure for the new Baxter State Park, and its value has been much appreciated across the years.

THE APPALACHIAN TRAIL

The Appalachian Trail is one of America's most famous and beloved long-distance trails. In his 1937 article "The Silver Aisle," Mainer Myron H. Avery had this to say about the trail he helped develop:

> Through somber-hued spruce and fir forests, across the depths of the Maine wilderness and its cathedral-like stillness—unerring in its course as a driven snow—lies a silvered aisle—the gateway to the finest of Maine's mountains,

lakes, forests and streams. With Maine's poet, those who travel this course of peace, beauty and solitude may indeed feel that—

This is the forest primeval, the murmuring pines
    and the hemlocks,
Bearded with moss, and in garments green, indis-
    tinct in the twilight.

Visions of earthly beauty, the joy of contemplation in lonely grandeur and the sense of physical well-being and mental relaxation, which grow out of exertion, are the lot of those who follow this path through its somber setting. For the white blazes of the Appalachian Trail lead far distant from the rush and clamor of highways and the wearying complexities of cities and towns. Time turns backward for a century, and it is as if one were retracing the journeys of the pioneers.[7]

The Katahdin region already had an Appalachian Trail when a group of people primarily from the mid-Atlantic states proposed in the 1920s to cut a trail along the ridges and mountain tops of the Appalachian Mountain chain from Georgia to Mount Washington in New Hampshire. An earlier trail by that name in the Wassataquoik Valley was cut in the 1880s from Katahdin Lake to the Great Basin. The use of that trail gradually diminished, and it was eventually abandoned altogether as folks began to reach the Great Basin in the 1920s via what we now call the Roaring Brook Road.

The northern terminus of the new Appalachian Trail (AT) was originally to be the summit of Mount Washington. When Myron H. Avery was elected chairman of the Appalachian Trail Conference he convinced the trail planners that the northern terminus should be the summit of Katahdin in his native state. When the change was finally approved, Avery and a cadre of friends began to lay out and cut the trail through Maine. They began on an August morning in 1933 at the top of Katahdin and over several seasons completed the work to the New Hampshire border across some 260 miles of mostly wilderness.

For the first five miles or so the AT utilized the famous Hunt Trail along the Hunt Spur to Katahdin Stream Campground. From there it followed old tote roads to Daicey Pond, down along Nesowadnehunk Stream, finally crossing the West Branch of the Penobscot. At first that crossing was over an old dam at Nesowadnehunk Falls. Later, in 1936 the Patten CCC crew built a suspension bridge and hikers could safely cross the churning waters of the river.

The AT has an interesting and storied history. Thousands have now made their way across the Appalachian chain to experience one of the great thrills of their lives, climbing Katahdin. Some accomplish that feat in one season; others spend a number of years, even a lifetime, hiking the AT one section at a time; some hike portions with no intention of hiking the whole 2,000 miles. All have been deeply touched by this experience, especially as the trail winds through so many wilderness or near-wilderness portions of Maine.

The hiker begins to see Katahdin in the 100-Mile Wilderness while traversing Gulf Hagas Mountain, the first peak in the White Cap Range, and then notices it dramatically at the Rainbow Ledges. A striking view then unfolds at Abol Stream, a view shared by ancient native peoples and the early Katahdin explorers, including Henry David Thoreau.

After crossing the Penobscot West Branch at Abol Bridge, the mountain looms dramatically as one reaches Baxter State Park. One of the most memorable views is from the Daicey Pond Campground where the Appalachian Trail Conference held its popular biennial meeting in 1939. Finally one sees the breathtaking view from the old lumber camp field at Katahdin Stream Campground as one begins the climb of the final 5.2 miles to the summit.

It is difficult to communicate in words the feelings that accompany these trail pilgrims as they climb the Hunt Spur to reach the Gateway, cross the fabled Tableland, and stand at last on the summit, tears of joy flowing freely and triumphantly. It was my personal privilege to be the Maine Appalachian Trail Club maintainer of the Hunt Trail for over twenty years, and I was always moved and inspired when I met these determined and dedicated people as they neared the end of their personal odyssey. I still reflect on how that Hunt Trail climb may have changed their lives—forever.

There are "2,000 milers" whose names are well known in the hiking community. Earl Shaffer was the first to hike the entire length of the trail from Georgia to Maine in one season in 1948. He turned around 50 years later and did it again in 1998 at the age of 79. Earl wrote this poem the night before his final climb:

> You love it and you fear it
> It is big and harsh and high
> A mass of ancient granite

Towering into the sky
From the Indians who revered it
To the climber of today
A symbol of a spirit
That can never pass away

Emma "Grandma" Gatewood hiked the whole trail in 1955 as a 67-year-old great grandmother, the first woman to do so. I can also see her in my mind's eye as she stood watching Katahdin before entering the woods to hike those last 5.2 miles. She and Earl Shaffer both later hiked the whole trail south from Katahdin.

Ed Garvey hiked the trail several times beginning in 1970 to gather vital data to enhance maintenance improvement and land acquisitions that became so important after the 1968 National Trails System Act was adopted by the U.S. Congress. I also imagine Ed seeing Katahdin from the campground before he headed up the mountain with his notebook in hand.

There is the remarkable adventure of Bill Irwin who, with his seeing-eye dog and companion, Orient, hiked the whole trail in 1990. The feat is even more remarkable when one learns that Bill could only "see" whether it was dark or light—nothing specific. He hiked more than half of his time on the trail alone. Unbelievable but true! Bill stood at the edge of that field at Katahdin Stream Campground and, no doubt, "saw" the end point of his personal odyssey in his own heart of hearts, touched and moved by his deep and abiding faith in God who, he believes, accompanied him and cared for him every step of the way. I shall always treasure my copy of his book about that hike, *Blind Courage*, with Bill's signature on one side of the frontspiece and Orient's paw mark on the other.

These are but a few of the thousands who have shared that experience of climbing Katahdin at the end of their adventure. All are special people, celebrated and honored by the spirits of that trail in the shadow of Katahdin.

EPILOGUE

Wilderness Preservation at Baxter State Park

FOREVER WILD! THESE TWO WORDS EXPRESS PROFOUNDLY PERCIVAL P. Baxter's dream and intent for the land he purchased to be set aside as a wilderness preserve. After more than a half-century, the words have acquired an almost mythic potency.

The words were used perhaps for the first time in 1955; they were carried in a legislative act by the state of Maine that sought to clarify and interpret words used in the Deeds of Trust that conveyed the land parcels from Baxter to the state. In the deeds, it is written that the land "shall forever be left in the natural wild state."

The Act declared:

> This area is to be maintained primarily as a Wilderness and recreational purposes are to be regarded as of secondary importance and shall not encroach upon the main objective of this area which is to be "Forever Wild."[1]

That passage, and especially those final two words, have been employed over and over again to defend the goal and design for maintaining the Katahdin region as a wilderness preserve. In the minds and hearts of those who love wilderness in general, and this wilderness in particular, the words will always be associated with Percival P. Baxter and the park that bears his name.

Forever Wild! No two words better express the need to strengthen all future efforts to preserve Katahdin as a wilderness place. Of course, that effort has not been, nor will it ever be, free of controversy and disagreement. Even so, we must never forget these words, the message they convey, and the important role they play in safeguarding this extraordinary area we have been visiting on our literary journey in the shadow of Katahdin.

THE AMERICAN WILDERNESS VISION

The Wilderness Act of 1964 very clearly states:

> [Wilderness is] an area where the earth and its community of life are untrammeled by man, where man himself is a visitor who does not remain. . . . [A wilderness must retain] its primeval character and influence, without permanent improvement or human habitation . . . protected and managed so as to preserve its natural conditions and which . . . generally appears to have been affected primarily by the forces of nature, with the imprint of man's work substantially unnoticeable, . . . [and which] has outstanding opportunities for solitude or a primitive and unconfined type of recreation.[2]

The American vision of wilderness has evolved and changed over the years. Before the first Europeans arrived there was no "wilderness." The lives of the native people were defined by a deeply spiritual kinship with nature. Nature was not to be feared; it was their home, their habitat, and their natural environment. They held all that surrounded them in great respect and sought to live in harmony with the sacred presence—the Great Spirit—they believed inhabited all natural things. The rhythm of the seasons was dictated by the rhythms of the natural world in which they lived.

Colonization brought a different approach. In time people came to believe that the wilderness needed to be tamed; it was useless and should be replaced. Wilderness was even dangerous, a barrier to be overcome, an obstacle to progress. Wilderness needed a master to bring it to cultivation so it might be productive; it was an enemy, not a friend. The American destiny was to control the wilderness, and so began the great westward expansion. Only that which could be controlled should remain in its natural wild state.

For many this was a biblical call to have dominion over all natural things—to own and then "husband" the world the Creator intended for human use. Much of humankind became separated from the natural world in its elemental form and thus separated from our roots.

As the land was cleared and the nation matured in the nineteenth century, wilderness gradually became less inhospitable, especially in the east. Appreciation grew for wilderness as a source of beauty and wonder, no longer to be feared and avoided. The beliefs held by many during that era, including Henry David Thoreau and Frederic E. Church, both of whom were inspired by Katahdin, slowly and inevitably evolved into the conservation movement of the late nineteenth and early twentieth centuries. National leaders proposed setting aside large tracts of wilderness land so they might be protected for the generations to follow. Yellowstone was made a national park in 1872; Yosemite National Park was granted federal protection in 1890; the Adirondack Forest Preserve was created in 1892. The National Park Service, the agency that now oversees the management of all national parks, was created in 1917.

President Theodore Roosevelt became one of the great champions of this public policy effort. He hiked to Katahdin's magnificent Great Basin and had stood on its summit in the summer of 1879. He never forgot this encounter with wilderness in Maine and at Katahdin; and later, conservation would become a hallmark of his presidency (1901–1909).

This period is also the context of Percival P. Baxter's early years of public service. There can be little doubt that Baxter was acquainted with the writings of Thoreau and later those of John Muir and Aldo Leopold. Muir advocated an appreciation of the spiritual dimension of wilderness; it was to be honored as a sanctuary. Leopold declared that "land must be regarded as a community to which we belong rather than a commodity belonging to us." All of these early advocates for preservation taught us that wilderness is as much an *idea* or a *presence*, as a *place*.

All these efforts culminated in 1964 when the U.S. Congress passed the Wilderness Act, creating the National Wilderness Preservation System. With this action, conservation of certain lands became national public policy, including preservation of special wilderness areas so their value to civilization would not be lost. This act, which has remarkably stood the test of time, became the cornerstone of a new effort to allow wilderness to teach us how to live our lives as partners with, rather than consumers of, of the land. In his book *Wilderness and the American Mind,* Roderick Frazier Nash states that during this period of time, a major paradigm shift took place.

> Some even began to reason that since the wilderness had been conquered, now it was time to conquer the self-destructive tendencies of civilization. Wilderness might be useful in that task as a symbol of restraint, an environmental base on which to build a legacy of limitation and sustainability. By the end of the twentieth century a vanguard of philosophers, intellectuals, and activists were even testing the deep ethical waters that accorded wilderness, and nature in general, existence rights totally independent of their utility to people.[3]

A WILDERNESS VISION FOR TODAY

Lessons of the past suggest the importance of molding a clear vision of public land protection for the twenty-first century. This vision must espouse many different levels of protection: urban green space, conservation easements, national and state forests and parks, and a host of other ways to ensure public access. In Maine, the Appalachian Mountain Club's Maine Woods Initiative, the West Branch Project, the Nature Conservancy's Katahdin Forest Project, local and regional land trusts, private gifts, and many other such efforts are helping to achieve land protection for public use. They all deserve our full support. Wilderness designation is also an important component of preservation and should take its place alongside other deserving efforts.

In the case of the Katahdin area, I argue for a level of preservation only slightly below the totally unspoiled, untouched, rarely visited wilderness designation advocated for some areas under national protection. I would suggest the following principles to guide such a vision:

• *Preserve the natural order for its own sake. Protection must represent an ethical obligation in and of itself to protect nature as it was created— unspoiled by negative human impact.*

We must conserve nature so that generations may experience the elemental forces that have shaped and continue to shape the world and the human community. Thoreau once described his profession as being "always on the alert to find God in nature—to know his lurking places." All members of the human community have the responsibility to do the same.

We have a moral responsibility to preserve certain areas for no other reason than the idea that they have the right to exist. It is, as Roderick F. Nash puts it, an act of "planetary humility." Natural forms of life have inalienable rights of their own, and they must be respected. Our lives are enhanced as we observe untouched environments; with that knowledge, we can better understand who we are and our place in life.

- *Manage human presence in wilderness so it will be in harmony with, rather than disturb, the natural order of the environment—the resource.*

A minimal degree of unobtrusive management is needed to protect the resource that is wilderness. If we leave the natural ecosystem undisturbed, we can observe the elemental ebb and flow of life. We become observers and visitors only, never dominators. Minimal human presence in wilderness is natural and authentic, but negative influence and impact is not acceptable. We must always walk lightly in wilderness places. Human presence must not be allowed to go beyond the point of harmony and balance.

- *Provide opportunities to get away from everyday human activity and achieve such a pure contact with the natural world that one gains perspective and insight upon returning to normal activity.*

Wilderness is a state of mind and heart. Wild places are fundamental to our survival in spirit. To know wilderness is to return to what Thoreau called an "original relation to the universe," a relationship he discovered as he climbed the granite sides of Katahdin. Eliot Porter once wrote that "a leaven of wildness is necessary for the health of the human spirit, a truth we seem to have forgotten in our headlong push to control all nature."[4] Through a kinship with undisturbed nature in our own secret places, we gain important spiritual insight and power. The ultimate value of wilderness lies in its effect on the human soul. Such an elemental kinship with nature must be cultivated, or we run the risk of becoming less than truly human.

BAXTER'S VISION
Armed with these guidelines and historical insights we turn to the vision of Percival P. Baxter and his "magnificent obsession" to preserve the Katahdin

area and much of the surrounding forest. In dealing with the Baxter dream we must reluctantly leave behind any hope of finding clearly enunciated principles or carefully crafted formal guidelines and precepts. Baxter never intellectualized a philosophy of wilderness. He did not write a book or leave us with a series of essays. He did not codify his views or set down guiding principles.

On the other hand, he knew exactly what he wanted. He had a simple instinctive sense of what wilderness should look like. As his views emerged and his land acquisitions accumulated, a philosophy that reflects the principles discussed earlier did indeed evolve, but it was articulated in different ways. He was careful about the language used in the Deeds of Trust that conveyed the land to the state of Maine. He wrote letters to friends, governors of Maine, the state legislature and its legislators, and Baxter State Park administrators. He made statements to the press. He even signed a legislative act that sought to interpret the meaning of some of the language in the Deeds of Trust.

From all those sources, a Baxter philosophy of wilderness preservation has, indeed, emerged. It is true that across the years he accepted a few compromises to enable the acquisition of the land or to clarify concerns not dealt with earlier. Some have labeled these as inconsistencies and even contradictions, and some of them were. In addition, there has been a long history of legal and legislative interpretations of his intentions from the time of his first land purchase in 1931. Even so, when one encounters the full force of his words, one cannot miss the clear sense of his intentions. Much like a puzzle, no one piece reveals the whole pattern or picture, but when the pieces are finally fit together the whole is revealed.

Some of the puzzle pieces are in the form of key phrases that sum up the Baxter vision. They are:

- "Forever . . . held in its natural wild state." (From the Deeds of Trust)
- "A sanctuary for wild beasts and birds." (From the Deeds of Trust)
- "Where nature rules." (From a speech given November 30, 1941)
- "Where creatures of the forest hold undisputed dominion." (From a speech given November 30, 1941)
- "Forever Wild." (From the 1955 legislative interpretation of the Deeds of Trust)

Other puzzle pieces are found in the cadence of Baxter's own words, and I invite you to discover the remarkable way in which Baxter's words echo the guiding principles I offered earlier.

- *Preserve the natural order for its own sake. Protection must represent an ethical obligation in and of itself to protect nature as it was created— unspoiled by negative human impact.*

> Very low human impact—unimproved.
> Most human use banned or at least limited.
> No increase in human use beyond the limits placed.
> No trappings of unpleasant civilization.
> No advertising.
> No commercial exploitation.
> No hunting except with cameras.
> No trapping.
> Only pleasant foot trails.
> Wildlife undisturbed and protected.
> A wildlife sanctuary.
> Creatures are to be safe from hunters.
> Plant species are to be left undisturbed.
> No lumbering except in the Scientific Forestry Management Area.
> The sound of the ax and of falling trees will never echo through these forests.
> The sole purpose of the donor in creating this park is to protect the forests and wild life within a great wilderness area unspoiled by man.
> Everything simple and natural, as near as possible to the conditions when only the Indians and the animals roamed the area.

- *Manage human presence in wilderness so it will be in harmony with, rather than disturb, the natural order of the environment—the resource.*

> A managed park that remains wild is not a contradiction.
> No more structures.
> Limited access for most vehicles.
> No aircraft.

No more roads other than the few unimproved old tote roads already in
place. No hard surfaced roads, ever.

Roads must never detract from the natural wild state of the park.

Hardening of the trail system for minimum impact.

Allow time for the area to be reclaimed by wilderness.

Should not be locked up and made inaccessible but used in the right
unspoiled way.

Forever Wild.

- *Provide opportunities to get away from everyday human activity and
achieve such a pure contact with the natural world that one gains perspective and insight upon returning to normal activity.*

Preserve the sense of wildness.

Purity of nature undisturbed.

A sense of mystery.

A place to experience solitude and quiet.

Simple primitive accommodations.

Simple campsites in the valleys, by the brooks, and on the shores of the
waters.

Simple log cabins and forest lean-tos.

Only small cabins for mountain climbers.

No more campsites.

No hotels.

Undisturbed beauty.

Reasonable fees—a park available to people of modest means and
abilities.

Users must expend effort to reach destination—the reward is partially
in the effort.

Mostly walking and backpacking.

One must be on one's own.

A place where nature rules.[5]

Taken all together this recital of words provides us with a remarkably
clear idea of Baxter's philosophy of wilderness. That philosophy is an essential guide to the protectors of Baxter State Park as they face the inevitable
challenges to its wilderness designation.

A CALL TO AWARENESS AND ACTION

The three guiding principles we have put forward, as well as Baxter's supporting vision, provide all who love wilderness a solid foundation for preservation efforts at Baxter State Park and elsewhere. As the future unfolds, there will continue to be, as in the past, unrelenting challenges to the wilderness status of this beloved place. The park is fortunate in having the clear, irrefutable language of the Deeds of Trust in place, but there will always be those who will test the limits of legal interpretation. We cannot let our guard down—ever. We must continue to be aware, alert, and vigilant to every challenge to the Baxter dream that this place be "Forever Wild."

The administrators and staff of Baxter State Park are to be commended for their faithfulness to the Baxter vision across the years. With very few exceptions, the park has kept to Baxter's instinctive sense of what wilderness should be like and translated that dream into action. Members of the staff continue to manage the park primarily as a wilderness preserve with recreational use as secondary. They recognize, as did Baxter, that though humans belong in the park, they must be there in harmony with the natural environment. Their recreational use must be, as Baxter once put it, "in the right unspoiled way."

The recently retired director of the park, Irvin "Buzz" Caverly, added his own key words to those of Governor Baxter, words that help define the wilderness values of this place. He often spoke of preserving a place where "nature will be at peace" and where those who manage the park will commit themselves in the future to make it even wilder within its borders than it is today.

Notwithstanding these commendable efforts, I would suggest three additional calls to action:

1. *Those who administer and manage the park—including the Baxter State Park Authority, the Advisory Board, and the staff of the park—must go beyond their present exemplary efforts on behalf of this wilderness resource.* They must be willing to take the initiative to solve some of the ongoing issues that could, if not confronted aggressively, compromise the wilderness character of the park. Vigilance in identifying potential threats is, of course, an important first step. We must all be willing to put limits on ourselves, and accept the idea that changes in behavior within the park may be needed. Such action may result in public criticism and

even ridicule, but it is part of the tough fight that must be accepted if the wilderness is to be preserved for future generations.

2. *Those who love the wilderness areas must also build on their active vigilance and be pro-active in their advocacy of wilderness values everywhere.* Citizens groups such as Friends of Baxter State Park, the Natural Resources Council of Maine, Maine Audubon, and many others must continue their active advocacy on behalf of the wilderness values at the park. These groups also have a role to play not only defending against challenges to wilderness, but also as friendly partners in the effort to be faithful to the Baxter vision. This is especially true for the Katahdin area, surrounded as it is by other lands not so restricted in their use.

The day is fast approaching when those who knew Governor Baxter personally and can vouch for his views on issues will no longer be in our midst. That reality, coupled with the fact that Baxter never formally codified his wilderness philosophy, presents its own serious challenge. With that in mind the Friends of Baxter State Park has gathered together, for the first time, all the materials relevant to Baxter's vision for the park. Copies of this multi-volume, annotated, compilation have been made available to appropriate state officials and as a public resource to the Maine State Library in Augusta and selected public libraries throughout the state.

3. *Finally, we must build on the sometimes elusive Baxter philosophy expressed earlier and be willing to utilize the best of wilderness thinking from the past, in our own day, and in the future to help us further define the guiding principles upon which we will make management decisions.* There may be loopholes we cannot now anticipate, and we must be prepared. There has, at times, been far too much reliance on what Baxter said or meant. That may not be enough to meet the challenges of the future. We must anchor our views in the Baxter vision, but we must be open to the voices of other wilderness advocates in order to stay faithful to that vision.

Katahdin will endure. Its storm-bitten granite lifts far above the timber de-sired of man, its boulder-strewn gorges and glooming precipices repel the feet of any but those hardy men and women who find joy in the primitive conquest of a mountain. Nothing can be taken away from it, for long ago the receding ice and the winter storms stripped it naked. Remote, inaccessible, it rises from the green inland ocean like an eternal symbol of the rock on which man and all his works are based. It is the solemn grandeur of elemen-tal things. It is the brooking spirit of a continent before the dawn. . . . May Katahdin always remain the lord of a lonely wilderness!

—Walter Pritchard Eaton[6]

NOTES AND SOURCES

PREFACE

1. Virginia Thorndike, *The Arctic Schooner, Bowdoin* (Unity, Maine: North Country Press, 1995), xii.

INTRODUCTION

Notes

1. Theodore Winthrop, *Life in the Open Air, and Other Papers* (Boston: Ticknor and Fields, 1863), 83.

2. Neil Rolde, *The Baxters of Maine: Downeast Visionaries* (Gardiner, Maine: Tilbury House, Publishers, 1997), 228.

3. William O. Douglas, *My Wilderness East of Katahdin* (Garden City, New Jersey: Doubleday, 1961), 267.

4. Edwin Bernbaum, *Sacred Mountains of the World* (San Francisco: Sierra Club Books, 1990), xiii. Text copyright © by Edwin Bernbaum. Reprinted by permission of Sierra Club Books.

5. Ibid., xv–xxii.

6. Ibid., xv–xxii.

7. Douglas, *My Wilderness*, 279.

8. *Portland Sunday Telegram*, November 30, 1941.

9. *Portland Evening Express*, June 20, 1957.

CHAPTER 1

Notes

1. Rev. John Sewall, "Let Loose in the Woods." *Maine Sportsman*, August, 1904, 224.

2. David S. Cook, *Above the Gravel Bar* (Milo, Maine: Milo Printing Company, 1985), 78.

3. John Giles, *Memoirs of Odd Adventures, Strange Deliverances, Etc. in the Captivity of John Giles* (Cincinnati: Spiller and Gates, 1869), 46-47.

4. Rev. Marcus R. Keep. From a series of articles in *The Bangor Democrat* beginning on December 7, 1847, describing his two 1847 trips to Katahdin, one by the ridge that now bears his name and the other to the Great Basin.

5. Fannie Hardy Eckstorm, *The Katahdin Legends* (Boston: Appalachian Mountain Club, 1942), 39.

6. Ibid., 51.

7. Molly Spotted Elk, *Katahdin: Wigwam's Tales of the Abenaki Tribe.* (Orono, Maine: The Maine Folklife Center, 2003), 16.

8. William O. Douglas, *My Wilderness East of Katahdin* (Garden City, New Jersey: Doubleday, 1961), 269.

9. Marion Whitney Smith, *Katahdin Fantasies: Stories Based on Old Indian Legends* (Millinocket, Maine: Millinocket Press, 1953), 3.

10. Edmund Ware Smith, *A Treasury of the Maine Woods* (New York: Frederick Fell, Inc., 1958), 169.

11. Eckstorm, *The Katahdin Legends*, 42.

12. Charles Watkins, *The Legends and Yarns of Katahdin* (Published by Charles Watkins, 1942) 170.

13. Ibid., 166.

14. Constance Baxter Marlowe, *Greatest Mountain: Katahdin's Wilderness* (Gardiner, Maine: Tilbury Press, 1999), 15-16.

15. *Wabanaki: A New Dawn*, VHS, produced by Dennis Kostyk and David 14 (1995; Hallowell, Maine: Maine Indian Tribal-State Commission)

Interviews and Correspondence

Connie Baxter Marlowe, John Bear Mitchell, Arnie Neptune, and James Neptune.

CHAPTER 2

Notes

1. John Giles, *Memoirs of Odd Adventures, Strange Deliverances, Etc. in the Captivity of John Giles, Esq.* (Cincinnati: Spiller and Gates, 1869), 45.

2. Ibid., 46.

3. Fannie Hardy Eckstorm, "History of the Chadwick Survey from Fort Pownal in the District of Maine to the Province of Quebec in Canada in 1764." *Sprague's Journal of Maine History*, June, 1926, 63.

4. Ibid., 83.

5. Charles Turner Jr., "A Description of Natardin or Catardin Mountain." Massachusetts Historical Society Collections, Second Series, 8, 1819, 112–116.

6. William D. Williamson. *History of the State of Maine* 1, 1936, 90.

7. Felix L. Ranlett, "Third Recorded Ascent of Katahdin." *Appalachia*, June, 1968, 43–47.

8. Ibid., 47.

9. I am indebted to Herbert Adams of Portland, Maine for his insight on this phenomenon.

10. John S. Springer, *Forest Life and Forest Trees*. (New York: Harper and Brothers), 205–208, and Edward S.C. Smith, "Larrabee and The Backwoods Expedition," *Appalachia*, February, 1926, 284–290.

11. Arthur H. Norton, "Over Old Trails Along the Penobscot and Wassataquoik." *The Maine Naturalist*, June, 1928, 56.

12. Herbert Adams, "Maine's First Official State Geologist: Charles T. Jackson, M.D., Chemist Extraordinaire." *Habitat*, Spring, 2000, 40.

13. Edward Everett Hale, "An Early Ascent of Katahdin." *Appalachia*, April, 1901, 282.

14. J.R. DeLaski, "Dr. Young's Botanical Expedition to Mount Katahdin." *The Maine Naturalist*, 1927, 52.

15. Henry David Thoreau, *The Maine Woods* (New York: W.W. Norton and Company, Inc., 1950), 274.

16. Marcus R. Keep, From an article in a series in *The Bangor Democrat* beginning on December 7, 1847, describing his two 1847 trips to Katahdin and the Great Basin.

17. Ibid.

18. Ibid.

19. Ibid.

20. Ibid.

21. State of Maine Acts and Resolves. February 19, 1859.

22. From an article titled "Marcus Keep, Explorer Pastor" in *The Portland Sunday Telegram*, September 15, 1940.

23. Ibid.

Interviews and Correspondence

Chris Huntington, Fran Mitchell, and Rodney Morgan.

CHAPTER 3

Notes

1. Charles E. Hamlin, "Routes to Ktaadn," *Appalachia*, December, 1881, 306.

2. Rev. Joseph Blake, "A Second Excursion to Mount Katahdin," *The Maine Naturalist*, June, 1916, 78.

3. Ibid., 79–80.

4. Marcus Keep, "The Scientific Survey—No. 8," *Aroostook Times*, September 20, 1861, 2.

5. Hamlin, "Routes to Katahdin," 308.

6. John W. Hakola, *Legacy of a Lifetime: The Story of Baxter State Park* (Woolwich, Maine: TBW Books, 1981), 38.

7. Rev. John Todd, *Summer Gleanings; or Sketches and Incidents* (Northampton, Massachusetts: Hopkins, Bridgman, 1852), 121–132.

8. Theodore Winthrop, *Life in the Open Air* (Boston: Ticknor and Fields, 1863), 59.

9. Ibid., 87-88.

10. Rev. John Sewall, "Let Loose in the Woods," *The Maine Sportsman*, August, 1904, 243–248.

11. Fannie Hardy Eckstorm, *Penobscot Man* (Somersworth, New Hampshire: New Hampshire Publishing Company, 1972), 145.

12. George Pickering, "A Tramp in the Shadow of Katahdin," *The Northern Monthly*, May and June, 1864, 147.

13. Ibid., 228–230.

14. George T. Sewall, *To Katahdin* (Gardiner, Maine: Tilbury House, Publishers, 2000), 65–66.

15. William W. Sewall, *Bill Sewall's Story of T. R.* (New York: Harper and Brothers Publishers, 1919), 2.

16. Nathan Miller, *Theodore Roosevelt: A Life* (New York: William Morrow and Company, Inc., 1992), 94.

17. William W. Sewall, *Bill Sewall's Story*, 114.

18. Ibid., Introduction.

19. *Island Falls, Maine, 1872-1972*. Compiled by Nina G. Sawyer, 1972, 82–83.

20. Capt. A.J. Farrar, *Down the West Branch* (Boston: Lee and Shephard Publishers, 1889), 188-195.

21. Lore A. Rogers, "My First Trip to Katahdin," *Down East*, May, 1960. 48. Reprinted by permission of *Down East* magazine. Copyright © Down East Enterprise, Inc., Camden, Maine. All rights reserved.

22. State of Maine Acts and Resolves, April 9, 1856.

23. I am indebted to Dr. David Field, Professor of Forest Policy and Forest Resources and Chair of the Department of Forest Management at the Univerity of Maine in Orono, for furnishing the information about the use of the chain measurement and its history.

24. State of Maine Acts and Resolves, March 30, 1859.

25. Hakola, *Legacy*, 28 [Quoting from the Expedition's Report].

26. Hamlin, "Routes to Ktaadn," 329.

27. *The Living Wilderness*, No. 26, Spring, 1949.

28. The Baxter Collection. Maine State Library. Folder 63, page 8 of the Address.

Interviews and Correspondence

Irvin "Buzz" Caverly, Dr. Peter Mason, and Castine (Maine) Historical Society.

CHAPTER 4

Notes

1. Lew Dietz, *Allagash* (New York: Holt, Rinehart and Winston, 1968), 56–59. Reprinted by permission of Henry Holt and Company, LLC.

2. G.T. Ridlon Sr., *Saco Valley Settlements and Families* (Portland, Maine: The Author, 1895), 12.

3. Fannie Hardy Eckstorm, "Lumbering in Maine," Chapter XXIV of *Maine: A History*, Edited by Louis Hatch (Somersworth, New Hampshire: New Hampshire Publishing Company, 1919), 691.

4. Ibid., 689–695.

5. Robert E. Pike, *Tall Trees and Tough Men* (New York: W.W. Norton and Company, 1967), 41. First published as a Norton paperback in 1984. Reissued 1999. Used by permission of W.W. Norton and Company, Inc.

6. "A Tramp in the Shadow of Katahdin," *Northern Monthly*, May 1863, 226–277.

7. Fannie Hardy Eckstorm, *Penobscot Man* (Somersworth, New Hampshire: New Hampshire Publishing Company, 1972), 234, 236–237.

8. Ibid., 3–22.

9. Ibid., 122–123.

10. Ann and Myron Sutton, *The Appalachian Trail: Wilderness on the Doorstep* (Philadelphia and New York: J.B. Lipincott Company, 1967), 155.

11. *Saturday Review of Literature*, June 25, 1949, 32

12. John S. Springer, *Forest Life and Forest Trees* (New York: Harper and Brothers, 1857). 158.

13. Alfred Hempstead, *The Penobscot Boom* (Self-published by the author, 1975), 63.

14. Ibid., 60. [The author is also indebted to Phil Palmer for his discovery of the meaning of the verb "ross" in logging usage].

15. *The Northern*. Newsletter of the Great Northern Paper Company. October, 1922.

16. Permission has been granted by Mr. Larry J. Woods of Dallas, Texas to tell, in his words, this story, which was based on an 1895 *Lewiston Journal* (Maine) newspaper account.

17. The author is indebted to Irvin "Buzz" Caverly, Director of Baxter State Park, for his account of the background of this story.

18. "Sandy Stream Song—An Episode of Hersey-Reed Lumber Operations of 1874," *Lewiston Journal Illustrated Magazine* (Maine), July 31, 1915.

19. Myron H. Avery, "The Story of the Wassataquoik, A Maine Epic," *The Maine Naturalist*, September, 1929, 83–84.

20. Arthur H. Norton, "Over Old Trails Along the Penobscot and Wassataquoik," *The Maine Naturalist*, June 1928, 70.

21. Edmund Ware Smith, *A Treasury of the Maine Woods* (New York: Frederick Fell, Inc., 1958), 165-166.

22. Myron H. Avery, "The Story of the Wassataquoik," 90.

23. Ibid., 96.

24. Myron H. Avery, "Katahdin and Its History," *In the Maine Woods*, 1939, 25.

Interviews and Correspondence

Herb Adams, Dana Brown, Irvin "Buzz" Caverly, Bernard Crabtree, Brendan Curran, Fred Fowler, Chuck Harris, and Tony York.

CHAPTER 5

Notes

1. *In the Maine Woods*, An Annual Publication of the Bangor and Aroostook Railroad, 1901

2. *Appalachia*, A Publication of the Appalachian Mountain Club, December, 1945, 559

3. *Lewiston Sunday Journal Magazine* (Maine), October 17, 1936.

4. From a Kidney Pond Camps promotional brochure found in the Baxter State Park archives.

5. *In the Maine Woods*, 1921, 119.

6. *In the Maine Woods*, 1933.

7. *In the Maine Woods*, 1940, 31–37.

8. Dr. William Horner, A History of Camp Phoenix. Unpublished. Permission given by the author.

9. Debsconeag Outing Camps Promotional Brochure, Bangor Public Library, 1907.

10. Ibid.

11. *Lewiston Sunday Journal Magazine* (Maine), October 2, 1920, 2.

Interviews and Correspondence

Al Barden, Elizabeth Beeuwkes, Irvin "Buzz" Caverly, Robert Chasse, Al and Suzann Cooper, Jim and Florence Daisey, Linc Daisey, Fred Fowler, the Reverend Hobart Heistand, Clarence Hilliard, Dr. William Horner, George Kerivan, Matt La-Roche, Eleanor Legassey, Joanne Monahan, Peter Pray, Wilmot "Wiggie" Robinson, Natalie Voisine, Howard Weymouth, Ray Woodworth, Anthony "Tony" York, and Jeanette York.

CHAPTER 6

Notes

1. Bruce Feiler, *Walking the Bible* (New York: William Morrow, Harper Collins Publishers, 2001), 393.

2. Fannie Hardy Eckstorm, *The Penobscot Man* (Somersworth, New Hampshire: New Hampshire Publishing Company, 1972), 5.

3. Walter Pritchard Eaton, "Lord of the Wilderness," *Scribner's Magazine*, July, 1925, 34.

4. Ibid., p. 36.

5. H. Walter Leavitt, *Katahdin Skylines* (Orono, Maine: University of Maine Press, 1942), 24.

6. Charles E. Hamlin, "Routes to Ktaadn," *Appalachia*, December, 1881, 315.

7. Herbert Whitney, "Builder of the Hunt Trail on Mount Katahdin Tells How He Did It," *Lewiston [Maine] Journal* Magazine Section, October 17, 1936.

8. Leavitt, *Katahdin Skylines*, 33.

9. *Guide to the Appalachian Trail in Maine, 1936*. A Publication of the Maine Appalachian Trail Club, 21.

10. Ronald Gower, "South From Katahdin," *Appalachia*, December, 1934, 193.

11. Leavitt, *Katadin Skylines*, 9–10.

12. Lester F. Hall Journal (Courtesy of Charlotte Hall Kirkpatrick and Edward Werler). Entry for 1938.

13. William Dawson, "The Eastern Approach to Mt. Katahdin," *Appalachia*, June, 1916, 335.

14. Leavitt, *Katahdin Skylines*, 10.

Interviews and Correspondence

Baxter State Park rangers, Irvin "Buzz" Caverly, Stephen Clark, David Field, Matt LaRouche, and Edward Werler.

CHAPTER 7

Notes

1. Lawrence Rosewell, "Ktaadn Basin," *Appalachia*, December, 1887, 26.

2. See Dabney W. Caldwell, *The Geology of Baxter State Park and Mt. Katahdin* (Augusta, Maine: Department of Forestry, 1972) for more information on the geology of the area.

3. H. Walter Leavitt, *Katahdin Skylines* (Orono, Maine: University of Maine Press, 1942), 49–50.

4. The Baxter Collection at the Maine State Library in Augusta, Maine.

5. Clayton Hall and Jane Thomas, with Elizabeth Harmon, *Chimney Pond Tales* (Cumberland Center, Maine: The Pamola Press, 1991), xii and 15-18.

6. Ibid., 25-26.

7. Ibid., 31-32.

8. Ibid., xii. [The story as told by Fannie Hardy Eckstorm is related in part in Chapter 1.]

9. Ibid., xii.

10. Baxter State Park Archives in Millinocket, Maine.

11. *Lewiston Journal Magazine* (Maine), March 1, 1958, 6A.

12. Chimney Pond Register (1930s and 1940s). Baxter State Park Archives, Millinocket, Maine.

13. *Appalachian Trail News*, a publication of the Appalachian Trail Conference, January, 1945.

14. From personal correspondence with Jane Thomas.

15. Charles D. Hubbard, *Camping in the North East Mountains* (Manchester, New Hampshire: Falmouth Publishing House, 1952), 94–96.

16. Rosewell Lawrence, "Improvements at Mount Ktaadn," *Appalachia*, June, 1888, 156.

17. *In the Maine Woods*, a publication of the Bangor and Aroostook Railroad, 1904, 151.

18. *The Northern*, a publication of the Great Northern Paper Company, May, 1923, 5–6.

19. *Guide to the Appalachian Trail in Maine* ("Katahdin" section). A publication of the Maine Appalachian Trail Club, 1933.

20. The Baxter Collection at the Maine State Library, Augusta, Maine has Marjorie Lee's account of her trip to the Great Basin.

21. Though he was given a copy of the page on which this song appeared in a songbook, the author has not been able to identify the title and publisher of the songbook.

Interviews and Correspondence

Bangor State Park rangers, Irvin "Buzz" Caverly, Bernard Crabtree, Brendan Curran, Ralph Robinson, Wilmot "Wiggie" Robinson, Jane Thomas, and Edward Werler.

CHAPTER 8

Notes

1. *Appalachia*, journal of the Appalachian Mountain Club. December, 1942, 268f.

2. Ronald Gower, "Katahdin Circumambulated," *Appalachia*. December, 1932, 394.

3. From an interview with Edward Werler.

4. From an interview with Irvin "Buzz" Caverly.

Interviews and Correspondence

Mildred Carter, Irvin "Buzz" Caverly, Douglas Christie, Bernard Crabtree, Brendan Curran, Ralph Robinson, and Edward Werler.

CHAPTER 9

Notes

1. Robert D. Richardson, *Henry David Thoreau: A Life of the Mind*. (Berkeley: University of California Press, 1986), 183.

2. Henry David Thoreau, *The Maine Woods* (New York: W.W. Norton and Company, Inc., 1950), 236.

3. Ibid., 249.

4. Ibid., 261–262.

5. Ibid., 266–268.

6. Ibid., 268–272.

7. Ibid., 272–274.

8. Ibid., 277–279.

9. Richardson, *Henry David Thoreau*, 181.

CHAPTER 10

Notes

1. *Mt. Katahdin* is now owned by the Yale University Art Gallery, New Haven, Connecticut.

2. Stephen May, "Pioneer Painter of Maine," *Down East Magazine*, November, 1989, 90.

3. Theodore C. Winthrop, *Life in the Open Air* (Boston: Ticknor and Fields, 1863), 51–109.

4. *Sunset*, dated 1856, is now owned by the Munson–Williams–Proctor Institute Museum of Art, Utica, New York.

5. Winthrop, *Life in the Open Air*, 51–109.

6. *Mount Katahdin* is now owned by the Addison Gallery of American Art, Phillips Academy, Andover, Massachusetts.

7. *Twilight in the Wilderness* is now owned by the Cleveland Museum of Art, Cleveland, Ohio.

8. Attributed to A.L. Holley, "Camps and Tramps About Katahdin," *Scribner's Magazine*, May, 1878.

9. Thomas Sedgewick Steele, *Canoe and Camera, A Hundred Mile Tour Through the Maine Forests* (Boston: Estes and Lauriat, 1882), 133.

10. From Chris Huntington's first draft of program notes written for the exhibition, Looking at Katahdin, The Artists Inspiration. L.C. Bates Museum, Hinkley, Maine, June 13–October 12, 1999. Courtesy of Chris Huntington.

11. *Katahdin from Millinocket Camp* is now owned by the Portland Museum of Art, Portland, Maine. It was a 1998 gift to the museum by the late Elizabeth B. Noyce.

12. Document OL.1885.18.A-B Olana State Historic Site, New York State Office of Parks, Recreation, and Historic Preservation. Used by permission.

13. William Howes Downes and Frank Torrey Robinson, "Our American Old Masters," *New England Magazine*, November, 1895, 302.

14. The Exhibition Catalogue, Frederic E. Church, Metropolitan Museum of Art, 1900.

15. Myron H. Avery, "Nineteenth Century Photographers of Katahdin," *Appalachia*, December, 1946, 222.

16. *Knife's Edge*, dated 1915, is now owned by the Maine State Library.

17. Jeanne Hokin, *Pinnacles and Pyramids* (Albuquerque: University of New Mexico Press, 1993), 117.

18. From Introductory Notes for Carl Sprinchorn: Realist Impulse and Romantic Vision, an exhibition organized by the Sordoni Art Gallery, Wilkes College, Wilkes-Barre, Pennsylvania, 1983.

19. From the Journal of Lester F. Hall. Entry for 1938, 55. Permission granted by Charlotte Kirkpatrick Hall and Edward Werler.

20. Ed Werler, *The Call of Katahdin*. (Yarmouth, Maine: Cranberry Knoll Publishers LLC, 2003), 130.

21. See Edmund Ware Smith, *For Maine Only* (New York: Frederick Fell, Inc., 1959), 89–104 and *Up River and Down, Stories from the Maine Woods* (New York: Rinehart and Winston, 1965), 169–187.

Interviews and Correspondence

Gerald Carr, Mac Day, Anne Hubert, Chris Huntington, Jym St. Pierre, Bill Silliker Jr., Edward and Martha Werler, and Ray Woodworth.

CHAPTER 11

Notes

1. Neil Rolde, *The Baxters of Maine: Downeast Visionaries* (Gardiner, Maine: Tilbury House, Publishers, 1997), 55–57.

2. Baxter referred to this visit in a short address he authored to be read on the occasion of the dedication of the Togue Pond Gatehouse in August 1967. The Baxter Collection, Maine State Library.

3. *Lewiston Journal Magazine* (Maine), October 2, 1920, 2–3. This is part of a long, rambling, often humorous account of the trip written by Arthur S. Staples a few months after the expedition.

4. Ibid., 4–5.

5. Ibid., 9.

6. The Baxter Collection. Maine State Library. Scrapbook No. 18, 33–55.

7. The Baxter Collection. Maine State Library. Scrapbook No. 3, 71.

8. Percival P. Baxter, "Mount Katahdin State Park," An Address Given by Hon. Percival P. Baxter, President of the Senate at the Annual Meeting of the Maine Sportsmen's Fish and Game Association, Hall of Representatives, State Capitol, Augusta, Maine, January 27, 1921. Printed by the State of Maine, Augusta, Maine, 3–14.

9. Percival P. Baxter, "Addresses 1921–1925" (Printed by the State of Maine, Augusta, Maine, 1925), Maine State Library Safe. Page 22 of the address is noted in the text.

10. Henry David Thoreau, *The Maine Woods* (New York: W.W. Norton and Company, Inc., 1950), 321.

11. The Baxter Collection. Maine State Library. Scrapbook No. 18, 33–55.

12. Communication to Governor Horace A. Hildreth and members of the Ninety-second Legislature. January 10, 1945, 117–119.

13. John W. Hakola, *Legacy of a Lifetime: The Story of Baxter State Park* (Woolwich, Maine: TBW Books, 1981), 73.

14. *Portland Sunday Telegram* and *Sunday Press Herald*. November 30, 1941, Section C, titled "Baxter State Park at Katahdin Now Complete with 112,945 Acres." The last paragraph was later condensed by Governor Baxter for use on a plaque at Katahdin Stream Campground.

15. From an Interview with Mrs. Myrle (Doris) Scott.

16. Trudy Irene Scee, *In the Deeds We Trust: Baxter State Park 1970–1994* (Standish, Maine: Tower Publishing, 1999), 301.

17. Quoted by Connie Baxter Marlowe in her *Greatest Mountain: Katahdin's Wilderness, Excerpts from the Writings of Percival P. Baxter* (Gardiner, Maine: Tilbury Press, 1999).

Interviews and Correspondence

Herbert Adams, Irvin "Buzz" Caverly, Neil Rolde, Doris Scott, Howard Whitcomb. Also used a 1980 taped interview with Helon Taylor by Peter Mills, who had served as a State Senator with Baxter, and Ken Spalding. Permission to use granted by Ken Spalding.

CHAPTER 12

Notes

1. Donn Fendler, *Lost on a Mountain in Maine* (Somersworth, New Hampshire: New Hampshire Publishing Company, 1978), Publisher's Note pages.

2. Baxter State Park Archives, Box 2.

3. Elizabeth Ring, "Fannie Hardy Eckstorm: Maine Woods Historian." From Jeanne Patten Whitten's *Fannie Hardy Eckstorm: A Descriptive Bibliography*. Northeast Folklore, Volume XVI, 1975, 45.

4. Fannie Hardy Eckstorm, *Penobscot Man* (Somersworth, New Hampshire: New Hampshire Publishing Company, 1972) Originally published in 1924.

5. Based on a story that first appeared in *Maine Sportsman*, December, 1897, 9.

6. "The Side Hill Gouger," *Appalachia*, December, 1940, 270.

7. Myron H. Avery, "The Silver Aisle," *The Appalachian Trail in Maine*, Maine Appalachian Trail Club, Augusta, Maine, and Bangor and Aroostook Railroad, Bangor, Maine, 1937, 5.

Interviews and Correspondence

Irvin "Buzz" Caverly and Donn Fendler.

EPILOGUE

Notes

1. State of Maine Legislative Acts. Private and Special 1955. Titled *Trust Deeds Interpreted.* Effective August 20, 1955. Chapter 2, Page 2.

2. Public Law 88–577, 88th Congress, S.4, September 3, 1964.

3. Roderick Frazier Nash, *Wilderness and the American Mind* (New Haven and London: Yale University Press, 2000), xiv.

4. Eliot Porter, *In Wildness Is the Preservation of the World* (New York and San Francisco: Sierra Club and Ballantine Books, 1962), 6.

5. *Percival P. Baxter's Vision for Baxter State Park. An Annotated Compilation of Original Sources.* Four-volume work published in limited number by the Friends of Baxter State Park in 2005. Available at the Maine State Library and selected Maine public libraries.

6. Walter Pritchard Eaton, "Lord of the Wilderness," *Scribner's Magazine.* July, 1925, 37.

Interviews and Correspondence

Irvin "Buzz" Caverly, Dean Bennett, and Howard Whitcomb.

GLOSSARY OF LOCATION NAMES

Abol   1. Aboljacknagesic was the name given to the stream that flows off the south flank of Katahdin, entering the Penobscot West Branch just above the falls that bears a similar name. Meaning: No trees, all smooth, bald country, bare. Likely referring to the open meadow-like area at the mouth of the stream. The area was called Aybol or Aybol Meadows by some early explorers. In 1874, the stream was identified by John M. Way Jr. as Sandy Brook.

2. Aboljackarmegus was the name given to the falls on the Penobscot West Branch just below the mouth of the stream that bears a similar name. Meaning: Smooth ledges, a clear reference to the nature of the falls.

Both of the names have across the years been shortened to Abol, the original native names now almost completely forgotten.

Ambajejus   (Several variations.) Meaning: Two currents—one on either side of an island. So named because of two large round rocks in the lake around which the river current flows.

Amberjackmockamus Falls   (Several variations.) Sometimes shortened to "Ambajack Falls." Meaning: Place where the water flows slantwise to the regular route.

Annis Brook   Named by timber operator Edward B. Draper for brothers George and Frank Annis. George Annis was the boss of the lumber operation on Pogy Mountain shortly after 1910 and later in the Upper Wassataquoik Valley (toward the Northwest Basin) where the brook is located. Frank Annis was also a lumber boss for the Draper Operation, and in 1911–12 built a sluice to bring logs from North Brother down into Annis Brook.

Avalanche Field and Avalanche Brook   Named for the East Slide avalanche that came down the southeast side of Keep Ridge in the mid-1820s. The Rev. Marcus Keep utilized this slide for his Keep Path, the earliest marked trail up Katahdin.

Balm of Gilead Brook   Flows west into Sandy Stream. The name refers to an aromatic resin or gum taken from a tree or shrub in ancient Palestine that was thought to have a number of medicinal and therapeutic properties.

Barnard Mountain   Named for a logger who worked along the Wassataquoik in the mid-nineteenth century.

Basin Ponds   These two small ponds (Upper and Lower) sit at the base of the Great Basin moraine, hence their name.

Baxter Peak   Originally named Monument Peak, the summit of Katahdin was renamed in 1933 to recognize Governor Percival P. Baxter's efforts to preserve the Katahdin area as a wilderness.

Bear Brook   Named in 1933 by H. Walter Leavitt while he was building the Leavitt Trail. Bears were attracted to the blueberries that grew there.

Bell Pond and Dam   Named for one of the lumber operators of the Tracey-Love Operations in the 1880s, the dam was located at the confluence of the South and Main Branches of Wassataquoik Stream. The pond lies northwest of the Wassataquoik and its waters flow into the stream not far from Inscription Rock.

Billfish Pond and Brook   Originally "Fillfish" on early maps, it was changed in the 1920s. It was said that in this pond one could get one's "fill" of fish.

Boody Brook   Named for Shephard Boody, an enterprising Bangor lumberman who in 1841–42 engineered the famous Telos Cut (Canal) that allowed logs to be diverted to Penobscot (American) waters.

The Brothers   Located northwest of Katahdin, these two peaks sit near one another, hence they are "brothers."

Burnt Mountain, Trail, and Dam   Refers to the scars from a large forest fire.

Burma Road   The road from Trout Brook to the Little East Branch was such a rough and muddy road that it was likely named for the famously rough 700-mile road in Burma.

Caribou Spring   The spring, not far west of the summit of Hamlin Peak, was used as a source of water by the caribou that frequented Katahdin's Tableland.

Cathedral Trail   Refers to the trail's three cathedral-like rock formations.

Caverly Pond and Lookout   Named in honor of Irvin "Buzz" Caverly, who retired as director of Baxter State Park in 2005.

Celia Pond   Origin uncertain, but because the name begins to appear on maps around 1913 it was likely named by Irving O. Hunt; also known as Faylor Pond.

Chimney Pond and Chimney Peak   Refers to a deep chimney-like cleft that separates Pamola Peak and Chimney Peak along the Knife Edge.

Mount Coe   Named for Ebenezer S. Coe, a prominent lawyer, civil engineer, and lumberman, who was also one of the first trustees of the Penobscot Lumbering Association.

Lake Cowles   Named for a member of the 1902 group that explored the Northwest Basin with Professor LeRoy H. Harvey.

Cross Range   This range of small peaks links the Brothers with Nesowadnehunk Field.

Dacey Mountain and Dam (Also Dace, Deasey, and Daisey)   Named for Hiram Dacey, who in the early- to mid-1930s established a farm along the Penobscot East Branch just above the mouth of Wassataquoik Stream to accommodate lumbermen and travelers.

Daicey (or Daisey) Pond   Known until the 1920s as Daisey (or Daisy) Pond, it was named for George Daisey, father of Charles Daisey, who was the proprietor of Camp Phoenix (sporting camp) for many years. The name Daisey has always been pronounced "day-see"; the change in spelling to Daicey Pond to match the pronunciation began to crop up in the 1920s and became permanent by the late 1930s.

Davis Pond   University of Maine Professor LeRoy H. Harvey proposed the name in 1903, after his 1902 exploration of the Northwest Basin.

Debsconeag   (Also Katepskonegan and other variations.) Refers to falls, deadwater, and lakes along the Penobscot West Branch. Katepskonegan was the original spelling, although Stepkonegin and Steptkenegen were also used. Meaning: Carrying place, high cliffs, and deep waters; ponds at the high place; ponds at the waterway; carrying place over a ledge or over rocks.

Depot Pond   This is the pond to the north (upstream) of the Basin Ponds. It was the site of a small lumber camp during the Great Northern Paper Company operation in the Basin Ponds area in the 1920s.

Draper Ponds, Trail, and Packhorse Trail   Named by Irving O. Hunt for Edward B. Draper, a lumber baron who ran an operation in the Wassataquoik region.

Dudley Trail   Named for Leroy Dudley, who for more than 20 years served as the beloved game warden at Chimney Pond.

Dwelly Pond and Brook   Likely named for one of the bosses of lumbering operations that took place in the area northwest of the Katahdin region.

Fort Mountain   Derived from a reference to this peak in the original account of Katahdin's first ascent by Charles Turner Jr. He indicated the English knew it by this name, leading to speculation Katahdin might have been ascended earlier than 1804.

Foss and Knowlton Pond and Brook   Named for two men, one of whom might have been Phineas Foss, who had a large timber operation in the area. The two built the road down the east side of Nesowadnehunk Stream before the dams were built in that area. Some old maps identify this as Knowlton Pond.

Foster Field   Named for lumberman Chuck Foster, who may have been in charge of the lumber camp at that location. The site is identified on early maps as "Foster's" or "Foster's Clearing."

Fowler Ponds and Brook   Named for one or more members of the Fowler family of Millinocket, Maine.

Freezeout Trail   Many speculate the name refers to the fact the trail follows the path of an old lumber road that was quite swampy and muddy, which would have made it easier to use as it froze. Loggers hauled barrels of water to spread on the road to facilitate the formation of ice.

The Gateway   The location of two large boulders marking the place where the Hunt Trail reaches the Tableland.

Grand Falls   The largest of the falls along Wassataquoik Stream.

Grassy Pond   Refers to the wet and soggy areas that surround this pond. At one time the Appalachian Trail passed along the shore of the pond on its way between Daicey Pond and Katahdin Stream Campground.

Great Basin   The spectacular glacial cirque to the north of Katahdin.

Greene Falls   May have been named for Walter D. Greene, Broadway actor and Maine guide, who—with Myron Avery—selected, built, and marked much of the original Appalachian Trail from Katahdin west in the early- to mid-1930s.

Hamlin Peak, Ridge and Trail   Named for Dr. Charles Edward Hamlin, professor of chemistry and natural history at Colby College and later professor of geology and geography at Harvard College.

Harvey Ridge   Named by the AMC to honor University of Maine Professor LeRoy H. Harvey, who explored the Northwest Basin in 1902.

Hathorn Streams and Ponds   Origin uncertain, but possibly named for Eben Hathorn, who was involved in the first West Branch logging operation in 1828.

Helon Taylor Trail and Pond   Named for the first supervisor of Baxter State Park (1950–67). The pond was previously known as Rat Pond for many years.

Hersey Dam   Named for William R. Hersey, of the Sandy Stream lumber operation.

Hinckley Brook   Origin uncertain, but possibly named for Josiah or Samuel Hinckley. The former was a partner in the charter to build a railway at Northeast Carry. The latter owned the clearing at the foot of the carry and helped people, including Henry David Thoreau in 1853, across the carry.

Howe Peaks and Brook   Named in 1935 at the request of Governor Percival Baxter to honor his friend Burton W. Howe, Patten lumberman, who arranged Governor Baxter's first visit to Katahdin in 1920, and to whom Baxter said he owed his interest in preserving the Katahdin area for the people of Maine.

Hunt Trail   Named by its builder, Irving O. Hunt (grandson of William Hunt of Hunt Farm), who in 1900 cut the trail along the southwest spur so his guests at Kidney Pond Camps could reach the summit of Katahdin.

Hunt Mountain   Prominent mountain seen from the old Hunt Farm site on the east side of the Penobscot East Branch. Named for William Hunt and his family, who established the farm in the 1930s to serve lumber operations and recreational travelers in the Wassataquoik Valley.

Inscription Rock   Named for the inscription cut into a giant Wassataquoik Stream boulder just above Grand Falls. It reads, "Tracey and Love, Commenced Operations, on Wissataquoik [sic], Oct. 16th, 1883."

Index Rock   A huge pointed boulder that protrudes in lonely splendor from the boulder-strewn slope between Pamola Peak and treeline along the Dudley Trail.

Katahdin   (Also Ktaadn, Kette-Adene, and other similar variations.) Meaning: The Greatest Mountain, the Highest Mountain, the Preeminent One. Because of the native meaning, the name should never be used with any other word. It should simply be called Katahdin and not Mount Katahdin. Katahdin Falls was once known as Kinaldo Falls.

Katahdinauguoh   The range of mountains to the west and northwest of Katahdin. The name seems to have been first used in print in 1829 by Moses Greenleaf. The native meaning is not entirely clear but may be another spelling of the Abenaki word "Katahdinaukee," which meant "the land around Katahdin."

Keep Ridge, Path, and Trail   Named for the Rev. Marcus R. Keep, who marked and cut the first formal trail to the summit of Katahdin in 1848. In the nineteenth century it was often called the Parson Keep Ridge by the AMC.

Klondike   Meaning: Hammer water—referring to driving stakes into a watercourse to make a salmon trap. The Klondike region to the northwest of Katahdin was first explored by George C. Witherle of Castine in 1886. The AMC adopted this name in 1922.

Knife Edge   The one-mile ridge between Pamola Peak and the Katahdin summit. The ridge was also called Knife's Edge, Saw Teeth, or the Knife Blade.

Leavitt Trail   Named for H. Walter Leavitt, who built this trail up Keep Ridge in 1933. The trail was abandoned when the road to Roaring Brook was completed.

Lily Pad Pond and Trail   Named by Irving O. Hunt.

Lookout Trail   Named for the view at the end of the trail northeast of Russell Pond.

Lost Pond   Several ponds share this identification in the Katahdin area, but the one between Foss-Knowlton and Daicey Ponds was named by Irving O. Hunt, because he had heard of a great trout pond in that general area but had trouble locating it for a long time.

Lunksoos   The native name for a wild beast similar to a panther or catamount that terrorized the native peoples in the area. The name is now used to identify a sporting camp located along the Penobscot East Branch. Pronounced "Lunk-a-soo."

Mammoth Dam   A large log-driving dam along Wassataquoik Stream, located just upstream from Grand Falls.

Marston Trail   Named for James L. and Philip Marston from Worcester, Massachusetts, who in 1953 received permission to build the trail from the Sourdnahunk-Millinocket Tote Road to the summit of North Brother.

Martin Ponds or Martin's Pond   Possibly meant to be Martan Ponds, in recognition of the animal species often found there.

Matagamon   (Several variations.) Meaning: Old exhausted lake, fished-out lake, grown up with weeds.

McLeod Camp and Trail   Named for the boss of an Ayer and Rogers lumber camp located along the South Branch of Wassataquoik Stream.

Millinocket   Meaning: Lake with many islands; dotted with many islands and coves.

Monument Rock   A large, upright rock at the edge of Nesowadnehunk Stream, downstream from Little and Big Niagara Falls. Because of its size it may have been considered by some an appropriate monument to the river drivers who lost their lives while logging.

Monument Line   Beginning in 1820, the first year of Maine statehood, an expedition was authorized by the Maine Boundary Commission to set an east-west base boundary line across the state from the Canadian Province of New Brunswick to the Province of Quebec. The line, completed in 1833, crosses the heart of the Katahdin region.

Moose Mountain   The official name for the mountain west of Sentinel Mountain, previously named Squaws Bosom.

Mullen Brook and Mountain   Likely named for a member or members of the Mullen family, many of whom were involved in logging in the region. Charles Mullen was a founder and early executive of the Great Northern Paper Company.

Murch Brook   The named recorded by Thoreau and others for what is now known as Katahdin Stream. Murch was likely a logger on the famed West Branch logging drives.

Nesowadnehunk   Variations include Sourdnahunk, Nesourdnehunk, and Sowdyhunk. Meaning: Stream that runs between mountains; swift stream between mountains or swift stream in a mountain ravine.

New City   A large logging depot camp near the confluence of the three branches of the Wassataquoik. Originally known as Russell's Camps, it was later named New City.

Niagara Falls (Big and Little)   Two major waterfalls along Nesowadnehunk Stream about a mile below Daicey Pond. The name is, of course, borrowed from the great falls along the Niagara River in western New York.

Nicatou or Nicketow   The place where the East and West Branches of the Penobscot River join together at present-day Medway. Meaning: The great forks; the river forks; where the route splits.

North Basin   The glacial cirque that lies north of the Great Basin.

Northwest Basin　The glacial cirque that lies northwest of the Great Basin. Called the West Basin by George Witherle in his late-nineteenth-century explorations and Northwest Basin by Professor LeRoy H. Harvey, who explored the area in 1901 or 1902.

Northwest Plateau　The extension of the Tableland northwest of Hamlin Peak.

Norway Falls　A falls along Wassataquoik Stream below Grand Falls.

OJI Mountain　During the early twentieth century, open rock slides on the mountain's southern face resembled the letters O, J, and I.

O Joy Brook　Named in 1925 by Clarence E. Holt, to express how he felt when he reached where the brook crosses Hunt Trail.

Old City　Large lumbering depot camp located downstream of Grand Falls along Wassataquoik Stream. It served as the central support camp for lumbering in the region before the timber cutting reached farther upstream. Also known as Tracy's Camps.

The Owl　Named because of its resemblance to an owl. Also known as Owl's Head.

Pamola　The god figure Native Americans believed dwelt at Katahdin. Natives have also used the name Bumole and other names for this god figure. Possible meaning is "come flying." Three concepts are expressed by this figure: Wuchowsen—spirit of the night wind; Storm-bird—huge bird-like creature; Human form—huge, spirit of Katahdin, lived inside the mountain with wife and two children.

Passagamet or Passangamet　Native meaning is unknown. Called Pescongamoc by Fannie Hardy Eckstorm. Identified as Passcomgomac Falls and Carry in 1904.

Penobscot　Meaning: At the rocky part; at the descending rocks or ledges; the descending ledge place.

Camp Phoenix　A sporting camp on Nesowadnehunk Lake named after a great bird in Egyptian mythology that, upon reaching the age of 500 years, threw itself on a burning pyre. From the ashes, however, the bird rose to new life. Twice in its history, the sporting camp has suffered major fire damage.

Pockwockamus　Meaning: Little muddy pond, little lake, muddy bottom.

Pogy　Possible native name for menhaden or poghaden, a small fish.

Polly Pond　Named for Florence Edwards "Polly" Eastman, the sister of one of I.O. and Lyman Hunt's regular "sports" at the Kidney Pond Camps. She apparently had great luck in fishing this then-unnamed pond. It is said that at one time she was the sweetheart of Lyman Hunt, though they never married.

Rat Pond　Probably named for muskrats that were often trapped there. Has been re-named the Helon Taylor Pond.

Ripogenus　Small rocks, gravel.

Robar Pond, Brook, and Dam　Named for Israel Robar, a semi-hermit who occupied a clearing along the lower Wassataquoik Stream. The site was later bought by the Ayer and Rogers lumber company.

Rum Mountain Trail and Pond   A wooded 3,361-foot mountain just south of Katahdin's South Peak.

Russell Mountain and Pond   The mountain is north of Katahdin and seen prominently from the pond. The pond is the center of Baxter State Park's wilderness and is the site of one of its campgrounds. Named for the boss of lumbering operations at the nearby New City depot camps.

Saddle Slide and Trail   Named for the broad saddle between Hamlin Peak and Katahdin's Baxter Peak, were the North Peaks Trail joins the Saddle Trail.

Sand Bank Trail   Blazed in the 1920s and built shortly thereafter by Madison Tracy and other citizens of Stacyville to provide access into the Wassataquoik Valley, the trail crossed the Penobscot East Branch near the Hunt Farm site, ascended Sand Bank Stream and headed northwest to Katahdin Lake.

Sentinel Mountain and Trail   Originally named "The Sentinel" because of the way it appears to stand guard over the Penobscot West Branch that passes along its southern base. It was renamed Mount Roosevelt for a short period early in the twentieth century to honor President Theodore Roosevelt.

Slaughter Pond and Trail   Named after a notable slaughter of moose on the pond that occurred one winter. Some say the deed was done by the late Jock Darling. Others say a group of hide hunters slaughtered thirteen moose and left the carcasses on the ice of the pond. I.O. Hunt reported that this happened in the late 1880s.

Slide Dam   Site of a dam that held back the waters of Nesowadnehunk Stream. So named because of a great avalanche from the slopes of South Brother and Mount Coe that dammed up the stream in the mid-1870s.

Snub Pitch and Brook   A logging road famous for its steep pitch. Loggers had to use a sled hooked to a cable to navigate parts of the road.

South Basin   The portion of the Great Basin where Chimney Pond is located. It is walled in by Pamola Peak and the Cathedral Ridge.

South Branch Pond and Brook   Named because the waters are supplied by the south branch of Trout Brook. It flows out of two large ponds—Upper South Branch Pond and Lower South Branch Pond.

South Peak   Peak along the Knife Edge southeast of Katahdin's Baxter Peak. Named Mount Cario by Marcus Keep in 1849; known in the 1870s as Excelsior Peak.

Spencer Cove   Named after Fred Spencer and his brother, who ran Camp Eureka by this site. The camp is now named Big Moose Inn.

Squaws Bosom   Refers to the rounded peaks of a mountain southwest of Doubletop Mountain. It was recently renamed Moose Mountain because of new laws in Maine that prohibit the use of names deemed offensive to Native Americans.

St. John Trail   Built and named in 1924 or 1925 by W.H. St. John, co-proprietor of Togue Pond Camps, the trail provided access to Katahdin from Avalanche Brook.

Strickland Mountain   Named for Major W. Hastings Strickland, the builder of the dam at the head of Telos Lake and a prominent Bangor lumberman operating in the Allagash region in the nineteenth century.

Tableland (Sometimes identified as The Plateau)   The vast, almost flat plateau at roughly the 4,500-foot level on the Katahdin massif. When viewed from the summit, it is clear that Katahdin was at one time much taller and a moving ice sheet cut away the top portion, leaving the tableland behind.

Tea Pond   Possibly named to recognize a shrub plant called Labrador Tea common in that area. It also might have been named for the dark color of the water there.

Thissel Brook and Bog   Likely named for James Thissell, a logger in the region.

Thoreau Spring   This previously unnamed spring on the Tableland (along the Hunt Trail) was finally named Governor's Spring in 1925 to honor Owen Brewster, governor of Maine who climbed the mountain that year. It was renamed Thoreau Spring in 1932 at the request of Governor Baxter to honor the great naturalist who visited Katahdin in 1846.

Tip Top   A flat, bare peak between the Northwest Basin and the North Peaks. The site of the Draper Company lumber operation early in the twentieth century.

Togue Ponds   Named for the togue fish that were plentiful there. On some early maps, it was named Katahdin Pond; on others, the upper pond was named Loon Pond, the lower Katahdin Pond. After the Great Northern Paper Company built a road across the isthmus, the two sections were named Upper and Lower Togue Ponds.

Toll Dam   The dam was built in 1879 by the Sourdnahunk Dam and Improvement Company along Nesowadnehunk Stream, a mile downstream from Daicey Pond.

The Tote Road   Known for many years as the Perimeter Road, the road circled Baxter State Park. The road has now been renamed the Tote Road to honor its original purpose and the loggers who worked in the region in the years before the wilderness park was proclaimed in 1933.

Tracy Horse Trail   Named for William F. Tracy, who took tourists to his camps by packhorses along this trail in 1927. Also known as Tracy Trail.

Tracy Pond   Named by I.O. Hunt to honor the Tracy family. The Wassataquoik Stream Trail is sometimes referred to as the Tracy Trail.

Traveler Mountains and Pond   The mountain peaks are east of the South Branch Ponds. Early river travelers thought this mountain traveled with them as they canoed down the Penobscot East Branch.

Turner Mountains (South, North, and East), Turner Brook, and Deadwater   Mistakenly thought to be named for Charles Turner Jr., the first non-native to ascend Katahdin. It was, however, named for the lumberman who first cut timber in the vicinity of these three mountains northeast of Katahdin.

Wadleigh Mountain, Brook, and Bog   Probably named for one or more members of the extensive Wadleigh family who were involved in early West Branch and Nesowdnehunk logging operations

Wassataquoik (also Sattacook)   Meanings: A clear running lake; bright and sparkling mountain stream; white, light-colored water; fish-spearing stream place; mountain stream or salmon river. The Penobscot East Branch is noted for its salmon, which used to be speared at night, by torchlight.

Webster Stream and Lake   Probably named for one or more members of the Webster family who were involved in lumbering activity in the area. The stream was known as Namadunkehunk (meaning "height of land stream") to native peoples.

Windey Pitch   Pronounced "wine-dee," the name refers to a steep pitch in the terrain that delayed the building of the tote road between Togue Pond and Roaring Brook for many years.

Windy Pitch and Windy Pitch Ponds   The record is unclear whether this should be pronounced "wine-dee" or "win-dee." I.O. Hunt reported that he had named it "wine-dee" because there were so many bends in the rapids in the part of the stream below the two Niagara falls. Others claim it was originally pronounced "win-dee," which referred to the gentle and distinctive sound of the winds in that area of the river.

Witherle Ravine   Named for George H. Witherle of Castine, Maine. Witherle made eleven expeditions into the Katahdin area between 1880 and 1901. His records shed much light on the region around Katahdin.

SELECTED BIBLIOGRAPHY

Though the Katahdin literature is quite vast I have chosen to list below only those works upon which I have heavily relied during the course of my research and writing. The Maine State Library has an exhaustive collection of works on Katahdin. That collection, along with those found in other Maine libraries, provides access to most of the resources covering Katahdin area history and stories.

COLLECTIONS

Myron H. Avery Collection. Maine State Library, Augusta, Maine.
Percival Proctor Baxter Collection. Maine State Library, Augusta, Maine.
Baxter State Parks Archives.
Maine State Historical Society Collection. Portland, Maine.
Old Maps from the Author's Private Collection.

BOOKS AND PUBLICATIONS

Published Works of Fannie Hardy Eckstorm.
Published Accounts of the Explorations of George H. Witherle and Charles E. Hamlin.
Hakola, John W., *Legacy of a Lifetime: The Story of Baxter State Park*. Woolwich, Maine: TBW Books, 1981.
Hempstead, Alfred G., *The Penobscot Boom*. Self-published by the author, 1975.
Leavitt, H. Walter, *Katahdin Skylines*. Orono, Maine: University of Maine Press, 1942.

Rolde, Neil, *The Baxters of Maine: Downeast Visionaries*. Gardiner, Maine: Tilbury House, Publishers, 1997.

Smith, Edward S.C., and Avery, Myron H., Compilers, *An Annotated Bibliography of Katahdin*. Washington, D.C.: Appalachian Trail Conference, November, 1936. First compiled in the 1920s and revised and updated a number of times, including a major reprinting in 1950.

Thoreau, Henry David, *The Maine Woods*. New York: W. W. Norton & Company, 1950.

JOURNALS AND PERIODICALS

Appalachia. Journal of the Appalachian Mountain Club.

In The Maine Woods. Annual promotional publication of the Bangor and Aroostook Railroad.

The Maine Naturalist.

The Maine Sportsman.

The Northern. Publication of the Great Northern Paper Company.

Sprague's Journal of Maine History.

GUIDEBOOKS

AMC Katahdin Guide. Boston, Massachusetts: Appalachian Mountain Club. Various editions from the 1920s into the 1950s.

Clark, Stephen, *Katahdin: A Guide to Baxter State Park and Katahdin*. Shapleigh, Maine: Clark Books, 2000.

Guide to the Appalchian Trail in Maine. Published periodically by the Maine Appalachian Trail Club.

Guide to Paths in the White Mountains and Adjacent Areas. Katahdin Chapters. Boston, Massachusetts: Appalachian Mountain Club. Various editions of the 1920s and 1930s.

Katahdin Section Guide. Published periodically in the past by the Maine Appalachian Trail Club.

NEWSPAPERS

Lewiston Sun Journal and *Lewiston Evening Journal*.

Maine Sunday Telegram and *Portland Press Herald*.

Bangor Democrat.

Bangor Daily Commercial.

INDEX